THINKING CREATIVELY
IN
TURBULENT TIMES

Edited by
Howard F. Didsbury Jr.
and the Staff of the World Future Society

World Future Society
Bethesda, Maryland
U.S.A.

Editor: Howard F. Didsbury Jr.

Manuscript Editor: Cynthia G. Wagner

Associate Editor: Susan Echard

Production Editor: Anne Silk

Assistant Editor: Tanya Parwani-Jaimes

Consulting Editor: Edward Cornish

Business Manager: Jefferson Cornish

Cover Design: Lisa Mathias

Published by:

World Future Society
7910 Woodmont Avenue
Suite 450
Bethesda, Maryland 20814
USA

International Standard Book Number: 0-930242-59-9

Printed in the United States

CONTENTS

EDUCATIONAL FUTURES

THE PENSION CRISIS

AUTOMATION'S FUTURE

HEALTH CHALLENGES

RENEWED IMPORTANCE OF A SPACE MISSION

RECREATIONAL FUTURES

PHILOSOPHICAL INSIGHTS/VALUES

SUSTAINABLE DEVELOPMENT

FOREWORD

We face the future in the midst of a tumultuous present that makes thinking creatively about human prospects as difficult as it is urgently necessary. Futures thinking offers hope, for it is among the most creative forms of thinking and can be applied to any human endeavor, from improving business innovation to understanding political change.

This collection of outstanding, forward-looking essays—prepared in conjunction with the World Future Society's conference World-Future 2004: Creating the Future Now!—provides a rich variety of ideas from some 40 thoughtful futurists. The men and women whose insights are assembled here bring their unique perspectives from all over the globe—Venezuela, Finland, New Zealand, Italy, Ireland, Peru, the Netherlands, Great Britain, the United States, and Canada—and from a cross-section of disciplines—biomedical science, economics, governance, business management, education, space research, psychology, engineering, and, of course, professional futures research.

The volume begins with an exploration of key technological change drivers and possible scientific breakthroughs in the years ahead, and then considers the need to deploy our foresight for improving the human environment. Next, we look at urban future as an essential issue today because growing numbers of the world's people are flocking into cities that are already straining to provide adequate resources to accommodate everyone.

Other aspects of the human future that will benefit from an injection of creative thinking—futurist style—are education, work and retirement issues, governance, health, space exploration, and even sports.

But the most profound questions challenging creative futurist thinkers have to do with our own humanity, the values we cherish, and the truths that may change as we pass through this age of white-hot turbulence.

The volume closes with reflections on sustainable development, for no human future can be created without attention to the planet, the homestead, on which we will build it.

The purpose of this volume is not just to lay the intellectual groundwork for those attending the conference, but also to keep these significant trends and ideas fresh in all futurists' minds afterwards. And the specific applications of creative futuristic thinking described in these pages should serve as an inspiration to all people setting out to create a better future for themselves, their businesses, or the world.

—THE EDITORS

THINKING CREATIVELY IN TURBULENT TIMES

EXECUTIVE SUMMARIES

I. THE PATH OF TECHNOLOGY AND SCIENCE

The Digital Future: An Alternate View
by Jan Amkreutz and Timothy C. Mack

Western society is well into the "Digital Age," the economic and social implications of which have provoked heated debate. While "Cassandras" worry over such issues as the dot-com bust and the potential displacement of humans in the coming Age of the Machine, a more realistic view of the digital future is needed.

Where Science Is Headed: Sixteen Trends
by Joseph F. Coates

The scope and impacts of science are enormous, so it is practical and necessary to analyze the trends marking the path of science into the future. The trends most likely to shape the overall scientific enterprise in the next decade or two include the blurring distinctions between science and technology and between basic and applied sciences; the fact that research is becoming more interdisciplinary, yet academia fails to note or support this interdisciplinarity; basic and applied research is rapidly globalizing, and in the United States this means science is in the hands of growing numbers of foreign-born researchers. Other trends include outsourcing of field work, the dominance of English as the language of science, pressure from science funders for results-oriented research, and the growing challenge of scientific authority by amateurs and hobbyists, as well as the significance of their contribution to the scientific knowledge base.

Microtechnology and Biological Design
by William Holmes

Microtechnology is the art of manufacturing products plainly visible under a light microscope. The convergence of microtechnology and biological design will have a profound effect on our way of life, yet nothing really new is needed—only incremental improvements of microtechnology products already in use. Cell-sized bioparts functioning like muscle, sensory, neural, and structural cells can be assembled into human-sized structures with biological characteristics. For instance, *bioclothes* will provide physical support and protection from cold and harm, while monitoring the body's shape, tension, motions, and internal physiologic signals. Modified cells within the body will be organized into a network for individual cell care, guided by their owners through bioclothes. Other developments: Robots, themselves biostructures, will assemble furnishings and even houses from bioparts. Small-scale, home-based manufacturers will flourish, ultimately leading to near self-sufficiency.

II. FUTURE-ORIENTED STUDIES

Traps in Futures Thinking—and How to Overcome Them
by Mika Mannermaa

Unsuccessful forecasts throughout history provide a wealth of lessons on how limited our ability is to think of the future credibly. The most-common traps in futures thinking are *"This is it!"* thinking, *paradigm blindness, trend-faith, cultural contempt, overenthusiasm* and *disparagement of everything new*. One example of the *"This is it!"* trap was the "End of History" discussion started by Francis Fukuyama, who failed to recognize that evolution on the globe has no end station. When thinking of issues like the global economy or ideologies, we should be aware that development is likely to continue for generations.

Strategies in futures thinking can help us avoid these traps. For instance, to overcome *paradigm blindness,* take care that you don't read only journals, magazines, and Web pages of your own discipline. In every organization trying to avoid traps in futures thinking and being thirsty for success, whether operating in business, administration, education, or in the academy, it would be good to have a kind of *disturbance generator* to keep you awake in front of the turbulent future(s).

The Political-Economic Pendulum: The United States Example
by John Smart

Historically, the United States has shifted back and forth, like a pendulum, from centralized, plutocratic political-economic domination to a decentralized, democratic culture. We are currently in a plutocratic cycle, but as the accelerating capabilities of technology empower individuals, we may see a swing back toward a more democratic political and economic atmosphere. Strategies that individuals can use to thrive in the digital future include becoming more comfortable using the Internet and other technologies for everyday activities, as well as honing your own professional technology skills and adopting the latest IT for your business.

Innovating for the Future
by Patrick A. van der Duin

Innovation processes are by definition forward looking, but innovation takes time. After the initial idea for an innovation has come up, new and future developments in the economy, society, and/or technology can render the idea obsolete. To create a commercially successful new product or service, innovators can benefit from the methods of futures research, such as gathering new information (or even knowledge) about future developments, so that current innovation processes can be adjusted. A case study shows how one R&D organization uses scenarios in its innovation processes.

Models of Change, with Examples of Key Issues in the Futures Studies Field
by Linda Groff

Change is the norm, but its pace is accelerating. Older models that help us understand change and its dynamic impacts include linear change, evolution, cyclical change, and dialectical change between thesis-antithesis-synthesis. Newer models of interest to futures researchers include step jump models (sudden shifts in a system without a prior breakdown), evolutionary spirals, series of S-shaped curves of breakdowns and breakthroughs, and chaos.

III. URBAN FUTURES

Imagineering Cities: Creating Livable Urban Futures in the 21st Century
by John Ratcliffe and Elzbieta Krawczyk

More than half of the world's population now lives in cities, and the forces of rapid technological change, expanding economic globalization, and profound cultural shifts mean that urban land-use planning and development are ever more important. Cities need to "imagine ahead and plan backwards." Case studies of Bilbao, Dublin, Lyon, and Vancouver show how different futures approaches can be applied to help urban planners and decision makers deal with issues ahead and envision and reposition their cities for the future.

The Rise of Telecities: Decentralizing the Global Society
by Joseph N. Pelton

The rise of overcentralized megacities is a dangerous trend, exposing countless millions to potential environmental catastrophe, rapidly spreading epidemics, terrorist attacks, and other threats. The answer is telecities, vast communication networks that are free from perils brought about by centralization. It is better to move and con-centrate ideas than people.

"Adding On" to the Nation: Housing a Bigger America
by David Pearce Snyder

US population will double in the next century, a daunting prospect for a nation already fighting a losing battle against urban sprawl. Architects and urban planners must strategize now to house, school, and transport an additional 290 million Americans, who also will be vastly different from today's Americans: They will be older, for instance, and increasingly living with impairments that all buildings and public facilities will need to accommodate.

IV. EDUCATIONAL FUTURES

How to Transform an Entire School System: The Future in the Present Tense
by Francis M. Duffy, John F. Horne III, and G. Thomas Houlihan

Challenges that educators face in their present when thinking about transforming their school systems include political pressure to improve schooling and emerging societal trends that portend great changes. From lessons learned in such case studies as the Chugach School District in Anchorage, Alaska, and Pearl River School District in Pearl River, New York, the authors offer strategies for transforming schools and school districts for the future, such as improving districts' relationships with their surrounding communities, including businesses.

V. THE PENSION CRISIS

The Opportunity of a Lifetime: Reshaping Retirement
by Michael Moynagh and Richard Worsley

A two-year project in the United Kingdom studying the future of retirement examined the reasons retirement is on the public agenda, notably the "pensions crisis" and longer life expectancy. The project also looked at the pressures on workers to retire later and how employers will respond, as well as the role of state pension arrangements in promoting a less age-based and more fulfilling view of retirement in the years ahead.

VI. AUTOMATION'S FUTURE

The Wolf Is Here: The Impact of Telepower
by Howard F. Didsbury Jr.

Society is increasingly challenged to do much, much more with fewer and fewer workers in worthwhile, well-paying jobs. Telepower increases our ability to meet this challenge, but at great cost: more fragmentation in society, replacement of humans and human contact with virtual reality and artificial intelligence, and growing risks to democracy and governance.

The Government of the Future is Intelligent: Citizen in Control, Government in Control
by Marcel Bullinga

Networked smart environments embedded with computer technologies may soon enable governments to download all relevant laws and regulations into every machine you use or building you enter, keeping you safer and making everything work better. This age of automatic law enforcement will mean more privacy for law-abiding citizens but less privacy for law-breakers—and consequently less crime.

VII. HEALTH CHALLENGES

Emerging Diseases: New Threats from an Old Nemesis
by Tyler A. Kokjohn, Kimball E. Cooper, and Laszlo Kerecsen

Infectious disease is not a thing of the past. Despite spectacular advances in medicine, some diseases are increasing as novel infectious agents appear, pathogenic microbes evolve, and etiologic agents expand into new geographic regions. Changing disease patterns can sometimes be linked directly to economic, medical, and environmental changes brought about by humans, but are often not foreseeable. The future challenge is to recognize and manage emerging diseases quickly to ensure they do minimal harm. Without directed surveillance and proactive mitigation efforts, emerging diseases could produce an unwelcome countertrend to hoped-for human health enhancements and projected life-span extensions.

The American Drug Abuse Epidemic: Policy Failures, Better Approaches, Societal Barriers
by Donald B. Louria and Amiram Sheffet

Over the past 50 years, there have been four simplistic approaches to illicit drug use: reduction in supply, long incarceration of users and small-time sellers, treatment of users, and mandatory urine testing of students and employees at work sites. Each of these has failed. Reducing supply is difficult given the constant demand and the potential profits. Long incarceration of nonviolent, small-time sellers and users is cruel, and does little except increase our already swollen jail population. Intensive treatment succeeds for only "motivated" users, and then only for about 30% (even less with follow-up of more than one year). Mandatory urine testing is an invasion of privacy, focuses on the wrong student population, and does not appear to work.

A better approach requires systems thinking; this allows a focus on interacting variables that either promote or reduce illicit drug use. Prevention requires a focus on reasons for drug use; two important reasons are peer pressure and boredom. One potentially effective approach is to involve young people in activities they find exciting and interesting so they have an antidote to boredom and drug-promoting peer group pressure. Primary prevention is a much better and, potentially, a far more effective approach. The drug scene can be reduced, but will be with us, to some extent, because of other societal and individual variables that encourage such use, including a sensate culture with a focus on hedonism.

VIII. RENEWED IMPORTANCE OF A SPACE MISSION

Using the Resources of Space to Provide Employment and Prosperity on Earth
by Lester Kuhl

The exploration of space will require a large resource commitment by a nation but with the correct project definition and financial approach such a project can be an asset to a nation's economy.

The current approach by the scientific community to solicit interest in space exploration as a "research project" is shortsighted and counterproductive. The major technical issues of the project have long been solved but the financial issues to pay for a project of this size have not been resolved. The exploration/commercialism of space can be a positive economic venture thereby making it a positive political venture. This venture can be used to generate "jobs" and not be thought of as one that is competing for resources of other national priorities. With this approach the exploration of space takes on a whole new meaning.

An alternative approach to exploring space focuses on constructing a transportation system first, then looking at possible financial approaches to pay for the development of the transportation system.

IX. RECREATIONAL FUTURES

The Future of Sport
by Robin Gunston

Sports, particularly the Olympic Games and team-based sports, have long been part of the human culture. Possible futures of sport will be influenced by trends such as the treatment of sport as entertainment and big business, the growing preference for individual rather than team sports, and the changes in club ownership, as well as terrorism and technological impacts. Four possible long-term scenarios are "Technosport," "Religiosport," "Machosport," and—the preferred scenario—"Valuesport." Global Community Games, a new worldwide, volunteer-led initiative, could become the key to achieving a better future of sport.

X. PHILOSOPHICAL INSIGHTS/VALUES

Future Life-Forms among Posthumans
by Jose Luis Cordeiro

As we begin to ride the wave into human redesign, the destination is still largely unknown. But despite all the unanswered questions, we have a number of clues that can help us speculate as to what we truly mean by the posthuman organism—including the striking acknowledgement that in all likelihood not just one type of posthuman awaits us, but several.

We will reengineer our biological constitutions and introduce silicon, steel, and microchips into ourselves. Some may choose to reside in computers as conscious wave patterns, while others will convert themselves into durable robots and venture out into space. Simultaneously, we will create entirely new forms of life, including artificial intelligence and perhaps even a global consciousness.

Humanity's monopoly as the only advanced sentient life-form on the planet will soon come to an end, supplemented by a number of posthuman incarnations. Moreover, how we reengineer ourselves could fundamentally change the ways in which our society functions and raise crucial questions about our identities and moral status as human beings.

Creativity, Innovation, and Visionary Thinking: Becoming All You Can Become
by Lynn Elen Burton

While it is true that extraordinary people like Leonardo da Vinci, Wolfgang Amadeus Mozart, Aung San Suu Kyi, Thomas Alva Edison, the current Dalai Lama of Tibet, and Oprah Winfrey, are all known for their unique genius, one can also identify many common characteristics underlying their successes. Examining creative thinking in terms of the Myers Briggs Type Indicator can help us understand how these extraordinary people tap into their strengths and abilities to create and think in innovative ways and to parlay their skills into success.

The Material Culture of Happiness
by Francesco Morace and Tiziana Traldi

Debates on the failure of capitalism to make people happy through wealth have focused much attention on the significance of the study of happiness for forming public policy. The Future Concept Lab has been following these debates and has undertaken a long-term research journey into the territory of happiness. This new field of social research can make a positive impact not only on policy making, but also on the world of consumption and on the private sector in general. Some key happiness trends could be employed in "happy marketing," a new perspective and new sensitivity toward the consumer world.

Tribe, Empire, or Global Commonwealth?
by W. Warren Wagar

The greatest issue confronting humankind in the 21st century is how we shall govern ourselves. Two powerful antithetical forces, tribalism and globalization, appear to be our only options, but there are others. Some argue that the United States can act as the world's policeman and the guardian of the new global economy, while others hope for a condominium of affluent powers, including the United

States, capable of jointly assuring stability in the world order. Proposals also abound for transforming the United Nations into the leading player in a new global security system. Unfortunately, for many reasons, none of these forces and projects can save civilization from unraveling in the course of the 21st century. The only sane alternative is a democratic global commonwealth, which today seems hopelessly out of reach, but may yet become attainable in the wake of crises so potentially lethal that they leave humankind with no other choice.

Evolving Future Consciousness through the Pursuit of Virtue
by Thomas Lombardo and Jonathan Richter

Society's increasingly intense focus on the present has led to a frenzied, fragmented world. People possess more wealth, material goods, and technological conveniences than ever before, but face chronic stress, anxiety, loss of control, deteriorating trust and connectivity, and escalating depression. Most importantly, our sense of the future is narrowing and weakening. A constructive approach for addressing these problems and improving the quality of our lives focuses on developing a core set of character virtues for the future: self-efficacy and self-responsibility; order, integration, and direction; courage, faith, and freedom; wisdom and the love of thinking; reciprocity and balance; and evolution and transcendence.

The Coming Conflict Between Science and Spirit
by William E. Halal

The nature of consciousness is one of the central issues of our time. Computer power should match the human brain about 2020, setting the stage for a grand test of a paramount scientific question: Is there a substantial difference between human intelligence and machine intelligence? New evidence supports the scientific view that consciousness arises out of the physical brain alone; other evidence supports the idea that a "spiritual" dimension indeed exists. One scenario depicts humanity bumping up against the limits of science, which would force us to recognize the *meta*physical qualities of humankind that lie *beyond information*. But an alternative scenario sees the study of consciousness producing a new scientific revolution, much as Darwin shattered the belief that humans differ from animals and Freud dispelled the conviction that human thought is rational.

Reflections on Teaching about Utopias: Oh, What a Lift That Phantom Offers!
by Arthur B. Shostak

Sociologists are strategic allies of futurists in the effort to understand the concept of utopia. Utopian study dates back to Comte and nowadays features the seminal work of Daniel Bell, W. Warren Wagar, Rosabeth Moss Kanter, and Wendell Bell, among many others. But we must now improve our teaching of the subject to ensure its place both in academia and in practical futures building. The neglect of utopias in sociology textbooks is both costly and unwarranted. Undergraduate students need academic attention to utopias. Fortunately, many fine new teaching aids are available, and teachers themselves can draw on their own classroom experiences helping young adults profit from this extraordinary topic.

XI. SUSTAINABLE DEVELOPMENT

New Paradigms in World Trade and the Global Economy
by Hazel Henderson

The traditional "Washington Consensus" theories of world trade are overly simplistic and ignore the new mobility of capital and the role of politics and powerful corporations in setting trade rules that are now seen as unfair and ignore social and environmental costs. A new model of sustainable world trade would build on the concept of *comparative advantage*—a cooperative "niche" strategy—as opposed to the current erroneous focus on competitive advantage.

The Future of Sustainable Development: A European Perspective
by Ruth Kelly, Lorcan Sirr, and John Ratcliffe

We are living in times of turbulence and complex changes without precedent in history. It is becoming increasingly evident that humans are an intrinsic component of nature, in that their actions affect both the biotic and abiotic environments, and are in turn affected by everything that shapes those environments. In evolutionary terms, population growth, societal restructuring, exhaustion of natural resources, and technological advancements have usually been so slow as to be indiscernible during an individual lifetime. However, in the past two centuries the global economy has shown exponential growth, transforming the character of the planet and especially of human life. If this rate of transformation is sustained without strategic planning for the future, the consequences for the long-term well-being of humanity are frightening. Anticipation of and preparation for the future are essential to achieving sustainable development. However, the potential for linking futures thinking to debates about sustainable development is very undeveloped at the global level. This paper examines the future of sustainable development in Europe, with specific reference to the application of the growing field of futures thinking as a vehicle to achieve it.

The Culture of Growth and the Culture of Limits
by Richard D. Lamm

Two opposing views of humanity's future—one espousing continued growth and the other cautioning us on limits—have led to a chasm of mutual incomprehension. But by examining the assumptions and prognostications of these two opposing views, we can see reality more clearly and make better choices regarding our use of resources for the future.

Opportunities and Challenges of the Future Transamazonic Connections in South America: What Could One Expect?
by Michael Edgard Ridia

Plans for creating transportation connections across South America's Amazon face numerous opportunities and challenges. The future viability of using ports in the Pacific Ocean for trade between the Brazilian Amazon regions and the Asia Pacific Zone depends on such factors as the unitary cost for different alternative routes. This paper analyzes complete estimates for the whole route, including all the multimodal connections. It also describes the impact of these connections in the Amazon Forest, including both economic opportunities and environmental risks. This analysis can serve as an example for other regions struggling to balance the goals of sustainable development with the pursuit of key projects in areas with immense natural resources.

THE PATH OF TECHNOLOGY
AND SCIENCE

THE DIGITAL FUTURE: AN ALTERNATE VIEW

by

Jan Amkreutz and Timothy C. Mack

THE DIGITAL THRESHOLD

It is a matter of general acceptance that Western society is well into the "Digital Age." What remains the subject of rather intense discussion are the economic and social implications of this "digital" transformation. While a subset of the economic possibilities can be discussed in the context of the "dot-com" boom and subsequent bust, the social factors, especially over the long term, remain more subtle. Many "Cassandras" have bemoaned the loss of human primacy in the emerging "Age of the Machine," and a popular series of films starring the governor of California plus innumerable science-fiction novels have spun out the dramatic elements of this scenario. However, there are also respected analysts of technology trends who have adopted this sobering viewpoint, to the degree that the issues surrounding our "digital future" now deserve a more detailed examination.

This article is not designed to provide *all* of this needed in-depth analysis, but will instead raise a series of questions specifically focused on the work of Ray Kurzweil, one of the most prominent proponents of this "ascendant machine" viewpoint. The highly respected creator of computer speech recognition systems and the optical character reader is known to those interested in the future of digital technology through his seminal book *The Age of Spiritual Machines*, in which he envisions a future ruled by artificial intelligence machines. Here is a summary of Kurzweil's vision:

> The intelligence of machines—nonbiological entities—will exceed human intelligence early in this century. By intelligence, I include all the diverse and subtle ways in which humans are intelligent—including musical and artistic aptitude, creativity, physically moving through the world, and even responding to emotion. By 2019, a $1,000 computer will match the processing power of the human brain—about 20 million billion calculations per second. This level of processing power is a necessary but not sufficient condition for achieving human-level intelligence in a machine. Organizing these resources—the "software" of intelligence—will take us to 2029, by which time your average personal computer will be equivalent to a thousand human brains. Once a computer achieves a level of intelligence comparable to human intelligence, it will necessarily soar past it.[1]

Jan Amkreutz *is principal of Digital Crossroads in Somers, Montana. He may be contacted at amkreutzj@centurytel.net.* **Timothy C. Mack** *is president of the World Future Society, Bethesda, Maryland. He may be contacted at tmack@wfs.org.*

The moment *when computer intelligence soars past human intelligence* is what Kurzweil has termed the "Singularity." This is a point at which well-known rules no longer work, and where something profoundly new emerges. However, it is clear to the authors of this article that this technological singularity is just one *manifestation* of a much deeper singularity: a singularity in the evolution of our universe. In Kurzweil's discussions about his singularity, it is not evident what the *essence* of the suggested post-human reality will actually be. Accordingly, this article will raise and discuss points of disagreement with Kurzweil's vision, and explore matters needing additional clarification. Hopefully, this discussion will stimulate a new dialogue concerning this very important area: the future of human nature.

DIGITAL PLAYERS

Are digital machines the showstoppers for human evolution that linger behind the curtain? According to Kurzweil, the emergence of "Robo Sapiens" as the dominant global species is only a few decades away:

> So technology itself is an exponential, evolutionary process that is a continuation of the biological evolution that created humanity in the first place. Biological evolution itself evolved in an exponential manner. Each stage created more powerful tools for the next, so when biological evolution created DNA it now had a means of keeping records of its experiments so evolution could proceed more quickly. Because of this, the Cambrian explosion only lasted a few tens of millions of years, whereas the first stage of creating DNA and primitive cells took billions of years. Finally, biological evolution created a species that could manipulate its environment and had some rational faculties, and now the cutting edge of evolution actually changed from biological evolution into something carried out by one of its own creations, Homo sapiens, and is represented by technology. In the next epoch this species that ushered in its own evolutionary process—that is, its own cultural and technological evolution, as no other species has—will combine with its own creation and will merge with its technology. At some level that's already happening, even if most of us don't necessarily have them yet inside our bodies and brains, since we're very intimate with the technology—it's in our pockets. We've certainly expanded the power of the mind of the human civilization through the power of its technology.

> We are entering a new era. I call it "the Singularity." It's a merger between human intelligence and machine intelligence

that is going to create something bigger than itself. It's the cutting edge of evolution on our planet. One can make a strong case that it's actually the cutting edge of the evolution of intelligence in general, because there's no indication that it's occurred anywhere else. To me that is what human civilization is all about. It is part of our destiny and part of the destiny of evolution to continue to progress ever faster, and to grow the power of intelligence exponentially. To contemplate stopping that—to think human beings are fine the way they are—is a misplaced fond remembrance of what human beings used to be. What human beings are is a species that has undergone a cultural and technological evolution, and it's the nature of evolution that it accelerates, and that its powers grow exponentially, and that's what we're talking about. The next stage of this will be to amplify our own intellectual powers with the results of our technology.[2]

In many writings, most notably in *The Age of Spiritual Machines*, Kurzweil describes the successors of the human race as non-biological machines with an intelligence that supersedes human intelligence. This is at the core of the alternate view presented in this paper: We agree with the essence of Kurzweil's vision, namely: (1) that evolution continues beyond the present; (2) that this continuation involves the evolution of intelligence (or at least the evolution of knowledge); and (3) that digital technology is the "condition sine qua non" for the future of evolution. The fundamental difference, in our view, concerns the implementation of future knowledge, the technological manifestations of that knowledge, and the way these manifestations relate to humans. As Jan Amkreutz explains in *Digital Spirit, Minding the Future*:

> Mental Evolution is coming to life, while biological evolution fades into the background continuing its journey to the baton of its own clock. *The gene has lost its dominance, the meme is taking over.* Variation and selection take on the added meaning of intention and purpose, design, and acceptation or rejection. Humanity has arrived at a singularity indeed. That singularity marks the end of the *Darwinian* evolutionary reign and the beginning of *mind-full* evolutionary expansion.[3]

In 1959, Arthur Summerfield was the Postmaster General in the United States under President Eisenhower. When asked about the future of mail, he envisioned that "before man reaches the moon your mail will be delivered within hours from New York to Australia by guided missiles. We stand on the threshold of rocket mail." Summerfield understood the essence of evolution for the future; pushing the limits of speed in the delivery of the mail. But e-mail emerged as the manifestation of that essential understanding. Like the US Postmaster General, we labor to extrapolate the tangible manifestations of today's realities, while sometimes missing the underlying intelligence or essence.

We always struggle to anticipate the novel manifestations brought about by groundbreaking technology. Overnight mail came along all right, but through the physical transportation of digital bits rather than atoms. We should: be prepared for the surprise of innovation, even when its full essence evades our understanding. Evolution continues, and the essence of that continuity is the expansion of knowledge, intimately coupled to the time-and-space-defying power of digital technology. New actors will emerge that harness that power. They will change the theater of our lives, change the rules to play by, and rewrite the storyline.

A DIGITAL STORYLINE

Ray Kurzweil grounds his vision in the expansionary power of evolution, and points to the emerging power—and intelligence—of digital technology. Although digital technology is arguably the most powerful technology in human history, and one certain to change the nature of all we do as humans over the next century, there are questions that beg for a closer look. Let us address some of these issues through an alternate view of the meaning of digital technology.

First, and largely because of digital technology, the evolution of human knowledge and hence of the human mind is just beginning, rather than ending. This broader evolution is already manifesting itself—not in natural biological alterations of the human brain, but in the conception, understanding, and creation of new knowledge constructs that shape the future. Kurzweil does in fact acknowledge this when he says:

> With DNA, evolution had an information-processing machine to record its experiments and conduct experiments in a more orderly way. So the next stage, such as the Cambrian explosion, went a lot faster, taking only a few tens of millions of years. The Cambrian explosion then established body plans that became a mature technology, meaning that we didn't need to evolve body plans any more.... Homo sapiens evolved in only hundreds of thousands of years, and then the cutting edge of evolution again worked by indirection to use this product of evolution, the first technology creating species to survive, to create the next stage: technology, a continuation of biological evolution by other means.[4]

There is no doubt that digital technology will catalyze human knowledge into a new and highly *digital* reality, while other technologies (such as nanotechnology and biotechnology) will serve as a means of rendering that reality into new physical creations. This digital reality—we are calling it *digeality*—is the hallmark of the larger "singularity" that humanity is entering. It will be manifested as a fundamentally new addition to the fabric of reality, one that flows from the human mind. And while the calculating power—and thus the creative power—of this new reality accelerates, so does the power of human minds. We don't have to wait for technology and human nature to merge, as that is already happening. On the far end of the spectrum, brain wave controls for machine-powered motion have already been successfully demonstrated in the laboratory. And the everyday impacts of this "merger" are already commonplace; whether it involves designing a new power plant using computer-aided design, creating a Web page, controlling a war in a virtual-reality control room, or simply running a "virtual" business from a cell phone. Nothing indicates that the human mind cannot deal effectively with increased complexity—or intelligence for that matter—without the need to fully comprehend everything about that complexity. The classic body-mind duality problem has just attained a new dimension: which "controls" what; i.e., does mental control digital or vice versa?

Second, the emergence of digeality—or new technology in general—does *not* mark a "singular" threshold in the history of evolution. Digeality is the expression of human knowledge in the language of bits, and is made accessible through the perceivable realities of sight, sound, and so forth. With digeality, humans have created a representation of the mental reality of humanity, a recon-struction of their understanding of the world. We can recreate past realities and imagine new worlds. This emerging *digeality marks the end of an earlier singularity that started with the creation of the first human thought*, some hundreds of thousands of years ago. Today, we are facing not a new and unique singularity, but the end of one that we entered when we became human. The merger of human intel-ligence and machine intelligence, as Kurzweil puts it, does mark the beginning of a new era, but it is not the ending of the human era, but merely another manifestation of the creative intelligence that makes us uniquely human.

Third, throughout the evolution of all life, nature has continuously added new features to existing creatures through evolution. In the course of its journey, nature crossed three metaphysical "thresholds." Each "crossing" expanded the diversity, versatility, and the psychic "decision space" available to extant entities, and added dynamic new properties that enhanced their further expansion. With the *First Crossing*, at the time of the Big Bang, nature brought forth the existence of our universe and the space-time continuum as we know it. With the *Second Crossing*, at about 4 billion years ago, nature added life, with the appearance of the first strand of RNA, DNA or living cells. Finally, with the *Third Crossing*, nature added knowledge, epitomized by the ability of humans to express their thoughts in forms independent of their biological limitations. The most important feature of each crossing was the increased autonomy of nature's creatures. These sequential degrees of freedom ultimately manifest themselves in human beings.

With the First Crossing, the reality of our existence appeared; we call it the physical reality. With the emergence of life in the Second Crossing, a second reality came with it—the reality that allows a living creature to navigate the physical world. From the jellyfish onward, this reality is epitomized through the functioning of a living brain. We call that reality the mental reality, which is central to the Third Crossing. It allows humans to make their way in the world. Now, the emerging digital reality has provided the tools to navigate all three realities. The man-machine "Singularity" that Kurzweil describes is actually the beginning of a new road of expansion. At the helm of that expansion will be a "new" human being, one that has extended its own phenotype to include a digital reality of human knowledge and the tools to efficiently apply that knowledge.

Fourth, the view of digeality as the extension of human nature does not imply a complete rejection of other "singularity" visions. On the contrary, technology is our means for creating new knowledge and rendering knowledge into useful forms. With the use of digital technology, the acquisition and the creation of new knowledge will certainly accelerate and set us on a course of conversion, a course where "the evolution of intelligence and the intelligence of evolution become less distinct,"[4] as George Dyson sums up in *Darwin Amongst the Machines*, a course that will ultimately unite the separate journeys of reality and knowledge and reach a point where the rendition of knowledge—digital or otherwise—becomes indistinguishable from the texture of reality itself.

Fifth, in the last few years, the vision of many advocates of artificial intelligence is changing. Perhaps it is frustration with the results. Maybe it is the notion that human "intelligence" involves more than problem solving, or the realization that neural networks cannot adequately capture the entire algorithmic essence of the human brain. Whatever the reason, several renowned AI experts have turned their attention to biology for new solutions. According to Rodney Brooks, director of the Artificial Intelligence Laboratory and Fujitsu Professor of Computer Science at the Massachusetts Institute of Technology:

> We have turned labs that were used to assemble silicon and steel robots into labs where we assemble robots from silicon, steel and living cells. We cultivate muscle cells and use them as the actuators in these simple devices, the precursors of prostheses that will be installed seamlessly into disabled human bodies. Some AI (artificial intelligence) Lab faculty who study how to make machines learn have stopped building better search engines and begun inventing programs

that can learn correlations in the human genome and thereby making predictions about the genetic cause of disease. We have turned rooms that used to house mechanical CAD (computer-aided-design) systems into rooms where we measure the cerebral motor control of human beings, so that eventually we can build neural prostheses for people with diseased brains. And our vision researchers, who used to build algorithm for detecting Russian tanks during the cold war, now build specialized vision systems to provide guidance during neurosurgery. Similar transformations are happening throughout engineering departments, not just at MIT, but throughout the world.[5]

The ultimate outcome of this effort is not yet clear. Perhaps AI experts will discover that, while kicking an old-time radio might bring its sound to life, kicking a stubborn algorithm is not as productive. Systems built from silicon and steel may not gain the independence from the thermodynamic forces of the universe as living organisms did. Likewise, these machines may not produce thoughts that acquire independence from their underlying flow of electrons, as humans have. Perhaps some functions of living organisms cannot be reproduced in machines. Does biology offer unique mechanisms that produce human knowledge? Is the secret of creativity hidden in the molecular organic structure of the biological brain? Is the human operating system written in the programming "language" of organic constructs? If so, we need to learn some fundamental things about human understanding and thinking, and enhance our ability to repair and augment our bodies, before we can "download" our brains. In the meantime, humanity will continue to build a plethora of robots from silicon, steel, molecules, and living components, as this creative impulse is an expression of what makes us human.

Over the past decades, digital machines have become ever more "alive," a fact that should be recognized with awe, pride, and admiration. At the forefront of these developments is the brilliance of the human mind, as they are the products of its thinking activity. Digeality expands our minds, connecting them over the Internet to the human knowledge in existence today. My "personal" digital twin can talk to everybody else's and connect me to the vast landscape of cultures, ideologies, mind-sets, and scientific theories that make up digeality. Therein lies the power of the Internet, not only as a tool of communication, but as an expression of the mental reality of the planet in all its richness and diversity. It reveals the true nature of our best scientific explanations of the evolutionary and relative nature of reality and the power and the adaptability of the human mind.

Sixth, the impact of digeality on our lives goes far beyond the possible rise of a new ruling class of "Robo Sapiens." After all, if machines solve all of our problems, perhaps life as "domesticated" creatures would have no responsibilities. We might even think that we are in charge. Who is to say whether your dog thinks that he is taking you for a walk or the other way around?

But enough of this idle musing, as it is not the same with human beings as with dogs, at least not until we face the gate to an entirely new threshold. Please don't misunderstand our meaning here. Humanity *will* build Robo Sapiens, non-living and "living" ones. Will they be intelligent? Probably, yes. But will they be smart? In *Our Molecular Future*, Douglas Mulhall explains why they might be:

> We may need artificially enhanced intelligence to understand nature's mysteries and the complexities that we're unleashing upon ourselves. If we're too squeamish about that, let's remember that we have the beginnings of such enhanced intelligence, in the form of computers that help us run everything from cars to life support, and implants that replace defective parts of our bodies. Moreover, if we want to stop killing ourselves by the tens of millions in violent conflict, we're going to have to get much smarter, because our genes haven't been able to solve that by themselves. This means addressing at least one probability: that the day of Homo sapiens may be numbered, either by nature's disruptive technology or our own. In a blink of the geological eye, we may be surpassed by our own creations or annihilated by nature's. Right now, we are not ready.[6]

The potential virtues and the perils of this technology are clear, as is the mindless way in which humans sometimes develop and apply those technologies. However, Mulhall's vision of being "surpassed by our own creations" is not so clear. Being "smart" also has to do with *intuition* and *imagination* or is driven by *intention*, *purpose*, and the amazing power of *curiosity*. In this sense, machines are *not* now nor may never be smart, while humans *are*. *Intelligence* is the source of knowledge that helps people make imaginative *and* intelligent choices. Intelligence is the essence of order: defining the knowable and the known, the predictable, the expectable, and the dependable. "Smartness," on the other hand, has the flavor of the unpredictable, of opportunity, the unknown, and the surprise of innovation. No change, no innovation, no scientific breakthroughs, no groundbreaking engineering insights, and no new expressions of art take place without this smartness. Smartness is just another word for "creativity with purpose."

Digeality provides both the accessibility to new renditions of intelligence and the tools to create new expressions of smartness. This can expand our human mental reality and elevate our human consciousness to new levels of understanding and operating reality. All of that human knowledge, the expressions of intelligence and also of smartness, can be embedded in the new reality of the digital world for everyone to see, hear, and touch them and to use them for the creation of new futures. All we have to do is to re-vision about our own evolutionary history and the evolutionary potential of the human mind. We have to stop using our "common-sense" static framework for the future and discover that such a framework acts only as a rearview mirror, pulling us back into Darwinian thinking.

Digeality presents us with a forward-projecting mirror that reflects the expansionary "nature" of nature: the nature of the universe, of biological life, and of human knowledge. This digital reality connects us and offers all of us the insights to make conscious changes for the future, as it reflects and projects our knowledge forward into the unknown. That is the spirit of the emerging digital reality. That is the digital spirit. Our minds are at the helm of the future of evolution, surrounded by the rest of nature: the known and the unknown, the knowable and the unknowable. We should power our boat with the engine of the knowable, while being properly humbled by the mysteries of the unknown and the unknowable. Our mind-sets then determine the direction of the boat. Determining that direction is the challenge we face, as evolution presents us with the ever-expanding repertoire of options and digeality expands that repertoire for everybody living today. The expansion of options is destiny, but choosing destinations is our responsibility—digeality takes away the alibi of ignorance.

Seventh, Ray Kurzweil foresees a merger of human and machine qualities, plus a looming impotence of *human* nature to deal with the realities of the future. We agree with the former and disagree with the latter. In Kurzweil's view, intelligent machines will create and disseminate intelligent solutions to the problems of the present and create a future that mankind can no longer understand. Artificial intelligence will reign in the form of a new self-bred type of algorithms that emerge from the complexity of man-made knowledge "seeds" sown in the fertile soil of networked silicon chips. These highly intelligent "spiritual machines" will create their own physical manifestations that act in the world. Helped on their way by human ingenuity, these creatures will reach beyond their present doll-like dependence on humans to become autonomous beings at the helm of the future, but it remains unclear within Kurzweil's scenario whether there will be a post-singularity "individuality"—e.g., distinctive machines that have different personalities. As Kurzweil explains:

> A key advantage of nonbiological intelligence is that machines can easily share their knowledge. If I learn French, or read *War and Peace*, I can't readily download that learning to you. You have to acquire that scholarship the same painstaking way that I did. My knowledge, embedded in a vast pattern of neurotransmitter concentrations and interneuronal connec-

tions, cannot be quickly accessed or transmitted. But we won't leave out quick downloading ports in our nonbiological equivalents of human neuron clusters. When one computer learns a skill or gains an insight, it can immediately share that wisdom with billions of other machines.[7]

In this scenario, personality is an arbitrary or perhaps optional feature of the machines. Who or what assigns these personalities? Emergence of a personality is impossible if everything is automatically shared in a digitally connected network of machines. When machine "A" downloads French, then all the other machines know French as well. Personality traits would be as pervasive—and invasive—as junk e-mail today. No individuals, just one big intelligent machine. Unless these machines produce innovative algorithms on their own, protect themselves from receiving junk personality traits or arrange a "machine-intellectual-property right" with all the legal trappings, every machine will have the same personality. Machines that can produce such algorithms are the dream of the artificial intelligence profession. To realize this dream, however, will require filling in formidable knowledge gaps.

IT'S ABOUT TIME

Filling these knowledge gaps may require a paradigm change in the scientific worldview itself: a change that involves our notion of space and time. But what if space and time are just illusions of our own human making? Or, to use Brian Greene's words in *The Fabric of the Cosmos*:

> Just as the hardness of a cannonball, the smell of the rose, and the speed of the cheetah disappear when you examine matter at the atomic level, space and time may similarly dissolve when scrutinized with the most fundamental formulation of nature's laws.[8]

If time and space could turn out to be just perceived manifestations of a deeper reality, they lose their power as measurement devices. Since Einstein showed that time is not the absolute dimension we thought it to be, and that acceleration is an accumulation of inertia, we have learned to take extreme care when we use time to measure anything at all. Quantum mechanics guides us even further towards a flexible interpretation of time. Ray Kurzweil, however, uses *time* and a derivative of time—*acceleration*—to build the philosophical foundation for the coming technological singularity. To quote Kurzweil:

> Thus the (double) exponential growth of computing is broader than Moore's Law.[9] And this accelerating growth of

computing is, in turn, part of a yet broader phenomenon discussed above, the accelerating pace of any evolutionary process.[10]

From this observation, Kurzweil derives his "Law of Accelerating Return," which explains that any evolutionary process accelerates and thus yields accelerating returns. These accelerating returns then—in the form of higher computing speeds—will reach a threshold, where something profoundly new emerges. The authors suggest that this "law of accelerating return" has things upside down. *Not that time leads to change, but—in evolution—change leads to time.* Change is the core of existence, right down to the basic vibrations of the fundamental strings that we call particles—to their patterns of energetic change. Change is a fundamental attribute of every existing, living, or thinking entity. Experience is the perception of change and, as such, experience *is* a manifestation of change. Time, in this view, is merely our human way to order experiences. We "undergo" a series of experiences, and we call the axis along which we order them "time." As David Deutsch says in *The Fabric of Reality*:

> We do not experience time flowing, or passing. What we experience are differences between our present perceptions and our present memories of past perceptions. We interpret those differences, correctly, as evidence that the universe changes with time. We also interpret them, incorrectly, as evidence that our consciousness, or the present, or something, moves through time.[11]

Time, then, has nothing to do with the emergence of anything that is new. We might, for practical purposes, use time to measure the speed of a new development, but we cannot use it to measure the nature of change itself. The speed of computers might accelerate forever, but that alone will not produce a fundamentally new reality. Digeality is now changing the human enterprise in fundamental ways today, but the changes that happen around us, be they e-commerce, e-government, or intelligent machines. And this is just the beginning of a re-visioning of our way of life, of war and peace, of family and professional life, and the institutions that govern and service us. Digeality will change our experiences and the way we experience. Digeality completes the toolkit that makes us human and will ultimately change our notion of time and its application to our lives. As Peter Russell notes in *The Challenge of Ever-Accelerating Change*:

> In conclusion, those who will best survive and even thrive in the coming times are those who learn to take back some of the time that accelerating change is taking away. We need to reclaim quality time to think, to rest, to allow ideas to bubble

and to let feelings surface. Time to nurture our relation-ships—both at home and at work. Our culture has developed a remarkable mastery of the material world around us; it is time now to develop a similar mastery of the inner world of mind. This is the next great frontier, not outer space, but inner space.[12]

For Peter Russell, time is of the essence, because time is about the quality of human experience. Isn't that what our lives come down to: the quality of our experiences? From the immense joy of holding a newly born for the first time, to the all-consuming pain at the departure of a loved one? Aren't those the moments when time does not seem to exist; when we truly *are*? When we focus on time, we are focusing on the abstract boundaries between experiences, ignoring the essence of living, thinking, and feeling. The quality of the human future will be determined by the quality of individual human experiences, not by time or any of the things that time tries to measure.

While it is true that the quality of the future is humanity's to squander, the history of nature speaks well for humanity's ability to transcend our own reality. That is a source of hope concerning human nature, which is the latest manifestation of nature's intel-ligence. No doubt there will be the false starts, missteps, and retracing our paths in the future, as in the past. But learning from mistakes is one of humanity's strongest suits, isn't it? Let's get to it!

NOTES

1. Ray Kurzweil, "The Evolution of Mind of the Twenty-First Century," *Are We Spiritual Machines*, Jay Wesley Richards, ed., Discovery Institute, 2002. Also available at: www.kurzweilai.net/meme/frame.html?main=/meme/memelist.html?m%3D19.

2. Ray Kurzweil, *The Intelligent Universe*. Originally published on Edge.com, November 7, 2002. Published December 12, 2002, on www.kurzweilai.net.

3. Jan Amkreutz, *Digital Spirit, Minding the Future* (1stbooks Library, 2003), 387.

4. George B. Dyson, *Darwin among the Machines* (London: Perseus Books, 1997).

5. Rodney Brooks, "The Merger of Flesh and Machines," *The Next Fifty Years, Science in the First Half of the Twenty-First Century*, John Brockman, ed. (New York: Vintage Books, 2002), 187.

6. Douglas Mulhall, *Our Molecular Future, How Nanotechnology, Robotics, Genetics, and Artificial Intelligence Will Transform Our World* (Amherst, NY: Prometheus Books, 2002), 312.

7. John Brockman, *After the Singularity: A Talk with Ray Kurzweil.* Originally published on March 25, 2002, on Edge.com. Interview can be found on www.kurzweilai.net.

8. Brian Greene, *The Fabric of the Cosmos: Space, Time, and the Texture of Reality* (New York: Knopf Books, 2004), 472.

9. Gordon Moore, one of the inventors of integrated circuits, and then chairman of Intel, noted in the mid-1970s that we could squeeze twice as many transistors on an integrated circuit every 24 months. The implication is that computers, which are built from integrated circuits, are doubling in power every two years. Since then, the rate of expansion established by Moore's Law has been met and sometimes exceeded.

10. Ibid., *After the Singularity.*

11. David Deutsch, *The Fabric of Reality* (New York: Penguin Books, 1997), 263.

12. See, Peter Russell, *The Challenge of Ever-Accelerating Change: Finding Inner Wisdom in Uncertain Times,* at www.peterussell.com/speaker/InSp.html.

WHERE SCIENCE IS HEADED: SIXTEEN TRENDS

by

Joseph F. Coates

While the scope of science is boundless, the contents massive, and the impact universal, it is still practical to see trends that mark the path of science into the future. Sixteen trends noted here are durable and likely to shape the overall scientific enterprise in the next decade or two. Trends within specific sciences are not covered.

1. There is a continuing blurring of the distinction between science and technology—This is most clearly seen in high-tech areas such as the production of computer chips, where basic science is increasingly called upon for help and new capabilities are rapidly employed. More generally, science is called upon where the identifiable limitations of current technologies demand a fresh basic look to find radically new avenues of improvement. The classic example of this is the telephone industry's needs for relief from unrealistic future demands on equipment and on its workforce, which led to the invention of the transistor.

2. The distinction between basic and applied science also continues to blur—This is extremely significant because it implies the breakup of the self-serving conceptual distinction made by academics. Obviously, academics prefer to see themselves as involved in basic scientific research, best characterized as self-initiated, with those in applied research assigned to a secondary and less prestigious status. In spite of all sorts of efforts to sustain the distinction, the differences between the two are fading quickly, in much the same way that the distinction between science and technology is fading. Practical needs and goals of the funders of research eventually shape, if not fully determine, the nature of the research enterprise. For example, federal funders are increasingly requiring a statement of the potential future benefits of proposed research. In many advanced projects, best illustrated by the space program or by military technology, the need to achieve some objective such as "a man on the moon by the year X" implies that plans specify large numbers of developments that are not possible at the time the plan is written. This situation frequently leads to "research basic to…." This again is an illustration of the crack in the academic monopoly on basic research since many of these basic research projects end up in the hands not of universities but of nonprofit and government laboratories and private contractors.

The two trends above link to a third trend in an important way because they show the shortcomings of the academic distinctions that are so important to maintaining the disciplinary categories at the university, and the associated performance necessary to progress up

Joseph F. Coates *is a consulting futurist, president, and principal of Joseph F. Coates Consulting Futurist, Inc., in Washington, D.C. He may be contacted at joe@josephcoates.com.*

an academic ladder.

3. Interdisciplinarity is increasingly important in research while largely ignored by academics and their universities—Almost all of the new leading-edge fields in science—genetics, brain research, and nanotechnology, as well as materials science, robotics, and automation—require interdisciplinary R&D. The university is by and large not comfortable in accommodating this intrinsic demand of contemporary research. As a partial mechanism for dealing with the need for interdisciplinarity they often set up "institutes," which are more often than not only loosely linked to the basic science departments' teaching and curricula.

There clearly are exceptions to this common behavior. One can see, for example, several programs at Harvard, MIT, and other distinguished universities getting into interdisciplinarity, especially in its graduate schools. But as a rule the bulk of American universities' interdisciplinarity can be seen as aspiration or as empty claims rather than as reality. Far too often, academic programs attempt to achieve interdisciplinarity by the stapler rather than by the true conceptual integration of research programs and the production of something truly interdisciplinary.

Again, interdisciplinarity in science is more and more being captured by federal laboratories, by federal contractors, and by large nonprofits such as SRI International. This is a pity because, first, it shortchanges the employers of the scientific workforce by training students too narrowly, in disciplines, while the action today is at the interface of disciplines. Second, it does the university a disservice by making it less viable as the primary or secondary place one wishes to go to in order to move into the most intellectually exciting research areas.

4. Credentialing in science is rapidly changing, expanding, and diversifying—This is a challenge to the traditional certifying by the university and is a response to the university's indifference and sluggishness in responding to new needs. The scientific enterprise is changing. Learning that is *ad hoc*, through freestanding courses or electronically based colleges, certifications by professional societies, and various other kinds of teaching and learning through the media, the Internet, and cassettes mark these forces for change. There is now also the credentialing beginning at high school that allows college credit for an expanding range of courses. There is the credentialing going on within corporations through in-house or contracted education and training programs for their own employees or contractors.

5. Globalization of both basic and applied research is rapidly progressing—This goes well beyond the two hundred years plus of globalization of science embodied in open literature exchange and international meetings. The current level of globalization involves the integration of research on global sites by research sponsors. Corporations such as Siemens or governmental agencies, looking for the highest degree of talent at the best possible cost, will buy that talent wherever it is.

Globalization has been facilitated by the end of the Cold War, which generated a super-abundance of cheap, highly skilled labor in the Iron Curtain countries, and by the more recent emergence of highly skilled labor in China, India, and to a lesser extent in other countries. The quality of that foreign talent is an attractive complement to the US base, in being stronger in theory but perhaps marginal in goals and commitment to practical applications.

Aside from the low cost and high volume of talent available, information technology is the single most important facilitator of globalized research. It can, for example, give the research organization a 16- or even a 24-hour day in R&D, as research activity passes through time zone after time zone to make a global circuit. Round-the-clock research accelerates the productive outcomes of a project and thereby offers the sponsor a potential advantage in meeting competitive goals.

In addition, information technology allows extremely effective management by more or less wiping out distance as a temporal factor. With a little experience or training, both R&D managers and staff learn to communicate effectively and economically through the use of groupware and broadband communications to exchange and discuss real-time details—whether graphic, tabular, or simply verbal.

6. Outsourcing is increasingly commonplace—It is virtually universal in some sectors of research and development, production, test, and evaluation. Field work is frequently outsourced. These tendencies are especially strong in the chemical sector and in information technology. In sectors with already extensive experience in outsourcing manufacturing, such as automotives, it is an easy and comfortable extension into outsourcing R&D. The key advantage is that it allows one to draw upon best available talent, while the cost is often lower and the flexibility much higher than if the work were conducted internal to the organization.

7. English is now the universal language in science—Scientists outside of the English-speaking world strive to be published in English-language journals. Young scientists—those under 40—are fully literate in English. The professional universality of English facilitates the globalization in outsourcing noted above. Possibly an exception to the universality is Japan. Technical and scientific results are often reported in both English and Japanese. But the difficulty of the Japanese language affords some advantage in which Japan can claim openness—and at the same time be relatively closed. This is accomplished by publishing many things, particularly in science policy, only in Japanese—and only much later, if at all, in English. It is not clear the extent to which China is engaged in similar publication policies in the planning globalization of its own R&D.

8. In the United States, basic and applied science is increasingly falling into the hands of foreign-born scientists, in training in

American universities and among those already established in their field—This has to be good for the global community of science, for foreign countries, and for businesses outside of the United States, since we are the outstanding training ground for scientists in almost every field. The policy issue needing to be examined is whether this growing dependency on foreign-born talent is good for the future of the US R&D establishment and for our general competitive position in the world. Heartfelt beliefs are no substitute for the absent research on this issue.

Recently a new issue has arisen that has not been adequately documented in terms of scope and significance. It appears to be quite common that a high-tech firm, usually an information technology firm, will fire high-priced native-born scientists and then make a plea to import foreign scientists at a substantially lower pay rate to fit a gap in its workforce. While that is the overall pattern, the details by which one can accomplish this are complex. This illustrates a side effect of globalization of talent, and it creates a domestic issue. What are the effects on the economic health and well-being of individual American scientists, engineers, and technologists and on their families? Should companies be allowed openly or by subterfuge to replace a citizen by a foreigner merely to enhance the corporate bottom line?

9. Physical science is still king of the hill, although biological sciences are fast coming to share that primacy, especially through genetics research, medical research, and brain research—The area where the most definitive research is conducted and hence the largest economic value continues to lie is in physical science and its derivative applications. My criterion for the status of the sciences is their ability to make definitive, unequivocal, highly reliable, and precise responses to current needs and questions through practical applications. There is no doubt that almost any question of a mechanical, engineering, material, or electronic sort can be answered definitively so that one can confidently make institutional, operational, planning, and personal decisions. The social sciences are still at the pre-definitive stage; that is, both theory and research often—if not usually—fall short of definite conclusions to shape policy, planning, and actions. They, however, should not be dismissed in public organizational decision making. They are able to inject an awareness of incompleteness, uncertainty, and openness into plans, programs, and projects that scientists, engineers, business people, and politicians may be too aggressively promoting. On the other hand, the social sciences, because they are still at a pre-definitive stage, too often have a strong ideological orientation and a less-than-even-handed approach to social, economic, and political issues. Regrettably, the social sciences in their relentless move toward more and more quantitative methods (apparently in some mimicry of physical sciences) have all too often given theory short shrift.

10. Physical and biological sciences are undergoing increasingly

important changes because of effects of information technology, particularly computers and telecommunications—Devices, equipment, tests, and analyses are moving to smaller and smaller scale, with the consequence that often incredibly large numbers of analyses and vast amounts of data are produced rapidly. Particularly in pharmacology, chemistry, and genetics, thousands of tests can routinely be conducted simultaneously on small-scale arrays. An interesting example of the practical effects is in forensic science, where incredibly small amounts of DNA evidence can provide definitive identification in a criminal situation.

Secondly—apparently at odds with the above—is that low-cost tools, equipment, and techniques now offer much broader opportunities for field work. For example, low-cost sensors and reporting devices can be put out in large numbers to collect a volume of information that was unthinkably difficult to gather 20 years ago. Sensors are now often in practice and surely in principle able to detect anything that one would want to detect. One sees this, for example, in the development of artificial noses to detect contraband material. Any physical phenomenon or biological material or other signal such as precursors to earthquakes can now be sensed or measured and hence contribute to the overall competence of the sciences in practical affairs and theoretical understanding.

Thirdly, simulation has become a tool in virtually every scientific area. Soon, nothing will be constructed until it has been planned, designed, tested, evaluated, and modified in cyberspace.

11. Ecology is the logical scientific base for all environmentalism and for the environmental movement—But regrettably progress is slow, underfunded, and without a sound theoretical base. One only has very general semi-quantitative and qualitative notions, such as "everything goes somewhere" serving as weak theory. Without an adequate scientific base we still see a tremendous amount of gratuitous conflict and disagreement with regard to environmental management and the future.

12. The scientific knowledge held by the public is pitiably thin and unreliable—Recurrent surveys sponsored by the National Science Foundation show the ubiquity of ignorance about science. The government is the primary potential source of remedy for this deficiency. But both the executive and legislative branches more or less sit on their hands. The National Science Foundation had its political misadventure decades ago in producing textbook material and has been gun-shy ever since. The most conservative inhabitants of Capitol Hill are ever ready to block educational, medical, or other information they find ideologically obscene and to punish the perpetrators by budgetary cuts or constrictive legislation. The president's education program promises "No Child Left Behind," but at least as far as science goes, it is a joke.

The primary consequence of this regrettable state of public ignorance is that, as more and more often scientific matters become public-policy issues, the population is left open to extremist, erroneous, or fantastic claims, unsound policy solutions, and a general intellectual mess of conflicting and faulty recommendations and ultimately bad laws, regulations, and policies.

13. Industry-sponsored basic research has more or less tanked—It is difficult to see much basic research with a truly long-term perspective, or beyond their immediate business interests, in the 25 or so top firms in terms of R&D investment. The amount of money industry spends on research is not strongly correlated with its basic nature. General Motors and Ford are among the nation's, and therefore the world's, largest funders of R&D. They have been right up there for decades, and yet can the reader name even one distinguished American scientist employed by either company, much less a Nobel laureate?

14. Hobbyists, ideologues, and amateurs are challenging traditional science in two separate ways—Many are literally challenging the reliability of research coming out of the established scientific community. This is clearly illustrated in the health and medical area. One has only to turn to the Internet to be confounded by the tremendous lot of truths, half-truths, lies, falsifications, and misunderstandings to be found there on any health issue. The Internet also widely propagates the occult and semi-occult. Many people still believe that something special went on at Roswell, and many people believe that there are extraterrestrials visiting us—and kidnapping some of us. Others still doubt that man has walked on the moon.

On the other hand, the development from hobbyist into an amateur scientist brings us all benefits. Now it is possible for thousands of people with surplus time on their computers to link into large-scale scientific experiments to do data processing, gratis, as public service. Repeatedly, amateurs are making astronomical discoveries of substantial importance.

The scientific community needs to develop better ways of coping with the ideologues and the ignoramuses and at the same time promoting scientific hobbyists and talented amateurs.

15. There is growing tension from the strong pressure for useful results—on schedule—in government, business, and foundation funding of R&D—The commitment to the bottom line in business is what underlies the pressure for scheduling what usually cannot be scheduled. It is not quite so clear what the driver for "results on demand" is in government funding agencies. The net effect is to drive out attention to what is and which must be uncertain in its outcome and timing. Science is now becoming a victim of a concept made famous in a different domain by Henry Kissinger: "The urgent drives out the important."

16. There is a continuing call for technology assessment, but not under that name—The Congressional Office of Technology Assessment, after a quarter of a century of distinguished service to Congress and therefore to the nation, was deep-sixed by a group of aggressive conservatives new to the Congress and not understanding how it worked or what support it needed. Technology assessment is not now conducted anywhere in the United States, but the cry for it comes up in many corners, including Capitol Hill. A recent example is Bill Joy's plea for better understanding of the future consequences of self-reproducing and intelligent robotics, genetics, and nano devices. His near-frantic plea for understanding showed that he was unfamiliar with the concept of technology assessment and what can be done and what had been done, but the plea is nevertheless justified. While the concept of TA is thriving in Europe and growing elsewhere in the industrialized nations, we who have the largest economy and the largest commitment to R&D and to the ubiquitous use of technology see our political and business leadership remaining staunchly indifferent to anticipating what side effects and unanticipated outcomes could be.

CONCLUSION

These notes on trends shaping the future of science do not cover the rich texture of forces more specifically shaping the individual sciences, nor do they probe the manifold pressures on public and private science policy. Nevertheless, they offer a framework for policy discussion and a pattern into which more detailed forces and factors can be integrated.

[Editor's note: This article appeared in the *Journal of the Washington Academy of Sciences*, Vol. 89, No. 3-4, Winter 2003.]

MICROTECHNOLOGY AND BIOLOGICAL DESIGN

by

William Holmes

MICROTECHNOLOGY AND NANOTECHNOLOGY

Microscopic technology has received much attention in the past few years, popularized by the word nanotechnology. However, nanotechnology designates the design and manufacture of devices one micron (1,000 nanometers) and smaller, down to atomic dimensions. In general, nanotechnology is experimental and speculative; working devices are few. Microtechnology describes larger devices, from one micron up to those visible to the naked eye, with many kinds of electrical, mechanical, and analytic devices already in production. Microtechnology benefits enormously from the simple fact that every step in the fabrication and assembly of microdevices can be guided by ordinary vision. One needs only a common light microscope. In contrast, vision in the nanotechnology range generally requires electron microscopes operating in a high vacuum.

There are already many products of microtechnology. Electronic devices lead with computer chips, complex analog circuitry, microlasers, flat displays, and the CCD arrays found in both video and still cameras. The same mask-and-etch methods used so successfully in electronic manufacture have been adapted for manufacturing microelectronic mechanical systems (MEMS) devices. Commercial products include sensors to measure force, acceleration, pressure, and temperature and movable micromirrors for switching light signals. Etched microfluidic devices are coming into use as chemical and biochemical microlaboratories.

MASS PRODUCTION METHODS IN MICROTECHNOLOGY

Each fabrication step in microtechnology acts in parallel on a large array of devices. Printing, a parallel process, extends to the various mask, etch, and spray techniques for making electronic circuits and MEMS devices. Arrays of master molds etched into a surface can simultaneously produce large numbers of mechanical parts by stamping or injection molding. The molds are reusable, greatly reducing costs.

Modified ink jet computer printers are sold for small-scale production of parts of arbitrary shape, building them by depositing microscopic drops layer by layer. The jets deposit liquids containing polymers or powders of solid materials such as metals and ceramics. The drops form a layer of complex shape that solidifies by evaporation of the solvent, chemical reaction, or laser beam heating. Complex

William Holmes *has been with the Digital Equipment and Monsanto corporations and in the Radiation Oncology Department of the University of Arizona Medical School. He may be contacted at bholmes2@mindspring.com.*

three-dimensional shapes are built up layer by layer to form a completed array of parts that may be further hardened by heating.

Arrays of hollow probes can assemble devices with multiple parts in parallel, adding each part simultaneously to an array of partially assembled devices. The parts can be picked up by applying a slight vacuum in the probes, then deposited on the growing devices with positive air pressure. Probes equipped with MEMS microgrippers are another possibility. Probes and laser beams can also directly join parts by applying adhesives or heat.

Microtechnology will move forward like standard technology, primarily by small steps that improve existing products in cost, reliability, and function. The products will become smaller and more numerous, decreasing in cost, following the history of microelectronics. When reliable devices reach sizes around 10 microns, they will enter the range of biological design, the "natural" size, the size of typical human cells. Products in this range will effectively merge the biological world with the world of human products. Homesteads can become nearly self-sufficient in basic needs; personal health care at the individual cell level will emerge. Our present limitations in land and natural resources will nearly disappear, by exploring, building, and even living in a microuniverse of immense size.

BIOLOGICAL DESIGNS IN MICROTECHNOLOGY

The cell is the basic construction unit of biology. Every human life starts from a single cell, which by a series of cell divisions, migrations, and differentiation produces an adult built from trillions of cells. Most human cells range in size from 10 microns upward, easily visible in considerable detail by a standard light microscope. Cells, of course, are extremely complex molecular factories. But they can also be viewed much more simply as biological parts that function similarly to those in manufactured devices. Thus, sensory cells for light, sound, touch, pressure, heat, and chemicals correspond to sensors for the same physical phenomena. Muscle cells correspond to actuators, networks of nerve cells to microprocessors. Various brick, shingle, and fiber-shaped cells correspond to similar mechanical counterparts. Collagen and elastin, the reinforcing and elastic fibers of the extracellular matrix, have their manufactured counterparts.

Clothes are a prime example of the potential for biological design: We can create clothes that provide physical protection from cold and harm, and even adjustable physical support. They can monitor the shape, tension, and motion of the body, as well as internal physiological signals. The clothes might contain facilities for communicating with the outside world by sight, sound, touch, and pressure. Such clothes deserve the name bioclothes. A few simple definitions will further clarify the principle of biological design:

- *Biopart*—a device functionally similar to some kind of cell, or cell fiber, designed to be assembled with other bioparts. Their size will range downward from the visible to cell size. Note that cells shaped like fibers can be quite long. Some human muscle cells are six inches long, while neuron axons can reach three feet.

- *Biostructure*—an assembly of bioparts; comparable to a biological tissue. Bioclothes are a type of biostructure.

- *Bionet*—bioparts connected by the equivalent of wires, or by wireless connections using sound or electromagnetic waves.

The development of biostructures with bionets will proceed incrementally using currently available devices as bioparts, since even simpler versions with fewer and larger parts will have many uses. Simple bioclothes are already in use, with a network of sensors woven into the cloth, a step towards clothing with the properties of skin. Successive reductions in device size will eventually arrive at bioparts of cell size and bioclothes that seamlessly serve as a versatile interface between the outside world and the body within.

NATURAL BIOPARTS FOR USING INSIDE THE BODY

Cells are natural bioparts. There are several hundred kinds of human cells, variously adapted to patrolling the body for infection and injury, processing multiple electrical signals, generating efficient motion, detecting chemicals, serving as molecular gatekeepers, and maintaining complex mechanical shapes. Modified cells can become internal bioparts, taking advantage of the enormous potential built into human cells and their obvious fitness to reside in the human body. Immune cells are the natural prototype; each cell's DNA is modified to recognize a single kind of foreign molecule among the millions of possibilities. Sensory neurons are suggestive prototypes for an internal bionet to report conditions within the body.

FUNDAMENTAL PROBLEMS

We live today with a number of limitations, frustrations, and fears that can be relieved by moving our technology into the microworld, specifically by using cell-size parts and modified cells as fundamental building blocks. The details are described in the next section.

Our Life as Industrial Parts

The industrial system of developed countries provides nearly all their inhabitants with enormous benefits—ample food and clothing; spacious, warm, dry living spaces; plausible expectations of a long, healthy life; freedom from grinding labor; and many opportunities for work and play. However, each of us is truly a part of a gigantic industrial machine, quite helpless without the coordinated actions of millions of others. We have lost the self-sufficiency of the simple hunter-gatherer societies from where we came. The fear of unemployment or, worse, technological obsolescence is never far from our thoughts. If we consciously move steadily towards smaller scale, more localized production, then small groups, families, and individuals can gradually regain control over their economic lives.

Personal Health Care

Most of us would like to direct our own health care, with confidence that we can prevent the diseases of youth and middle age and that old age will be long, productive, and enjoyable. We can only attain such a goal by stages, gradually developing the ability to monitor the inner workings of our body down to the cellular level, intervening locally when problems arise. We will clearly need to establish some kind of network of cell-size "parts" within our body to interact with individual cells. The network will probably be composed of our own cells, modified to report problems and apply remedies.

How Does the Mind Work?

We lack a basic understanding of why we think and feel the way we do. A personal-observation network within the brain, operating with cell-size "parts," probably modified neurons, can provide us with insight into our actions. Those with serious deficiencies can gradually remedy them by controlling activities of specific neural circuits, even inducing the growth and connection of new neurons where necessary.

Finite Living Space and Resources

We are running out of land, clean air, and water. Competition for land and resources leads to economic and political strife and, even worse, to a pessimistic feeling that only drastic restrictions can prevent future catastrophes. Moving our technologies into the microworld will not directly create more land. We will still need to grow enough to eat, relying on increased crop yields and reduced population growth. However, construction of houses and clothes with imbedded microparts can drastically reduce the energy needed for heating, cooling, lighting, and transportation. People can stay at home yet effectively travel for work or pleasure by projecting their senses and physical actions through bioclothes. By projecting ourselves into microscopic spaces, our psychological and functional sense of space will be enormously expanded as we effectively enter an immense microuniverse.

Security and Freedom

Our security problems range from crime to terrorism to outright war. Surveillance is one answer, by spy satellites, by ubiquitous TV monitors, by spies and undercover agents, and by examining everyone's electronic transactions. Surveillance can be seen as a threat to liberty; public oversight is required. In addition, there are fears of potential dangers imposed by our own products, ranging from the highly credible (nuclear bombs) to the remotely possible (nano-robots). Credible fears need credible public policies to handle them.

THE MICROTECHNOLOGY APPROACH TO FUNDAMENTAL PROBLEMS

Forsaking Our Lives as Industrial Parts—The Road to Self-Reliance

Two historic forces are converging on the workplace: Adam Smith and robotics. Smith envisioned production broken into small steps that any semiskilled worker could master. For 200 years the steps have become more defined, and the workplace more precise, as specialized machines have supplanted skilled motions. Computers are repeating the same process, reducing routine paper work and decision making to rules, then automating their application with computer programs.

Robots replace the simplified manual operations of the worker with a mechanically flexible machine guided by a computer. Robots are beginning to automate the hand-eye skills of those human operators who handle work pieces and assemble them. Incremental improvements in both workflow precision and robot adaptability will continue. Workers will become supervisors; fewer and fewer will be needed. Service jobs such as retail sales, cleaning, and landscape maintenance are subject to the same trends. Even security services will automate by sending video camera and microphone signals to programs for detecting suspicious activity.

Increasing automation will also bring a positive benefit: the potential of working at home. The speed of our electronic communication networks is rapidly nearing the capacity to send sight as well as sound to nearly every home. Sound and vision are digitized and reproduced with excellent fidelity by microphones, earphones, television cameras and monitors. These two senses alone are sufficient for performing many jobs from home. However, controlling mechanical motion from home requires the transfer of human motions to the workplace and returning touch and force sensations for guidance. The communication channels will have sufficient capacity, since visual signals require more bandwidth than signals for the tactile sensations and motions of the hands and arms. However, the equivalent devices for conveying touch, force, and motion are not as fully developed as those for vision and sound. Remote manipulators have been used for many years but are quite specialized. Remotely controlled assembly robots will need a shape resembling human hands and arms, with appropriate touch and force sensors. The home worker will control the robot with tactile gloves that convert finger, hand, and arm motions into digital signals transmitted to the robot and that convert incoming signals into the sensations of force and touch on the hands and arms.

The tactile gloves and robots now in production are crude biostructures. As microtechnology improves, tactile gloves will evolve into full bioclothes, while robots for remote manipulation will evolve into devices that reproduce the full range of human movements and transmit the tactile sensations and forces encountered back to the bioclothes. Such robots will be *teleforms*, the logical extension of the telephone and television to touch, force, and motion.

Remote operation will enable many to work at home. The possibilities will increase greatly as assembly robots become available to the consumer. Assembling products under contract may become a cottage industry. Consumers can also become producers, turning the home workshop into a small factory for making many of the products they would otherwise buy. Hobbyists already make boats and small airplanes from scratch and assemble antique cars from kits. Some make their own furniture, renovate their house, or even build a new one. Many gardeners grow major portions of their diet. Home weavers make unique fabrics from yarn; many more make their own clothing from fabric. Knitters convert yarn directly into clothes. These activities take substantial time and skills. Small robots can do much of the routine work, enabling the home worker to achieve some of the self-sufficiency of earlier times, when each homestead produced most of its requirements.

Many basic production methods began as purely hand operations and are still used for small-scale and one-of-a-kind operations. Glass blowing, forging, casting, and injection molding are examples. The lenses in high-precision microscopes and telescopes were ground using hand tools until well into the 19th century, with surface accuracy in the high nanometer range. Hand tools alone can produce nanotechnology.

Chemistry and biochemistry are inherent microtechnologies, actually nanotechnologies, since the basic "parts" are molecules. Practically any synthesis or analysis can be run on a micro scale. Ten thousand or more distinct chemicals are routinely deposited by arrays of probes on a small glass surface for running parallel analyses, with applications such as detecting gene mutations. Microbiology is another inherent microtechnology. A single microorganism can multiply indefinitely. Although many households now grow a few microorganisms as starters for sourdough breads, yogurt, tempeh, and cheeses, the security implications of general-purpose facilities for microorganism culture in millions of homes are obvious and are considered below.

Microtechnology has further implications for self-sufficient households. Large, human-size objects can be built from microparts, emulating biology. A two-by-four is simply a large number of empty cells with cellulose walls, attached together by other biomolecules acting as glue. Fabrics start as microdiameter fibers of cotton, wool, or synthetic polymers spun into thread and yarn, then further combined by weaving, sewing, and knitting. Ceramics, stone, and metals are conglomerations of small microcrystals. Biostructures from clothes to furniture to houses can be assembled from a supply of inorganic, organic, and manufactured microparts. They might include sensors for temperature, light, sound, chemicals, and even bacteria. They could adapt in shape and strength, change color, communicate, report on internal problems, and perhaps even repair themselves. Variations on microprobe arrays could assemble such structures. As always, the path downward will be incremental, increasingly useful functions emerging as the microparts decrease down to cell size.

The nearly self-sufficient homestead may seem like an ideal, a long time in achieving. Yet the goal is important. Our livelihoods will be increasingly threatened. Our need for agility in guessing job trends and retraining will grow steadily. The more we can do for ourselves, the more self-confident we will feel. Larger groups from families to small towns to small countries will also benefit by a move to small-scale production. A higher degree of local self-sufficiency in the smaller and more impoverished countries, especially within culturally distinct regions, could go a long way towards relieving the world's economic tensions.

Personal Health Care

Although health and life depend on the coordinated actions of our cells, we are nearly blind and totally clumsy when we need to intervene. We can neither fix nor replace individual cells. Surgical intervention destroys thousands with every stroke of the knife. The natural, safe, effective way to guide health care requires inspection and intervention by "objects" no larger than single cells. Genetic diseases and metastatic cancer pose the most obvious needs. Action at the cell level seems best for treating cardiovascular problems like damaged heart muscle fibers and fatty deposits in small vessels. Many degenerative neurological diseases, including some major mental diseases, seem to involve small, distinct networks of neurons. Intervention requires treating the affected cells, while sparing other neural structures in the brain.

Cell care will require constant investigation of conditions within the body in order to guide rational therapy. The patient will become the primary observer, not the physician, a long step towards medical self-care. In brief, bioclothes can monitor major physiological processes from the outside—heart activity, respiration, muscle tone, body motion, temperature, and, periodically, the contents of the breath and urine. Sonic pulses can obtain further information on the shape and motion of interior organs, including the heart. Sensors within the body can monitor the content of blood and tissues and perhaps details of blood flow. These sensors would report to the bioclothes, probably by radio signals, possibly using wire-like extensions up to the skin for better transmission. The sensors need not be cell size, just small enough so that adjacent tissues are not severely crowded. As in all microtechnology, even crude test and reporting methods will be of great value, incrementally modified to smaller and more numerous detectors until cell size is reached.

Intervention at the cell level will require cell-size bioparts. By far the best candidates are one's own cells, which are the proper size, have enormous potential from their DNA, and are naturally compatible with the individual's own immune system. White cells and neurons are both strong candidates. White cells are mobile, capable of moving from the bloodstream and wandering or residing among the cells in tissues. They modify their DNA to recognize one type of molecule among millions of possibilities. Some white cells recognize and attach to specific molecules on a cell surface and secrete (destructive) substances inside. Neurons detect electrical pulses, sound, and chemicals and produce signals by secreting small packets of neurotransmitters. They can extend their axons and dendrites like probes into tissues, often guided by specific molecules on cell surfaces. They have the potential to send and receive signals between the depths of the body and the surface of the skin.

Neurons and white cells would need modification to act in a cell-care network, perhaps by DNA inserted as minichromosomes, viruses, or bacteria, one per cell, incapable of replication. Modified cells or manufactured bioparts could be guided to the proper tissues within the body by recognizing and attaching to specific molecules on cells in the destination tissue. Sound or short wavelength radiation could also serve as guides by scanning the tissue with focused beams converging to a small volume, a method used in radiation therapy and surgery. Crossed beams of differing wavelengths could provide more exact specificity. The modified cells or bioparts would need the capabilities of sensory cells to respond to the sound or radiation. Once a certain number were placed, they could guide further ones into position by secreting special guidance molecules, much like cell movements are guided during embryonic growth.

A true cell-care network of bioparts, whether modified cells or manufactured devices, will report interior conditions to their owner visually and verbally at any level of detail, from organ to cells. The network will care for tissues by secreting appropriate biomolecules, by removing defective cells, by stimulating stem cells to divide, or even by replacing defective cells or nuclei with new ones derived from culture of the person's own cells. Bioparts in the tissue would serve as beacons to guide the replacements to the proper location. True guided imagery for health care will at last become possible.

We can develop cell care incrementally by starting with skin cell care of the epidermis and the underlying dermis. The mechanical problems of access are much less, since bioparts can be introduced directly through the skin. Skin diseases, scarring, and aging provide plenty of medical and psychological motivation.

How Does Our Mind Work?

The immensity of our brain is staggering. If we could enlarge the brain 1,000 times, its 100 billion neurons would be the size of marbles, with root-like fibers extending long distances before coming to rest on other neurons. The entire mass would be a mound hundreds of feet high and wide, tightly packed and intertwined, an impenetrable jungle. Fortunately the brain's structure is not sheer chaos, but divided into a large number of connected networks. Cells with similar function are grouped together, recognizable by their shape, pattern of electrical activity, repertoire of signaling molecules (neurotransmitters), and connections to other groups. We have learned the basic functions of some of these regions by MRI, correlating mental activities like reading with increased blood flow in certain regions. More information comes from the unfortunate victims of brain injuries, strokes, and tumors, whose lost functions are correlated with the regions damaged. Further insight comes from animal studies using very fine wires to measure the electrical activity of single neurons while the animal performs a simple action. These measurements show the activities of single cells, but are necessarily extremely limited in number.

Cell care of the brain will require a genuine network of bioparts, a true bionet, probably built with modified neurons. The complex shapes and mechanical entanglement of neurons require bioparts of cell size to prevent disruption and act effectively on the right cells. Eventually individuals will establish cell-care networks in their brains, sufficient to observe their own neural activity in detail, correlating activity with their conscious perceptions of sight, sound, touch, and muscular actions. The network will be totally under the control of their owners, communicating with their bioclothes. Explorers will investigate their minds by deliberately introducing electrical and chemical signals to enhance or inhibit specific neural networks, learning in the process how their conscious sensations, motivations, and emotions work together and how their memories are related to consciousness.

The origins of mental diseases, uncontrollable emotions, and powerful compulsions will become clear, based on the shared self-knowledge of many. Those with a severe disability can use their network of neural bioparts to correct it. If there is an imbalance of neurotransmitters in certain areas, they can secrete corrective neurotransmitters or inhibitors. If the neurons are damaged, the cell care methods used elsewhere in the body can restore them. If there are too few neurons in a group, the network can stimulate local stem cells to grow new ones and establish chemical gradients as paths for growing connections to other neurons.

It will be possible to train the brain by mental action, much like physical exercise strengthens muscles. Neurons change the density of their projections and their production of neurotransmitters and receptors in response to their level of activity. When neuron function is well correlated with mental action, one can devise appropriate mental exercises to change groups of neurons to function optimally. Those who are willing can improve selected mental abilities and achieve their personal version of optimal mental health. Psychiatry and neuroscience will finally meet.

Finally, insights may be gained on how to attain entirely new mental capabilities hitherto unknown. For example, three primary colors are perceived: red, green, and blue. Combining these three within the brain creates all our other color perceptions. Discovering how this happens could lead to proposed neuron circuits that would combine four primary colors to create color perceptions never experienced. We may be on the verge of exploring an undiscovered world of consciousness—new colors, new emotions, directly perceiving space in three dimensions, hearing an entire musical piece at one time, and sensations literally inconceivable within the limits of our present neural structures. The daring and curious will explore their own brains, personally directing the growth of novel neural structures, describing what they find as best they can to the rest of the world.

More Living Space and Resources—The Microuniverse

Humanity is pressing the earth's resources. Some pressure comes from those who have barely enough to eat. However, the growing numbers who eat well still have unquenched desires for living space and "stuff." Only agricultural technology and population constraint can cope with the food problem, but microtechology can help with the rest. Bioclothes will communicate with teleforms anywhere on earth, potentially reducing the energy spent for commuting and travel. Closer to home, miniature teleforms will let us create complex microenvironments on small pieces of property. Suppose one were magnified a thousand times, a mile-high giant. A glance from any airplane shows that human beings would be invisible, most buildings minuscule, trees and forests tiny plants, even mountains just rocky ground with interesting shapes. Nothing has actually changed, just our psychological perceptions. If we reduced our size a thousand times, the most ordinary plot of land would seem a million times larger; a single room could hold a billion visually similar. This thought experiment can become real, using bioclothes to project our perceptions and actions into a microteleform. Our immediate surroundings can become a *microuniverse*.

Hobbyists already build elaborate miniature environments with working parts, such as miniature railroads covering multiple rooms. Children's dollhouses can be quite detailed, while adults have built elaborate miniature rooms and whole palaces, some displayed in museums. Aquariums are miniature seafloors with fish selected to fit the space. Given miniature tools, and perhaps miniature robots to help, one can use teleforms to build, work, and play in one's own environments. A person can even walk in the environment by using extended bioclothes equipped with a floor that moves like a treadmill of constantly changing shape. The user will have the sensation of walking while actually staying in one place. User and teleform will move together, effectively walking on the microenvironment terrain. Even sports are possible if the players' teleforms and bioclothes are responsive enough.

These miniature environments can be as natural as one wants. There are plants and animals of all sizes down to microns, with fascinating shapes and colors. Rocks have beautiful crystalline structures even at magnifications of one thousand; gravel can become rocky hills. The outdoor lover can create a terrain of great complexity to enjoy and explore.

Closer to home, one can turn a room or even a box into a livable palace, even sleeping in it (while actually lying in one's extended bioclothes). In practice we will have as much psychological space as we want, with huge reserves unused.

Security and Freedom

Security is a fundamental need in any society: freedom from economic hardship, ill health, and physical harm, whether from common criminals, fanatic terrorists, or outright war. The gradual introduction of microtechnology will continue to reduce economic hardship by increasing productive capacity, both industrial and individual. Ill health will become increasingly rare as microtechnology and biotechnology combine to eventually become personal cell care. However, reasonable fears of potential harm from ordinary criminals, terrorists, and hostile nations will become a driving force for ever-increasing surveillance. Sensing devices for sight, sound, chemicals, and microorganisms are bound to proliferate, becoming smaller and smaller as they become ever more numerous. Eventually a pervasive surveillance network may emerge, extending from city streets and buildings into the countryside and even into the air. Computers will recognize individuals by face, walk, and voice, recording what buildings and cars they enter and leave and who they are with. A complete account of everyone's public movements can be stored—even indoor movements in public places.

Controlling the quantity of information gathered and who can use it will become a major issue for all of us. There are two extremes—public access or government investigators only. If everyone can look, whole countries and eventually most of the world will become one global village where everyone knows the other's business. However, open information will neutralize the power that secret knowledge brings. If governments alone can monitor these databases, they will obviously have too much power. At the very least, data collection by the government should always have citizen oversight, preferably by rotating groups of citizens. In general, an individual should be able to see what his or her data files contain. The objection that openness will impede investigations will become less valid, as public surveillance makes it more and more difficult to actually commit crimes.

TECHNOLOGICAL FEARS

Nuclear bombs are the classic example of danger from technology. Atom bombs have been a grave danger for more than 50 years. The established nuclear powers still own a perilous number of bombs, and there are several countries trying to join the club. Surveillance by spies and spy satellites has been a major source of stability by producing believable estimates of the quantity and quality of atomic weapons and discouraging most other nations from developing their own weapons. Bioweapons merit comparable attention, since it is relatively easy to grow microorganisms anywhere in the world with relatively simple equipment. The best defenses will be partly political, fostering a worldwide system of committed governments, each working internally to prevent such activities. However, direct defenses will also be necessary. We will need to obtain an extremely detailed knowledge of the characteristics of microorganisms that are potential bioweapons and develop rapid microdetection methods that are cheap and widely deployable.

A final fear, armies of nanorobots, is a very remote possibility. Forty years of robot research has yet to produce a plausible human-size robot soldier. Shrinking such robots to microscopic size may well be impossible and is certainly far beyond our present capabilities. Insect and mite-sized weapons are more plausible. If they materialize, they will resemble non-reproducing bioweapons. A dense surveillance network, matching their size and numbers, can detect and destroy them, emulating the biological design of our immune system.

A final note. Secrecy will not stop the spread of technology. Secretive nations will blind themselves, spreading suspicions by their own secrecy, while falling behind the rest of the world.

SIGNPOSTS POINTING TO MICROTECHNOLOGY

We can judge how rapidly microtechnology is progressing by the appearance and practical use of the following capabilities. Most already exist in rudimentary form.

The Road to Self-Reliance

Robots that can recognize, handle, and assemble typical objects found on assembly lines.

Home maintenance robots that can clean indoor surfaces and maintain lawns.

A device emulating muscle action with reasonable energy efficiency.

An efficient fuel cell or fuel-powered generator no bigger than a pea.

Bioclothes with the force and tactile capabilities for remote manipulation.

Personal Health Care

A sensor (e.g., for glucose) of any size, embedded in tissue for months without immune reactions, accurately reporting glucose levels to detectors on the surface of the skin.

An embedded device controlled from the skin that releases accurate doses into tissue or blood for months.

Cell size or smaller constructions, like white cells, platelets, bacteria, viruses, or liposomes, that bind nearly exclusively to specific cell types.

Bioclothes for continuous personal monitoring of the heart, general motion, muscular tension, etc.

The Microuniverse

Bioclothes working with a robot manipulator that duplicates human hand-arm movements at one-tenth size, with full magnified vision.

Security and Freedom

A public surveillance/observation network usable by both the public and the government.

PREDICTIONS

The future depends on our goals as much as our technical knowledge. Sustained effort turns "mights" into "cans," and "cans" into "wills."

The Road to Self-Reliance

We can move to a largely self-sufficient society, with outside resources available to all.

Personal Health Care

We can attain personal health care over a long healthy life.
We might extend life by continuous cell repair or replacement.

How Does Our Mind Work?

We can attain our personal vision of mental health, with a deep understanding of our psyche.
We might cultivate our brain to attain powers and skills others possess by birth.
We might possibly extend our brains so as to attain new powers of emotion, sensation, and intellect.

The Microuniverse

We can enter and live, almost entirely, in a vast microuniverse.

Security and Freedom

We can create a society that values freedom first, security second, and provides both.

A Prediction on Predictions

The public perceptions of most of the above predictions will change in the next few years from "futuristic" (the next century) to "possible" (the next generation) to "obvious" (relevant to all of us).

IT IS THE NATURE OF HUMANITY TO CREATE AND EXPLORE

Human consciousness stretches back into prehistory perhaps to pre-human times. During this time our mental life has evolved far beyond other species. Our language, literature, art, music, tools, dwellings, crops, machines, science, and religion are mental states made visible, audible, and tangible through our hands and body. Every human product has a corresponding mental representation in the nervous system. Although humanity and all its products remain a part of nature, human nature has become a creative mental force, always exploring, never static. The collective human minds of the world transcend our individual minds in knowledge, abilities, beliefs, and visions, forming a kind of mind or spirit of humanity. Since we are nearly blind to our inner selves, we inevitably explore inward and downwards into the microworld within our bodies, following the injunction "know thyself."

FUTURE-ORIENTED STUDIES

TRAPS IN FUTURES THINKING—AND HOW TO OVERCOME THEM

by

Mika Mannermaa

FUTURES THINKING—A MERIT LIST

Despite the fact that systematic futures research is a phenomenon born and strengthened only after the Second World War, futures thinking has a long history. Actually it is as long as is the known history of human beings. How good are we in thinking of the future(s)? Here is an incomplete merit list of our competencies in this field:

"Inventions have long since reached their limits, and I see no hope for further developments."
—Roman engineer Julius Sextus Frontinus, A.D. 10

"Heavier than air flying machines are impossible."
—Physicist Lord Kelvin, 1895

"1930 will be a splendid employment year."
—US Department of Labor, 1929

"The Japanese don't make anything the people in the US would want."
—Secretary of State John Foster Dulles, 1954

"By the turn of this century, we will live in a paperless society."
—Roger Smith, chairman of General Motors, 1986

"I predict the Internet...will go spectacularly supernova and in 1996 catastrophically collapse."
—Bob Metcalfe, InfoWorld, 1995

The history of unsuccessful forecasts is a massive cornucopia offering a wide variety of juicy examples. Wallowing in them is, however, useless, if we do not learn from our mistakes. Our ability to think of the future credibly is limited by many factors, like inadequate basic data, knowledge and wisdom, bad methods or bad use of good ones, but also some specific *traps of futures thinking*. The most common of them are *"This is it!"* thinking, *Paradigm blindness, Trend-faith, Cultural contempt, Overenthusiasm* and *Disparagement of everything new.*

Mika Mannermaa *is managing director of Futures Studies Mannermaa Ltd. in Piispanristi, Finland. He may be contacted at ttmanner@netti.fi.*

"THIS IS IT!"

When the Roman engineer Frontinus announced already 2,000 years ago that everything that there is to be invented has been invented, he fell into the trap of *"This is it!"* thinking so familiar to us all. It is tempting to think that some technological or other development has come to the end of its path, and "nothing new under the sun" is left to be expected.

The collapse of the biggest societal experiment in the world history from 1989 was a surprise to all. During the decades of the Cold War after the Second World War people learned to think that *the existing status quo* in world politics would be forever. Not a single futures researcher, political scientist, historian, politician, or business leader made a protest, when the leader (or dictator, if you wish) of the German Democratic Republic, Erich Honecher, announced in the beginning of 1989 that the Berlin Wall would stay upright for at least the next hundred years. It doesn't help much, if you in parenthesis in a subordinate clause in one of your six scenarios wrote that "something like this might happen." But nobody made a clear statement, with a loud voice, that "Hey guys, listen to me, from 1989 the socialist bloc will start collapsing!" *"This is it!"* when it came to the global political status quo.

But then the world changed. The collapse of the socialist bloc was interpreted by the well-known societal philosopher Francis Fukuyama as the end result of the evolutionary battle between the two great ideologies, the Western market liberalism and Socialism. Survival of the fittest meant that the Western view was the winner.[1] In his own way Fukuyama, too, fell into the trap of *"This is it!"* thinking. As it must have been obvious, Fukuyama's theses were opposed by many. Perhaps the best known is Harvard professor Samuel Huntington's article in the journal *Foreign Affairs*.[2] His main argument was that the great civilizations—Western Christianity, Orthodox world, Islam, Confucian philosophy (China), Japanese culture, Hinduism, African, and Latin American cultures—are fundamentally different to the extent that the future is featured by tensions and conflicts between them. Issues related to cultures bypass economic factors in importance, which at the moment operate as the most powerful actors globally. Encounters of cultures strengthen their inner cohesion and emphasize differences between them. Ideas of a single common world culture, meaning the dominance of the Western thinking or a birth of a new culture as a result of some sort of melting process of the present cultures, on the other hand, are implausible. The World Futures Studies Federation arranged a world conference on the theme *Coherence and Chaos in Our Uncommon Futures—Visions, Means, Actions* in 1993.[3] "Uncommon" referred both to the unknown nature of the future and to the varied concepts of reality expressed by the different cultures, which are strange to each other. Different interpretations and educated guesses about these questions were presented in the conference, but, for example, the idea of a global uniform culture was commonly considered both implausible and undesirable.

PARADIGM BLINDNESS

The claim of the famous physicist Lord Kelvin that flying machines, which are heavier than the air, like aircrafts, are impossible, represented a mode of thinking that might be called *paradigm blindness*. Thomas Kuhn presented his well-known concept of paradigm originally in his book *The Structure of Scientific Revolutions* in the beginning of the 1960s.[4] The word paradigm comes from the Greek word *paradeigma*, which means a mode or pattern of thought. To Plato, paradeigma meant the real world of ideas, of which the visible world is only a reflection. The Kuhnian concept of paradigm is related to scientific problem solving, which becomes a guiding thought-model in a certain discipline and which creates a new research tradition (e.g., Darwin's theory of evolution or Einstein's theories of relativity). The idea of *scientific revolutions* used by Kuhn has to do with paradigm shifts: For example, Einstein gave birth to a revolutionary paradigm shift with his theories of relativity. In between paradigm shifts there exists, according to Kuhn, a period of "normal science." During those periods, scientific activities stick to the predominant paradigm.[5]

Experts in a discipline learn the existing wisdom, paradigm, or doctrine telling them what is the predominant way of thinking accepted by the scientific community in the field at a specific time. How do you make science, what are the accepted methods, what kind of empirical data is to be used, what is the nature of the results, what are the dominating results now, into what direction should new research be directed and how should the students be guided, which are the leading journals, and who are the biggest gurus?

The idea of paradigms can be generalized outside of the domain of science, too. Similar pressure to stick to one's own paradigm concerns industrial leaders who have run their factories for 30 years, city mayors with the same life and work experiences, and members of all informal "jolly good fellows" networks, like freemasons, rotary clubs, feminist groups, religious sects, factories for raising "political broilers" for parties, and other clubs for elevating the spirit and feeling of togetherness among their members.

This phenomenon can also limit our thinking and prevent us from seeing essential factors outside of our paradigm. The pressure to think in a similar way with our fellow men and women, and pure *paradigm blindness,* is lurking among us all constantly and everywhere.

Marshall McLuhan once thought that "We don't know who discovered water, but we are pretty sure it wasn't a fish." Every now and then it makes sense to take some distance from our normal paradigm in order to see better—and further. It may pay off to make a visit, for example, to the seminars, meetings, and Web pages of "others"—even "enemies." One may get good ideas and new perspectives even on familiar issues.

TREND-FAITH

In 1929, just before the Great Depression, when announcing that the next year will be a great year for employment (implying good prospectives for the economy in general, too), the US Department of Labor made a gross forecasting mistake by leaning on *trend-faith*. Believing in trends is a natural and typically human way to think of development and the future. If an object of observation has changed according to a certain pattern—e.g., followed *linear or exponential growth, cyclical fluctuations,* or *some combination of them*—people easily think that the same pattern will hold true in the future, too. For example, econometric models using several variables, parameters, and equations express this message in a more complicated way than straightforward trend extrapolations, but basically the question is about the same thing: continuing the *pattern of change* discovered in the past into the future. Unchangeability must be included in these patterns, too. If something has not changed in the past, and you believe that it will not change in the future either, you apply one special case of trend thinking.

Basic postulates in *trend-faith* are thus *unchanging change* and *unchanging nonchange.* One important expression of *unchanging change* is the idea of *cyclical variations*—seasonal fluctuations or long waves (Kondratieff). These variations are identified from the past data, and it is thought that they will continue to exist in the same way also in the future. At least implicitly, several *ceteris paribus* assumptions are made. It is thought that factors that are outside of the research topic, like environmental issues, values, global factors, or technologies in economic forecasts, do not produce surprises: Their impacts remain the same as they were in the past. Another way to put this is to say that in trend thinking you believe that *the structures do not change.* Structural changes or breaks are clearly outside the reach of trend thinking.

One version of *trend-faith* is the so-called *railway thinking.* According to it, nations are considered to be like trains following each other on the same tracks. Some nations are further in their development, but all of them are supposed to follow the same path. A modification of railway thinking, called the model of *flying goose,* was adopted in Japan after the World War II. According to it, societies are following each other on the same development path, but those latecomers come closer and closer to the leading ones. The Japanese were cleverly applying the "second best strategy," copying technologies developed in the leading-edge countries, and finally became number ones in some branches and innovations.

For example, in the 1960s many societally important trends in the Western countries were "well-behaving" in the circumstances of strong economic growth. At that time, trend forecasts didn't always fail, at least not in the short run. Since that period the economic environment has been more turbulent, and at the moment the credibility of economic trend predictions becomes close to zero, if the forecasting perspective is longer than a few months. A coolheaded conclusion, based on studies of aptness of economic forecasts, is that *it is primarily an accident if an economic prediction hits even close to the target, even though the forecasting perspective would be only six months or so.*

Nowadays, trend thinking can be used for producing a kind of reference scenarios, business-as-usual descriptions of the future. After producing them, one can start constructing the truly interesting alternative scenarios.

CULTURAL CONTEMPT

US Secretary of State John F. Dulles expressed *cultural contempt* when announcing in the 1950s that the Japanese will never make anything that the Americans would like to have. As we know, he was totally wrong. During the last decades, Japanese high-tech products from Panasonic, Sony, Toyota, Nissan, etc., have conquered the world of the American consumers.

Generalizing somewhat, it seems that the danger of falling into the trap of *cultural contempt* is *directly related to the past success of the actor in question,* like a government, national culture, a dominating company, even a single person: "We are so good that we don't need to try!" Correspondingly, sensitivity to one's own vulnerability seems to be inversely related to the issue of how great a future it used to have in the past. The hungriest for change and development are usually those who have not yet reached success—in economy, politics, culture, science, sports, etc. Perhaps it wasn't an accident that the losers of the Second World War—Japan, Germany, Finland— created the best economic success stories after the war.

In economy, the trap of *cultural contempt* can go off in a situation that Harvard professor Michael Porter has called a phase of wealth-centered economy.[6] In that phase, the growth of economy is based primarily on the prosperity created earlier. It is tried to be maintained by purchases of companies and mergers, not by investments into production capital and by innovations. One chases for quick profits, and industrial activities with their entrepreneural risks are left to the background. Companies and other economic and societal actors are trying to hold on to the positions achieved in the past, competitiveness is weakening, motivations among the business leaders and employees are lowering, and salaries are rising more rapidly than productivity. The economy drifts into a state of under-investments and scarce innovations. In international competition, those companies possessing real competitive advantages make successes and buy companies from countries having a wealth-centered economy. Actually *a wealth-centered economy is the beginning of national decline.* If a society is staring into the past and sticks to the benefits achieved earlier and does not create anything new, it cannot maintain its prosperity in the long run.

Philosophy of *wealth-centered economy* and *cultural contempt* among the leading economic and political actors is a destructive combination. *New society is created by new organizing principles and actors.* Multimedia software and applications are not produced in refrigerator factories or paper mills. Free-market economy, at least in theory, takes care that the companies falling into the thinking trap of *cultural contempt* and rigidity (wealth-centered economy) face serious troubles in confronting the future. Societal organizations are able to live longer "over their age" than economic ones.

Sometimes we come to a situation where we have to conclude that a barn is a barn, and it does not turn into a skyscraper, no matter how much color we paint on it. If we don't realize it, and stick to the thinking trap of *cultural contempt*, someone else will take care of the job of structural change for us.

OVERENTHUSIASM AND DISPARAGEMENT OF EVERYTHING NEW

If Roger Smith and many other prophets of the 1980s had been right, we should not have any papers on our desks, in our briefcases, seminar halls, offices, or elsewhere in society. On the other hand, according to Bob Metcalfe, who still acts as a big ICT guru (e.g., in the MIT's *Technology Review*), there should be no Internet after 1996.

Smith and Metcalfe failed badly, but due to different reasons. *Overenthusiasm* and *disparagement of everything new* as attitudes towards the future represent the same false thinking pattern, *exaggeration*, but, the opposite extremes of it. When a new technological or other development is in its embryonic phase, especially if it is understood as being something promising, it is easily hoped and believed to come true more rapidly than what will be the case in reality. The paperless office is a good example.

The opposite of *overenthusiam* is *disparagement of everything new*, of which Metcalfe made himself guilty. It happened during a time when the Internet, thanks to the new World Wide Web technology, had just started to spread out from the academic world to other spheres of society.

In addition to pure technological problems, both *overenthusiam* and *disparagement of everything new* are related to the problematique of how to identify, out of the new possibilities offered by technological development, those ones that satisfy our real needs in the long run as private consumers, business leaders, experts, in our hobbies, etc. Which technological—and in principle, economic or societal—innovations will become parts of our consumer and other behavior patterns, improving our life quality, increasing the effectiveness of our work, and making our businesses successful, which will only be passing fads, if even that much?

For example, the mobile phone is an innovation that indisputably has been useful for us and increased our feelings of comfort. In only a little more than 10 years it has changed our everyday life and work so deeply that it makes sense to speak of a clear cultural change. The key word here is accessibility. Our employer, colleagues, family—everyone—assume that we can be reached by mobile phone all the time. If we insist not to be involved in this new culture, we will become disabled as workers, and "odd fellows" as members of a family or in a tribe around some hobby. E-mail and Internet have reached a similar status.

As important as it is to identify those technological and other "weak signals" that satisfy our real needs in the long run, it is also important to understand which of the many offerings of technologies and salesmen do not fall into that important category. Who still remembers tamagotchis?

THE WISDOM OF HINDSIGHT IS SWEET—BUT NOT EVERYTHING WENT WRONG

Some traps in futures thinking into which it is easy to fall were presented above. The description was not exhaustive. As examples of other thinking problems, into which, however, we will not dive more deeply in this article, the following can be mentioned:[7]

- An estimate of the future (possibly a forecast) has an impact on the real development and on itself in a self-fulfilling or self-destroying way. It is very difficult in advance to evaluate these kinds of consequential influences, as well as impacts of second, third, etc., degrees and the significance of feedback loops—future happenings have impacts on the new statements of the future.

- The future is not made only by prime ministers and business leaders but by housewives and by others, too. Putting together all the possible actions of the potential futures actors creates a mass of futures alternatives, which is impossible to totally "govern" by any means available.

- Subjectivity, even total irrationality, in addition to all rational planning has its impact on how the future realizes itself, no matter whether we like it or not. There exist feelings, self-censorship, lying, religious and ethnic fanaticism in economy, politics, and culture. Terrorists are there, shaping the future, independently of how lunatic we consider this phenomenon to be. There is no rational way to mentally control irrationality.

• Even the most "objective" researcher possesses many indirect, even unconscious, values and hypotheses in her/his studies. One can never get rid of them totally, and one should make the adopted values as explicit as possible.

• Data is always inadequate. We should remember what Karl Popper wrote about future inventions: They cannot be known in advance. The same is inevitably valid when it comes to their consequences. And no matter what is the nature of the empirical data—large and superficial or deep but small—it is always restricted.

As we all know, evaluation on how good a statement of the future (not necessarily a forecast) is in relation to the real development can only be made afterwards, a posteriori. It may take decades before we can consider whether a statement of the future was good or not. People love to practice hindsight of wisdom, because we are so good in it.

Due to the traps in futures thinking and other reasons, estimating happenings in the future has often been quite unsuccessful. Everything, however, didn't go wrong. At best, futures studies have shown convincing long-term perspectives and probably had impacts on the societal development processes. We also keep constantly saying that the future is unpredictable and that it should be thought of as alternatives only. We can construct an amount of "n" scenarios based on varying key assumptions, but we know that the one that realizes itself into the present reality at some point of time in the future is # "n+1." Practically always. Why, then, spend time and money for this seemingly useless effort to understand the future? My answer is that by thinking of those "n" possibilities you will become better prepared for the unknown, truly realizing one, too. And one thing is certain: The future materializes itself into the present *somehow.*

Even in futures studies accumulation of knowledge and understanding may be real, even though we cannot *know* the essential facts of the future.[8] If you have read hundreds of reports, articles, and books of the future, and made them yourself, too, you should have learned something, both methodologically and substantially. You ought to have a broader perspective and deeper understanding of what might be essential in the future than, for example, a business leader or an engineer, who both have their involvements elsewhere. After practicing his profession for 20 years, a carpenter is justifiably proud of his professional skills and experience. Why don't we?, Are we somehow more stupid, unable to learn or something?

There are fortunately examples of phenomena that were spoken among the futures researchers long before public political, economic, and other debate started—and actions were taken, too. In the following, just one example is briefly described.

One of the best examples is related to the relations between human activities and nature (which we usually call the *environment* due to our self-centered attitudes), and the limitations of these relations. One of the pioneers in the field, Bob Jungk, published his book *Tomorrow Is Already Here* already in the 1950s. Rachel Carson's *Silent Spring* came out in 1962, and the research team at MIT led by Dennis Meadows published their work *Limits to Growth* in 1972. It was not until the United Nations' World Commission of Environment and Development (the so-called Brundtland Commission) published its report *Our Common Future* in 1987, when the establishments (governments) in many countries really started to take these extremely serious questions into their agendas. *Our Common Future* started a boom of ecologically sustainable development.

At this point it should be remembered that *the only purpose for presenting statements of the future is not to make self-fulfilling prophecies.* The other important motivation is *to construct futures prospects in order to start processes that prevent those prospects from coming true.* There might be other motivations, too, like an attempt to mess up things.

It is extremely problematic and often practically impossible to measure the influences of futures statements on real developments. For example, it is very difficult to say what the impact was of the theories of one of the most influential futures researchers of all times, Karl Marx, on the societal courses of events during the last 150 years or so. How much did his theory on impoverishment of the labor class affect the birth of the labor movement and the birth of the Nordic welfare societies? What if he had never presented his theory publicly? This question belongs to the domain of contrafactual study of history. What about his theory on the accumulation of capital? At least we are witnessing it every day these days—just think of the mergers of the global giant companies in the field of media or the role of Microsoft.[9]

CONCLUSION: HOW TO OVERCOME TRAPS IN FUTURES THINKING

A quick guide for avoiding traps in futures thinking:

- *"This is it!"*: Simply don't ever think like this! Evolution on the globe has no end station, at least not as long as the sun keeps on heating us. Even though in cultural evolution we are able to destroy much of our environment, cause the extinction of thousands of species, fight against each other, etc., still we are probably not able to destroy all the life on the earth. When thinking of the minor issues, like global economy or ideologies, development is going to continue generations from our times.

- *Paradigm blindness.* Take care that you don't read only journals, magazines, and Web pages of your own discipline. In scenario and strategy groups, use as multivaried expertise as possible.

Visit the domains of the "strangers." If you are a business director, do something stupid: Take part in a seminar of a radical activist group, go to a Britney Spears concert, read some Charles Bukowsky. Every now and then avoid your colleagues; don't take part in futures studies conferences only.

• *Trend-faith.* Don't ask whether an important trend is going to break down. Ask when the breakdown will take place! You can start by making a list of trends you think have been "well-behaving" during, say, the last 30 years. If you are able to name any such trend, keep on asking yourself, is it going to behave well in the future, too? For how long? And based on what assumptions? If after this process you still believe in the continuation of this trend, be sure that you make some checking after half a year or so.

• *Cultural contempt.* Is your company overwhelmingly superior compared with all the competitors, are you the greatest and most successful, are you happy? Yes or no? If yes, start thinking quickly! Others are not that bad. If you fall into your self-satisfied sleep, the others will be awake and lurk behind your back. They are greedy for success, which they haven't experienced yet. Sergei Bubka won seven world championships in pole vault between 1983 and 1997. Was the first championship in 1983 the reason for winning the next six ones, or did he do some work for them?

• *Overenthusiasm and disparagement of everything new.* Everyone who has spent some time in a work community can probably name some overly enthusiastic persons eager to grasp any exciting idea, as well as persons who seem to have adopted as their life mission an attitude which says that you have to disparage every new idea presented by someone, especially if the idea somehow differs from the normal way of thinking. Actually, both of these extreme attitudes may be valuable in, for example, a strategic scenario project in a company, if you take care that neither of them starts to dominate the thinking of the scenario group. A group consisting only of neutral, well-behaving bureaucrats will probably not produce anything interesting.

In every organization, trying to avoid traps in futures thinking and being thirsty for success, whether operating in business, administration, education, or the academy, it would be good to have a kind of disturbance generator (DG) to keep you awake in front of the turbulent future(s). The tasks of a DG include *asking* odd questions concerning the basic assumptions and modes of operation in the organization from the futures perspectives, *identifying* new important weak signals in the operating environment—in the economy, technology, world politics, societal issues, environment, values, etc.—having potential impacts on the organization's development, and *producing* innovations related to products, services, customers, modes of operation, strategies, and scenarios.

A DG can be a person, a propeller-head hanging around and reporting on interesting phenomena to the top leaders. It can also be formed of regularly organized futures studios at the top level of the organization in question. In some bigger companies, a DG has been organized more systematically using, for example, the company's Intranet system for collecting new megatrends, weak signals, and other important futures phenomena. The system also applies tools for organizing and prioritizing these phenomena, and the results are being used in the systematic scenario and strategy work of the company, as shown in Figure 1.

FIGURE 1 - MONITORING SYSTEM OF WEAK SIGNALS AND MEGATRENDS IN A COMPANY

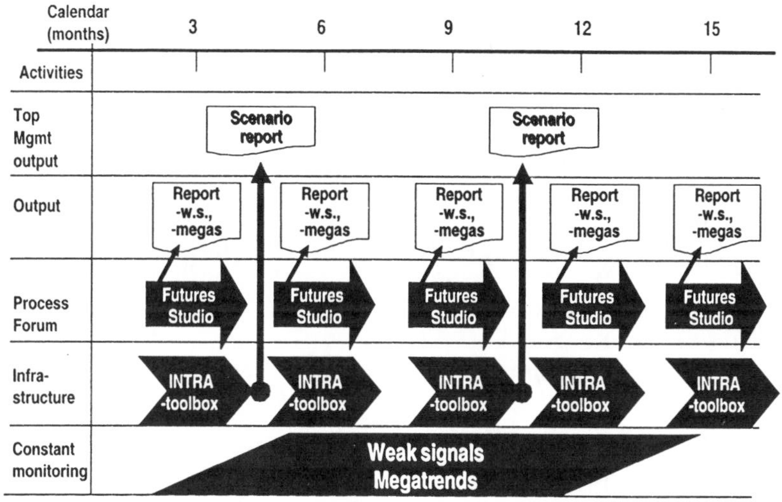

It is important to understand, however, that a DG is not so much a business unit, person, or procedure as it is a *new culture in the organization*. It represents shifts in cultural thinking: from trends to breaks, from past to future, from sleep to awareness, from hierarchies to networks, from machines to organisms, from arrogance to sensitivity—and from unchange to change. *Long live the Disturbance Generators!*

REFERENCES

Bell, Wendell. *Foundations of Futures Studies. Vol 1.* (New Brunswick, NJ: Transaction Publishers, 1997), 365.

Fukuyama, Francis. *The End of History and the Last Man* (New York: Free Press, 1992).

Godet, Michel. *Creating Futures: Scenario Planning as a Strategic Management Tool* (Paris: Economica, Paris, 2001), 269 s.

Gordon, Theodore J. "The Methods of Futures Research," *The Annals of the American Academy of Political and Social Science*, 522, July 1992, 25-35.

Huntington, Samuel P. "The Clash of Civilizations?" *Foreign Affairs*, Vol. 72, No. 3 (1993), 22-49.

Kuhn, Thomas S. *The Structure of Scientific Revolutions* (Chicago, IL: University of Chicago Press, 1962).

Kuhn, Thomas S. (1979) "Second Thoughts on Paradigms," *The Structure of Scientific Theories*, ed. Frederick Suppe (Chicago, London: University of Chicago Press, 1979), 459-499.

Mannermaa, Mika. "Futures Research and Social Decision-Making. Alternative Futures as a Case Study," *FUTURES*, Vol. 18, October 1986, 658-670.

Mannermaa, Mika. "In Search of An Evolutionary Paradigm for Futures Research," *FUTURES*, Vol. 23, May (1991), 349-372.

Mannermaa, Mika. *Linking Present Decisions to Long-Range Visions.* Selection of Papers from the XI World Conference of the World Futures Studies Federation (WFSF), ed. 1992, Budapest. Vols. I and II, 511 pages.

Mannermaa, Mika. "Multidisciplinarity, Methodologies and Futures Studies," *Futures Research Quarterly*, Vol. 16, No. 2, Summer 2000, 5-20.

Masini, Eleonora. *Why Futures Studies?* (London: Grey Seal Books, 1993).

Porter, Michael. *The Wealth of Nations (Kansakuntien kilpailuetu)* (1991), Otava, Keuruu.

What's Up in Science (Tieteessä tapahtuu), March 2002.

NOTES

1. Fukuyama, 1992.

2. Huntington, 1993.

3. Mannermaa; Inayatullah; Slaughter, 1994.

4. Kuhn, 1962.

5. Margaret Masterman calculated that Kuhn had used the word paradigm in 22 different meanings in his influential book. So, the concept is apt to many interpretations, see Kuhn 1979, 459-460.

6. Porter, 1991.

7. Cf. Bell 1997, 243-246; Gordon 1992, 26; Masini 1993, 47-53; and Godet 2001, 20-31.

8. Something we do know, for example, there exist *true statements of the future.* I can say: "In 2045 a hundred years have gone by since the establishment of the United Nations." There are also *statements that are true now and in the future,* too: "In a certain algebra 1+1=2," is true in 2004, but also in 2500. In principle, *historical statements,* when being true stories, are as true in 2100 as in 2004, but here we cannot be sure. We cannot go back and make empirical observations on how the Second World War really happened. Many of us have a roughly similar understanding of those happenings, but there are differences too. It has also been pointed out that the history has usually been written by the winners, and very often by males. We can be pretty sure that Saddam Hussein's story of the Iraq War is quite different from George Bush's view. Finally, *natural laws,* like gravity, should hold true in the future, too (even though we cannot be sure in the deepest sense). It makes it possible to predict, for example, the timing of solar eclipses hundreds of years before they happen. But all these examples are pretty *trivial,* when it comes to our task as futures researchers to say something *essential* about the future(s).

9. Taking up Marx in this way should not be interpreted as giving support to the Marxist parties in politics. On the other hand, Marx should not be condemned as guilty of all of the stupidities, for which real socialism fell. In a similar way, one should not consider the father of liberalism, Adam Smith, as responsible for all *those* stupidities, which Bush's regime is causing.

THE POLITICAL-ECONOMIC PENDULUM:
THE UNITED STATES EXAMPLE

by

John Smart

One of the broadest questions we as developmental futurists, systems theorists, and students of accelerating change can ask about any complex system (an organism, a political structure, an economy) involves the natural constraints on its dynamics. Very few physical systems in the known world undergo sustained acceleration for long. In fact, only computation, as a generalized process, appears to accelerate indefinitely, which suggests it occupies a very special place in our universe. Most elements and attributes of complex systems seem to follow cyclical developmental dynamics. Understanding the cycles can give us great insight into their relative importance in creating the future, in our observed world of continuously accelerating technological and computational change.

Let's turn now to US history. Among the first things many of us learn in high school civics is that our country has a government based on democracy and an economy based on free enterprise. We certainly are a uniquely pioneering and privileged nation, but reality is more complicated than we were initially taught.

Complex systems like governments and economies can be shown to be on a cyclic pendulum between more decentralized (e.g., democracy-promoting, reformist, progressive, free enterprise) and more centralized (wealth-, power-, and control-concentrating; big business; plutocratic) forms of existence. This same cycle is seen in all living systems, from the life cycle of *dycostelium*, the slime mold, which reliably cycles between independent foraging and group aggregation in reproduction and crisis, to the various patterns of *Homo sapiens*, the self-aware hominid, which engages in predictable oscillations between differentiated independent experience and joining together for a range of reproductive and social functions.

With regard to the political and economic structure of US society, where we are on this natural pendulum at any particular time may be a function of both our recent history and a range of internal and external sociotechnological developmental trends. While it seems an admirable goal to dampen its swing, the central dynamic of the political-economic pendulum may be impossible to eliminate. Like our diurnal rhythm, this pendular cycle may represent an optimal approach to developing political economies in which biological human beings play an integral part.

Several Greek philosophers first observed a natural political cycle from democracy to plutocratic dictatorship/tyranny and then to revolution or reform that restores a measure of democracy and restarts the cycle. The economist Joseph Schumpeter, among others,

John Smart *is president of the Institute for Accelerating Change in Los Angeles, California. He may be contacted at johnsmart@accelerating.org.*

describes a similar developmental cycle in emerging economic sectors, beginning with multiple new enterprises, moving to oligopoly and near monopoly and rigidity, followed by a phase of "creative destruction" and divestiture as the dinosaurs either learn to reinvent themselves or are replaced in a world of rapidly changing technologies and business models. But even though it was first observed more than two thousand years ago, the pendular swing from democracy to plutocracy and back through reform is quickly forgotten in the heat of day-to-day debates.

We presently inhabit a highly plutocratic era. Furthermore, while there are some signs of growing citizen empowerment, those willing to look closely will find that most of today's trends are still working predominantly against greater democracy at the present time. As Fareed Zakaria notes in *The Future of Freedom* (2003) even with the best of our social activism we continue to subtly drift into an increasingly "illiberal democracy" in the United States, as measured by growing elite and special-interest privilege, growing corporate and institutional power versus personal rights, increasing media centralization and social conservatism, US unilateralism on the world stage, and relative loss of resources and standards for the development of the education, skills, and leadership capacity of our youth.

History reveals that our country has experienced several prior periods of high plutocracy, of poor citizen empowerment and comparably few educational resources, of economic policies that favored various social elites, the rich, and big business at the expense of the common person. We have experienced both "hands off," government-minimizing plutocracies, passively transferring control to the wealthy, and ones that actively used state power to advance the interests of the privileged over the common citizen. In either case, plutocratic periods can be defined by a move from relative political freedom to relative control and by the loss of personal wealth of the majority relative to those of elites. But as we will note, the political-economic system always swings back from hierarchical (plutocratic) to network (democratic) control whenever social and technological conditions have sufficiently advanced.

Recounting our country's arc of history, first recall the extreme plutocracy in 18th century America under King George III, the government that incited the American Revolution of 1776. This dynamic was a classic example of the Greek cycle mentioned earlier. The many generations of active democratic action seen after our revolution were rooted in the passion of populists like Thomas Paine and Adam Smith, and egalitarian presidents like Thomas Jefferson (1801-1809) and James Madison (1809-1817). The reforms of this era became ingrained in our constitution and its amendments and in a climate that guaranteed greater political and economic freedoms here than in any other previous environment. Along with an open immigration policy for the type of self-driven people drawn to our country, an unparalleled program of multiethnic integration, and our abundant natural resources, these revolutionary reforms have been the foundation of the American economic miracle during the 19th and 20th centuries.

Consider next the racial plutocracy that was broken by the US Civil War (1861-1865). This war also led to a sharp decrease in states' rights, however, so we may note that, while one political issue swings democratic, another may swing plutocratic at the same time. Political pendulums that involve historically underrepresented groups are also often slow to build momentum. One example is the gender plutocracy that persisted in America from 1776 to the Nineteenth Amendment in 1920.

Perhaps most importantly with regard to the political climate, historians like Ronald Inglehart (*The Silent Revolution*, 1977; *Cultural Shift in Advanced Industrial Society*, 1990; *Modernization and Postmodernization*, 1997), Michael Schudson (*The Good Citizen*, 1999), and others make the case that maturing industrial societies are continually reforming, broadening and refining their political values. As Inglehart's global surveys show, the most prominent effect of technological development is that it makes every developed nation more tolerant and focused on individual advancement over nationalist or ideological causes. As our technology runs ever faster each year, in diverse and subtle ways it prods us to exercise our personal rights and to establish increasingly local autonomies. We move from coarse-grained to fine-grained control of the quality of our environment. The evolutionary development of technology, while it does alternate between plutocratic and democratic applications, does not itself appear to be on a pendulum like political and economic systems. Instead, technology seems to be engaged in an accelerating phase transition to a substantially new regime. This transition, the technological singularity, is considered at length in other essays. I refer the reader to those for more information.

The remainder of this essay will consider pendular swings in political and economic systems and suggest that simple and self-correcting patterns may be discerned.

In at least four clear periods since the birth of our republic, the political and economic pendulum has pushed us toward either monied special-interest control (a political plutocracy) or wealth concentration (an economic plutocracy) or some combination of both. As we will see, we are currently in the throes of the fourth major political-economic plutocratic surge. But before we become unduly alarmed, it helps to realize that during each of the prior three surges either wealth concentration or elite privilege or both were effectively reversed soon after, both by the vagaries of a competitive and technologically changing environment and through scores of new democratic laws and institutions. Let's now consider each of the four periods in greater detail.

The first major swing to extreme political-economic plutocracy (1780-1900), emerging as it did in the aftermath of the world's greatest democratic revolution, took over a century to reach its extreme. Big business favoritism grew steadily after the American Revolution, but it markedly accelerated after 1865 in the post–Civil War era of industrial revolution, peaking during the Gilded Age (Mark Twain's derisive term for this period), the last quarter of the 19th century, when the monied interests and the new multi-state corporate trusts rose to great power.

Publicly, big business excess peaked during the scandal-plagued administration of Ulysses S. Grant (1869-1877), but plutocratic conditions continued for a while further under the mixed presidencies of Grover Cleveland and Benjamin Harrison (1885-1897), which were nominally against special interests but also actively against labor, and which were responsible for the passage of an initially useless and toothless Sherman Anti-Trust Act of 1890. The democratic reversal finally came at the end of William McKinley's smoothly pandering, Ronald Reagan–like tenure of 1897-1901. At this point the balance swung back during reform president Theodore Roosevelt's (1901-1909) trust-busting and "Square Deal" administration. A wave of populism, reacting to the robber barons of the late 1800s, initiated a broad series of reforms beginning in the 1890s, including the first clearly successful strikes of the US labor movement (1890s-1920), the first child labor law (1906), and, perhaps most crucially, the Sixteenth Amendment, which created the progressive federal income tax of 1914, a fundamental strategy to counter the natural, gravitational, plutocratic tendency for "property to attract property."

Since then it has turned out that such democratic instruments as income, property, and estate taxes and the requirements of social insurance are more than sufficient to control the rich-poor gap, given that they are always augmented in the long run by turnover resulting from competition and the natural unpredictability of the market. Furthermore, as scholars like Gary Hamel ("The Quest for Resilience," 2003, *Harvard Business Review*) have argued, this natural volatility and wealth turnover increases as technological change accelerates.

Brad DeLong, in his 1997 essay "Robber Barons," summarizes the work of a number of scholars who have shown that wealth concentration steadily increased in the top 1% (5%, etc.) of US society from 1776 to the 1865 Civil War. This unexpected calamity caused wealth to drop acutely but did not change the underlying plutocratic climate, which fostered substantial wealth concentration again from 1870 to 1900.

The second major swing to an extreme of political-economic plutocracy (1920-1930) was much shorter. While wealth concentration was eroding after 1900 (and especially after 1914 and the new taxation and regulation environment), the elite were doing their best to avoid their new economic strictures by increasing their political influence in government. This influence was stemmed for a time during the progressive eras of Theodore Roosevelt (1901-1909), and

Woodrow Wilson (1913-1921). But it pushed forward under Republican William H. Taft (1909-1913) and especially under the combined laissez-faire capitalist Republican tenure of a scandal-plagued Warren Harding, a passive Calvin Coolidge, and a protectionist Herbert Hoover (1921-1933). During this period leading up to the Great Depression, the country increasingly gave way to political plutocracy, special-interest pandering, small business Ponzi schemes (named after Charles Ponzi's massive fraud with his Security and Exchange Company in 1920), and generalized big business unaccountability and favoritism.

No one presently has a definitive theory of the factors that catalyzed the Great Depression of 1929-1939, but systemic under-regulation during laissez-faire capitalism, speculative excess, and the job disruptions induced by increasing automation (assembly lines) all played an important role. In the end, this traumatic event allowed an opportunist reformer, Franklin D. Roosevelt (1933-1945) and his "New Deal," in a series of dramatic new statutes and guarantees for the common citizen, to rapidly reverse economic and power stratifications that had been accumulating for decades. Among many other advances (and some predictable boondoggles), his administration introduced the Fair Labor Standards Act of 1938, which institutionalized the 40-hour workweek, the minimum wage, and numerous other democratic firsts. Harry S. Truman (1945-1953) continued this pushback toward democracy with such acts as racially integrating the armed forces under significant opposition, firing an errant General Douglas MacArthur, which reasserted civilian control over an increasingly powerful military, and guiding the Marshall Plan for Europe to become a policy of redevelopment, not of punitive reparations or political control. But during Truman's second administration the elites again began to gain noticeable privilege and power.

The third swing to extreme political-economic plutocracy (1950-1965) was also comparatively brief. During this era we saw the rise of the military industrial complex and the multinational corporations (MNCs) under Dwight D. Eisenhower (1953-1961). This was accompanied by increasing civil rights abuses in the 1950s under McCarthyism, the House Un-American Activities Committee (HUAC), and the Red Scare. The ominously restrictive feel of this period climaxed during the Cuban missile crisis of October 18-29, 1962, historically the closest the United States would ever come to open military engagement with our Cold War adversary, the Soviet Union. But these plutocratic-autocratic excesses were again broadly rolled back, beginning during the presidency of John F. Kennedy (1961-1963), and the pushback was accelerated by the escalating catastrophe of the Vietnam War (1961-1970). Even during the Republican and often control-oriented presidencies of Lyndon Johnson and Richard Nixon (1963-1974), this new era was marked by dramatic civil rights reforms, leading to generalized racial integration, women's rights, equal opportunity in employment, and many other substantial civil liberties and economic advances for the common citizen. It also saw permanent cultural revolutions in youth attitude, sexuality, and tolerance of sexual diversity.

Perhaps the greatest lesson of the return back from the third swing is that we can change the balance rapidly (in ten years, in this case) if we determine our government is too restrictive or our economy is too unregulated. The shifts always seem to be catalyzed either by particularly egregious plutocratic mismanagement (British tyranny, robber baron excess) or some opportune social catastrophe (Civil War, Great Depression, Vietnam War) that the citizenry uses to suggest that political or economic authorities have temporarily overstepped their legitimacy and need to be democratized by the network in which they are embedded.

Another implicit lesson in this long-term pendular dynamic is that both plutocracy and democracy can develop to excess. Consider that if too much power is given too quickly and too broadly to the hierarchy, as occurred in restrictive McCarthyism, or to the popular network, as occurred during the idealistic 1960s, we discover that most of the plans being made in that state of the system simply won't work for the long term. Think of either HUAC blacklists or hippie communes as two classic examples of idealistic unsustainability at both poles of the pendulum. Consider the meme of "mobocracy," or Fareed Zakaria's (*The Future of Freedom*, 2003) observations on the dangers of giving too much voting power on complex issues directly to the citizens of illiberal democracies without the insulation of plutocratic elected representatives. Balance and tolerance must be maintained in order to create any lasting political-economic structure that integrates all the important social actors.

The fourth swing out to excessive political-economic plutocracy (1975-2004) while not nearly as long as our first 120-year swing, has lasted a surprisingly long time at almost three decades to date. Beginning in the mid-1970s, upper-class wealth begun to accelerate upwards again. Recapping causes of the swing back to economic democracy prior to the 1970s, DeLong notes:

> After 1900 the concentration of wealth began a slow decline. Wars—and the higher taxes and inflation that accompanied them—took a heavy toll of the financial wealth of the rich. Stock market booms (like the 1920s and the 1960s) saw wealth concentration take a step upward; but prolonged bear markets (like the 1930s and the 1970s) eroded wealth concentration. The coming of the social-democratic social insurance state eroded wealth concentration: near-universal education boosted the productivity and wages of those near the bottom of the pyramid, progressive income and estate taxes trimmed some wealth off the top, and explicit government wage policy—minimum wages, restrictions on connections between

finance and industry, and support for union-centered collective bargaining—shifted the distribution of income and wealth toward labor without producing mammoth amounts of classical unemployment (see Lindert and Williamson, 1976). ...Whatever the causes, wealth concentration fell, and further in the 1960s as a result of the expansion of social democracy and in the 1970s as a result the collapse of the real value of the stock market and the inflation of the 1970s.

But now, in 2004, we have returned to a strongly plutocratic era, in both political and economic terms. The activist Ralph Nader was among the first to chart what he terms a widening "democracy gap" that has been growing in the United States since 1979. Kevin Phillips, in *Wealth and Democracy*, 2002, powerfully makes a similar case, with much unfortunate lamenting. The *NY Times* columnist and economist Paul Krugman has also written a valuable book, *The Great Unraveling: Losing Our Way in the New Century*, 2003, that rails against the plutocratic excesses of the Bush presidency, one that paints the picture of an unusually centralized and privilege-loving United States here in the early 21st century.

Such chronicles are enlightening but they are also often jeremiads, predicting that the excess will continue unchecked to the ultimate ruin of the nation, unless we heed the author's personal prescription for salvation. Such manifestos almost always ignore, perhaps for dramatic effect, the fact that complex adaptive systems, whether they be weather systems or world economies, always correct themselves. The most important question, given the dynamic, is when and where the balance should be or will likely be restored. We've seen shrill calls to social action in other areas (environment, overpopulation, social norms) in increasing frequency since the consciousness-raising era of the 1960s. While these often help us to effect important change, their sky-is-falling perspective always has the ring of inauthenticity to it. Complex systems are much more subtle and resilient than that.

When one realizes the pendular nature of political-economic systems, these predictions can be put in the context of self-balancing dynamics. Books like Paul Ray's *Cultural Creatives: How 50 Million People are Changing the World*, 2001; Stephen Moore and Julian Simon's *It's Getting Better All the Time*, 2000; or Bjorn Lomborg's *Skeptical Environmentalist*, 2001, highlight the stunning material and social advances that the average person has continued to reap under our increasingly centralized, plutocratic, special-interest capitalism.

Yes, we've seen ridiculous increases in corporate pay at the top of the economic hierarchy, again since the early 1980s. When groups like United for a Fair Economy report, arguably, that the richest 1% of the population owns 38% of its wealth while the poorest 40% owns only 0.2%, we know that today's extreme plutocratic trend is again ripe to reverse itself. But when? We've recently seen the encouraging rise of initiative politics, which, with the help of rich opportunists, the general public is increasingly using to recall any politicians, regardless of party, who preside over economic downturns, as occurred with California Governor Gray Davis in 2003. This new political accountability is one of several soft signs of the growing power of the citizen in our increasingly communication-enabled environment.

The popularity of reformers like John McCain (and democratic issues like the McCain-Bradley campaign finance reform bill) also shows that we are ready to make some progressive changes, even though the momentum has not yet gathered major force. All it takes is to look at some significantly more egalitarian countries, like Finland, to see just how much farther we might eventually go. In 2004, Finnish police gave a record $216,900 speeding ticket to Jussi Salonoja, 27, one of their country's richest men, under a system where traffic fines are linked to an offender's income.

Not only traffic, but all kinds of fines and judgments under tort law might one day be treated in this highly democratic manner. But don't expect that level of legal progressivism here in the United States for many years to come, as it would take away the privilege to selectively ignore the law that our elite have long enjoyed.

The Internet-driven appeal of talented populists like Howard Dean in 2003-2004 is another indicator that countervailing democratic tendencies are always able to come to the fore when we want them to. Curiously, the Dean phenomenon occurred with only e-mail and today's primitive social software (e.g., Meetup.com) and without electronic democracy and secure digital identities, which are at least another decade or two away from implementation. At the same time, the fact that Dean, the true reformer, could not generate long-term momentum within the Democratic party is another soft indication that the plutocratic swing, though slowing down, is still not ready to shift its direction, for now at least.

How much further can the present plutocratic swing go? Will it require the convergence of a broader network of progressives, an emerging "Digital Democracy," and an appropriately timed catastrophe (e.g., a milder variant of our historical Great Depression or Vietnam War) to help us reverse the shift? If so, we may be in for a surprisingly long wait, as there is nothing currently transpiring—not our Middle East military activities, our presently accelerating tech outsourcing economic disruption, or even our deficit spending debacle—that presently looks to be disruptive enough to catalyze reversal of the cycle, though time will tell, of course.

Should there be significant and sustained economic repercussions to the United States based on economic globalization, our tremendous deficits, or other unpredictable factors (war, terrorism), we would likely see a powerful response by the citizenry to bring democratic reform politicians into office. But if we don't see a five- or ten-year recession while we rebalance our budget and are instead able to "grow through" the deficit, which seems at least possible, if highly uncertain in these still very human-dependent, pre-singularity years, then our country's current plutocratic trajectory might continue on through several more political administrations, slowed but not yet checked.

While we might look forward to a progressive revolt during a second Bush term with a sour economy and an associated catastrophe, today's smooth and media-oiled plutocracy might instead profitably continue well into the 2010s, perhaps even all the way to the citizen-empowering intelligent Internet, linguistic user interface (LUI era) of the 2020s. But once we reach that incredibly networked environment (see singularitywatch.com/lui.html for more on the LUI) the pendular dynamic must surely shift back toward the democratic pole, at least far enough to correct many of the worst social, economic, and political imbalances that have accrued in the favor of elites over the latest plutocratic swing.

So in our ongoing civil liberties debates about the incursions of the Patriot Act and other potentially alarming centralizations of power, it helps to remember that the McCarthy Era led to the Civil Rights Era within one decade. Consider how quickly the reversal can occur when we all decide we want it. It helps to remember the slowly but steadily growing voting power of the average citizen in an increasingly networked nation. It helps to remember that these issues have pendular dynamics, and the pendulum can swing back as rapidly as circumstances require.

Finally, as mentioned at the beginning of this essay, regardless of the state of the political-economic cycle we can expect that global technological acceleration will continue unchecked. For now, the progression to a technological singularity (singularitywatch.com/), an imminent era of human-surpassing electronic intelligence, remains the most important and least understood story of the present era of human history.

Now that we have discussed the political-economic dynamic behind our great nation's present environment, I'd like to briefly venture into some analysis and policy considerations regarding an important social problem in applied futurism, the education of America's youth. As practical, change-oriented futurists, we must consider our activism in the context of our present highly plutocratic and unilateral political era, several decades before the arrival of both the LUI and any subsequent greater-than-human computer intelligence.

DIGITAL ACTIVISM: YOUTH EDUCATION IN THE PLUTOCRATIC AND UNILATERAL UNITED STATES OF THE EARLY 21st CENTURY

First, a brief statement of the problem: While they have gained abilities in a few new areas, today's children know either a little or a lot less about a large number of specialized subjects and skills than their "better-schooled" parents did at their age.

This is a simple consequence of our increasingly automated society. We can tick off a growing list of capabilities (food preparation ability, home building, automotive repair, mathematical ability, reading and writing ability, logical reasoning, critical argument, etc.) that are no longer as carefully learned—or studied at all—by today's youth. Such skills have been deprioritized in an increasingly fast-paced and complex world. It shocks some of us to realize that there are kids growing up today who may never become proficient at reading a physical map if they are given regular access to GPS navigation PDAs and modern cars from birth. What does this mean for the future?

To some, this powerful trend toward an increasingly automation-enhanced, computer-enhanced living is disturbing. Yet in the context of globally accelerating technological change, we cannot conclude that today's youth are less prepared for 21st-century society than someone who has devoted precious time and brain space to becoming adept at the older manual skills.

In our map reading example, if GPS map readers become exponentially more affordable, ubiquitous, and powerful each year, manual map reading may eventually become as poor a skill choice as learning to handweave textiles became in the 20th century. Essentially, once the new technologies are effective, the manual skill loses economic value every year forward by comparison to the technological alternative.

Let us ask a few Socratic questions to elucidate the issues. Are today's children more cortically stimulated than the kids of a generation ago? Most certainly so. Do they have earlier social maturity and a more nuanced emotional intelligence than their parents? Several studies have reached this conclusion. But do today's children have better analytical and critical thinking abilities? Are they more independent thinkers? Most likely not, by many of our traditional measures at least. Here lies the crux of the issue.

We all know that youth math and science abilities have fallen significantly in recent generations. Perhaps the definitive study in this area is the Department of Education's National Center for Education Statistics Trends in International Mathematics and Science Study (TIMSS). TIMSS has been conducted in 1995, 1999, and 2003 (data pending). The 1995 results ranked US 12th graders 19th out of 21 countries in math and 16th out of 21 in science. What's more, the relative performance of US eighth graders in 1999 was worse than for fourth graders in 1995. And we've seen several studies argue that a number of related critical thinking and motivational skills are also less developed in today's "MTV generation" than in the past.

At one level we've all caused this outcome, because we've collectively allowed a plutocratic swing to emerge in our society, a culture where there aren't strong economic and social incentives for every citizen to learn such skills in competition with all the other enticements of modern life. Rather than dive further into the data regarding homework, aptitude scores, and time spent thinking or learning about mathematical and scientific topics, let's simply grant the point and consider possible solutions we might implement in coming years.

It hurts to realize that a technology-enabled fallback in education for independent thought has occurred in our plutocratic and unilateral United States of the early 21st century. Regardless of how many technological skills our youth are learning, it disturbs us to see that they have also, at least in the last few decades, become noticeably less analytical, less able or inclined to understand and objectively evaluate the dynamics of the society they live in. The ability to think independently is a part of the human experience we *don't* want to see automated. To use an important word from biology, societies that suffer this fate become "clonal," like China under Mao or Afghanistan under the Taliban. Clonal societies are intellectually homogenous, internally weak, and rapidly surpassed by heterogeneous ones. We don't want to think that our country may be heading in this direction.

We will briefly address this educational fallback in the remainder of this essay. How can we, as activist futurists, improve analytical and critical thinking in today's youth? How can we make a stronger and more critical liberal society, the necessary base for any healthy democracy?

Perhaps most importantly as developmental futurists, we should recognize that the fallback in youth abilities has occurred not only due to the political and economic climate, but, far more importantly, as a result of the technological one. We are currently engaged in a momentous systems transition from human-based to machine-based educational infrastructures on this planet. We live in a world where the old-guard hierarchical, human-centric educational infrastructure is currently being taken apart and reorganized by our emerging network-based electronic educational infrastructure (digital television, first-generation Internet, video games, cell phones, etc.). We can expect to see the new electronic ecologies continue to outcompete the more humanizing, more mature, but substantially slower and older biology-based infrastructures during this transition period.

As I've noted many times before, first-generation technological systems are often dehumanizing (see Smart's Third Law of Technology, singularitywatch.com/laws.html). While today's early digital systems can easily grab the eyeballs and brain space of our youth and push a lot of raw information, they also deliver much less filtered wisdom and can't yet offer high levels of personalization, motivation, outcome monitoring, or efficiency. Such systems divert children from the many advantages of the old infrastructure, but without yet offering much real education within the new.

But wait until the intelligent, linguistic user interface (LUI)-based Internet in 2020 (see: singularitywatch.com/lui.html for more on the

LUI) then ask this question about critical thinking skills in technologically advanced countries. By then, if accelerating trends in computation continue as they have for the last century, our digital personalities will be our best coaches and educators, and human performance will have moved to a whole new amazing level that only the future-aware among us truly appreciate today. Our political and economic desires for increasing personal empowerment, development, and democracy will be tremendously aided by the networks of tomorrow. The pendulum will finally swing back with a vengeance.

As activist futurists, most of us want to catalyze this deeply humanizing transition. To that end, systems theory offers us at least four obvious options—political, economic, social, and technological levers of change. All of these play an important role, but as Archimedes reminds us, technology is the "lever that moves the world." Let's consider each briefly for some insights in that regard.

First, let's recognize that political systems are the oldest dialogue of change. I would argue that they were eclipsed in power by economic systems after the rise of mature mercantilism (1500s to 1700s), aided by the Industrial Revolution in the 1800s. Economic systems were then transformed by social (mass consumption) and technological systems (mass production) in the 1920s, and ultimately surpassed in importance by technological systems with the dawn of the digital age in the 1950s. Political systems are, grossly, the least relevant lever of accelerating change.

The US political system is presently engaged in a deeply plutocratic and unilateral swing. To me, this argues strongly that powerful political solutions to our national educational problems are highly unlikely to be forthcoming. Indeed, I expect they will be the least effective strategies in the present environment. The vested interests have no strong reason to change the status quo. I stand in solidarity with them, but we must also realize that any educational futurist trying to effect change politically today is in for a very difficult fight.

There is some partial justification for our current administration's unilateral outlook on the world. Leaders are needed in times of crisis, and it does seem very likely that we lead the world in understanding and modeling the way that technology is going to impact culture on the planet, including the way technology is going to build national security, a fundamentally important human need in all world cultures. Furthermore, the tolerant, multicultural, rights-oriented, representative democracy we are building here seems to be a global attractor.

But all this gives us no right to think that, because we lead in certain ways, the world revolves around us: It decidedly does not. What the United States is going to learn over the next two decades is that the developing nations are going to advance economically much faster than we are in an absolute sense.

US society today is an example of the saturation in productivity that occurs when you continue to throw more and more physical goods, wealth, and increasingly pandering programs of higher education at individual human beings. We have an epidemic of obesity, we are less willing to work hard than ever before (though we are fortunately still more productivity- and competition-oriented than several socialist European nations), and we require a burgeoning variety of entitlements and creature comforts. Our youth are attention-distracted by endless entertainment choices.

America remains an innovation engine, to be sure. There is yet a chance that our economic productivity will continue to exceed that of other nations, perhaps even China, given our service sector, for several decades. But our growth rate must be flat by comparison to the emerging nations for deep computational reasons. Futurist Glen Hiemstra uses the excellent word "rationalization" to describe the globalization outsourcing we are seeing today. Don't think globalization, think "rationalization" of the world's workforce. The next several decades will see a leveling of what has been an increasingly irrational and unsustainable income differential between global haves and have-nots. Today's IT outsourcing is only a feeble early example of what will come the better our global technological and legal infrastructure becomes. Our own music in Earth's symphony will be joined by, and collectively exceeded by, many others as hundreds of millions of the world's most enterprising and underpaid workers are connected to and educated by the emerging intelligent global web.

When we consider economic systems as levers of change, especially in the context of our globalizing economy, we realize that there are also problems attempting to effect educational change in the United States in coming years. In a plutocratic era, many commercial forces will be closely allied with the existing educational power structures, far more concerned with protecting their jobs than creating reform. While they will be open to ventures for improving children's education that fit with their conservative agenda, big textbook and other educational companies are, in general, unlikely to initiate transformational programs for improving the quality of educational systems today.

Furthermore, considering our global economy, we are increasingly realizing that the dominant economic dynamic of coming decades will not be centered around the United States. Now that we have a good first-generation Internet and global connectivity, the Internet economy has discovered that far more productivity can be gained by preferentially developing the emerging nations. Because computing and networks have unified economic and cultural interchange, all enterprise is increasingly able to form international partnerships to seek global solutions.

Let me make a clear prediction that the information, income, and wealth gaps between First and Third Worlds, which grew throughout the 20th century, will be narrowing in the 21st. We see unmistakable signs of this already. Because globalization is a strongly non-zero-sum game, we are definitely going to see the US standard of living increase in this process. But it will increase far less than the emerging nations' standards in coming years, making up for past imbalances, as it should.

The United States is only 4% of the world's population. By simple mathematics, the Third World tech support staff will soon outnumber the First World's five to one, perhaps eventually even ten to one. We can't expect US youth, presently grappling with the consequences of our culture's material success, to provide the dominant tech support for the most important transition coming our way: the building of the next-generation planetary Internet, a linguistic user interface, and all the amazing global technological intelligence and new economic enterprise that tomorrow's network will enable.

It is the hungry emerging nations' youth who will do the bulk of IT tech support for Earth's next-generation Internet economy in coming decades, just like the hardworking Chinese and Irish immigrants built out the railroads, the dominant network of 19th century. If we are foresighted and global in our education, US youth can creatively collaborate and partner with the world's workforce in this monumental task, and they will do so on their own initiative in increasingly powerful groupware and simulation environments in coming decades in myriad ways we can scarcely imagine today. We are heading into a truly global transition, now that we have the network to do so (the first-generation Internet). The sooner we realize this the better we will be able to help our youth participate meaningfully in the rapid economic development now occurring in emerging nations.

Many of today's social systems, at the cultural level, have their own problems as levers of change. They can be expected to aggressively perpetuate consumerist distractions in a highly plutocratic society. As Dean Kamen notes, dominant youth heroes in today's United States are athletes or entertainers bent on pushing you product, individuals who certainly play a valuable role in society but who have disproportionately displaced many of the great social welfare and justice role models of science, industry, medicine, or politics that our 19th-century youth idealized. We know we are in an era of cultural poverty when dominant musical genres of the modern era celebrate sex, money, power, fame, and ego in simplistic terms, rather than personal advancement, global awareness, empathy, and the more nuanced human needs.

This is not a tirade against modern culture, merely a recognition of one of the many costs of extreme plutocracy and unilateralism in any advanced industrial nation. We can fight this to some degree, but much more effectively at the personal and small group levels than at the broader cultural level. Again, we have to be conscious of our environment and its natural constraints.

That leaves us with technology, the fastest growing and most dynamic segment of current society, as the major lever for affecting the problem of youth education today. While some technologies enforce the hierarchical status quo and perpetuate what scholar Richard Rhodes in *Visions of Technology*, 2000, calls "structural violence," many others promote openness, distributed intelligence, transparency, and other strongly democratic values. We must learn the difference and advocate for appropriate technologies.

I see at least two powerful personal strategies for practical implementation of the technological lever on education by futurists today. The first is learning how to use technology to increase your own and your children's educational sophistication, and the second is using it to create local businesses that have, as a clear goal, the effect of increasing the intelligence, independence, wisdom, and worldliness of their employees and customers, both young and old. Let me close with a few brief words on each of these strategies to spur you into your own additional research.

For your family, you could start by reading any of a number of interesting surveys of the social effect of computing technologies, such as Don Tapscott's *Growing Up Digital*, 1999. Get a subscription to a few good computer magazines, like *Smart Computing: In Plain English*, or *PC Magazine*. Use the Internet on a daily basis. Create a personal Web site. Post your digital pictures to it.

Get broadband, and get your grandparents on broadband. Start having webcam phone conversations with them (Apple's iChat AV is excellent). Buy goods on eBay.com and use PayPal to support the emerging global digital marketplace for consumer goods. Sell your used goods there as well, or take them to your local AuctionDrop.com warehouse, where they'll sell them for you on eBay themselves for a small fee. Use Amazon.com to buy your books. Use Netflix.com to rent your DVDs. Try dating through a good Internet relationships site like eHarmony.com. Buy your clothes through places like LandsEnd.com, who will keep your measurements online, to simplify future clothing decisions. Do your banking with an online bank, like Everbank.com. Get a penpal in a foreign country through an Internet café, and support his or her family financially and interpersonally. Upgrade your operating system, software, and computer regularly. If you haven't already, get your kid digital.

For your business, you might start with Slywotsky and Morrison's *How Digital is Your Business*, 2000, or Bill Gates's *Business at the Speed of Thought*, 2000. Ask yourself how you can employ youth who are interested in learning information technology (IT) skills and how you can use IT and other technologies to improve your business. Sometimes it's better to spend a lot less money, a lot smarter, on slightly older technologies. Look for ways where you can replace existing processes and systems with mature, cheap, dependable technologies.

Unless you are a market leader, be careful about spending money on unproven new business technologies. Watch other technology adopters carefully before you spend, and use the Internet for competitive intelligence. When you are considering spending nondiscretionary income on technology for competitive advantage, *always* study a technology carefully first, and spend only after you understand value inherent in the older, cheaper, and more mature technologies.

Finally, if you want to understand and selectively employ some of the newest technologies that are leading us to the next-generation intelligent Internet, you might start with John Patrick's *Net Attitude*, 2001. You can also review some of my Internet essays on the linguistic user interface, or LUI, as mentioned earlier. A new, increasingly intelligent conversational computing infrastructure and interface is coming, both to the Internet and to every device with a wireless connection, one that will arrive incrementally between now and 2025 by most estimates. Systems theory gives us every reason to expect that the LUI, personality capture, persuasive computing, and other intelligent interface technologies are going to usher in a much smarter, more self-actualized, less culturally controlled, more democratically active, empowered youth.

What we do every day can either accelerate or delay the coming transition, so ask yourself how you can be a digital activist for educational empowerment in your daily life.

INNOVATING FOR THE FUTURE

by

Patrick A. van der Duin

INTRODUCTION

This paper discusses how futures research is linked to innovation. It reports generally about a current research project that investigates how qualitative methods of futures research are used in innovation processes at commercial companies, and specifically about a case study at KPN Research.

The domain of the present research is:

• *Commercial companies*—Leaving exceptions aside (e.g., Reger, 2001; Burmeister et al., 2002; Van Oirschot, 2003), there is not much scientific and critical research available about the use of futures research within commercial organizations, as opposed to the amount of research into futures research in the public sector (e.g., Martin and Irvine, 1989; Tijink, 1999; Cuhls, 2001). Research into the use of futures research at commercial companies would fill in a gap. Coates (2001) underlines this: "Far too little has been written about how the study of the future is conducted or used in the business community in the United States and Europe."

• *Qualitative methods of futures research*—Given the large amount, large diversity, and (subsequently) many ways of classifying methods of futures research (e.g., May, 1996; Glenn, 1999), this research limits itself to methods of futures research that are (predominantly) qualitative by nature. Another reason for this focus is that during the innovation process, especially in its early stages and compared with qualitative information, it might be expected that not much quantitative data is available yet, which makes the use of quantitative methods much more difficult and less likely. Qualitative methods might be more helpful, then, since qualitative information is more available. In this research the scenario method, roadmapping, and trend analysis are taken into consideration.

• *Innovation processes*—Innovations, whatever their type or effect, do not fall from the sky. They are developed by innovators from an idea into a new product, service, process, or other type of innovation. Innovation processes can take place in different ways. We can distinguish four generations that have evolved between the end of World War II and the present (Rothwell,

Patrick A. van der Duin *is a research fellow at Delft University of Technology, Delft, Netherlands. He may be contacted at p.vanderduin@tbm. tudelft.nl.*

1994; Niosi, 1999). These successive generations show that, for instance, innovation processes have become more complex and linked closer to the strategy of a company, and increasingly involve a cooperation between several companies rather than taking place within a single organization.

The research goal is built upon five standpoints:

1. Futures research is carried out in different ways, for different goals, and with different methods by many commercial companies (Bürgel, Reger, and Ackel-Zakour, 2000).

2. Innovation is an important driver of competitive advantage for both commercial companies and the national economy of countries. Nevertheless, innovation processes have a high failure rate.

3. Futures research is used by commercial organizations in innovation processes.

4. Much research into the use of futures research within governmental or nonprofit organizations has already been done.

5. No literature is present about how futures research is specifically used in innovation processes in commercial companies.

Based upon these five standpoints, it can be concluded that the use of qualitative methods of futures research in innovation processes within commercial companies is challenging and potentially fruitful. By addressing this area, valuable knowledge is gained on how the use of methods of futures research is actually taking place and how (in principle) it improves innovation processes that (too) often do not result in commercial successes. The goal of this research is therefore: *To investigate the use of qualitative methods of futures research in innovation processes in commercial companies.*

The research goal has an empirical, theoretical, and practical (or instrumental) aspect:

1. Empirical: It is the first research into the use of (qualitative methods of) futures research in innovation *processes* at commercial companies.

2. Theoretical: The findings of this research are used to construct a theoretical framework that describes the relationship between qualitative methods of futures research and innovation processes (at commercial companies).

3. Practical (instrumental): The findings of this research (as expressed in the theoretical framework) can support both futures research and innovators at commercial companies in their application of qualitative methods of futures research in innovation processes.

FUTURES RESEARCH AND INNOVATION

Futures research is used in innovation processes. Many authors have related innovation to the concept of future, and in some cases even consider the use of futures research in innovation processes crucial for the success of an innovation, or argue that at least it can contribute positively to the quality of an innovation process (and the possible subsequent commercial success of the developed innovation). Du Preez and Pistorius (1999) state: "One of the major challenges in the management of innovation ... becomes one of managing the technological future." And: "There is a growing awareness that the ability to identify emerging technologies as well as the ability to assess the sustainability and demise of mature technologies are important elements in the process of managing technology" (p. 216). In addition to this, Cooper (1980) already found in the 1980s that the innovator's knowledge and feeling of future market developments is the second most important factor for explaining the viability of innovation projects. And De Jong and Kerste (2001) refer to research done by Cobbenhagen, Hertog, and Pennings (1994) that shows that successful innovating companies had put factors on their agenda that would become important for successful innovation in the 1990s, already five years earlier than their less successful competitors. On a company level, Johannessen, Olaisen, and Olsen (1999) state that in the knowledge economy the innovation-led company must, among other capabilities, "be able to formulate visions about future opportunities," and must have "the ability to visualize or identify pictures of future opportunities and turn them into reality, as well as a sense of optimism and faith in the future." Twiss (1992a) has even considered it worthwhile to include in his innovation-management audit a specific question about the use of futures research: "Do we use exploratory techniques to identify and predict future trends, e.g., brainstorming, scenario analysis, and Delphi?" Floyd (1997) at his turn devotes a chapter to techniques and tools (such as extrapolation, Delphi, and market pressure forecasting) for assessing the rate of change of technology and how it can be used for innovation strategies, and Van Lente (1993) considers the role of (technological) expectations and promises as an integral part of the innovation process. Furthermore, Lin (2001) states that the success of an innovation is strongly dependent on the extent to which its potential future has been researched: "The competitive value of any innovation depends on our ability to evaluate its future novelty, usefulness, risk, and cost. Our ability to do this depends on our understanding of how it will be used in the future, and the expected consequences and results of this use." Finally, Tidd et al. (1997) describe an example that shows the importance of looking into the future for innovation. The example is about the electrical industry, which in the 1960s and 1970s expected that nuclear technology would be the energy source of the future. Nuclear energy failed to do so, and companies in the electrical industry later discovered that "the main revolutionary opportunities and threats for them came from the virtual costless storage and manipulation of information provided by the semiconductor." It can be assumed that a timely recognition and understanding of these developments would have prevented energy companies from investing (too) much money in a faulty technology.

The link between futures research and innovation can be further established by discussing two concepts: the lead time of an innovation and the uncertainty of an innovation process.

The Lead Time of Innovation

Although many organizations put great effort in reducing the lead time of their innovation processes (Braaksma and Bruins, 1998), the development of many innovations still takes considerable time. Agarwal and Bayus (2002) have compiled a sample of 30 important product innovations (such as the automobile, the turbojet engine, and the microcomputer) and have calculated that the time between invention and commercialization is on average almost 30 years. During this development time, many developments and changes in, for instance, technology or business can take place. Following this, Twiss (1992b) states: "Nowadays, technical lead times are often so long that a market can be lost before a proper response is made." And (ibid., p. 132): "During the period the new product is under development market needs may change or they may be satisfied by a competitive product or an innovation based upon a different, and perhaps superior, technological concept." This means that a current idea (for an innovation) not necessarily has to be a successful innovation at a future date when it is introduced into a market. In between many changes might have taken place that could counteract the potential market success of the idea. Collingridge (1980) views the lead time of an innovation in terms of his "dilemma of control." This dilemma refers to the fact that "the social consequences of technology cannot be predicted early in the life of the technology. By the time undesirable consequences are discovered, however, the technology is often so much part of the whole economic and social fabric that its control is extremely difficult" (ibid., p. 11). Collingridge has little faith in changing the course of the development of a technology or innovation during its lead time. It shows that Collingridge is skeptical of assessing the future (social) consequences of the development and implementation of a new technology, and he holds the opinion that a more diverse development of technology can be of much value in coping with this dilemma. Collingridge's dilemma is a clear example of the notion that different changes that can occur between the first idea of a technology and its implementation later on, expressed, in this case, in undesirable social consequences. Collingridge's skepticism of predicting the consequences of a technology might be eased, however, if he would consider besides *predicting* the future of a certain technology also the possibility of *exploring* it, which might result in more information about these possible social consequences.

To develop a view in which future developments might influence the idea, an organization can make use of futures research. Futures research thereby prevents an organization from investing time, money, and other resources in current ideas that might not be potentially successful innovations in the future. In different stages of the innovation process, an organization collects information and knowledge about how the innovation eventually will look or how it will be used when it is finally introduced into the market. Based on that information, the innovation process is adjusted or even stopped. This is a reactive (or defensive) attitude towards the use of futures research in innovation processes. That is, the feasibility of an idea (or even a patent) for an innovation is evaluated during the innovation process by assessing the impact of future developments on the idea (or patent).

Alternatively, an idea (for an innovation) can also benefit from new developments that occur during the development time. For example, an idea might initially not be technologically feasible, but new technological developments can make the idea possible after all. Or, initially there might not be a need among (potential) users for a product, but certain developments in society and in the market might create a need for the product that makes it interesting enough to develop. This is a more proactive (or defensive) attitude towards the use of futures research in innovation. That is, a company (or a combination of companies) tries to enhance the feasibility of an idea (or patent) by bringing it more in line with (possible) future developments. Some companies even try to influence the course of future developments so that it benefits their ideas for innovation. This, of course, is only possible even to a certain extent for large companies or combinations of companies who operate on a worldwide scale. A recent example is the cooperation between multinationals such as Philips, Sony, Microsoft, and HP that are developing products and services in the field of "ambient intelligence."

Rip (1995) adds to all this that the influence of developments on an innovation does not stop after the market introduction but continues during its diffusion: "The eventual shape of a technology, its usage, and the way it is embedded in society can be very different after 5, 10, or more years than it looked at the beginning." This is also known as "reinvention" (Rogers, 1992).

The Uncertainty of Innovation Processes

In every innovation process it is very difficult to know in advance how an idea will evolve in the future and which developments it will encounter: "For we are now concerned with two dimensions of uncertainty—that of the innovation itself, and of the environment into which it will be launched at some future date" (Twiss, 1992b). Twiss (ibid., p. 180) describes the example of the Concorde, of which the operational economics were influenced by uncertain (economic) factors that were not seen when the development started, such as price competition in airline fares, decreased purchasing power of the airlines caused by economic downfall, and sharply rising aviation fuel prices. In addition to that, Twiss (ibid., p. 6) refers to Bright (1968): "Bright attributes a great deal of this uncertainty to the difficulty of forecasting the technical and social environments into which the new technology will be launched some years later. This difficulty must be recognized. Yet there is little doubt that the very high level of failure stems at least in part from the absence of a systematic attempt to match a new technology to future market needs."

So innovation processes are inherently uncertain and difficult (Trott, 1998; Schepers, Schnell, and Vroom, 1999; Osawa, 2003) and have, for instance, an economic, technological, and/or societal nature. In the words of Freeman and Soete (2000): "The chain of events from invention or specification to social application is often long and hazardous." During an innovation process, companies must make decisions about how to cope with uncertain developments that (might) influence the innovation, and these decisions might have uncertain and unexpected consequences for innovation at their turn. Van Asselt and Rotmans (2002) have constructed a taxonomy of uncertainty in which they distinguish between two classes of uncertainties, each with different sources. First, there is uncertainty due to *variability*, with sources such as societal randomness (social, economic, and cultural dynamics) and technological surprise. Second, there is uncertainty due to *limited knowledge*, with sources such as lack of observations/measurements and conflicting evidence. Both classes are also related to each other: "Due to variability in combination with limited resources to measure and obtain empirical information, reality exhibits inherent uncertainty and unpredictability. As such, it contributes to limited knowledge" (ibid., p. 80). Because in this research uncertainty is mainly considered with respect to (possible) future developments in different fields, uncertainty due to variability is the most applicable class of uncertainty.

So at the start of and during the innovation process there are often a lot of uncertainties (e.g., technical, regulatory, or commercial) that can have many different sources. For instance, Will there be any need for our product when it is introduced into the market? Or, Is this idea technically feasible? That is, Are we going to develop sufficient technical knowledge to make this idea possible? In addition to this, Trueman (1998) states that the amount of uncertainty is related to the type of innovation. That is, a radical innovation is more uncertain (and more risky) than an incremental innovation because the development of a radical innovation involves more dimensions, such as new product, new technology, and new market. By using methods of futures research in innovation processes, companies in principle can recognize and subsequently cope with this uncertainty. Futures research can provide an overview and assess the effects of certain developments. It can make organizations aware of these potential trends.

CASE: KPN RESEARCH AND THE "INNOVATION CHAIN"

A case study has been done at KPN Research, the R&D department of Dutch telecom operator KPN, that uses a method named the "Innovation Chain" (IC), in which scenarios were used in an innovation process. The goal of the IC was to bring customers and experts together to think about innovation and can be viewed as a process plan to come from a rough idea to cooperation on a certain topic. The IC had five successive steps:

1. Current situation: Analyzing the problems of a company with regard to innovation.

2. Future exploration: The problem (or opportunity), the company, and its customers are projected into four scenarios.

3. Future vision: The generated information of step 2 is condensed to *one* future vision on the topic by finding out what the red threat is through the four scenarios and the topic that has been projected in these scenarios.

4. ICT-strategy: After assessing a vision for the future, a "road" from now into that future is determined, which has actions that need to be taken to achieve the vision.

5. ICT-services: Because the IC aims at finding out new ICT-products and services by which customers of the IC could better reach and communicate it with their customers, the IC ends with this step, thereby making the future vision and strategy more specific.

An important input to the IC were four scenarios that have been built in a project named "Destination 2005." The scenarios were:

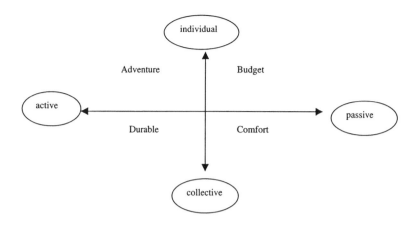

Adventure (Short Summary)

The "adventure" scenario is based on egocentric fun lovers who, above all, crave more excitement, variety, and pleasure in their lives. They are out to have a good time with lots of thrills. Life is a fairy tale and society is the theme park where it is played out. Everyone is shamelessly selfish and unwilling to conform to established social patterns. They are even less prepared to make any kind of sacrifice for others.

Budget (Short Summary)

In this scenario, the European economy is facing problems. The economic bubble has burst, resulting in a period of economic and social decay. Many companies have gone bankrupt, and the housing market has collapsed. As a result, economic growth is far more sluggish than in the 1990s. People work relatively hard at highly irregular hours in an attempt to turn the tide.

Comfort (Short Summary)

The key words to describe this scenario are "comfort" and "usefulness." Its catchwords are "reduced complexity," "time saving," and "rationalization." After the turn of the century, society responded to an increasingly complex world by expressing a collective desire for control and comfort. Consumers no longer want to choose from a whole range of options, but want companies and organizations to provide products and services that are fully tailored to their needs. The most popular organizations are those that provide sound service and do the thinking for their customers.

Durable (Short Summary)

This scenario focuses on the quality of life and is opposed to the idea that progress usually means "more." People are tired of innovations and have slotted into a new mind-set, giving them more time to enjoy nature and each other. Success is no longer measured according to income and possessions, but according to well-being and social behavior. Rejecting the constant desire for more has become a valued way of thinking. People no longer want to be manipulated by advertising and promotional campaigns. Consumerism is less rampant.

RESULTS

The case study has brought up the following results:

The Place of the Scenarios of "Destination 2005" in the IC

The scenarios were used in the second part of the IC, that is, the phase in which the future of a certain topic or problem is being explored. The scenarios' main function was to inspire people to think about the future and to come up with new ideas. The scenarios were not used to assess the value of certain ideas about innovation. But several interviewees said that this was not sufficient and that the scenarios should be supplemented by trends that were focused on the business sector of the customer involved. By doing this, the IC could better focus on the problems and practices of the customer, which would extend the use of the outcomes of the IC. A few interviewees said that those trends could indeed play an important role in the follow-up, that is in the latter phases of the IC. But, as a few other interviewees said, the risk of supplementing the scenarios with trends is that the inspiring character of the scenarios is endangered since trends have a much more one-directional character than scenarios and cannot include as much variety as different scenarios can.

The Need for Custom-Made Scenarios

The use of the corporate scenarios that originally were developed specifically for KPN show that scenarios do not have to be necessarily custom-made, despite the claim of scenario-guru Arie de Geus that "nothing is as boring as another man's scenarios." But from the interviewees, especially customers of the IC, it can be concluded that de Geus's remark is not necessarily true, at least not in this case. If the scenarios have a strong societal character and focus on end-users (i.e., consumers), participants of the IC could also project their own company and business in those scenarios. One of the "inventors" of the IC said that a big advantage of the scenarios was that they could be made clear in a very short time period because they were so appealing to the users. Although from the interview it became clear that users could not always quickly reproduce the names of the scenarios (despite the attention the project group devoted to come up with names easy to remember), they all had much less difficulty in describing the general character of the scenarios. The relation with the former conclusion is that supplementing the scenarios with trends aimed at the business sector of the client of the IC would make the scenarios more custom-made.

The Use of the Corporate Scenarios as Scenarios?

The scenarios of the "Destination 2005" project describe different possible futures in 2005. However, from the interviews it became clear the scenarios were not always used as such in the IC. Often the scenarios were considered as market segments, which means that the scenarios were used to look at the *current* market instead of possible markets in the future. One of the IC-facilitators did not consider this a problem as long as the scenarios would make the users of the IC (and the scenarios) stretch their minds and think about the future. Nevertheless, if the scenarios are viewed as (current) market segments, it is very difficult to consider them as possible futures. Also, on a few occasions one scenario was chosen to work out in further detail, often for practical reasons or because the client had the opinion that the chosen scenario would suit them the best. This obviously conflicts with the idea behind scenario thinking as a tool to make and use several possible future images.

The Spin-Off of the IC to Other Innovations Projects

Almost all interviewees said that the IC had not resulted in any specific innovation, only a plan for innovation. But they also said that the IC and the scenarios had indeed a positive effect on other current innovation projects. One KPN account manager confirmed this and said that he obtained an order from another project because the customer told him that the IC and the scenarios convinced him that KPN was the suitable partner for him. One person at KPN Research who was involved with the IC even said, knowing this story, KPN Research should have a business in which KPN Research gets a certain percentage of the turnover KPN would make at that customer. So, although the IC had not resulted in any specific innovations, let alone the possible success or failure of that innovation, it did influence other innovation projects of KPN and its customers in a positive way.

The Expert's View

The "Destination 2005" project was carried out by *Future*

Scanning, a sub-department of KPN Research occupied with doing futures research. Although it was not directly involved in building the concept of the IC, its role and position in the IC was unquestioned. But this position is not undisputed in activity in KPN Research with regard to futures research. *Future Scanning* was not involved in the trend analysis that had been carried out for the making of the strategy of KPN Research for 2002. Almost no interviewee could exactly explain why this was so. Some of them (especially those responsible for or involved with innovation policy) said that they knew too little about the IC, so it did not cross their minds when they were making the trend analysis. But almost all interviewees said that it is an odd situation when what they sell to their customers is not being used for internal causes. One interviewee said that he was willing to do an experiment and to apply the IC to the innovation policy of KPN Research. One interviewee said that he had some regret about this and that the next time he definitely would make use of their expertise because during the process of spotting and analyzing trends he had encountered some problems that he found difficult to solve by himself. When he was asked why he had not made use of *Future Scanning* he could not immediately respond to that, but after some thinking he came up with that KPN Research consists of experts on all kinds of subjects and that being an expert automatically means that you also are able to form an opinion about the future of your own area of expertise. This would mean that a separate group of futures researchers would be superfluous. A reply to this would be that spotting future developments is one thing, and the experts of KPN Research might indeed be good at this, but analyzing the spotted trends and assessing which consequences the spotted trends mean for, for instance, innovation policy is a different expertise, as the interviewee from above found out when he encountered problems with carrying out the trend analysis.

In line with this, the people from *Future Scanning* position themselves as "future *process* experts" as opposed to "future *content* experts." This means that their main expertise is how to apply methods of futures research, whereas the "experts" give input that can be seen as the raw material on which the methods are being applied. This positioning makes the futures researchers within KPN Research not superfluous, because they are the people within KPN Research who have the skills and experience to apply these methods.

REFERENCES

Bright, J.R. *Some Management Lessons from Technological Innovation Research,* National Conference on Management of Technological Innovation, University of Bradford Management Centre, 1968.

Bürgel, H.D., G. Reger, and R. Ackel-Zakour. "Technology Foresight: Experiences from Companies Operating Worldwide," *International Journal of Services Technology and Management,* Vol. 1, No. 4

(2000), 394-412.

Burmeister, K., A. Neef, B. Albert, and H. Glockner. *Futures Research and Business: Practices, Methods, Perspectives* (Essen: Z_punkt GmbH Büro für Zukunftsgestaltung, 2002).

Coates, J.F. "The Future as a Factor in Business Planning and Management," *Futures Research Quarterly*, Vol. 17, No. 3 (Fall 2001), 5-11.

Cobbenhagen, J.W.C.M., J.F. Hertog, and J.M. Pennings. *Changing Successfully: Core Competencies and Business Processes* (Deventer: Kluwer Bedrijfswetenschappen, 1994).

Collingridge, D. *The Social Control of Technology* (London: Frances Pinter (Publishers) Ltd., 1980).

Cooper, R.G. (1980). "Project NewProd: Factors in New Product Success," *European Journal of Marketing*, 14 (5/6) (1980), 277-291.

Cuhls, K. "Foresight with Delphi Surveys in Japan," *Technology Analysis & Strategic Management*, Vol. 13, No. 4 (2001), 555-569.

De Jong, J., and R. Kerste. *The Power of the Idea: Better Results by Innovative Behavior of Employees* (Schoonhoven: Academic Service, 2001).

du Preez, G.T., and C.W.I. Pistorius. "Technology Threat and Opportunity Assessment," *Technological Forecasting and Social Change* (1999), 216-234.

Floyd, C. *Managing Technology for Corporate Success* (Aldershot: Gower, 1997).

Freeman, C., and L. Soete. *The Economics of Industrial Innovation* (Cambridge: MIT Press, 2000).

Glenn, J. (ed.). *Futures Research Methodology* (Washington: American Council for the United Nations University, CD Rom: Version 1.0, 1999).

Johannessen, J.A., J. Olaisen, and B. Olsen. "Managing and Organizing Innovation in the Knowledge Economy," *European Journal of Innovation Management*, Vol. 2, No. 3 (1999), 116-128.

Lin, Ian B. "Innovation in the Networked World," *Innovation and Imagination at Work* (Roseville: Australian Institute of Management/McGrawHill, 2001).

Martin, B.R., and J. Irvine. *Research Foresight. Priority-Setting in Science* (London: Pinter Publishers, 1989).

May, G. *The Future Is Ours* (London: Adamantine Press, 1996).

Niosi, J. "Fourth-Generation R&D: From Linear Models to Flexible Innovation," *Journal of Business Research*, 45 (1999), 111-117.

Osawa, Y. "How Well Did the New Sumitomo Electric Project Ranking Method Predict Performance?," *R&D Management*, 33 (2003), 343-350.

Reger, G. "Technology Foresight in Companies: From an Indicator to a Network and Process Perspective," *Technology Analysis & Strategic Management*, Vol. 13, No. 4 (2001), 533-553.

Rip, A. "Introduction of New Technology: Making Use of Recent Insights from Sociology and Economics of Technology," *Technology*

Analysis & Strategic Management, Vol. 7, No. 4 (1995).

Rogers, E.M. *Diffusion of Innovations* (New York: The Free Press, 1995) 4th Edition.

Rothwell, R. "Towards the Fifth-Generation Innovation Process," *International Marketing Review*, Vol. 11, No. 1 (1994), 7-31.

Schepers, J., R. Schnell, and P. Vroom. "From Idea to Business—How Siemens Bridges the Innovation Gap," *Research-Technology Management* (1999) 26-31.

Tidd, J., J. Bessant, and K. Pavitt. *Managing Innovation. Integrating Technological, Market and Organizational Change* (Chichester: John Wiley & Sons, 1997) 1st Edition.

Trott, P. *Innovation Management and New Product Development* (Harlow: Pearson Education Limited, 1998).

Trueman, M. "Managing Innovation by Design—How a New Design Typology May Facilitate the Product Development Process in Industrial Companies and Provide a Competitive Advantage," *European Journal of Innovation Management*, Vol. 1, No. 13, 44-56.

Twiss, B. *Managing Technological Innovation* (London: Pitman Publishing, 1992a).

Twiss, B. *Forecasting for Technologists and Engineers. A Practical Guide for Better Decisions* (London: Peter Peregrinus Ltd., 1992b).

Van Asselt, M.B.A., and J. Rotmans. "Uncertainty in Integrated Assessment Modelling. From Positivism to Pluralism," *Climatic Change*, 54 (2002), 75-105.

Van Oirschot, R. *Future Management: The Paradox of a Controllable Future* (Amsterdam: Uitgeverij Business Contact, 2003).

MODELS OF CHANGE, WITH EXAMPLES OF KEY ISSUES IN THE FUTURES STUDIES FIELD

by

Linda Groff

INTRODUCTION TO MODELS OF CHANGE

First we will look at characteristics of how futurists view change—including the fact that change is seen as the norm, and that the pace of change is speeding up today. Then we will look at a number of different models and examples of change and evolution. If it is possible to say that evolution—in any area of our lives—goes through certain detectable stages, then one can ask: How does one get from one stage to the next; i.e., what is the process of change from stage to stage? This paper looks at a number of different models of change—including older models, as well as more recent models of particular interest to futurists today, along with examples of change that seem to illustrate each model. In looking at all the models together, a very good overview of much literature and issues in the futures field is presented.

The models and examples of change and evolution to be examined include the following. The older models of change include linear change (the classical 19th-century Western model, as well as Charles Darwin's model for biological evolution); cyclical change through sequential points (the classical Eastern model); cyclical change through nonsequential points; cyclical change between two points or poles over time; and dialectical change between thesis-antithesis-synthesis. The models of change and evolution of particular interest to futurists today include accelerating growth with "doom and gloom" examples (the megacrisis variables) and accelerating growth with positive, breakthrough examples (areas of technological, societal, and human potential), and an S-curve (of accelerating growth followed by "limits to growth" within an existing system relative to its environment) leading to one of three possible responses—steady-state growth, a breakdown of the system, or a breakdown followed by a quantum jump or breakthrough to a whole new system level. Additional models of interest to futurists today include a step jump model (where one suddenly shifts to a higher system level without any prior breakdown); an evolutionary spiral (combining elements of the Eastern circular model of change, but spiraling upward with each circle to a new level, implying a direction of change to evolution over time—the Western, linear idea); a series of S-curves to breakdowns to breakthroughs over time; the alternation between order (predictable, recognizable change within a system) and

Linda Groff is director of Global Options Consulting, Playa del Rey, California. She is professor of political science and futures studies and coordinator of the Behavioral Science Undergraduate Program at California State University-Dominguez Hills, Carson, California. She may be contacted at ljgroff@csudh.edu.

chaos (a sudden shift to unpredictable, unrecognizable patterns of change) as outlined in chaos theory—where the pattern of the whole is also repeated in ever smaller parts of the whole; and finally, two versions of the acceleration of accelerating change.

HOW FUTURISTS VIEW CHANGE

There are a few common perspectives that futurists share about the processes of change transforming our world and how they look at change. These principles include:

• Futurists do not claim to predict the future. Indeed, there is no one future, but instead many alternative futures exist in any present situation. These alternative futures include possible futures (anything—positive or negative—that could happen in the future), probable futures (what is most likely to happen in the future—in general or in some specific area), and preferable futures (what one would most like to have happen in the future). The goal is to make preferable futures more probable, and also to anticipate not only probable futures (what is most likely), but also possible futures, which though unlikely, if they occurred, could have a big impact.

• The present is a product of what people created in the past, while the future is a result of what people are creating and doing right now. We are currently creating the world that we will be living and working in five to 20 years from now, in Earl Joseph's view (1970s), which is probably significantly shortened today, given the very rapid pace of change. People must therefore be empowered to see how their current thoughts, ideas, and actions or inactions ("sins of commission or omission") are creating their own futures—both individually and collectively.

• The future is never just an extension or repeat of past trends; there are always new developments and unexpected events, as well as unanticipated breakthroughs and breakdowns or crises, that change the future from what we expected—which is another reason why futurists never claim to totally predict the future. The interaction of so much change happening in so many different areas of life today can also create consequences that are not always anticipated.

• Futurists all agree that change is the norm and that the pace of change is speeding up enormously today. From events of recent years, it also appears that change—and evolution—can happen very quickly, once it finally occurs. Examples of this include the fall of the Berlin Wall; the fall of communism first in Eastern European countries, then in the Soviet Union; and the breakup of the Soviet Union into 15 independent states. It is also interesting that none of these developments was really predicted by any of the experts studying these areas ahead of time. This also indicates the increasing unpredictability of events transforming our lives—which principle of unpredictability is also a key feature in most of the new scientific paradigms (or overarching worldviews under which scientists do their research) today.

• One of the most important factors propelling change today is the escalating rate of technological change, innovation, and breakthrough, which is in turn restructuring all our institutions and eventually even our collective thinking—though there is always a lag effect here. One consequence is that many of our institutions today are somewhat outmoded and dysfunctional, although some sectors of society are changing faster than others. In general, business changes faster (because it has to to survive) than does government or education. Our thinking also has to change—to accompany larger system levels of interaction and partial integration today (global and larger regional blocs), as well as the decentralization of society and institutions within countries, and even the breakup of nation-states, in some cases—if we want to be able to solve problems facing the world today. Nonetheless, antiglobalization protests (on social, environmental, and job issues), followed by the black-and-white thinking of both bin Laden (in his attack on the World Trade Center and Pentagon on September 11, 2001) and of the United States and the United Kingdom (in their attack on Iraq), have all tended to increase opposition to various aspects of globalization, which is nonetheless continuing.

CHANGES THROUGH DIFFERENT STAGES (A, B, C, D)

When we look at the future, the key questions are:

1. Assuming that the pace of change will continue and that the future will be different in certain important ways from the present, then what are the likely stages that we will go through to get there? And what different stages have we already gone through relative to any area of change? These stages of change can be represented as follows:

$$A \rightarrow B \rightarrow C \rightarrow D$$

Examples of the process of evolution or change through successive stages include each of the following cases:

• Evolution through the biological stages of life and aging (which all humans share) and the related culturally learned rituals to observe and honor these biological stages of life and rites of passage (which differ from culture to culture). These stages include birth, infancy, childhood, adolescence/young adulthood, middle adulthood, older adulthood, and death.

• Evolution historically through different types of technological and related societal stages of civilization, including hunting and gathering age, agricultural age, industrial age, information age, and postinformation age (whatever that will be called—perhaps the biotech age or the inner-outer space age). What is significant is that each of these periods or ages is occurring at an ever faster pace of change than the previous stage, and that each stage represents a break from the past, which new stage could not have been predicted by extending trends from the previous stage.

2. What is the *process of change* through these different stages in any given area of our lives? In short, what models will best explain the processes of change occurring in different areas of our lives today? The remainder of this paper will focus on some of these models of change and evolution, with relevant examples of each model.

FIGURE 1 - LINEAR, PREDICTABLE CHANGE (A CHANGE IN A LEADS TO A PREDICTABLE CHANGE IN B)

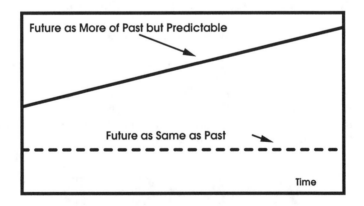

One of the most common and popular models of change is the linear growth model, in which the future is seen as more of the past; i.e., as an extension of past trends. In a linear growth model, the future is also seen as predictable; i.e., there is an equal absolute number of units of increase per unit of time. Another way of saying this is that change from one stage to the next is by slow, gradual change.

Examples of this linear growth model include:

• What most people would like to believe the future will be like (because it is predictable), but what it often is not—especially today.

• Classical Western cultural worldview, from the 19th century, which assumes that linear progress is the norm and that the future is predictable and an improvement upon the past. Also sees change as slow and gradual.

• Darwin's theory of biological evolution, which posited that biological evolution—from one species to the next—was via slow, gradual change. Darwin then looked for evidence of this slow gradual change from one species to the next in the fossil record, but had difficulty finding such evidence.

• The Newtonian (or 19th century Old Physics) model of reality as a clockwork universe, where a given change in A always leads to a predictable change in the quantity of variable B. (This view is seriously challenged today by the uncertainty and unpredictability principles in various new scientific paradigms, including the New Physics and Chaos Theory as examples.)

FIGURE 2 - CYCLICAL CHANGE THROUGH SEQUENTIAL POINTS OR STAGES

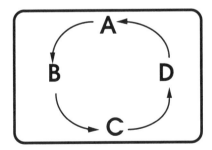

In this model, change is cyclical and proceeds through a series of repeating points or stages—in a definite, recurring, set order.

Examples of this model include:

• The most common example of cyclical change through sequential points is the progression through the four seasons of the year—spring, summer, fall, and winter—always in the same order.

• The classical, most common view of nature and history in many non-Western, including Eastern, civilizations and cultures, as well as indigenous cultures; i.e., history repeats itself, just as the cycles of nature repeat themselves.

• Also P.R. Sarkar's model (based on the Indian caste system) of the rotation of power within any society between four main groups (or castes within Indian society): the military or warrior caste, the intellectuals or academics, entrepreneurs or business-people, and workers or masses of people. The model can begin anywhere in the cycle, but power rotates among these four groups in a set, predictable order. Each group comes to power because it offers something that society needs at the time, and which the previous group in power was unable to offer. However, with time the weaknesses or shortcomings of each group surface, requiring a new group to come to power that can provide this needed quality.

For example, when there is too much disorder in society, the military takes power to restore order. They reestablish order, but then lack sufficient new ideas, so the intellectuals next come to power. The intellectuals have good ideas, but they don't know how to get anything done, so eventually the entrepreneurs or businesspeople come to power. They know how to get things done, but they become too greedy, so eventually the workers or people must rise up and take back power. They redistribute power, but are too anarchic, so eventually the military must come to power again to restore order, and the process continues again, as before.

What is particularly interesting is that the history of the Internet has followed these same stages, or at least the first three of these four stages, beginning with the military. The Internet began as an effort by the Advanced Research Projects Agency (ARPA) in the US Department of Defense to find alternative pathways to send information between two points, A & B, if there was a nuclear war and one route was wiped out. In the next stage, academics began using the Internet to share information. In this stage, the ethic was the free sharing of information and ideas and research. In the next stage, which we are clearly in today, the entrepreneurs and businesspeople start using the Internet, seeking ways to sell products, expand their businesses, and also cut costs of doing business by selling directly to customers. In this stage, the ethic of the Internet changes to making money instead of sharing information freely. If this model is correct, then the next stage of the Internet will be the people and workers all gaining access to the Internet as well.

Indeed, the Clinton-Gore administration stated that, in the information age—when access to ideas and information is the basis for power in society—the goal must be that everyone eventually gains access to the Internet. It's a good goal, not just nationally, but also globally.

FIGURE 3 - CYCLICAL CHANGE THROUGH NONSEQUENTIAL POINTS OR STAGES

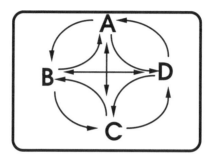

In this model, change is cyclical and proceeds through a series of repeating points—but not in any particular set order.

Examples of this model include:

• Alternations in fashion or hair styles, with periodic returns to earlier styles, but in no set order.

• Rotations of people in leadership positions or jobs within an organization, but in no set order.

FIGURE 4 - CYCLICAL CHANGE BETWEEN TWO POINTS OR POLES OVER TIME

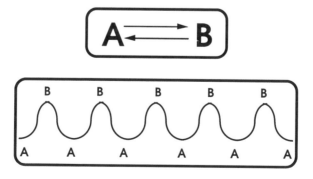

In this model, change alternates between two points or polar opposites over time, as seen in the above diagrams.

Examples of these models include:

• Liberal-conservative swings within a political system—whether that system is democratic or not. Apparently such changes occurred in the former Soviet Union, not just in Western political systems.

• Alternations within an economic system between expansion and contraction, or boom and bust. For example, Kondratieff, a Russian economist, claims to have discovered such cycles of boom (25 years) and bust (25 years) within the capitalist economic system. Based on the 1930s Depression, he and his followers thus predicted that another Great Depression would occur in the capitalist business cycle in the 1980s—exactly 50 years after the earlier Great Depression. While recessions have happened, no great depression has yet occurred. Some people, such as Ravi Batra, have then extended their predictions of such a depression from the 1980s to the 1990s. Others, however, claimed that, with the increasing productivity provided by the Internet and other high technologies, the old capitalist business cycles had been replaced by a "new economy" operating under new rules, allowing for a longer period of economic expansion than previously possible, before some kind of correction or at least recession was necessary. This "new economy" expansion collapsed with the "dot-com" and stock market crash beginning in 2000.

• Alternations between sensate/materialistic values and ideational/spiritual values within Western civilizations historically, as expounded in the work of Pitirim Sorokin (at Harvard University in Sociology in the 1930s). He predicted back in the 1930s that Western civilization had become so materialistic that in the future it would be replaced by either ideational/spiritual values or by some combination of spiritual and material values.

Finding the Higher Unity That Unites Polar Opposites Today

As we move towards more interdependence within our very diverse, global society today, there is a tendency towards the dynamic balancing of polar opposites within a whole systems context, creating a complex systems view of reality, rather than adversarial relations between opposites that see themselves as separate and therefore unconnected, as in the past—especially in the West. (Nonetheless, the current black-and-white worldviews of Al Qaeda, and the Bush administration in response, show an opposite trend, which in this writer's view is out of touch on both sides with the mind-set needed for an increasingly interdependent world.)
Examples include the following:

• Politically, more people call themselves "independents" in the

United States, voting on candidates rather than by party.

• Economically, the trend towards more worker ownership of companies dissolves the old adversarial relations between owner and workers.

• Concerning spiritual and/or material values underlying civilizations, more people today—in both Eastern and Western cultures—seem interested in creating lives that honor both spiritual and material values, not either-or.

FIGURE 5 - DIALECTICAL CHANGE BETWEEN THESIS, ANTITHESIS, AND SYNTHESIS: INTERACTION BETWEEN TWO POLES OR OPPOSITES LEADS TO NEW SYNTHESIS

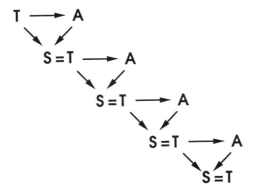

Another interesting model of change is the dialectical process of thesis, antithesis, and synthesis, in which the interaction between two points, A & B, instead of alternating back and forth between polar opposites (as in the above example) produces something new out of the interaction. Thus, an initial position or state (thesis) leads to its opposite (antithesis), which interact with each other, eventually producing something new—a synthesis, which contains elements of both the thesis and the antithesis. This synthesis becomes a new thesis and the process starts all over again.

Examples of this model include:

• George William Frederick Hegel applied the dialectic to an idealistic view of history.

• Karl Marx's materialistic view of social class conflict working through history accepted Hegel's dialectical view of the change process, but took Hegel's basic assumption of an idealistic view of reality and "stood Hegel on his head"; i.e., he instead applied the dialectical method to a materialist view of reality and history, which worked via social class conflict as the engine of historical change.

• A more current example might be capitalism (which began with the industrial age) leading to socialism (an industrial age critique of capitalism) leading to a new global economy (in the information age) that potentially transcends both capitalist and socialist economic systems. So far, however, it looks like only socialism, but not capitalism, has been transformed. People speak of a new global economy today, but it is based only on capitalism.

INTRODUCTION TO MODELS OF CHANGE OF PARTICULAR INTEREST TO FUTURISTS TODAY

The remaining models of change covered in this paper are models that have been of particular interest to futurists in explaining many of the changes currently sweeping the planet. These models include accelerating growth, S-curves, three different responses to S-curves (steady state, breakdown, and breakdown followed by breakthrough), step jump, evolutionary spirals, S-curves to breakdowns to breakthroughs over time, the alternation between chaos and order, and two versions of the acceleration of accelerating change.

Introduction to Accelerating Growth Model (An Equal Percentage Increase Per Unit of Time), with Both Negative and Positive Examples

The next models of change deal with accelerating, or exponential growth, where there is an equal percentage increase per unit of time. Growth begins slowly, but accelerates over time and sometimes is out of control before people realize there is a problem. Because so many areas of life are undergoing accelerating growth rates today, futurists argue that it is necessary to recognize such growth rates early on, if we are to be responsible in, and develop adequate policies for, dealing with such change before it gets out of control (also compare Figures 6 and 7 below with Figure 15).

FIGURE 6 - ACCELERATING GROWTH WITH NEGATIVE "DOOM AND GLOOM" EXAMPLES

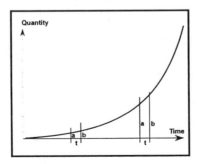

Examples of this model include:

• Growth rate of interrelated global "megacrisis" variables, including rates of population growth, food consumption, energy consumption, environmental pollution, and depletion of the earth's nonrenewable resources.

• Growth rate at which species are becoming extinct today.

• Growth rate in costs of health care and university education in the United States.

Note: The above growth rates often lead to "doom and gloom" views of the future. But these growth rates in megacrisis variables have led to social movements to deal with these crises, including:

• Appropriate/intermediate technology movement and related voluntary simplicity movement (1970s).

• Sustainable development movement (1990s), sometimes also called the regenerative design movement.

FIGURE 7 - ACCELERATING GROWTH WITH POSITIVE, BREAKTHROUGH EXAMPLES

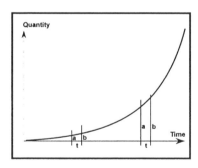

Examples of this model include:

• Growth rate of technological inventions and innovations; i.e., an explosion of high technologies, including information age technologies (computers, telecommunications, robotics, and now also the Internet, World Wide Web, multimedia, and virtual reality); space age technologies (building on information age technologies); and biotechnologies including genetic engineering/recombinant DNA/gene splicing, nanotechnology, and cloning.

• Growth rate of people and groups interested in personal growth, spiritual consciousness and transformation (Peter Russell), and various psychotechnologies.

• Growth rate in social and organizational technologies, releasing social and human potential within organizations.

Note: The above growth rates often lead to positive breakthrough views of the future. They imply that continued growth is desirable and possible in the future.

Introduction to S-Curves (Accelerating Growth Followed by "Limits to Growth") Leading to Three Different Possible Consequences

After a period of accelerating growth, a period of "limits to growth" within a given system can be reached, where the environment does not contain enough resources to support further unlimited future growth of the components or species within that system. When this "limits to growth" point is reached, it creates a major crisis in the system. There are at least three different ways that the system can respond to this "limits to growth" or crisis situation, which follow:

FIGURE 8 - S-CURVE (ACCELERATING GROWTH FOLLOWED BY "LIMITS TO GROWTH") LEADING TO STEADY-STATE GROWTH

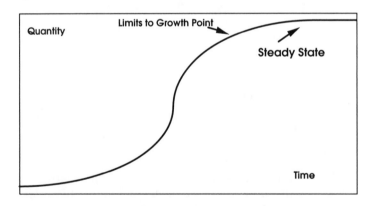

In this model, growth levels off after the Limits to Growth point is reached.

Examples of this model include:

• Sustainable Development, or steady state economic growth, which is advocated as the goal by many people today who are concerned about increasing global population, finite world resources, protection of the environment as our life support system, and creating the foundation for economic development for peoples all over the world, including in developing countries. It is generally recognized that there are not enough resources on earth for everyone to live at the standard of living of some people in the developed world, where there is also much waste of energy and resources.

• Regenerative Design Movement—which recognizes that nature will regenerate itself, "if" we take care of it and do not take from nature at a faster rate than it can replenish itself.

FIGURE 9 - S-CURVE (ACCELERATING GROWTH FOLLOWED BY "LIMITS TO GROWTH") LEADING TO BREAKDOWN

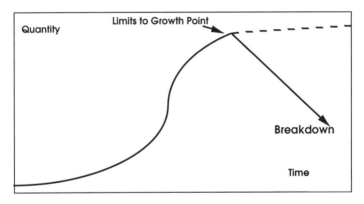

In this model, breakdowns and further crises occurs within a system after the limits to growth point is reached.

Examples of this model include:

• Epidemics of diseases leading to an increasing number of cases, including deaths (after which immunities and vaccines often develop, leading to decreased cases).

• Increasing population of a species within an environment with finite resources leading to a sudden drop off of a population once limits to growth are reached.

• A sudden catastrophe such as a meteor or comet hitting the earth, creating dust in the atmosphere, which blocks sunlight to the earth, killing plants, then animals, leading to the extinction of a species, such as the dinosaurs 65 million years ago.

• Similar projected effect of nuclear winter today—if a nuclear war occurred, filling the air with dust and blocking out sunlight, thereby killing off life on earth.

FIGURE 10 - S-CURVE (ACCELERATING GROWTH FOLLOWED BY "LIMITS TO GROWTH") LEADING TO A BREAKDOWN OF THE SYSTEM FOLLOWED BY A QUANTUM JUMP/BREAKTHROUGH TO A NEW SYSTEM LEVEL

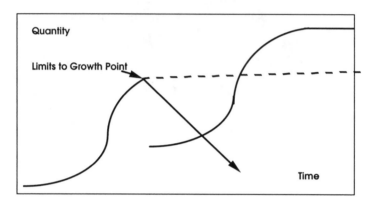

Here, a breakthrough to a whole new system level follows an initial breakdown of the system, which in turn followed a "limits to growth" point being reached within a system.

Examples of this model include:

• Breakthroughs to all kinds of new technologies—information age, space, and biotechnologies including genetic engineering, and nanotechnologies—none of which are simply extensions of earlier technologies.

• Alvin Toffler said that the Information Age could never have been predicted from the Industrial Age; it was a break from the past, not an extension of past trends—ushered in by new technology.

• The destruction of World War II (breakdown) leading to the Manhattan Project and to the splitting of the atom and development of the atomic bomb (technological breakthrough), after which Einstein said: "Everything has changed [re: the destructive powers of technology with the atomic bomb] save our thinking," which needs to change if we are going to use this technology responsibly—to support life, not death.

It is hard to anticipate such breakthroughs because something totally new appears. For example, a caterpillar looking up at a butterfly says, "You'll never get me up in one of those," not realizing that a butterfly is what its own future will be!

ADDITIONAL MODELS OF INTEREST TO FUTURISTS TODAY

FIGURE 11 - STEP JUMP MODEL: A SUDDEN CHANGE TO A TOTALLY NEW STATE OR SYSTEM LEVEL

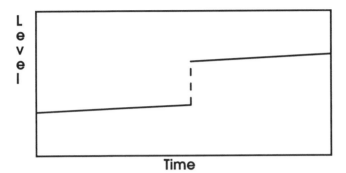

In this model there is a sudden jump to a totally new system level. It is interesting to compare this model with the previous S-curve (accelerating growth to limits to growth) followed by break-down and then breakthrough model. In the step jump model, the shift to a new system level occurs suddenly and without any need for some prior breakdown in the previous system, or crisis first, to trigger or drive the next breakthrough. In short, in the step jump model there is no pain necessary before a breakthrough or gain is possible. Obviously this is the model that individuals or organiza-tions would prefer as the basis for change, but unfortunately, in most cases it is much more likely that some degree of breakdown or crisis in a system or organization or person's life is necessary before people are willing to explore new ways of doing things, leading to an even-tual breakthrough.

Examples of this model include:

• Change from ice to water to steam at set temperatures.

• Sudden advent of the atomic age, with the successful splitting of the atom (although some years of research preceded this breakthrough event). The point here is that once the atomic and nuclear genie was out of the bottle, there was no turning back to an earlier age where such knowledge was not known.

• "Aha" creative insight or new idea or sudden understanding of a relationship between things, which one didn't understand before.

• First view of earth from space as a beautiful living planet, giving us a totally new image of the earth as an interdependent whole without national borders separating peoples on earth.

• Possible future breakthroughs to a totally new state if, for example, contact were suddenly established with extraterrestrial life.

FIGURE 12 - EVOLUTIONARY SPIRAL: COMBINATION OF CYCLICAL/EASTERN MODEL AND LINEAR/WESTERN MODEL OF REALITY

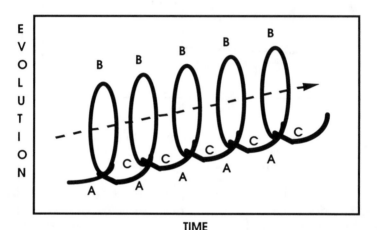

In this model of an evolutionary spiral, crises (A) within an existing system trigger design innovations (B) which then usher in a new stage of evolution (C). This is a nice model because it combines the Eastern cyclical model with the Western linear model (of intentionality or a direction of change running through evolution). Note: today many other opposites (such as these cyclical and linear views of reality) are coming together to create a complex systems view of reality as the new global cultural paradigm for the 21st century.

Examples of this model include:

• This evolutionary spiral, with the "arrow of time" running through it, is used by various people writing on evolution. Examples include: Barbara Hubbard's evolutionary spiral, where crises within an existing system (A) trigger design innovations (B), which then usher in a new stage of evolution (C); and also the model of cosmic evolution, with the arrow of time running through it, which is used by the Wright Center of Tufts University, where their stages of evolution include particulate, galactic, stellar, planetary, chemical, biological, and cultural stages.

• Evolutionary examples of past design innovations, ushering in new stages of evolution, include the invention of photosynthesis in plants and the invention of sexual attraction between opposite sexes for reproduction, replacing earlier division of cells for reproduction.

• Today some people believe so many changes are occurring—in so many different areas of our life and at such a fast pace of change—that we may be in the process of a major evolutionary jump in what it means to be a human being, beyond what any of us can totally understand.

FIGURE 13 - A SERIES OF S-CURVES (ACCELERATING GROWTH FOLLOWED BY "LIMITS TO GROWTH") LEADING TO BREAKDOWN OF THE SYSTEM AND THEN TO A QUANTUM JUMP/BREAKTHROUGH REPEATED OVER TIME

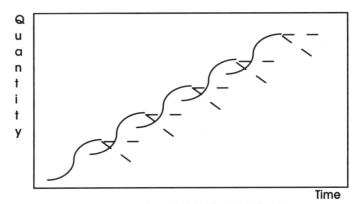

Periodic Quantum Jump Model of Evolution Over Time

This is the same model as Figure 10, except that this is graphed over time (also compare this with Figure 16).
Examples:

• Hunter-gatherer to agricultural to industrial (to atomic) to information/communication ages and societies and beyond.

• Model of the stages of evolution in Duane Elgin's book *Awakening Earth*, including the following eras, and the type of consciousness associated with each stage:

- Archaic era: contracted consciousness.
- Awakening hunter-gatherer era: surface consciousness.

- Agrarian-based civilizations/era: depth consciousness.
- Scientific-industrial era: dynamic consciousness.
- Mass communication and global reconciliation era: reflective consciousness.
- Global bonding, Gaian building and celebration era: oceanic consciousness.
- Surpassing era: flow consciousness.
- Initial maturity of planetary civilization: integral awareness.

FIGURE 14 - CHAOS THEORY: ALTERNATION BETWEEN ORDER (RECOGNIZABLE AND USUALLY PREDICTABLE PATTERN OF CHANGE WITHIN A SYSTEM) AND CHAOS (AN UNRECOGNIZABLE PATTERN OF CHANGE)

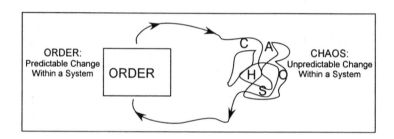

In this model, a recognizable, predictable pattern of change within an existing system can suddenly change or shift into a turbulent, chaotic, unrecognizable pattern. Out of this chaos, however, a "strange attractor" emerges, around which a new pattern and order occurs. The universe thus alternates between order and chaos. The pattern of the whole also repeats in ever smaller parts of the whole—a characteristic of fractal geometry, the geometry of chaos theory. Fractal geometry also seems to explain patterns found in nature. A big debate is whether the mathematics of chaos theory can actually explain sudden changes in systems in different areas of life—thus being a true new scientific paradigm—or whether chaos theory is just a nice metaphor for the fact that our lives are sometimes orderly or chaotic. Chaos theory has been used as a model to try to scientifically explain a number of phenomena, some of which are noted as examples below.

Examples of phenomena that chaos theory has tried to explain include:

• Volatility of weather patterns. Note the increasing unpredictability of weather patterns in the world today. Also, a butterfly flapping its wings in one hemisphere can effect the weather patterns in another hemisphere, since everything is interdependent.

- Drops of water from a faucet suddenly changing their pattern.

- The heart suddenly going into erratic fibrillations.

- Fluctuations in the stock market.

- Random firing of neurons in the brain.

Introduction to the Acceleration of Accelerating Change

There are at least two different models of change that illustrate the acceleration of accelerating change—a topic of current interest. In the first instance, the percentage rate of change in a given unit of time (from point a to b) increases *within* the same evolutionary curve or cycle of change over time. In the second instance, the acceleration of accelerating change occurs when one moves from one evolutionary curve or cycle of change to the next. These two models are illustrated in Figures 15 and 16, respectively, with examples of each.

FIGURE 15 - THE ACCELERATION OF ACCELERATING CHANGE—FROM ONE UNIT OF TIME TO THE NEXT WITHIN THE SAME EVOLUTIONARY CURVE OR CYCLE OF CHANGE

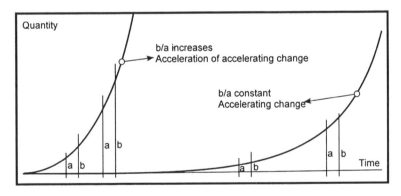

In this model, the percentage rate of change in a given unit of time (from point a to b) increases *within* the same evolutionary curve or cycle of change over time—illustrated in the left portion of Figure 15 above. This can be contrasted with Figures 6 and 7, Accelerating Growth, where the percentage rate of change throughout the evolutionary curve is constant—illustrated in the right portion of Figure 15. This can also be contrasted with the next model, Figure 16—a different version of the Acceleration of Accelerating Change.

Examples of this model include:

- The latest evidence today is that the galaxies in the universe are accelerating in the rate at which they are moving apart from each other. If this continues—which is now the dominant view of astronomers—then our physical universe will end in some kind of cold death: first the stars will burn out, removing the main energy/heat source to support life, and many billions of years later, matter may totally decay, leaving only elementary particles too spread out to interact with each other, i.e., entropy. Before this happens, people (if left on earth) will only be able to see our Milky Way, Andromeda, and other local galaxies—a lonely universe indeed. (The opposite outcome—that the universe will collapse back in on itself into a big crunch or heat death—thus seems less likely at present.)

• Similarly, in the early evolution of our physical universe, there was a period when there was an acceleration in the number of new stars being formed (followed, however, by a slowing down of the rate of new star formation later).

• In biological evolution, there was a period—the Cambrian Explosion—when the number of new species of animals suddenly exploded (followed, however, by a slowing down in the rate at which new species came into existence).

FIGURE 16 - THE ACCELERATION OF ACCELERATING CHANGE—BETWEEN ONE EVOLUTIONARY CURVE OR CYCLE OF CHANGE TO THE NEXT

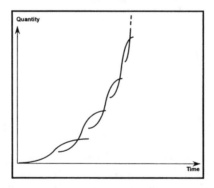

There is a second type of Acceleration of Accelerating Change, where there is an acceleration or increase in the percentage rate of change from one evolutionary curve or cycle of change to the next. This can be compared to Figure 13, where there is a series of S-curves over time (as here), except in Figure 13 the percentage rate of change within the accelerating part of each S-curve is constant over time, whereas in Figure 16 this percentage rate of change increases from one growth curve to the next.

Examples of this model include:

• In technological-societal evolution, it is clear that the Agricultural, Industrial, and Information Revolutions—Alvin Toffler's famous three waves or periods of change—each occur in ever shorter periods and faster rates of change than the previous period(s), with each new period ushered in by new technologies which end up totally restructuring all societal institutions and even mind-sets and worldviews. Thus, the Agricultural Age lasted thousands of years, the Industrial Age lasted 200-300 years, and the Information Age will only last approximately 30-40 years. Figure 16 thus appears to be more accurate for graphing these three waves of change, even though people often illustrate these three waves with Figure 13 instead.

• If we look at the physical evolution of the universe, biological evolution of species, the cultural evolution of technological-societal change and ideas, and finally the evolution of consciousness, each subsequent type of evolution (which all work through us as human beings) occurs over ever shorter periods of time and at ever faster rates of change.

• In conclusion, it seems that there are periodic bursts of change throughout different areas of evolution, often followed by a levelling off in the rate of change for a period of time (the famous S-curve), to be followed later by new bursts of qualitatively new types of change. It also appears that in most cases, each subsequent period or cycle of change (i.e., each subsequent S-curve) occurs at ever faster rates if change than the previous cycle of change.

CONCLUSIONS ON MODELS OF CHANGE

Having gone through all these different models of change, and examples of each model, what conclusions can one reach about the processes of change and evolution transforming our world and the universe today? Many different models of change have been explored, along with examples of each. Here are some tentative conclusions:

• No one model explains all examples of change or evolution.

• Different models of change and evolution have also been favored by different cultures—especially Eastern and indigenous cultures vs. Western cultures traditionally. Different periods of human history have also favored different models to explain the changes that they were undergoing. Earlier cultures and civilizations favored more predictable models of change (whether linear or cyclical), while such models seem less appropriate for the world today.

• Given that the pace of change seems to be greatly accelerating today, new models of change seem necessary to explain what people are experiencing. The fact that many areas of life are undergoing accelerating rates of growth today seems to indicate that we are in a period of massive change on this planet, with both positive and negative examples.

• The rate at which change is accelerating may itself be further accelerating today, and may have also occurred periodically in different areas of evolution in the past, to sometimes be followed by a decrease in the percentage rate at which change is accelerating after that.

• Many of the new scientific paradigms (discussed in separate writing) have models of change that include uncertainty and unpredictability, where a system can suddenly break down and then have a breakthrough to a new system level, or can suddenly shift from order into chaos and then a new order.

• This is a huge topic deserving further study.

[Author's Note: It is almost impossible to cite an adequate bibliography because this is my own summary and synthesis of an exposure to a wide range of issues in the Futures Studies field over many years. This paper will therefore forgo a formal bibliography. The first version of this presentation was put together for a futures panel organized by Walter Truett Anderson for William Shatner. I am greatly indebted to my late husband, Paul Smoker, for making computer versions of many of the diagrams used in this paper, and also to Jan Amkruetz for doing several additional computer diagrams recently.]

URBAN FUTURES

IMAGINEERING CITIES: CREATING LIVABLE URBAN FUTURES IN THE 21ST CENTURY

by

John Ratcliffe and Elzbieta Krawczyk

THE CONTEXT

The 21st century is being recognized as the "century of cities." More than half of the world's population now live in cities, and the importance of urban environments has become even greater over recent decades. Cities are the key centers of human activity and the engines of economic growth throughout the world, a world that has been dramatically transformed and is more complex, more competitive, and better connected than ever before (Ratcliffe, 2002a). Rapid technological change, expanding globalization, profound cultural shifts, and new economic trends have brought about a whole range of fresh opportunities and challenges. Traditional ways in which cities were planned and managed turn out to be less relevant and less sustainable in times of an accelerating pace of change and greater complexity in the global environment. Nowadays cities search for new, more effective ways of dealing with existing problems and measures that would help them to avoid further turmoil ahead. They look for a preferred future state and the means that would help them choose the path leading to it so as to create attractive and productive urban environments for inhabitants, business, and visitors.

This paper is set around the adage: "Imagine ahead—plan backwards." It explores the challenges facing 21st-century cities and their governments; it identifies the difficulties the planning profession encounters in times of accelerating change and increasing uncertainty for the future; it examines the nature and role of the futures approach in the city context; and it demonstrates how various cities, such as Bilbao, Dublin, Lyon, and Vancouver, reposition themselves, envision their futures, and deal with the challenges and opportunities that lie ahead.

Increasingly, it is recognized that cities, in order to create sustainable competitive environments, need to transform their planning policy and practice to encourage active business and civic engagement in concerted planning and decision making. Vision, leadership, and collaborative action lie at the foundation of building sustainable and competitive cities in the future. Futures approaches such as prospective and foresight, and techniques, such as scenario planning and visioning, can play an important role in developing preferred futures, creating a platform for collaboration between dif-

John Ratcliffe *is director of the Futures Academy, Department of the Built Environment, Dublin Institute of Technology, Dublin, Ireland. He may be contacted at john.ratcliffe@dit.ie.* Elzbieta Krawczyk *is a Ph.D. student in the Department of the Built Environment, Dublin Institute of Technology. She may be contacted at elzbieta.krawczyk@dit.ie.*

ferent actors, and formulating specific actions and broad policy proposals.

CONTEMPORARY URBAN PLANNING AND ITS CHALLENGES

Planning, although concerned with the future by definition, for many years has mostly been concentrating on shaping the physical form of cities and securing the provision of adequate services for their inhabitants. Planning agencies became actively involved in budgeting, land development, social-service funding, administration of various programs and projects, and other short-term activities (Isserman, 1985). Planners, however, have generally tended to separate the physical form from the social, economic, and environmental aspects rather than treating all these elements in an integrated manner (Gaffikin and Morrissey, 1999). Planners, the "visionary profession," whose role "is to lead from the present to the future" (Isserman, *op. cit.*), arguably have lost their creativity and innovative thinking in order to respond to the current needs, future projections, and crises on the ground.

Planning has neglected time and the future in order to fulfill present spatial demands (Isserman, *ibid., APAJ*, 2001, and Ratcliffe, *op. cit.*). The methods used in spatial analysis and territorial planning have advanced greatly, but the methods for coping with the time dimension in planning have not been developed to the same extent. It is increasingly being recognized that the planner's toolkit for exploring the future needs to be improved and broadened (Ratcliffe, *ibid.*).

Traditional planning systems are based on the model that can best be described as "predict and provide." The policies are developed and decisions are made on the basis of evidence that is usually gathered through observation of historical trends such as population, demand for various types of infrastructure—housing, schools, leisure, retail, and the like. These trends are projected into the future through the application of a range of techniques, mainly quantitative. Typically such trend projections have several hypotheses, usually the case trend, the desirable alternative, and the worst-case option. Often a set of wild cards is added and some sort of cross-impact analysis is carried out in order to integrate all the elements and choose the option that will then be implemented. This model leads to the reinforcement of the present situation into the future and makes it more difficult to think of other alternatives (Serra, 2001).

Reinforcement of past and present trends, however, is no longer an option. The emergence of powerful new drivers of change makes it impossible to act in a "business as usual" way. Competition for investment, increasing social and environmental pressures, and unexpected cultural transformations force towns, cities, and regions to discover how to respond to new tendencies, tackle them in a comprehensive and integrated manner, learn how to anticipate what lies ahead, and strive to create more livable and attractive environments.

In this way, contemporary urban planners and decision makers have come to recognize a whole range of fresh challenges that face them:

• The need to find effective ways of understanding the urban embroglio that cities have become and the global context within which they function.

• The need to anticipate future change that may and will influence cities.

• The need to find new ways in which the broad community and its various constituent interest groups can actively be engaged in planning and managing their cities in order to shape their urban environments according to their chosen values and perceived needs.

• The necessity to comprehend that it is not enough anymore simply to be responsive; it is essential to be proactive.

In order to tackle these challenges, planners and decision makers have sought new approaches and methods to assist them. The futures field is proving to be one of the most fruitful sources of methods and techniques currently being adopted for city planning and urban areas around the world.

FUTURES IN THE CITY CONTEXT

The future is not a probable place we are being taken to, but a preferred place we are creating. The tracks to it are not found and followed, but made by laying and constructing the trail.

—Ellyard, 1993

Futures methods facilitate dealing with the complexity of systems and the uncertainty of impending change. They help to anticipate what lies ahead and to build images of the most desirable future. They also set a philosophical and psychological background for re-thinking the present in the light of the future. The futures field raises a number of questions that assist in creating mind-sets ready to deal with upcoming matters and events in a constructive and creative way.

Futures, prospective, foresight, scenario planning, and urban visioning can successfully be used in promoting urban-planning processes in order to foster the sustainable development of prosperous cities and towns in a manner that favors a more holistic, inclusive, integrative, and creative approach (Ratcliffe, 2004). They assist in the development of a widely agreed vision of where the place in question wants to be in 20, 50, or 100 years time (Gaffikin and Morrissey, 1999), and they help to set a path towards this desired state.

The methods most often used are visioning, and scenario planning. Visioning is a process in which communities values, desires, and hopes for the future of their city or region are combined into an image of the place in its preferred future state (Kitsuse and Myers, 2000). Visioning promotes an inspiring and creative approach to "remaking the purpose" (Gaffikin and Morrissey, *op. cit.*) of places in decline, struggling with social, infrastructural, and environmental problems, or places looking for their own identity and position in the global context. Gaffikin and Morrissey (*ibid.*) recognize a role of vision planning in attempting to end the old segregation between various city dimensions and in integrating these elements in order to ensure a holistic approach towards development. They look at long-term visioning as a method that "looks far enough ahead to avoid the immediate concerns about 'feasibilities' such as cost." Visioning helps to establish "where" we want to go and also "why." The "why" question leads to discussion of the values and principles underlining the vision of preferred future and enables the engage-ment of the wider community in this debate. The engagement of all sectors of society, often representing diverse interests, in the visioning process gives the opportunity to exchange their views and come to a common conclusion. It is much easier to discuss diverse points of view and seek a compromise using the future as a "blank canvas to sketch from" than to deal with present problems and dilemmas that seem to be largely unchangeable and very difficult to solve (*ibid.*).

Another method sometimes used on its own, or as a part of prospective or visioning exercises, is scenario planning. The scenario method is a powerful technique supporting decision-making processes. Scenario stories describe what cities might be like a few decades ahead and stimulate thinking about what is really desired and what policy proposals are needed in order to achieve that preferred state. The scenario process is an important technique in itself, as it develops an understanding of what type of forces will shape urban environments and how these forces can act and interact with each other.

IMAGINATIVE CITIES

> Successful cities seemed to have some things in common—visionary individuals, creative organizations, and political culture sharing a clarity of purpose.
>
> —Charles Landry, 2000

Over the past decade, cities and city regions around the globe have been undertaking various exercises aimed at setting the direction for their future development. These exercises have different structures, budgets, timescales and time horizons, and methodologies. They have also been initiated for different reasons and by different organizations, but there are similar experiences shared by all of them.

This paper presents examples of four cities: Bilbao, Dublin, Lyon, and Vancouver, illustrating the exercises that were undertaken in order to develop preferred future visions for these respective cities. Despite the differences in the way these exercises were conducted, a number of common threads can be identified:

- Leadership.
- Collaboration between all actors within the city/metropolitan region.
- An holistic approach towards urban space.
- The importance of the actual process—not just a product.

Leadership had a significant role to play in initiating and conducting the process in three cases. The individual leadership of Raymond Barre (mayor of Lyon) and Josu Ortuondo (mayor of Bilbao) led to the setting up of Millenaire 3 and *Bilbao-Metropoli-30*, bodies respectively responsible for the development of a future vision and related implementation plans. In Dublin, it was the leadership of an organization, the Dublin Chamber of Commerce. The Chamber of Commerce decided to develop a vision for the city in 20 years time in the absence of other similar initiatives. It was felt that Dublin, after a period of high economic growth, had reached a plateau and that fundamental rethinking of the future direction of the city was needed in order to sustain competitiveness and enhance the quality of life.

Collaboration by all actors within the city/metropolitan region was deemed an essential foundation for the projects in every case. It is widely recognized that "the collaborative process helps to develop rich solutions and ensure that the ownership of the solutions are rooted in the community so that they will be implemented" (Cities PLUS, 2004). In Bilbao, Lyon, and Vancouver, representatives of all sectors (public agencies, business community, citizen groups, experts, and academics) were invited into the process and took an active part in building and implementing the common vision. In Dublin, although the vision itself was developed by the business association, it has been recognized that it can be realized only if all the stakeholders in the city ultimately take ownership of the vision and commit themselves collectively to common action. With this in mind, the Dublin Chamber of Commerce intends to use the vision as an invitation to a grand debate about the future of the city, in which all actors and agencies would engage.

Dublin 2020 Vision

Ireland witnessed exceptional economic growth during the "Celtic Tiger" era. It resulted in the major physical, social, and cultural transformation of its capital, Dublin. Although the city has reached a significant international status, it is struggling with a number of critical infrastructural and social problems. In order to sustain Dublin's competitiveness and to achieve balanced development, these problems need to be solved. But it is also being recognized that the city needs to have a vision of where it wants to be in 10, 20, or 50 years' time and develop a strategy that would set a path to this imagined city state.

In response to this need, the Dublin Chamber of Commerce undertook in late 2003 to develop a vision for the city in the year 2020. The vision was developed through a structured process (Prospective through Scenarios) by a group of selected experts on strategic planning coming from various business sectors, the Chamber's members, over a period of eight months.

The vision portrays Dublin as:

"A knowledge city," in which lifelong learning and personal and civic development are on the daily agenda, where civic and environmental attitudes are formed at the beginning of the learning cycle, and where teaching how to think creatively and independently is a part of the curriculum.

"A great European city," which is well known in Europe for its distinct cultural identity and trademarks, where citizens feel and act as stakeholders, and where living is safe, comfortable, and convivial.

"A city that works," because growth is planned and managed, resources are utilized in an efficient way, and public services such as transportation, waste management, energy, and water supply meet the highest standards.

"A highly competitive city," which attracts highly qualified labor and encourages R&D, where enterprise and entrepreneurial culture are promoted and a fiscal regime and regulations support business and innovation.

"A city wisely governed," by a directly elected mayor, who ensures implementation of plans and enforcement of policies, a city with its own transparent financial system, in which central and local government powers are in balance, and citizens, the business community, and public authorities work together to ensure its optimal development.

Within each of the above themes, the Dublin Chamber of Commerce proposed a number of key policy measures that need to be introduced and a series of actions required for the vision to be realized.

Dublin Chamber of Commerce recognizes that in order for the vision to be realized the support of key stakeholders involved in the city development is required. Therefore, the first step that should be undertaken is the establishment of a Forum for Dublin that would bring together all players within the city—local authorities, business community, citizens, academics, environmental groups, and so forth. The Forum would facilitate further debate on the future of the city and ensure delivery of policies and actions required for achieving the vision agreed by the Forum.

Lyon Millenaire 3: "21 Priorities for the 21st Century"

Lyon is the third-largest city in France. Once it used to be the main French city and a major European center. It has a long business tradition that continued through the centuries and sustained the city's thriving prosperity and international position. Lyon's status has declined with the rise of Paris and as a result of the administrative changes in the 1960s. Lyon then became a capital of the new Rhone-Alps region, but its role was not recognized by other economically independent sub-regions like the Saint-Etienne (Le Gales, 1994). A highly fragmented and weak local government system, urban sprawl, social problems, and the need to improve the competitiveness of the region underlined the development of the Millenaire 3 project.

The Millenaire 3 program was launched in 1997 by Raymond Barre, mayor of Lyon and president of Greater Lyon. The project aimed at providing the conurbation with a comprehensive, integrated development program consistent with the sustainability principles that would enable Lyon to improve its international ranking and achieve social cohesiveness (EDURC, 2000).

The Greater Lyon area has approximately 1.3 million inhabitants, and its territory is divided among 55 municipalities. One of the great challenges for the project was to bring all these towns together so as to create a coherent whole and then engage the representatives of all groups (local government agencies, business circles, academia, and community groups) into the development of the strategy.

The Millenaire 3 approach was based on the assumption that planning for the future can no longer be left entirely to specialists and that it should be based on the cooperation of all actors involved in shaping the city. The approach led to the synergy of three functions: public debate, networking of actors, and projects. The vision developed within the Millenaire 3 framework describes Greater Lyon through five strategic-policy themes:

- An international, culturally receptive city.
- An attractive, livable city.
- A city that fosters the spirit of enterprise.
- A city conducive to lifetime learning.
- A city putting consultative democracy to work.

Within each of these policy themes a number of more-detailed objectives was specified. The total number of priority objectives was 21, thus: "21 Priorities for the 21st Century."

The project helped to establish a stable relationship based on trust between the civil society and Greater Lyon. It brought back the desire for genuine public debate, encouraged networking of stakeholders representing various areas, and provided fresh visibility for non-mainstream actors and forces rising within the metropolis. Millenaire 3 contributed to emergence of projects arising from the civil society.

Revitalization Plan for Metropolitan Bilbao

Bilbao, situated in the Spanish Basque Country, within its metropolitan border is a home for about 1 million people spread around 30 municipalities. Traditionally, the economy of the city was based on steel and shipbuilding industries. As a result of the global shift from industry to a service-based economy, Bilbao has been struggling with severe economic, social, and environmental problems. The fears for the future of the city led to the mobilization of local actors and the undertaking of extensive planning action in 1992. A public and private partnership body—"Bilbao-Metropoli-30"—was founded in order to develop a new vision for the future of the metropolitan region and prepare a regeneration plan divided up into easily legible projects (EDURC, 1999).

The regeneration plan for Bilbao was based on a comprehensive integrated approach. The overall aim of the plan was "to improve the welfare level and the quality of life of its inhabitants through the improvement of the urban environment and the international economic competitiveness of the metropolis" (TRANSLAND, 1999). In order to realize the plan, a set of eight critical issues was identified:

1. Investment in human resources.
2. Service metropolis in a modern industrial region.
3. Mobility and accessibility.
4. Environmental regeneration.
5. Urban regeneration.
6. Cultural centrality.
7. Coordinated management by the public administration and the private sector.
8. Social action.

The methodology used for the development of the strategic plan was based on participation and evaluation. Committees comprising experts, representatives of different sectors, and decision makers took part in all phases of the process: planning, implementation, and evaluation. Evaluation is an essential part of the process. In this phase the impact of new facilities on the city's overall situation is considered, as well as the social impact of the measures undertaken.

A holistic approach towards the urban environment was another characteristic common for all four projects. The methodologies applied in these exercises enabled participants to look at their cities as entireties. It has been recognized, especially in the Vancouver case, that "the key to sustainability requires determination to focus simultaneously on all dimensions: social, economic, and environmental; short term, medium term and long term; from the local to global levels" (Cities PLUS, *op. cit.*).

Another characteristic common to these projects was recognition of the importance of the process by which the visions were developed. Bringing the right agencies and people together to share their perceptions and ambitions, and enabling them to think creatively and flexibly together, is frequently as valuable as the particular findings derived from the effort (Ratcliffe, *op. cit.*). One of the participants from Vancouver, Ron Clarke, summed it up thus: "The process generates informed choices. It is not about seeing the future, and it's certainly not about guaranteeing an outcome, but it is about defining a rich and intellectually robust and defensible process. Win, lose, or draw, we've already gained immensely" (Cities PLUS, *op. cit.*).

The Long-Term Plan for Greater Vancouver

The 100-year plan for Greater Vancouver was developed as Canada's response to an international competition on Sustainable Urban Systems Design, sponsored by Gas Union. The project was run through cooperation of the Sheltair Group (a private planning consulting company), the GVRD (the public sector client), the Liu Institute for Global Issues (a university-based think tank), and the International Center for Sustainable Cities (a civil society organization). The 18-month-long process evolved into a dialogue among 500 individuals and organizations representing public, private, and civil sector actors.

The approach adopted by Vancouver involved three main phases:

1. Envisioning the future of the region.
2. Exploring the options.
3. Implementing the plan.

The overall process was based upon the Adaptive Management Framework, which could be described as a pyramid that has a vision for the desired future at the zenith, and then is built from more detailed levels, including goals, targets, strategies, and implementation policies and technologies.

The Greater Vancouver Regional District (GVRD) recognized the project as very beneficial for the establishment of new partnerships, clarification and stimulation of the commitment to urban sustainability, and creation of learning networks at the regional, national, and international levels. The project represents a substantial change in planning practice towards integrated comprehensive planning. In the past, the GVRD would develop its strategic direction from a series of separate plans each with its own vision, goals, timescales, and structures, while this plan treats the urban system as an integrated whole.

It has been recognized that the 100-year horizon helped to look forward leaving behind current preoccupations and vested interests. The extrapolative and backcasting scenarios were powerful tools in the process, which was as important as the plan itself.

FINAL THOUGHTS

In order to create attractive environments for their inhabitants, business, and visitors, 21st-century cities need to be creative and innovative, proactive, and open to new opportunities. Their future should be build upon values and principles promulgated and proclaimed by their citizens. Collectively built visions should mobilize people and resources into collaborative action. Futures methodologies can assist in fulfilling these aims through the provision of adequate approaches and techniques. Cities such as Bilbao, Dublin, Lyon, and Vancouver, as well as many others, have accepted these challenges and initiated actions to meet them. Again, it bears repetition to state that the central message and major change in mind-set in all this is: "Imagine ahead—plan backwards."

REFERENCES

Cities PLUS, "A Sustainable Urban System: The Long-Term Plan for Greater Vancouver" [Internet], www.sheltair.com/library_usp.html (accessed February 26, 2004).

EC Conference on Regional Foresight. December 13, 2001. Dublin. "Territorial Foresight: More than Planning, Less Than Prospective" J. Serra, [Internet], foren.jrc.es/Docs/Conference/conprog.htm (accessed July 21, 2002).

EDURC. "Bilbao" in *European Cities in the Making*, Newsletter of the Working Group "Development Strategies in Major European Cities," No. 1, February 1999.

EDURC. "Lyon" in *European Cities in the Making*, Newsletter of the Working Group "Development Strategies in Major European Cities," No. 15, September 2000.

Ellyard, P. (1993) quoted in "Goals and Objectives: A Vision for Our Community" [Internet], www.cityofdiamondbar.com/home/index.asp?page=282 (accessed February 27, 2004).

Gaffikin, F., M. Morrissey (ed.) *City Visions: Imagining Place, Enfranchising People* (London—Sterling, Virginia: Pluto Press, 1999).

Isserman A. "Dare to Plan: An Essay on the Role of the Future in Planning Practice and Education," *Town Planning Review*, Vol. 56, No. 4 (1985), 483-491.

Journal of the American Planning Association, Vol. 67, No. 4, Autumn 2001.

Kitsuse A. and D. Myers. "Constructing the Future in Planning: A Survey of Theories and Tools," *Journal of Planning Education and Research*, Vol. 29, Summer 2000, 221-31.

Landry, C. *The Creative City: Toolkit for Urban Innovators* (London: Earthscan, 2000).

Le Gales, P. "Lyon" in Harding A. (ed.) *European Cities towards 2000: Profiles, Policies and Prospects* (Manchester: Manchester University Press, 1994).

Ratcliffe, J. (2002a) "Imagineering Cities: Creating Future 'Prospectives' for Present Planning," conference paper presented at Turkish Real Estate Seminar III, May 2-4, 2002, Istanbul.

Ratcliffe, J. (2002b) "Scenario Planning: An Evaluation of Practice," [Internet], www.dit.ie/DIT/built/futuresacademy/whoweare/scenarioplanningdoc (accessed February 11, 2004).

TRANSLAND (1999) "Metropolitan Bilbao, Spain: Strategic Plan for the Revitalisation of Metropolitan Bilbao," available from www.inro.tno.nl/transland/cases_nonprio/bilbao.pdf (accessed September 23, 2003).

ULI (Europe) Conference. January 22, 2004. Paris. "Imagineering the Competitive City," J. Ratcliffe [Internet], dit.ie/futuresacademy/whoweare (accessed February 19, 2004).

THE RISE OF TELECITIES: DECENTRALIZING THE GLOBAL SOCIETY

by

Joseph N. Pelton

Modern technological progress is essentially one-way: Once major innovations occur—regardless of whether they are helpful or harmful—they cannot simply be undone. They are almost always here to stay. During the last several millennia, we have seen "progress" as a set of trends towards megacities: increased urbanization and technological development; higher capacity and faster transportation systems; concentrated and centralized infrastructure for energy, water, and sewage; and expanded police, military, and weapons systems.

In the 21st century, these trends will accelerate, according to some urban planners, architects, and industrialists. There will be more centralization, more urbanization, and greater concentration of people in high-rise urban structures. Models of such a future of high-tech megastructures, with dense concentrations of populations, are visible everywhere. We already see this ill-advised vision of the future in huge skyscraper megastructures in Kuala Lumpur, Shanghai, Taipei, and most remarkably in the redesigned World Trade Center.

These exotic and exciting testimonials to high-rise technology and centralization are as awe-inspiring as they are wrong-minded and potentially destructive. The 21st century demands a new direction—a megashift in value systems and a move toward electronic decentralization. The future of human, intellectual, and economic relationships will be based not in the traditional city, but in the *telecity*—a global community whose life, direction, and functioning are shaped by telecommunications.

THE END OF THE MEGACITY

Telecities will supersede megacities for several reasons, including the drive toward clean air, reducing pollution, energy conservation, more jobs based on services, and coping with the high cost of urban property. Now we must add the need to cope with terrorist threats in a high-technology world.

Western mind-sets were clearly jolted in the wake of the terrorist attack on the World Trade Center in New York City and attacks in Indonesia, Saudi Arabia, and elsewhere. But the risks posed by 20th-century patterns of urbanization and architecture have yet to register fully with political figures and leaders of industry. The Pentagon, for example, has been rebuilt *in situ* rather than distributed to multiple

Joseph N. Pelton *is executive director of the Arthur C. Clarke Institute and director of the Space and Advanced Communications Research Institute at George Washington University in Washington, D.C. He may be contacted at ecjpelton@ aol.com.*

locations and connected by secure landlines and broadband wireless systems. Likewise, the reconstruction of the World Trade Center complex still represents a massive concentration of humanity and infrastructure. This is a remarkably shortsighted and dangerous vision of the future.

The security risks, economic expenses, and environmental hazards of overcentralization are everywhere, and they do not stop with skyscrapers and large governmental structures. There are risks also at seaports and airports, in food and water supplies, at nuclear power plants and hydroelectric turbines at major dams, in transportation systems, and in information and communications systems.

This vulnerability applies not only to terrorist threats but also to human error, such as system-wide blackouts in North America in August 2003 and in Italy in September 2003, and natural disasters such as typhoons, hurricanes, floods, and earthquakes. Leaders and planners are only slowly becoming aware that overcentralized facilities are the most vulnerable to attack or catastrophic destruction.

There is also growing awareness that new broadband electronic systems now allow governments and corporations to safeguard their key assets and people in new and innovative ways. So far, corporations have been quickest to adjust to these new realities, but some governments have begun to adjust as well.

In Japan, for example, the 1995 Kobe earthquake not only killed many people but also wiped out transportation, fiber-optic communications systems, and key infrastructure for many months. The government decided to place satellite earth terminals throughout the country at post offices to ensure communications back-up in times of disaster. More than 4,000 small satellite terminals are already in place, and soon a total of 10,000 will provide the Japanese with a level of secure communications far exceeding any other country's capabilities.

The United States, Europe, and other regions should look to the Japanese model to mitigate the impacts of terrorist attacks or natural disasters. Backup data centers, distributed wireless and satellite facilities, and a new emphasis on replacing classic megacities like New York City and London with telecities will likely ultimately represent a key trend of the 21st century.

Today, most communications providers and satellite system operations are beginning to provide managed network services that are safer from natural disasters and terrorist attack. Basic issues to carefully consider include the following.

- *Reviewing key facilities* to ensure that they are not clumped together, built in flood zones, or built in structures that are not hurricane and earthquake proof. (Verizon put much of its wireless antenna systems for Manhattan on top of the World Trade Center, for instance, and in Florida, the construction of several teleports has been allowed in flood zones.)

• *Strategic planning* to place government and corporate offices in locations that are not only more decentralized, protected, and cheaper, but also where their data and communications centers will be more protected.

• *Decentralizing* all critical infrastructure wherever possible.

• *Reorganizing corporations* to allow them to work as distributed information systems so as to conserve energy, reduce commuting time, improve the environment, and sharply reduce capital and operating costs.

• *Designing better and "smarter" airports, transportation, and energy systems*, with greater attention to disaster and terrorist risks and their implications.

In short, there are many key facilities of the 21st century that need to be conceived in different ways and designed to be smarter, more distributed, and more resilient.

GOODBYE TO COMMUTING

The world is a much smaller place today than 40 years ago, when the age of satellites and fiber-optic networks began. These electronic systems now link billions of people via telephone, radio, television, the Internet, and so on. Everything from astrophysics to *I Love Lucy* to religious ceremonies at the Vatican are instantly available via satellite-linked modems, even in the rain forests of Brazil and the frozen shores of Antarctica. In the age of the telecity, concentrations of people, government facilities, and other infrastructure are simply not necessary and can only serve to increase risks and elevate costs and pollution.

Fiber-optic and coaxial cables, satellite networks, terrestrial wireless, and other transmission systems allow instant and broadband broadcast and electronic exchange on a planetary scale. Today, fiber-optic networks are capable of transmitting hundreds of terabits per second within the world's most advanced countries. Advanced satellites allow more than 200 countries and territories to achieve instantaneous linkage via telephone or the Internet. More than 100 million satellite terminals located everywhere serve a global cast of users. Satellite-user terminals are now interlinked via an amazing combination of broadcast, fixed, navigational, and mobile satellites. In another decade, that number of terminals will likely grow into the several hundreds of millions. In another two decades, that number might even exceed a billion and be so pervasive that we may own several satellite terminals, including one that we wear within a suit coat or on our arm like a wristwatch.

Satellite-user terminals will continue to shrink in size and cost and "disappear" within our clothing or briefcase or into handheld personal data assistants. A flip-down eye loop will provide multimedia information from anywhere on the planet or even outer space colonies.

In such a world environment, an organization could transfer operations from the world's most expensive (and potentially vulnerable) locations to lower-cost suburbs, rural locations, or another country entirely. No need exists for mass commutes to move millions of people into massive high-rise compounds. New electronic and optical systems will be able to provide true "telepresence" anytime and anywhere at virtually no cost.

Global business via satellite and fiber is already commonplace. Electronic funds transfers worldwide were projected to approach $400 trillion during 2003. As impressive as the growth rates in information services around the world have been during the past four decades, this is nothing compared to what will soon be. Studies by Pioneer Consulting and other organizations suggest that e-business and electronic services could increase by an order of magnitude in the next five years.

WORKING FROM HOME OR HAWAII

Rapid, fundamental shifts in work patterns and in corporate organizations are already occurring in the United States and around the world. Hewlett-Packard, for example, has some 40,000 teleworkers at home or at remote work sites. In Japan, NEC continues to expand its network of remote telework centers to bring workers together electronically, since it can no longer afford to build new workspace in the heart of Tokyo. Although these efforts began through IT networking based on terrestrial cable technology, more-flexible satellites will provide the wireless networks of the future.

The Yankee Group estimates there are more than 15 million teleworkers in the United States. They and other market forecasters, such as the Gartner Group and Nielson's, expect this number to rise to more than 50 million by 2010. Similar patterns of growth are expected in Europe, Canada, Japan, and elsewhere around the world. Broadband satellite links are well positioned to fuel this trend due to their flexibility of interconnection, universal coverage, increasing ability to support Internet-protocol based local and wide area networks, and ever cheaper micro-terminals.

There are also more than a million international teleworkers worldwide. Twenty years ago, hourly labor wages were well below the cost of international tie-lines, but now the cost of international information networks are a small fraction of the cost of skilled personnel. We see a continued growth of "lone eagles"—people who decide to locate their service businesses in scenic Hawaii or Switzerland. From their electronic perches, service providers can provide information or consulting services around the world via broadband connections.

People in dozens of emerging economies already telework via fiber or satellites for companies in the United States or Japan. Insurance companies in the northeastern United States have tele-workers in the Caribbean providing word processing and data entry, while Japanese companies hire low-salary computer software development engineers in India, Pakistan, or South Korea. Programmers from Bangalore to St. Petersburg are essentially providing data and IT services around the world live via satellite. The question is whether new broadband networks will beget telework and more worldwide teleservices or the other way around, with the demand for telework-based services begetting new "telepresence" systems. The most important question is whether these trends are driven by the pursuit of new economies of operation and labor markets, by environmental savings, or by the desire to protect population and critical systems against terrorist attacks.

MOBILE MONEY

A few decades ago, the world banking community invented new electronic funds transfer (EFT) systems to move money more efficiently across countries and around the globe. The driving benefit of such systems was to reduce the float of capital that was unavailable for use while checks were being cleared through banking systems. Today, we understand that the benefits of electronic banking are far more extensive than just reducing floating cash. The entire world of banking has been revolutionized. It is not only more efficient and faster, but also more global. And now with the Internet, EFT systems are increasingly integrated with the new world of e-commerce and e-trade.

Between 1997 and 2003, EFT value soared from less than $50 trillion to nearly $400 trillion, more than the combined economic product of all the countries and territories of the entire world. These statistics alone should underscore the true importance of trans-national EFT. Satellite, wireless, and cable-based electronic fund transfers represent the hub of global enterprise. Such electronic cash is therefore central to the idea of an emerging "worldwide mind."

Without the satellite and fiber infrastructure to support the flow of electronic funds, the world economy would grind to a halt. A frontal assault on this system by cyberterrorists could be a nearly lethal blow to global economic prosperity. Of course, such vulnerability is only the beginning: Information networks control energy grids, transportation systems, water systems, dams, and flood-control systems. The great challenge is, therefore, to provide new forms of security for all aspects of 21st-century telecommunications, including media redundancy, improved code and authentication systems, and enhanced cyberlocation.

OTHER TELECITY REVOLUTIONS

More people will need education and health care in the next two generations than have ever been educated or treated since the beginning of human civilization. The technology that makes possible the delivery of health and education services more effectively across long distance and to remote areas must not be confused with the core objectives themselves. The new way of looking at governmental services is to seek ways to deliver more and better services to more people. A corollary is that one must use the most effective technology and system in order to deliver services more effectively and with the most up-to-date information.

Media can and will assist in this great challenge, but the tool must never be confused with the social need. These teleservices must reach the most remote and isolated spaces and with the most up-to-date information. In some cases, satellites and/or fiber networks can also conserve substantial amounts of energy and provide financial savings, but this should be considered a side benefit rather than the object of telecare, telehealth, and tele-education.

BRIDGING THE GAP

For the last half of the 20th century, there were broad concerns about economic and information gaps among the world's nations. The rise of terrorist attacks has increased awareness of the risks that such gaps entail.

There have been continuing charges of neo-colonialism and exploitation of emerging nations by multinational corporations. The advent of the World Trade Organization, free trade coalitions, and e-commerce has tended to increase rather than ameliorate some of those concerns. On one hand, international trade originating from developing countries is increasing as a percentage of the world's total, but much of that trade can be traced to multinational organizations ("North-to-South"). Although telecommunication developments seem to offer new hope and opportunity, the concerns remain. Telenetworks can help bridge the digital divide if planned and implemented in the right way. This must be considered part of the 21st-century telecity conception.

The roughly 2 billion people in developing nations that lack basic services must be considered a challenge not only for the poorest countries, but also for the stability of the world's economic and political systems. What seems clear is that wireless communications and satellite networks often represent the best hope for enabling sustainable development in emerging countries.

Fiber-optic networks and high-end computers do not address the basic needs of many emerging economies. Satellites allow "South-to-South" communications and programs and facilitate tele-education, telehealth, and the growth of services in developing countries. The spread of e-commerce, Internet, and other modern services will most likely come via wireless and satellite technology to the world's poorest or most isolated nations. Certainly satellites and low-cost technologies are not a panacea, but they do represent solid ways of addressing basic needs in Africa, Asia, South and Central America, and the Middle East. It is key to recognize that the critical pathway to success in the delivery of these services relates to the educational and health content and not the delivery system.

FUNDAMENTAL SHIFTS AND EMERGING PATTERNS

Today, information available to our global society is accelerating at exponential speeds. Electronic networks and satellites interconnect even the most remote areas. The nature of learning, communications, and social interchange is being totally transformed via distance learning, international scientific collaboration, access to the Internet, and the global reach of corporations and electronic commerce.

As the rate of speed in the circulation of information accelerated, new ways of obtaining, storing, and sharing information have evolved. The final trends regarding the development, sharing, protection, and refinement of information in the 21st century are still evolving and have yet to be fully understood. One thing that is now clear is that satellites and broadband fiber-optic networks will make the world ever more visually oriented and less text-oriented. We have yet to understand the full implications of this change. But just as more and more information depreciates the value of any one intellectual item, more and visual information also likely depreciates both visual and text information.

The pattern by which information is circulated is changing, and quickly so. Many factors drive this changing pattern, including global reach, increasing speed and volume of the information being circulated, the magnitude and educational level of the populations of modern countries, the ownership patterns of media by private and public entities, the interaction of news with sports and entertainment, and the falling costs of computing and communications.

Thus, information is becoming not only increasingly visual, but also almost randomly prioritized in terms of its meaning, importance, or relevance. The unexpected results include information overload, decreased vocabularies, and educational systems that create more specialization and fewer broadly educated generalists or systems analysts.

The speed and low cost of modern transmission systems appear to be major drivers in this transformation, not only in the most developed countries but also around the world. The fact that television entertainment, sports, movies, and multimedia-based games and e-commerce now dominate traditional telecommunications networks and the Internet appears to represent a fundamental shift in the world today—with much more to come tomorrow.

MAKING LIVES BETTER

The digital revolution has made more information available to more people, faster, and from more varied types of media and applications. Perhaps the most important application of telecity technologies may be to save the environment.

NASA's Mission to Planet Earth and Earth Observation System provide us with air, water, land, glacier, and pollution data. Increasingly, sophisticated and high-resolution multispectral sensors, side-looking and synthetic aperture radar, infrared, thermal mapping systems, and other devices allow us to collect data from all over the world. But we need communications satellite technology to transfer this data from remote sensing satellites to data analysis centers and then to users, wherever they may be.

Global information networks are now creating truly global corporations, supporting electronic immigrants (transnational telecommuters), and supporting telework and telecommuting for tens of millions of workers around the world. Tele-education, telehealth, and telegovernment are megatrends of the new millennium. These networks are essential to linking scientists together to carry out big projects and support supercomputer processing to help protect against natural disasters. The key is not only to do this effectively and at low cost, but also to provide the coverage and bandwidth to be able to do it quickly and accurately. It is also important to allow the right person or organization to obtain the right information at the right time—that requires decentralization.

Often our short-term calculations are at odds with the interests of our children and grandchildren. Issues we must address include:

- We must find applications and benefits of satellite system and fiber operators that go beyond merely developing networks that are faster and cheaper.

- We must create not only better electronic and photonic machinery, but also improved educational, medical, social, and cultural systems that serve the needs of future generations. We need to create economic and political systems that are wise enough to look beyond short-term material and monetary gains.

- As we move from national and regional to international and global economic, social, and cultural networks and systems, we must learn to use new technology not only to transact business faster and at higher volume, but also to improve the human condition. We must improve security, environment, world peace, prosperity, and sustainable livelihood for ourselves and for our progeny. Business and management schools must teach future managers how to embrace distributed networks and form effective electronic teams across the world.

• Finally, we must find ways through economic, legislative, regulatory, or judicial systems for controlling the use of digital information systems to produce a higher quality of life, protect privacy, offer greater environmental protection, and sustain human life. Updated energy and clean air acts must give new emphasis to and rewards for telecommuting, distributed organizations, and 21st-century management systems optimized for a service economy.

"ADDING ON" TO THE NATION: HOUSING A BIGGER AMERICA

by

David Pearce Snyder

The Census Bureau expects the US population to double during this century. In a nation already fighting a losing battle against urban sprawl, this is a daunting prospect. *An entire additional America!* Where will we put another 290 million of us, plus another 200 million job sites and classrooms for 50 million more students? And won't we have to pave over millions of acres of farmland with new freeways?

For most industries and professions, the size and make-up of the population 30 or 50 years from now is of very little consequence to their day-to-day decision making. The restaurant manager, police officer, and factory worker are concerned almost entirely with the present. But an architect's creations can have a service life of 30, 50, or 100 years. Today's designs will have to remain serviceable, pleasing, and economically efficient for a continuously changing user population. Today, for example, 35 million Americans are 65 years old or older (13% of the US population). By 2025, it will be 65 million; by 2050, 85 million; and there will be 175 million Americans over 65 by century's end: nearly one-third of us. Property owners and public-works offices alike are gloomily anticipating the costs of retrofitting their facilities to accommodate an increasingly impaired population.

OLD FOLKS AT HOME...AND AT WORK

Back when we were an industrial economy, it was widely assumed that people who reached 65 would retire from work and move to purpose-built retirement communities for a well-deserved rest. But AARP surveys have found that 45% of baby boomers plan to keep working into their 70s, and that 27% expect to work into their 80s! What's more, those of us who *do* retire are unlikely to move to a purpose-built adult community anytime soon. According to a recent survey conducted by developer Del Webb, 86% of US employees born before 1946 plan to remain in their current homes when they retire. The great majority of Americans want to "age in place."

One reason why most Americans plan to stay employed into their 70s is that most of us no longer physically "labor" for a living. In 1935, when our Social Security System was set up, over one-half of all US jobs were in farming, manufacturing, or construction. Forty years of work on a farm or an assembly line left most people eager

David Pearce Snyder *is a consulting futurist at The Snyder Family Enterprise in Bethesda, Maryland (www.the-futurist.com). He may be contacted at snyder fam1@aol.com.*

for retirement. But today, 80% of us work in services. And, while some consumer service work does involve physical activity (such as letter carriers, baggage handlers, and auto repair), two-thirds of our service workers—56% of *all* US jobs—are in white-collar positions that primarily involve the gathering, processing, analyzing, applying, transmitting, storing, retrieving, and disposing of information.

FROM VERTICAL TO VIRTUAL WORKPLACE INTEGRATION

During the 20th century, *both* the mass production of manufactured goods *and* the processing of masses of information were labor-intensive operations whose infrastructure requirements gave architects substantial employment—e.g., sprawling factories and warehouses, towering office blocks, and the cities and suburbs to house dense concentrations of workers and their families. But today, just as automation has already squeezed millions of jobs out of manufacturing, the computer and its Internet infrastructure are eliminating billions of paper transactions and records and millions of clerical jobs.

Our new capacity to move masses of accurate data around the world instantaneously has given US employers "virtual access" to high quality professional and technical employees in distant low-cost labor markets. Forrester Research, the Cambridge, Massachusetts, technology consultancy, recently forecast that 3.3 million US white collar jobs will be off-shored during the next 15 years, including 185,000 architects. Ernst and Young's real estate practice has estimated that exporting 3.3 million white-collar jobs will reduce domestic demand for office space by 50 million square feet per year through 2017!

The same high-speed Internet "info-structure" that makes it possible for employers to outsource professional and technical services to foreign markets also facilitates domestic outsourcing. Growing numbers of major employers—International Paper, BP, Bank of America, British Airways, etc.—are contracting out entire administrative functions (computer systems, human resources, facilities management, financial services, logistics, procurement, etc.) *both* to reduce their overhead costs *and* to free up management's time and attention to focus on the organization's "competitive competencies."

The US Bureau of Labor Statistics (BLS) expects the "Business Services" portion of the US economy to grow by 50% (5 million jobs) during this decade—*twice as fast as any other sector*—as more and more employers pay other firms to provide their administrative services. In these "distributed enterprises," the inputs of multiple independent components are "virtually integrated" over the Internet. Core employees, subcontractors, contingent workers, and independent consultants collaborate with each other from dispersed work sites that are increasingly being equipped with large, high-resolution, flat-panel displays that permit high-resolution videoconferencing and shared white board work space.

As growing numbers of private and public sector organizations transform themselves from vertically integrated, labor-intensive bureaucracies into lean, virtually integrated networks of high-performance specialists, US economic productivity-improvement rates are expected to continue their recent seven-year rise. This will keep profits and wages high and inflation low. But it will also sustain continued career-ending job eliminations throughout all large corporate and government institutions. Displaced middle-income professional, managerial, and technical employees will swell the ranks of the nation's contingent white-collar workforce: millions of part-time, temporary, and contract employees, many of whom will work out of their homes, along with tens of millions of salaried tele-commuters and millions of self-employed.

During the 1990s, a limited number of employers offered "flex-place"—or telecommuting—as a family-friendly arrangement to retain valuable personnel in a tight labor market. But since the recent recession, a growing number of employers have begun *to mandate* telecommuting for large numbers of their white-collar workers, as a means of cutting their corporate real estate costs. "Home-basing" will be the next phase of disaggregating our vertically integrated Industrial Era enterprises, following "outsourcing" and "off-shoring." A recent survey of major Silicon Valley employers (Intel, Sun, Cisco, H-P, etc.) found that those firms anticipate reducing their office space requirements by 15%-20% during the next 24 to 36 months, purely by adopting telecommuting as general corporate policy. Consulting firms with 30 to 50 employees have simply dropped their office space leases at renewal time to become networks of home offices with conference rooms in cyberspace.

WORK IS WHERE YOU DO IT

The organization of the postindustrial workplace has begun to emerge. By 2015, 20%-25% of all gainful employment will take place in the home. Just as the aging of Americans will require retrofitting all commercial, public, and residential space, so too will the wide-spread shift of commercial work into the household. The nearly $100 billion that US households currently spend each year on residential modifications—including home offices, granny-flats, and caregiver accommodations—will grow dramatically. Local government in traffic-choked cities will offer tax incentives to encourage home employment as a means of reducing gridlock and air pollution. Health insurers—and federal healthcare policy—will increasingly promote home care as a superior, less-costly alternative to institution-al care for most dependent adults. Hospitals and doctors have already begun to use wireless Internet to remotely monitor and medicate patients in their homes.

From now on, the routine lifetime uses of *all* dwellings will include not only traditional social and domestic functions, but commercial employment, senior living, convalescent care, and distance learning as well. The return of marketplace production to households will, in turn, revitalize older residential neighborhoods and their local retail businesses. Meanwhile, the continuing migration of white-collar work out of commercial buildings—and out of the country—will leave a lot of empty office space in need of an architect's hand to convert it into luxury flats, home/office condos, affordable housing, or *(shudder)* data hotels.

FROM LIVING ROOM TO WORKING ROOM

These are truly transformational times. A dramatically different future is just a few years away. Architects must offer their clients practical long-range visions that will accommodate the inevitable changes that lie ahead. A century ago, Frank Lloyd Wright invented the *living room* to accommodate the altered lifestyles of the emerging "leisure class," who had been newly made prosperous by the maturing Industrial Revolution. Now is the appropriate moment in time for architects to invent the *working room* for a newly "leisured class," made redundant by the Information Revolution. In the past, home-based workers have typically set up their offices in bedrooms left empty by their grown children. But today, nearly two-thirds of college students return home to live after graduation—the so-called "baby boomerang"—in order to keep their expenses down while they pay off their tuition loans.

Not only are US families housing 50% of their young adult off-spring, but 20% of US workers report that they are caring for one or more of their older relatives. The baby boomers are becoming the "sandwich generation." At the same time, boomer couples—over half of whom both work full time—will be experiencing the transformational turbulence of downsizing, outsourcing, and off-shoring. It is entirely reasonable to assume that one or more members of a sandwich generation household will find themselves unexpectedly thrust into America's rapidly growing, part-time, home-based, self-employed contingent workforce. Purpose-built working space will be an increasingly essential feature of the American home for the foreseeable future.

By 2030, America will have added nearly 60 million more people—25 million households. Will we have discovered an acceptable alternative to urban sprawl by then, or will we still be carpet-tiling the countryside with subdivisions? Will 100 million of us still haul a ton of steel, glass, and rubber to and from work each day? Will we have developed a means of mass-producing attractive, affordable living spaces by 2030, or will the developers and politicians keep us imprisoned in the stick-built 20th century housing paradigm? Will we still be warehousing growing numbers of our dependent elderly in institutional settings, or will we have begun to integrate our older relatives into our new extendable households? Could family-based infilling reduce the pressure for urban sprawl and diminish the inter-generational competition for resources in an aging America?

The recent recession and its jobless recovery may have temporarily left many architects with empty order books, but the spreading application of our rapidly maturing information technology is already leading us to reinvent our principal institutions. The great challenge facing US architects today is not to design a fitting memorial for the victims of 9/11 or an optimal replacement for the World Trade Center. It is to design basic components of the built environment that will accommodate the changing realities of daily life and work in the 21st century, including the addition of an entire second America.

EDUCATIONAL FUTURES

HOW TO TRANSFORM AN ENTIRE SCHOOL SYSTEM: THE FUTURE IN THE PRESENT TENSE

by

Francis M. Duffy, John F. Horne III, and G. Thomas Houlihan

THE PRESENT TENSE: WHY SCHOOL DISTRICTS NEED TO TRANSFORM

Political Pressure to Change

It's a fact of life for school districts: Standards, assessments, and accountability are the triple engines driving school improvement into the 21st century (Duffy, 2002). This is not necessarily a bad thing. Consider what Vicki Phillips (in Duffy and Dale, 2001), the highly regarded former superintendent of schools in Lancaster, Pennsylvania, and now Pennsylvania's State Superintendent of Schools, says about the role of standards in this triad:

> ...I also know from firsthand experience that clear, high, measurable standards can provide a framework for teaching and learning that is richer, deeper, more rigorous, and more accessible to all students than ever before. Our children would be better served if we worked together to ensure that the promise of standards bears fruit, and not our fears. The answer is not to throw out the best tool that is at hand, but rather to help states, districts, and schools use that tool wisely and well (p. 107).

The pressure for setting standards, conducting student assessments, and holding educators accountable comes primarily from state and federal governments. Some observers characterize this pressure as "legislated learning" (Wise, 1979, 1988). Legislated learning provides for uniform and tight alignment between student-performance outcomes and the curriculum, between the curriculum and teaching, and between teaching and testing (Sergiovanni, Burlingame, Coombs, and Thurston, 1999).

Given the political pressure to change, the ideal improvement strategy should be periodic whole-district transformation followed by periods of continuous improvement (Duffy, 2004). In the absence of educators leading change in their districts, the predictable dynamic will see federal and state governments ordering school systems to

Francis M. Duffy *is an author and a professor of Change-Leadership in Education in the Department of Administration and Supervision at Gallaudet University in Washington, D.C. He may be contacted at francis.duffy@gallaudet.edu.* **John F. Horne III** *is a practicing organizational consultant and president of ChannelMarker Consulting in Tempe, Arizona. He may be contacted at chanelmark@aol.com.* **G. Thomas Houlihan** *is the executive director of the Council of Chief State School Officers (CCSSO). He may be contacted at tomh@ccsso.org.*

to change. The pressure for change and the need for districts to become more proactive in changing what they do will increase as emerging societal and economic trends reach their tipping points and spread rapidly.

Emerging Trends Portending Great Change

The trends featured here focus primarily on those affecting the United States. As with any forecasting, the arrival of unexpected "wild cards" could alter the direction on one or more of the identified trends. However, the long-term trends projected to have the most significant impact on the shape of school systems seem to have a high probability of becoming reality and will, therefore, have a significant influence on school systems throughout the United States.

Social trends. During the period 1965-1975, school-aged children in the United States represented a substantial proportion of the population, and two-parent families were in the majority in approximately 85% of family households, according to United States Bureau of Census records. In the year 2000, census records indicated less than 25% of all households in the United States were two-parent families with children. The number of single-parent households in the United States increased by 25% during the period 1990-2000.

Overall, projections to the year 2010 indicate a further drop of five percentage points in the percentage of households with children under age 18 years. Marx (2002) in an article on future trends in education reports that by 2020 persons aged 55 an older (30%) will outnumber persons aged 18 and younger (25%) as a percentage of the total population (p. 32). The financial impact of this ratio will also be significant. In 1940, there were 42 workers for every retiree. Currently, this ratio is 3.2 workers to one retiree. By 2030, it is projected to be 2.2 workers to each retiree. The costs of retirement and medical care will be supported by a smaller and smaller worker-retiree ratio in the coming decades.

Finally, in the United States, an increasing proportion of children in schools will be immigrants. The US Census Bureau estimates that immigrant children will comprise 22% of the school-age population by 2010. In addition, it projects that the majority of school-age children will be members of a racial/ethnic minority by 2030.

Implications of social trends. In 1995, the "US federal budget dispensed nearly ten times as much in benefits to each senior citizen as it did to each child" (p. 110), reported Peter G. Peterson, former US Secretary of Commerce. As the baby boomer wave moves inexorably toward mass retirement, it is highly likely that the focus of the United States will significantly shift to issues associated with aging. The child population "bulge" that moved through the population during the 1960-1980 era stamped its own priorities on the country's policies that culminated with the creation of the US Department of Education (1979-1981). Ironically, this same cohort priority on funding K-12 education in the years ahead than their own parents did during their era.

Increasing concerns around health care and income security are likely to take precedence over education in the allocation of public resources. Nevertheless, the school-age population will continue to grow in terms of raw numbers and result in demands for new or renovated school facilities. To exacerbate the situation further, older homeowners concerned about income security may be resistant to increases in property, sales, or other forms of taxation to fund education in their communities. This, in turn, will compel school systems to develop alternate funding formulae to meet the needs of school-aged children.

Increasing child poverty levels, shifts in ethnic demographics, expanding levels of single-parent households, and surging levels of learning disabilities among students will likely pressure school systems to provide additional services such as health care, after-school care, and specialized learning methodologies without substantive increases in funding levels. As a result, "free" public education may turn to an income-based sliding fee scale for non-core academic services.

Economic trends. The Bureau of Labor Statistics (BLS) projects that total job potential in the United States will rise from 146.6 million in 2000 to 167.8 million in 2010. However, the US workforce is estimated to grow from 140.9 million in 2000 to 157.7 million in 2010. This means that by 2010 there will be a 10 million worker shortfall for all available positions, including in the field of education.

Further, the BLS estimates that employment needs in education will rise 19% during this period while demand from other employment sectors will have an average increase of 25%. This means that the education sector may need to hire 20% of all the 16.8 million new workforce members during the next 10 years to meet replacement and growth projections. This hiring goal represents an almost insurmountable challenge to the field of education given the competition in the general marketplace for talented young men and women.

BLS data suggest that the educational services industry was the second largest industry in the economy in 2002. Employees in this industry are older than average, with 47% over the age of 45 years compared with 38% of employees in all industries combined. By 2008, approximately 23% of elementary school teachers, 31% of secondary school teachers, and 40% of education administrators will enter the 54-64 year old age range, of which 85% will choose retirement. The American Association of Colleges of Teacher Education (Kantrowitz and Wingert, 2000) expects the supply of teachers to expand a modest 3.6% between 1998 and 2004 and only at a 1.2% rate for the years 2005-2010. US census data show that the student population will continue to rise at a significant rate until 2005, when it is projected to level off.

Finally, during 2002 it was reported that approximately 15 states in the US had reduced educational spending to cope with shortfalls in other parts of their state budgets. This reduction in educational spending contrasts with the fact that school districts will face sharply escalating costs for employee health benefits and retirement payouts during the remainder of the decade.

Implications of economic trends. School systems have historically lagged 10-15 years behind commercial organizations in making structural changes to their systems. It is expected that school systems will emulate the merger model of other organizations in the 1980s as a means of coping with increasing operational costs. In the near term, this is likely to result in a wave of schools and school district consolidations to create "mega-school" complexes. These merged operations are likely to reduce costs but ultimately result in lower student achievement and an increase in parental dissatisfaction. In turn, middle- to upper-income parents are likely to defect to alternate school options such as charter schools, homeschooling, and private schools, thus creating "poverty pockets" in a number of school districts. Ultimately, a "weighted-voucher" system will be developed to encourage a more even distribution of student types across the entire school system in a community. These vouchers will give schools within school districts increased funds for taking students with characteristics such as poverty, learning disabilities, and residential disadvantages.

Flat or low-increase funding for school districts, increasing student enrollment, and teacher and administrator shortages will force a transformation of the traditional design and functioning of school districts. New organizational structures within school districts will likely incorporate experienced building-level master teachers supervising a team of teachers who design and monitor classroom activities and para-teachers preparing standardized lesson plans, content testing and grading, and homework correction. K-12 schools will utilize a CEO model in place of the present school principal arrangement. This building-level administrator will focus on budget development, appropriating money, marketing, recruitment, and planning while leaving curriculum development matters to master teachers within their respective schools. As schools within districts take on more autonomy, local school boards will diminish in authority and ultimately transform into Community Relations Boards responsible for building support within the community and eliciting corporate or private funding to enhance services within schools.

Information economy demands. In 1991, the US Department of Labor published a report titled "What Work Requires of Schools." In this report, basic "information economy" skills were identified as lifelong learning, communication, creative adaptive thinking, personal management, and group participation effectiveness and leadership. Over the past 10 years, numerous reports from a variety of global sources have consistently reiterated the need for a shift in focus to these skills consistently.

Information technology innovations up to this year (2004) have yet to be integrated fully and broadly in school systems to expand teacher productivity, individualize instruction, or to create networks with resources outside a school system's boundaries. This lack of integration is supported in a 1999 report by the Education Commission of the States, which noted that "computing devices are becoming smaller, cheaper, more powerful and—perhaps most important—more connected with one another. So far, the impact of digital technology on K-12 education has been relatively minor..." (p. 12). Further, teacher surveys routinely report that teachers feel their training and proficiency in information technology is inadequate.

The challenge of keeping pace with rapid technological innovation and "churn" in the global marketplace has pressured employers to seek employees with strong learning capabilities and flexible skills. This need for more knowledgeable and skilled employees has motivated many business groups to shift from supplemental financial support for schools to a more direct involvement with schools within districts. Irving Buchen (2003) notes this trend in an article on future trends in education when he said, "Driven by a desire for a well-trained and motivated workforce as well as a sense of social responsibility, many CEOs have forged partnerships with schools" (p. 48).

The concepts of accountability and return-on-investment have appeared in education in part as a response to mismatches between school curriculum, school district needs, and rapidly tightening budget constraints. Yet, the demand for accountability is increasing (as noted earlier in this article). Even business stalwarts such as Peter Drucker have called for more accountable schools; Drucker notes "education has become much too expensive not to be accountable.... (Expenditures) have skyrocketed from 2% of GNP around 1913 to 10% eighty years later" (Drucker, 1993).

Implication of information-economy demands. New school models will proliferate as a response to both the call for more emphasis on information-economy skills and increasing pressure for more individualized instruction. The early signs of this shift to more diverse instructional models can be seen in the emergence of cyber/home schooling, charter schools, and industry-specific schools. Accountability will continue to be a driving theme for a number of education stakeholders. The current turmoil surrounding "high-stakes testing" will ultimately calm and result in a single national "basics examination" modulated by a variety of other assessment tools designed to reflect individual student strengths. This trend is already seen in college entrance processes and employment hiring practices.

Final thoughts about emerging trends. Senge, Cambron McCabe, Lucas, Kleiner, Dutton, and Smith (2000) say "schools are not 'broken' and in need of fixing. They are a social institution under stress that needs to evolve" (p. 52). In the United States and much of the Western world the basic model for schooling has remained unchanged for over a century. It is, by and large, a labor-intensive bureaucratic institution funded by public resources but with little accountability for student outcomes. This original design was a good match with a work world with fixed-skill needs, a large labor pool, and a public unquestioning about the expenditure rate. Virtually all these factors have changed or are in the process of changing. Yet, school systems by their very nature are conservative and slow to embrace these changes.

Ideally, whole school systems would collectively engage in transformational change. However, this has rarely been the case to date. Hope glimmers with those maverick or breakaway schools that are able to envision a desirable future and have the fortitude to resist the pressure to stay unchanged. These early models of how to transform can ultimately become role models for other school systems that desire to transform.

One role model school is Rover Elementary School, a public institution in Tempe, Arizona, that embraced the concepts presented in the 1991 report *What Work Requires of Schools* (cited earlier). Educators in that school engaged in whole-school transformation to meet the future needs cited in that report by integrating development of student leadership opportunities, teamwork, and adaptive thinking skills into its core curriculum. Buchen (2003) in an article in *The Futurist* magazine called Rover School a "futures lab." Through persistent success and dogged determination, this school's model eventually influenced the district system to make changes (Horne and McClelland, 2001).

Another school that can serve as a transformation role model is the Horizon Community Learning Center, a K-12 charter school in Phoenix, Arizona. This school is a role model for other schools because of the way it stimulated the desire for change among parents in its community by integrating with its traditional academic curriculum future-oriented skills for students such as daily involvement with project management and teamwork.

Whether significant change comes to school systems in the United States is not in question. The relevant question is whether change will come in the form of a national commitment like the nation of Singapore or in a more haphazard fashion as has historically been the case in the United States. Regardless of the process for change, schools like Rover Elementary School and the Horizon Community Learning Center will become important role models for other school districts that want to engage in transformational change.

REAL WORLD EXAMPLES OF WHOLE-DISTRICT CHANGE

It is a fact that political pressure on school systems to improve is significant. It is a fact that there are important social, economic, and technological trends that will have varying levels of impact on school systems. So how can educators transform entire school systems to anticipate and respond quickly to these pressures and trends?

Answers to the above question are found in both practice and the literature. In practice, state departments of education in some states are working with local school systems to help them create and sustain systemic (i.e., whole-district) change. These examples serve as powerful role models for other states not yet involved with whole-district change. In the literature, state-of-the-art principles are emerging to guide the development of methodologies to transform entire school systems (Duffy, 2004). Highlights from the field and a summary of these innovative principles are found below.

Examples of Whole-District Change

There is a growing number of real-world examples of whole-district change, such as the Chugach School District in Anchorage, Alaska, and Pearl River School District in Pearl River, New York, the first two Baldrige Quality Award winners in education. Another school district that is engaging in whole-system change is the Metropolitan School District of Decatur Township in Indianapolis, Indiana (visit the Web site for this project at www.indiana.edu/~sys chang/decatur/bios/biographies.html). School districts that participated in a study by the Learning First Alliance titled "Beyond Islands of Excellence: What Districts Can Do to Improve Instruction and Achievement in All Schools" (Togneri and Anderson, 2003) were:

- Aldine Independent School District, Texas
- Chula Vista Elementary School District, California
- Kent County Public Schools, Maryland
- Minneapolis Public Schools, Minnesota
- Providence Public Schools, Rhode Island.

Other significant whole-district improvement efforts are being initiated by state departments of education. The guiding principle behind many of these state-level initiatives is the notion of creating and sustaining strategic alignment among all parts of the education system (Duffy, 2004).

Creating alignment is perhaps the most significant and critical decision to be made in a system of education if it wants to move toward higher levels of performance. One alignment model used by the North Carolina State Department of Education is shown in Figure 1. This model suggests that alignment begins by setting state standards for education and then working to make sure that every level of the education system, right down to the individual learner, is in alignment with those standards.

Strategic alignment is in consonance with principles of systems thinking and systems improvement. With systems thinking, the old notion that individual schools within school districts could "just do their own thing" is replaced by a focused consensus on what represents important results within the education system, and in most cases this focus is on student and employee performance.

FIGURE 1 - STRATEGIC ALIGNMENT OF THE EDUCATION SYSTEM

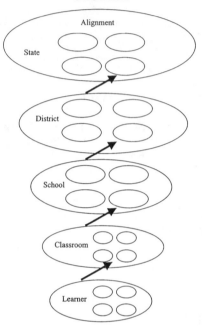

Source: North Carolina Partnership for Excellence

There is ample evidence to lend credence to this focus on alignment and systems. The state of North Carolina immediately comes to mind (for a detailed analysis of student achievement results in North Carolina, please visit www.ncpe-online.org). Led by the business community within the state, a concerted effort began in the mid-1990s to tie higher education performance to the fundamental principles of quality management (Deming, 1986) and the Baldrige Quality Framework (2003).

In applying the principles of quality management in conjunction with the notion of creating strategic alignment, professional development for educators was held simultaneously for both schools and school system personnel and every employee of the State Department of Public Instruction. As a result of this concerted effort to create and sustain systemic change, North Carolina's student achievement gains have led the nation in every category available over the past six to eight years, and many in North Carolina attribute this significant increase to the focus on systems thinking and the professional development that accompanied the Excellent Schools Act of 1996-1997.

North Carolina is not the only state that has data to support this approach. Indiana's General Assembly passed legislation in the late 1990s providing funds to train every employee in the Department of Education in the same principles used in North Carolina. Local school systems were even allowed to use the Baldrige Quality Framework in lieu of traditional accreditation processes. And the results from Indiana mirror that of North Carolina—NAEP scores have increased, SAT scores have improved, and dropout rates have decreased.

Other states that have joined in this focus on systems thinking include South Carolina, Maryland, New Mexico, Ohio, Texas, and Illinois. In all of these states, student performance has increased continuously over time.

State departments of education and local school systems that wish to engage in transformational change, especially in response to political pressure to change and emerging societal trends identified earlier, need to learn how to engage school systems in transformational change. This learning must include information about system redesign methodologies specially designed to create and sustain systemic change and strategic alignment. There are methodologies emerging that are designed for this purpose (e.g., Reigeluth and Garfinkle, 1994; Duffy, 2002, 2003). Whatever methodology is selected or designed, we believe that it must be based on contemporary principles for navigating large-scale change (Duffy, 2004). These principles are described next.

THE FUTURE: HOW TO TRANSFORM AN ENTIRE SCHOOL SYSTEM

It is clear that transforming a whole system requires three sets of simultaneous changes. These sets are characterized as three paths. Moving a school system along these three paths simultaneously will require applying eight key principles for navigating whole-district change. The three paths and the eight principles are described next.

Three Paths Toward High Performance

Path 1: Improve a district's core and supporting work processes. A school district's work process is a sequenced instructional program (e.g., a K-12 instructional program) conjoined with classroom teaching and learning (Duffy, 2002; Duffy, 2003). In the lexicon of systems improvement, the term for this work process is "core work."

Core work is maintained and enriched by supporting work. In school districts, supporting work roles include administrators, supervisors, education specialists, librarians, cafeteria workers, janitors, bus drivers, and others. Supporting work is important to the success of a school district, but it is not the most important work. Classroom teaching and learning is the most important work.

When trying to improve a school system, the core and supporting work processes must be improved. Further, the entire work process (e.g., preK-12th grade) must be examined and improved, not just parts of it (e.g., not just the middle-school program or not just the reading program). One of the reasons the entire work process must be improved is because of a systems improvement principle expressed as "upstream errors flow downstream." This principle reflects the fact that mistakes made early in a work process flow downstream, are compounded, and create more problems later on in the process; for example, think about what happens to youngsters in high school when there are early errors in their elementary math and reading programs that prevent them from gaining mastery of those subjects.

Path 2: Improve a district's internal "social architecture." Improving work processes to improve learning for students, teachers and staff, and the whole school system is an important goal, but it is still a piecemeal approach to change. It is possible for a school district to have a fabulous curriculum with extraordinarily effective instructional methods but still have an internal social "architecture" (which includes organization culture, organization design, communication patterns, reward systems, and so on) that is de-motivating, dissatisfying, and demoralizing for teachers and staff. De-motivated, dissatisfied, and demoralized teachers and staff cannot and will not use a fabulous curriculum in remarkable ways. So, in addition to improving how the work of a district is done, improvement efforts must also focus on simultaneously improving a district's internal social "architecture."

Path 3: Improve a district's relationships with its external environment. Improving a school district's work processes and internal social "architecture" is important, but it is still a fragmented approach to district-wide improvement. A district can have a fabulous curriculum and highly motivated teachers, but lack the support of its community. A district lacking community support is not an effective district. So a systemic approach to improving a school district must also simultaneously improve a district's relationships with its external environment.

A school district is an open system. An open system is one that interacts with its environment by exchanging a valued product or service in return for needed resources. If educators want their districts to become high-performing school systems, they need to have a positive and supporting relationship with stakeholders in their districts' external environments. But they can't wait until they improve their work processes and social architecture to start working on these relationships. They need positive and supporting relationships to make the important changes they desire. So they also have to improve their districts' environmental relationships at the same time they start improving their work processes and social architecture.

It is our hope that all this is making sense because the principle of simultaneous improvement is absolutely essential for effective organization improvement (e.g., see Pasmore, 1988; Emery, 1977; Trist, Higgin, Murray, and Pollack, 1963). In the literature on systems improvement this principle is called joint optimization (Cummings and Worley, 2001).

Eight Principles for Navigating Whole-District Change

There are eight principles that we think should be used to create a framework for any methodology to transform entire school systems (Duffy, 2004). These principles are summarized below.

Principle #1: A school district's external environment is complex and unstable. The environments within which school districts find themselves are increasingly complex and unstable. This complexity and instability is being driven by the triple engines of standards, assessments, and accountability (Duffy, 2002). In complex and unstable environments, school districts need to be able to plan for the future while also being able to respond quickly to unanticipated events.

Principle # 2: The capacity to anticipate the future and respond quickly to unanticipated events is partially a function of an organization's internal social "architecture." A school district's social architecture includes its culture, communication patterns, power and political dynamics, the reward system, policies and procedures, and organization design. Social architecture has a significant influence on educator's capacity and willingness to plan for the future and to respond to unexpected events. A new social architecture for school systems that would increase capacity and willingness would have the following distinguishing characteristics. It would:

- Favor skill-based work, professional knowledge, and networked relationships.

- Be anchored to a network of teams with their collective knowledge, talent, and resources.

- Create broad and easy opportunities for participation and communication.

- Connect people to each other and to resources in ways that help the school district as much as possible to take charge of its own destiny (as opposed to being externally regulated and externally forced to improve).

Principle #3: Biological metaphors most accurately describe how social networks function. The biological metaphor that seems to work best for organizations with a networked internal social architecture is "ecosystem." In nature, some ecosystems offer scarce opportunities for life (polar ice caps), while others offer overflowing opportunities (equatorial jungles). If a school system is thought of as an ecosystem, it too can offer scarce or abundant opportunities for success. Scarcity or abundance of opportunities in school districts depends on that district's organizational mental model that guides people's thoughts, feelings, and actions. If most people in a district choose to think, feel, and act like their district can never improve, it will not. If most people in a district choose to think, feel, and act that their district does have the creative potential to move the district toward breath-takingly higher levels of performance, they can and will make that journey. The power of choice, either individually or collectively, has been repeatedly proven to have an extraordinary effect on human performance. Or, as Jean Paul Sartre once said, "We are our choices."

Principle #4: Creating a web of accountabilities using networked teams doesn't mean that authority and control are surrendered to the networked "mob." In all school districts, the voice of leadership must still be present and heard even though significant steps are taken to redesign leadership positions so incumbents can practice effective transfor-mational leadership instead of being caretakers of the status quo. Without the voice of leadership from the top of a school district, people freeze in place when there are too many change options to be considered. Without some element of leadership at the top, the many at the bottom are often paralyzed by an overabundance of choices. The creation of a social architecture that honors and uses formal leadership roles while simultaneously creating and sustaining networked teams will provide powerful moments for creating innovative ideas to improve student, faculty and staff, and system learning.

Principle #5: A networked social architecture stimulates creativity and innovation. Creativity and innovation present breathtaking oppor-tunities for improvement. As opportunities for improving schooling emerge and are taken, still newer opportunities will begin to emerge at a faster rate. This is somewhat like the financial principle of compound interest. Therefore, change leaders need to find ways to help educators seize opportunities, succeed at using them, and then help others build their success on earlier successes. This creates compound organizational learning.

Principle #6: Peak performance is an illusion. In the 21st century environment for a school district there are multiple performance peaks that evoke images of the Rocky Mountains where some peaks are lower than others. What if the peak a district sits atop is low compared to others, but folks inside the district don't realize it? Wouldn't the perception of being at peak performance be an illusion?

All school districts sit atop a performance peak, no matter what that level of performance might be. The path to the next higher performance peak is not a straight "as the crow flies" line. A clear view of the next higher level of performance is not a straight shot forward and upward. There is only one way to get to the next higher peak—a district has to go downhill before it can go back up. It has to become temporarily less effective, less skilled, and less successful.

The "first down, then up" principle applies to organizational performance, too, especially as informed by Seyle's (1956) General Adaptation Syndrome theory. This theory suggests that when an organization is stressed (e.g., by the requirements of change) that system's performance will first go downhill before it climbs back up to a new level of performance. The problem for school districts is, however, that the more successful a school district is the less inclined it is to let go of what it does and move down the performance curve toward the edge of chaos (a phrase coined by Roger Lewin, 1992). This capacity to let go has to be built into a school system.

The "first down, then up" journey happens when educators start questioning their success. Not everything they do has to be abandoned completely, but everything they do needs to be questioned completely. During this questioning, they must be open to stunning opportunities for innovative ideas to improve student, teacher, and system learning.

Principle # 7: School district improvement models must move from the concept of change to concept of flux. The field of organization improvement is moving away from the concept of change to the concept of flux (Kelly, 1998). While change focuses on creating new programs, ideas, and so on, flux is about managing creative destruction followed by rebirth. Flux breaks down the status quo while creating a temporary foundation for innovative puzzle solving and a rebirth of an organization. Innovation destroys the status quo by introducing breakthrough innovations to a system. The quest for innovation in a school district must be unending, and robust innovation is only sustained by a school district hovering at the edge of chaos but never falling over the edge.

Principle # 8: Don't solve problems, seek opportunities. Focusing on seeking opportunities instead of problem solving builds and sustains creative and emotional energy for organization renewal and implies a positive approach to innovation. Lippit (1980) confirmed that people tend to perform more productively and develop better long-term plans when working on positive goals and visions rather than focusing on solving problems. Focusing on exciting opportunities releases creative energy and keeps people engaged over a longer period of time. Thus, instead of asking "What's wrong?" educators seeking opportunities to improve their school systems can ask these questions: (1) "What future do we want for our system?" (2) "Where are we now?" and (3) "What do we need to do in order to create a desirable future?"

CONCLUSION

This article is based on the premise that a school system's journey to the future can only begin in the present. The "present" for school systems is colored by significant political pressure for requiring school systems to comply with standards and assess student achievement frequently, and then to hold districts accountable for results. The present is also being defined by near-term and long-term social, economic, and technological trends. This present state of affairs for school systems has created significant challenges for educators and policy makers who wish to transform entire school systems.

Despite the challenges, there are contemporary examples of school systems engaged in transformational change. Several of these were highlighted in this article. These real-world examples included local school districts, as well as state departments of education. One state department of education in particular was showcased; that is, the North Carolina Department of Education's effort to improve schooling in their state.

The real-world examples of whole-system change were followed by a presentation of a three-path strategy to transform school systems. We also stated our belief that movement along these paths must be guided by a set of eight principles that define contemporary approaches to navigating complex, rapid, and systemic change. These principles were also described.

REFERENCES

Baldrige National Quality Program (2003). Education criteria for performance excellence. Accessed on February 15, 2004, at www.quality.nist.gov/PDF_files/2003_Education_ Criteria.pdf.

Buchen, I. "Education in America: The Next 25 Years," *The Futurist*, Vol. 37, No. 1 (January-February 2003), 44-50.

Cummings, T.G., and C. Worley. *Organization Development & Change* (7th Edition) (Cincinnati: South-Western College Publishing, 2001).

Deming, W.E. *Out of the Crisis* (Cambridge, MA: MIT Center for Advanced Educational Services, 1986).

Drucker, P.F. *Post-Capitalist Society* (New York: HarperBusiness, 1993).

Duffy, F.M. *Step-Up-To-Excellence: An Innovative Approach to Managing and Rewarding Performance in School Systems* (Lanham, MD: Scarecrow Education, 2002).

Duffy, F.M. *Courage, Passion and Vision: A Guide to Leading Systemic School Improvement* (Lanham, MD: Scarecrow Education and the American Association of School Administrators, 2003).

Duffy, F.M. "Navigating Whole-District Change: Eight Principles for Moving an Organization Upward in Times of Unpredictability,"

The School Administrator, 61 (1) (January 2004), 22-25.

Duffy, F.M. *Moving Upward Together: Creating Strategic Alignment to Sustain Systemic School Improvement,* No. 1, Leading Systemic School Improvement Series (Lanham, MD: Scarecrow Education, 2004 in press).

Education Commission of the States (January 1999). *Future Trends Affecting Education* (Denver, CO: Author).

Emery, F.E. *Two Basic Organization Designs in Futures We Are In* (Leiden: Martinus Nijhoff, 1977).

Horne, J.F., and S. McClelland. "Leveraging Change Within A School District," F.M. Duffy and J.D. Dale eds., *Creating Successful School Districts* (Norwood, MA: Christopher-Gordon, 2001), 237-254.

Kantrowitz, B., and P. Wingert. "Teachers Wanted," *Newsweek,* October 2, 2000, 37-39.

Kelly, K. *New Rules for the New Economy: 10 Radical Strategies for a Connected World* (New York: Penguin Books, 1998).

Lewin, R. *Complexity, Life on the Edge of Chaos* (New York: Macmillan Publishing Co., 1992).

Lippitt, R. *Choosing the Future You Prefer* (Washington, DC: Development Publishers, 1980).

Marx, G. "Ten Trends: Shaping a Future for Students and Schools," *Arizona School Boards Association (ASBA) Journal,* Spring 2002, 32-35.

Pasmore, W.A. *Designing Effective Organizations: The Sociotechnical Systems Perspective* (New York: Wiley & Sons, 1988).

Peterson, P.G. *Gray Dawn: How the Coming Age Wave Will Transform America and the World* (New York: Times Books, 1999).

Phillips, V. "Finishing the Race: A District Perspective of Standards-Based Reform," F.M. Duffy and J.D. Dale eds., *Creating Successful School Systems: Voices from the University, the Field, and the Community* (Norwood, MA: Christopher-Gordon Publishers, 2001).

Reigeluth, C.M., and R.J. Garfinkle. *Systemic Change in Education* (Englewood Cliffs, NJ: Educational Technology Publications, 1994).

Senge, P., N.H. Cambron McCabe, T. Lucas, A. Kleiner, J. Dutton, and B. Smith. *Schools That Learn: A Fifth Discipline Fieldbook for Educators, Parents and Everyone Who Cares About Education* (New York: Doubleday Books, 2000).

Sergiovanni, T.J., M. Burlingame, F.S. Coombs, and P.W. Thurston. *Educational Governance and Administration* (4th Edition) (Boston: Allyn & Bacon, 1999).

Seyle, H. *The Stress of Life* (New York: McGraw-Hill, 1956).

Snyder, D.P., G. Edwards, and C. Folsom. "The Strategic Context for Education in America: 2000 to 2020," H.F. Didsbury Jr. ed., *21st Century Opportunities and Challenges: An Age of Destruction or An Age of Transformation* (Bethesda, MD: World Future Society, 2003), 155-177.

Togneri, W., and S.E. Anderson. "Beyond Islands of Excellence: What Districts Can Do to Improve Instruction and Achievement in

All Schools—A Leadership Brief," (Washington, DC: Learning First Alliance, 2003).

Trist, E.L., G.W. Higgin, H. Murray, and A.B. Pollack. *Organizational Choice* (London: Tavistock, 1963).

US Department of Labor, Bureau of Labor Statistics. Accessed on March 12, 2004, at www.bls.gov/home/htm.

US Department of Labor, Employment and Training Administration. *What Work Requires of Schools* (Washington, DC: Author, 1991).

Wise, A.E. *Legislated Learning: The Bureaucratization of the American Classroom* (Berkeley, CA: University of California Press, 1979).

Wise, A.E. "Legislated Learning Revisited," *Phi Delta Kappan*, 69 (5) (1988), 329-332.

THE PENSION CRISIS

THE OPPORTUNITY OF A LIFETIME: RESHAPING RETIREMENT

by

Michael Moynagh and Richard Worsley

BACKGROUND

The "pensions crisis" and longer life expectancy are forcing policy makers and employers throughout the world to think again about retirement. This report looks at the future of retirement policy in Britain over the next 20 years. It takes for granted that people will need to work till they are older and asks: What will be the implications for retirement and old age? Will retirement as we know it be postponed for a few years? Or will retirement be reshaped, to become less age-related and more fulfilling?

The report is part of the work of the Tomorrow Project, launched in 1996 to support individuals and organizations in thinking and gaining new insights about the future. The Project addresses a wide range of topics about the future of people's lives in Britain over the next two decades. As part of this work, we have undertaken a two-year research project on the future of retirement, with support from six organizations.

Reshaping Retirement is a study of the future rather than a conventional research report. It draws on various types of research material, including research literature, a series of consultations, and a program of focus groups.

The report is structured not around particular drivers of change, such as demographic, economic, and social developments, but around issues that will have a decisive impact on retirement in the next two decades—what will happen to the labor market for older people, to state pensions, and to lifetime savings for retirement?

The key issue for retirement is how to square the triangle of longer life expectancy, adequate retirement incomes, and younger workers' desire to increase their current living standards. Our starting point is that people will resolve this conundrum by working till they are older. The recent reversal of the trend to early retirement will continue, and growing numbers will work beyond the state pension age.

As this happens, three questions will have to be tackled. How will the transition out of employment be managed? Given that Britain's labor market is likely to remain highly polarized, will the state pension system prevent those at the bottom of the earnings league slipping into old-age poverty? What will be done to encourage people to increase their long-term savings?

Michael Moynagh and Richard Worsley are co-directors of the Tomorrow Project (a UK charity researching the future of people's lives, www.tomorrowproject. net). Copies of the full report, of which this paper is a summary, may be ordered from r.worsley@virgin.net, and the Project may be contacted at the same address.

Linking these issues is an overarching theme: How will old age be experienced in the future? Will it be more of the same, but just starting at an older age? Or will retirement be reshaped so that many more older people mix part-time work with extended leisure and have higher incomes with which to enjoy their old age, bringing about a much more positive view in society of the aging process?

To develop this theme, our report is structured as follows:

• Chapter 2 asks why the future of retirement is on the agenda now.

• Chapter 3 looks at factors that will shape the labor market for older people and offers two scenarios.

• Chapter 4 discusses the future of state pension arrangements and, again, offers two scenarios.

• Chapter 5 considers the future of lifetime savings and offers two further scenarios.

• Chapter 6 draws together the scenarios in chapters 3-5 and presents two final, generic scenarios. It suggests how we can create the best possible future.

UP FOR GRABS: RETIREMENT ON THE AGENDA

Retirement is a relatively modern concept. Until recently there has been a trend to longer retirement, which is now being questioned. Lower fertility rates will reduce the size of the working population, making it harder to fund state pensions and other benefits for older people; later retirement is an obvious part of the solution. People are working for fewer years but retiring for longer, which is financially untenable; again, later retirement is an obvious answer.

Tackling poverty among older people has become a political priority and will remain so because of Britain's polarized labor market, but the current solution—means testing—is unpopular; later retirement in return for a higher state pension for all is the most realistic alternative. Many people will not have saved enough for their retirement if it lasts for as long as it does now; they may have to postpone retirement instead. The government is starting to make it easier for people to stay on at work.

Finally, retirement is on the agenda because over the next 20 years we have an opportunity to transform how we think about it and to improve the quality of life for older people. Instead of our lives being divided "horizontally" on the basis of age, for many people they are becoming more "vertically" sliced, with transitions—between work and learning, for example—at many different ages.

A key difference is that individuals have greater choice over these transitions. Although choice is severely constrained for people on lower incomes, living standards are likely to continue to rise, which will expand choice, to an extent, even for them.

"Liquid lives" could make imposed retirement at a certain age a thing of the past. Might traditional retirement be replaced by greatly expanded choice and by a dramatic shift in how old age is viewed— as a period of human flourishing before a final stage of dependency?

FETTERED OR FREED? WORK IN LATER LIFE

The pressure on workers to retire later will mount, but how will employers respond? Will they simply postpone retirement, forcing older people to work till they drop? Or will they introduce more flexible forms of employment, tailor-made to the needs of older workers?

Change will not be easy. Today's concept of retirement is deeply entrenched and will not transform overnight. Many people still see retirement as both a reward for hard work and a right to an extended period of leisure. This view is reinforced by the experience of many older workers, who often find jobs stressful and exhausting—an experience that is likely to persist.

Encouraging more-flexible employment, with work lasting till later in life, may be seen as chipping away the right to retirement and damaging to older people's health, and be strongly resisted. At the same time, age discrimination by employers could further entrench current patterns of employment by older workers.

However, employers will also have to respond to four pressures in the labor market.

Drivers of Change

Legislation is due in the United Kingdom by 2006 for equal treatment in employment on grounds of age, including the likelihood that compulsory retirement ages (at least up to 70) will be outlawed. The form of the legislation and the manner of its implementation will help to determine whether retirement will be postponed or reshaped. Pressure may build within the European Union for further legislation to encourage employment by older workers.

Skill shortages, which loom in many UK sectors, may be a second spur to a different view of retirement, as parts of the economy become more labor intensive than less, technology slices away fewer jobs than expected, the demand for skills rises, the supply of young people entering the workforce begins to tail off, and skill mismatches persist. Employers may respond by investing in labor-saving equipment or by recruiting more immigrant workers, but the recruitment of older workers will be their main strategy. How well will employers respond to older workers' needs?

The aspirations of older workers will be important. They will be influenced by the continued expansion of choice (not only for the better off, but for those on lower incomes as living standards rise), by caring commitments to relatives, and by the likelihood that older workers will want employment that is less demanding but still worthwhile.

Commercial constraints may make it difficult to create high-quality flexible employment. These will include the size and location of the business, increasing consumer demands, and heavy competitive pressures on costs. Will attracting older workers be seen as costly and difficult, or as vital for competing in tighter labor markets?

Two Scenarios

Retirement postponed. In this scenario, employers respond with "more of the same" over the next 20 years. They meet the growing economic need for people to work into their late 60s by effectively postponing retirement rather than reshaping it. Older workers acquiesce, despite their health concerns, because they need the money.

The public retains its deep-seated attachment to retirement as a right. Age discrimination at work remains deeply entrenched. Most employers remain cautious and unimaginative. Older workers end up remaining full time in good quality jobs, if they have them, or trading down to part-time, more marginal employment, which narrows the opportunities for lower-paid workers. Retirement is still broadly age-related, though at a later age, and the routes into it remain inflexible.

Retirement reshaped. In this scenario, retirement is not postponed but reshaped, so that it is far less age-related. Routes out of work are more flexible—driven by a generation of older workers who have lived fluid lives, value choice, and demand more flexibility in retirement, so that they can continue work but without feeling too stressed and worn out. Skill shortages have become so acute that employers are clamoring for older workers. Employers respond by creating more flexible patterns of work.

By 2025 the traditional concept of retirement has begun to change. Aging begins to be seen as an opportunity for fulfillment rather than the continuation of punishing employment. Retirement is becoming less age-related, and the pathways out of employment more varied. Although a substantial proportion of people still leave work in their late 60s, a growing minority continue into their early 70s—and some even later. It is too early to say that retirement has been totally reshaped, but the way retirement is framed has changed.

PATCHING UP OR LASTING REFORM? THE FUTURE OF THE STATE PENSION

The state pension system makes a statement about the nature of retirement. It gives younger people a rough idea of when they can expect to retire, and by being strongly age-related props up a traditional view of retirement. A rewarding old age requires an adequate income, but many pensioners are in poverty now. Will the state pension promote a less age-based and more fulfilling view of retirement in the years ahead?

Drivers of Change

The present state pension system is under challenge from many quarters. It is criticized for being too complex, for containing disincentives to save, for failing adequately to address poverty, for being ill-attuned to longer life expectancy, and for being costly to the taxpayer. There is widespread agreement that the system will have to be overhauled at some stage.

Yet there are strong political constraints in the way. These include the long-term costs of improving state pensions when set against other demands on the public purse, fears that the benefits of improvement would go to those who need it least, opposition on health grounds to requiring older people to work longer in return for pension reform, and a lack of consensus over the desired nature of reform.

Two Scenarios

More of the same. In this scenario, government tries to make the current system work. Elements of the state pension are improved and indexed to earnings. These steps lift many pensioners off means-tested benefits.

Government meets the additional costs from savings elsewhere and by phasing in an increase in the state pension age to perhaps 67, starting in the early 2030s.

Lack of consensus drives government to a minimalist approach, designed to keep in tact as much of the present system as possible. No additional steps are taken to make state pensions more flexible as a further encouragement to phased retirement.

A flexible state pension. This scenario is more radical, though it is presented as the further evolution of the current plans.

A new "Flexible State Pension" is phased in from 2030 and indexed to earnings. It is paid to everyone, irrespective of their contribution records, on a residency basis and at a flat rate, set just above the poverty line. Eventually, when all pensioners are covered, the Flexible Pension makes means-tested benefits for this age group largely redundant.

Individuals have increased choice over when they start to receive their Flexible Pension. They can take it any time between ages 60 and 80. The value of the pension is adjusted downward if taken before age 70 and upward if taken later. Anyone who settles for a reduced pension requires an annuity (or equivalent), which will guarantee that their retirement income, including the state pension, remains at the level of the Flexible Pension or higher.

The substantial net costs of the Flexible Pension are met by raising the state, or "central," pension age, probably to around 70, phased in over a 10-year period, starting in the mid-2030s. People whose lifetime earnings average out at close to the poverty line receive a slightly higher pension.

The age at which the full Flexible Pension becomes payable is adjusted automatically to reflect changes in life expectancy, with those affected notified well in advance of the date at which the full pension becomes payable.

The new Flexible State Pension supports the reshaping of retirement. It further erodes the notion that older people enter a stage of life that is strongly age determined. It embodies the principles of choice and flexibility. It lifts the incomes of the poor, helping them have a more fulfilled old age.

WITH OR AGAINST THE GRAIN? THE FUTURE OF LIFETIME SAVINGS

The government hopes that there will be a strong shift to saving for retirement through an occupational or personal pension scheme. But this seems unlikely under present arrangements.

Drivers of Change

Many workers will remain reluctant to save. One reason will be that Britain's polarized labor market persists, leaving a good number too poor to do so. Will those on middle to higher incomes who can afford to save for retirement save enough? Many are not doing so now.

In the future, savings by middle earners will be curtailed by breaks in full-time employment (for example, to look after children), by additional financial commitments (notably paying more for higher education and other government services), by the costs for some of family breakdown (living on your own is a lot more expensive than with another person), by the strong allure of day-to-day consumption, and by longer expectancy, which makes it harder for young people to imagine their old age and plan for it.

Defined benefit schemes will gradually wither away. Until now they have proved highly attractive, not least because employers carried most of the risks. But the spread of these schemes has gone into sharp reverse. They are seen as too costly and risky for employers. Employers are using the closure of final salary schemes to new members as an opportunity to cut their pension contributions to the new schemes and to transfer the risks to individuals.

Defined contribution schemes will be unattractive to many people. Mistrust is widespread following a succession of scandals and recent collapses in the financial services industry. Despite reducing costs, the industry's cost structure is ill suited to a low inflation age, with lower nominal returns on investment. Equity-based pensions involve considerable risks for the individual, even if investments are moved into bonds as retirement approaches.

The huge range of pension products, complicated charging structures, and complex tax treatments (despite government's proposed simplification) leave consumers confused. Has the industry ended up in the wrong business? It sells an extensive range of products when most people would benefit from a simpler range. It sees itself as selling pensions, when what most people need is regular financial advice.

In short, it provides customized pensions and standardized advice, when perhaps what most people need are standardized pensions and more customized advice.

Persuading people to save will be a huge challenge. Solutions may lie in better advice and information, including the imaginative development of pension forecasts so that they attract more media interest and comment. Another solution might be to compel individuals, employers, or both to contribute a certain annual amount to pension schemes, though this would carry high political risks.

Alternatives to pensions may become more attractive. These alternatives could include equity release schemes through which people raise income on their homes, and inheritance.

Two Scenarios

Compulsion plus. In this scenario, employers are obliged to contribute a minimum of 5% of each worker's earnings to the individual's personal or occupational pension. To encourage contracted-out workers to save more, employers are required to match the contributions of individuals up to a total of 9%. So if a person put 5%-9% of his or her salary into a pension, the employer would have to match it.

Despite this new incentive, workers remain reluctant to increase their savings substantially. So in 2011, as part of the reform of state pensions, compulsion is extended to individuals (and retained for employers). The state pension age is raised, perhaps to 67. Private pensions are expected to follow suit, giving individuals longer in which to save.

Compulsion removes the need for tax relief on contributions to private pensions, which is phased out. The abolition of tax relief funds a substantial cut in income tax, making compulsion politically acceptable. Compulsion rather than choice becomes a key feature of the pensions regime.

Lifelong savings account. This scenario adopts a more flexible approach to lifetime savings—a different way of thinking about savings altogether. The Lifelong Savings Account bundles together various current savings schemes that attract government support.

This new approach to savings is designed around the life cycle rather than around retirement alone, as currently with pensions. It encourages people to save for immediate needs, as well as more distant ones, by acquiring "assets" that they want now, but which can also boost income in old age. These "assets" consist of housing, learning, and old-age income.

Individuals are encouraged to travel through life with a Lifelong Savings Account, into which they put contributions when they can, and from which they can make withdrawals to purchase three types of assets: property, work-related learning that will push up their income, or a pension. These purchases attract government financial support up to a ceiling, replacing the support that is given to other current forms of savings. They also attract (compulsory) employer support, again replacing employer contributions to pensions.

The Lifelong Savings Account is kick-started with a much-enhanced "baby bond," perhaps financed by receipts from inheritance tax. An annual savings forecast is a further feature.

To qualify for matching contributions, the Lifelong Savings Account is held in a designated bank or building society account, but only with banks and building societies that offer financial advice independent of the sale of financial products.

The scenario responds to reservations about a one-size-fits-all approach to savings and works with rather than against the short-termism of consumer behavior. It encourages savers to spread risks and enshrines the values of choice and flexibility needed for the reshaping of retirement.

TRAVELING TO THE FUTURE

We pull together the scenarios in the previous three chapters into two final, generic scenarios, which provide alternative maps for policies on retirement, the state pension, and savings for old age.

Two Scenarios

Putting it off. Retirement is much as we know it today, but it starts later. The beginning of retirement remains age-related, but the age is merely postponed. Routes into retirement remain inflexible, and fulfillment in older age is jeopardized by inadequate income. The financial preparation for retirement is squeezed into a one-size-fits-all straitjacket, which ignores the fluidity and diversity of many people's experiences.

Employers are reluctant to devote management time and other resources to creating flexible work for older people. A relatively tepid approach to pension reform reinforces existing views of retirement. Inflexible savings are still the road to inflexible retirement.

Liquid lives. This scenario looks very different. Its foundations are laid during the first quarter of the century, although its main features are not fully apparent till some 25 years later.

Retirement is no longer a distinct phase of life. People can mix-'n-match work and more extended leisure, with more numerous routes out of full-time employment. Indeed, the distinction between working life and retirement becomes so blurred for many people that eventually the notion of retirement itself comes into question. The financial preparation for retirement is released from its traditional straitjacket. Individuals have more savings options, backed by state and employer financial support. They can tread a more flexible financial path to a more flexible old age.

The need to encourage flexible employment becomes a policy priority. The Flexible Pension cuts pensioner poverty, enabling those on low incomes to enjoy a somewhat more fulfilling old age. Lifelong Savings Accounts embody the values of choice and flexibility to reshape lifetime savings, so that people are more willing to save, acquire more assets, and are able to use these assets to support their old age.

Our Preferred Future

Liquid lives would erode the dominant role of age in retirement arrangements. It would offer older people more choice and flexibility and more opportunities for fulfillment and self-improvement. It would transform the experience of old age and have a "ripple down" effect on younger age groups—not least by making their work more flexible: Flexible work for older people would influence the terms and conditions of younger workers.

Even if few active steps were taken to reshape retirement, social forces may bring it about in any case. Might it not be better to work with the grain of those forces? Many of the milestones along the *liquid lives* route are in place already.

Retirement and the financial preparation for old age could be reshaped bit by bit over the next two decades, so that by 2025 the foundations would have been laid for a very different approach to later life and a more flexible, fulfilling, and rewarding old age.

AUTOMATION'S FUTURE

THE WOLF IS HERE: THE IMPACT OF TELEPOWER

by

Howard F. Didsbury Jr.

The dramatic and continuing, if not actually accelerating, technological advances resulting from the melding of computers and telecommunications—what is referred to as "telepower"—taxes the imagination when it comes to trying to visualize its far-reaching ramifications. More exactly, telepower "occurs when telecommunications, artificial intelligence, and data processing power are successfully harnessed for profit, personal satisfaction, military advantage, pleasure, or prestige." This statement made by Joseph N. Pelton in a recent important book on the subject is a succinct summary of the essence of this new force.

RESERVATIONS ABOUT TELEPOWER

There is much about this complex dynamo of change to admire and, no doubt, encourage. Pelton, in his 1990 book *Future Talk*, subtitled *Global Life in the Age of Telepower*, presents a concise, authoritative overview of the awesome dynamo. Pelton enthusiastically catalogs many of the positive effects and options presented by telepower, an agent for positive human advancement. However, he is also mindful that telepower can, without the exercise of human wisdom, vigilance, and responsibility, become a genuine threat (termed by Pelton "Teleshock") to a humane existence. Unless we recognize the need to "humanize" the "Super-speed" and "Super-smart" characteristics of these technologies, "we will be playing with fire."

One valuable function of futurist speculation is that of attempting to foresee likely harmful or undesirable results of scientific advances and technological ingenuity. In doing this, futurist speculation serves as "early warning signals" that are designed to elicit prudent reflection and timely action. To take one example, teleshock poses the threat of persistent technological unemployment. A standard response to this early warning signal is a recitation of the story of the little boy who cried "Wolf!" And with this the warning is casually dismissed. However, the fact that the wolf ultimately does appear is overlooked. To the perceptive, the advent of telepower and teleshock is clear evidence that the wolf is here.

Over a decade ago, I produced a brief paper entitled "The Serpent in the Garden," published in 1982 in *Communications and the Future*, which dealt with a few of the likely effects of the "telecommunica-revolution," a term then much in vogue. As I noted, "Many see in this revolution the realization of a technological paradise—

Howard F. Didsbury Jr. *is director of Special Projects for the World Future Society and president of Alternative Futures Research Associates, Washington, D.C. He may be contacted at didsbury@wfs.org.*

comfort, ease, and convenience for all.... But look more closely and one sees a serpent lurking in this paradise!" The serpent was a symbol of unanticipated, undesirable effects. The enthusiasm and excitement associated with the advent and expansion of telepower calls forth a restatement of serious reservations about the unalloyed benefits of the latest—and continuing—advances.

FRAGMENTATION OF SOCIETY

For example, telepower may further accelerate the ideological and value fragmentation of American society. The vast increase in cable channels and other means of communication may mean a rapidly increasing loss of commonly shared assumptions, values, and attitudes throughout the nation. Another undesirable effect of a multiplicity of carriers may be the increasing proliferation of "special interests" and their power. One consequence of this will be the diminished concern for "the public interest" understood as the general, common good devoid of narrow partisanship or ideological demands. Each interest group, highly organized and committed to its own agenda first and foremost and strong enough to exercise "veto power" over policy formulation, can make the effective functioning of democratic government virtually impossible.

THINGS REPLACING HUMANS

Another ominous aspect of the impact of telepower is the marked tendency in a world of "virtual reality" and marvelous speedy, smart machines to have "things" replace human beings and human contact. To preserve humaneness, people need people and warm human interaction. This fact is ignored at great peril to the human psyche. As telepower augments the artificial environment in which human beings live, the effects may be grave. In such an environment, humans vicariously experience life more and more removed from the real world. The long-range detrimental effects of such an existence may be profound. The short-range consequences are apparent. It is conceivable that one of the causes of many mental health problems in a high-tech society stems from the stresses and strains of its sheer artificiality, its foreignness to living as a human being in some communion with nature.

Like Anteus of classical Greek mythology, who was invulnerable while his feet touched the earth, human beings may need to draw refreshment and strength from the actual experience of nature's realm. Will the vicarious enjoyment of living be further enhanced electronically? Will "appearance" be substituted more and more for "the real thing," for "reality"? The mania for substitution—machines for muscles, computers for minds, drugs for sensations, and other ever-increasing ingenious substitutions—may ultimately find a substitute for being human!

DANGERS OF ELECTRONIC DEMOCRACY

Still another reason for apprehension is the likely effects of telepower on the functioning of democratic government itself. The potentialities of telepower for enhancing participatory democracy are greeted ecstatically by its egalitarian admirers. They are fascinated by its prospects for genuine democracy. Instantaneous electronic plebiscites will end voter apathy or sense of powerlessness. Plebiscites will be held on political, social, and economic issues confronting society. The electronic plebiscite, we are advised, restores genuine democracy. It provides an opportunity for all to participate actively in the political process and dispels, once and for all, feelings of alienation. From this perspective, adjectives fail to describe adequately the many wonderful results that will follow the arrival of popular instantaneous plebiscites. And that may be.

Nevertheless, there are some good reasons for having second, less sanguine, thoughts about the whole prospect. For one thing, as everyone knows, there are as many fads and fashions in ideas (economic, social, and political) as there are in clothes. They come and go with notable swiftness. In the realm of style, no harm results from this; in matters of statecraft, law, and society, the results could be chaotic if not calamitous. Popular fickleness on issues is demonstrated repeatedly by the results of polls. What is a burning issue one day becomes a dead issue a short time later.

Secondly, there are the dangers that arise from ignorance, hysteria, and passion—not to mention problems created by sensationalism and the oversimplification of difficult, complicated, issues. Electronic plebiscites would create a field day for the politician with the catchy slogan and the easy, simple solution. It is chilling to think that one's freedom or survival might hang upon the electronic whim of one's neighbor—a neighbor who might be a passionate ignoramus, a religious fanatic, or a well-meaning, completely uninformed person. Who could rest secure a single night in such a society?

CONCLUSION

Some years ago, long before "virtual reality" was conceived (save in science fiction), Lewis Mumford in his *Transformation of Man* (1956) posted an early warning signal about scientific and technological substitutions that would replace the human role:

Will not science also provide an effortless mechanical orgasm, thus doing away with the uncertainties of human affection and the need for bodily contact; a necessary aid to artificial insemination? The contempt for organic processes, the willful effort to replace them, at a price, with mechanical equivalents [in the present context of scientific and technological advances: telepower and genetic engineering] have only begun to show their hand.

These brief notes on some of the negative aspects of the much-heralded telepower age may suggest that the Golden Age that many envision may not be as golden as we are led to believe. This being the case, prudence dictates that thoughtful, concerned people everywhere should strive to anticipate undesirable effects of this dynamic force without delay. They should seek to formulate policies to prevent or at the very least alleviate the inhumane effects of telepower/teleshock. Informed, timely action may achieve some good; inaction secures mischief.

THE GOVERNMENT OF THE FUTURE IS INTELLIGENT: CITIZEN IN CONTROL, GOVERNMENT IN CONTROL

by

Marcel Bullinga

In the future, citizens will be more "in control." Technology will provide the tools for self-service and self-control: many self-service dashboards, one self-service card, and a self-service mobile. It will allow us to perform continuous checks: Is the air polluted, is this taxi driver cheating on me, is this doctor licensed? It also will allow us to control any use of our own personal data and to prevent misuse. This will greatly enhance our privacy. Big Brother is nonsense.

At the same time, government will gain power as well. Technology will provide government and society at large with tools for a safer society and for automatic law enforcement. Permits and licenses will be built into cars, trains, buildings, and doors. Laws will automatically distribute themselves into our physical environment. All machines, doors, and buildings will become updateable—like Windows updates itself on your desktop computer.

Innovation in government will be about creating this intelligent, transparent world. It is the only way to cope with rising fraud, global crime and diseases, accidents, and disasters. Decent citizens will gain privacy, and criminals will lose it. For our future defense, we may have to go back to the protection the old medieval city once gave us.

GOVERNMENT IN CONTROL, SAFER CITIZEN: AUTOMATIC LAW ENFORCEMENT

Making rules and enforcing them is an important government task. Right now, laws are written down on paper and enforced by people. I think in future all rules and laws will be molded into expert systems and into chips. These chips will be molded into cars, doors, and buildings—that is, our physical environment. That means that no longer will police officers and other government personnel exclusively enforce the law; our physical environment will enforce the law as well. I call this trend automatic law enforcement.

A few examples illustrate my point best. A modern cigarette machine only allows you to purchase cigarettes if you are of legal age: a fact that is put on a smart card. You put the smart card in the machine, you wave at it, or you wave at the barkeeper and he will open the machine. The smart card is the key to legal services or products, in this case cigarettes. If you are not of legal age you do not get any illegal product or service.

In the same way, an elevator could stop working if the govern-

Marcel Bullinga *is a futurist and trendwatcher for the Dutch government. He is an international speaker about innovation and the future. He may be contacted at info@futurecheck.nl.*

ment license that is embedded in the elevator has expired. If it has not expired and if the elevator still meets all government demands, then it just keeps working.

The most interesting machine in terms of automatic law enforcement is the intelligent car, which, to be precise, doesn't exist yet. Starting this future intelligent car is like launching an Apollo spacecraft. It performs a lot of network checks before it actually starts. Are you the rightful owner? If not, then the car doesn't start. Are you in some kind of police record? If yes, then the car doesn't start. Are the safety belts on? If not, then the car doesn't start. Only when the car and you have met all these network checks in milliseconds, then the car starts—which is a nice thing for a car to do. You won't have to do much; the car is of course self-steering. While driving, you pay road taxes by the mile, and it is impossible to drive into a silence area or to exceed the speed limit. (That is not fiction; this kind of real-time government control has been tested already in satellite-steered cars.) The motor continuously checks if it meets the environmental laws. If not—well, I don't exactly know what might happen then, but you think of some interesting real-time punishment! Stealing the car, or any other intelligent machine, will be useless; it simply will not work in the wrong hands.

Basically, the intelligent car is a *transparent space*. All kinds of databases about car and owner are coupled with government databases. No, Big Brother does not come in here, since this coupling is for good reasons: owner's safety, traffic safety, health safety, antitheft, antifraud…. Who can oppose that?

Updateable Laws, Updateable Machines

In future, government will not supply paper laws anymore but will supply open standards software and send this software, in real time, to all these meanwhile intelligent, cars, buildings, and machines. It can be done because these machines will be updateable. Intelligent appliances, machines, and products mean that these appliances become self-aware. They have an ability to make some sort of decision and are self-enforcing. In my opinion, the following laws could be translated into automatic law enforcement: environmental laws, traffic laws, safety laws, bookkeeping rules, and all social security involving proof of identity. In future, when asking reports and statistics from companies, government will use a company's existing software to extract and upload the reports automatically and on the other hand download the licenses in real time. Think of Windows updating itself. In the same way, we get machines updating themselves with new rules.

If the value of the digits is guaranteed, if the context and the ownership of the digits is guaranteed and somehow packaged in the same data, then we could get something like an intelligent beer tap. It is an existing commercial product. It taps beer, of course, and there is a link between the tap and the pay desk. So no way you can make false statements about how many beers you have tapped this year.

If we can make a connection between the beer tap and the pay desk, we can also make a link to the Tax Service Department and transfer the VAT in real time. We are using our mobile already for many more purposes than just phoning. We pay the waiter's bill, the parking ticket, train ticket, and it is a voting machine. We pay taxes in real time and get back bonus points from government or company.

The European Central Bank is trying to create intelligent money. They want to put a chip in paper money for guaranteed authenticity. I don't understand why they don't get rid of the paper and just stick to the chip!

Back to Medieval City

Do you know anything about those beautiful medieval cities? I just love to read about them in historic novels. They were the center of creativity, and the people trading in it added lots of value to the nation. Well, we did not really have nations at that time. It was more like cities bonding with other cities and sharing power or competing for it. And the citizens guarded their city very well. There were huge walls and gates. At the gates one could try to get into the city, but everyone was checked thoroughly and if you could not contribute to the city, or if you were a criminal, then you were not allowed inside.

In modern times, we left all this behind us. We created nations, we created free movement of persons, and in the last century we opened up our borders. I think we will see a countertrend because of illegal or harmful immigration and the real-time spread of diseases. Think of SARS and mad cow disease. Specialists say we will encounter things much worse than that. This countertrend means we will be forced to go back from unlimited openness to limited access. We will have to go back to the old defense mechanism of medieval cities. The previous national borders will be replaced by new physical city borders and by virtual administrative borders.

You can see it happening in Rome and London and Singapore. What is Rome famous for, besides being a wonderful ancient city? It has this video tracking system installed for the purpose of reducing congestion. People in the police force all over the world argue that we should not only use that system for tracking cars but also for tracking people: checking who wants to get in and preventing them from doing that if they are illegal or criminal.

The point is that technology allows us to leave at rest all decent citizens and their privacy, and to bother only the criminals. It is not about searching everyone on the streets and in the planes—that is a really scary future!—no, technology selects the bad guys whom we should check out more carefully. Technology is the only way of combining the fight against terrorism with a decent civil society.

Self-Service Privacy Dashboards: More Than We Ever Thought Possible

One of the fun things in digital technology is that it is able to cloak information; that is, cloak personal information and only use aggregated statistical information. So, yes, driving in an intelligent car means you are monitored, but, no, your privacy is not lost. No one knows it's you who is driving there or why, unless you choose to reveal your status to people you trust. Unless your employer wants to track and trace you for good economic reasons. Unless you make an accident happen in a hit and run. When you hit someone and you drive on without taking care of the victim, the car itself will reveal your identity in real time to another car, a passenger, a nearby police agent. The same goes for a virtual transaction. You can spend your money anonymously, but if you try to spend it twice, the system reveals your identity and location. If you use fraudulent data, like false solicitation forms or nonexisting claims, the system will discover it, will cancel the transaction or deny entrance.

So, please stop talking about Big Brother in the digital age. It is a nonsense story. If you want to be concerned about anything, be concerned about Japanese schoolgirls using cameras in mobile phones to take pictures of you in the supermarket or the sauna and publishing them on the Net, or about English schoolboys using Bluetooth-failures to harass passersby with real-time SMS-spam.

POLICY IMPLICATIONS OF THE FUTURE

I have shown you seeds of a few possible futures. I have not shown you *the* future; it does not exist. Innovation is about analyzing the future, marking where you want to be in say 2010, and making deals in the present to get there. Be ahead of change before it hits you. I list the policy implications of the future trends mentioned in this article, both strategic and tactical.

What parts of the list you feel attracted to depends completely on your vision of the future, your culture, your local norms and values. Whether it will be *citizen in control* or *government in control* is up to you.

Strategic Policy, Socio Trends

• The extreme wealth generated in the last decade by selling and reselling houses is fake. It will get back on us in time. Mahatma Gandhi said it: Lasting wealth is created only by working hard. So start working again!

• Working hard is best done where it pays off: in innovation. All innovation, in services, organizations, and products, is about knowledge and knowledge only, be it creating new knowledge or applying current knowledge. If you want to stay ahead in the international rankings, start educating people, start combining research areas from the user's point of view. If the neighboring country already has invested heavily in nanotechnology and biotechnology, you will probably not be able to keep up anymore, so change horses. I suggest embedded software ("intelligent world," remember, is dependent on that) and intelligent logistics; i.e., smart knowledge, in general.

• Privatization is not a matter of ideology. *Does it work or not* is the only question. Do not privatize any vital public service or government monopoly (such as energy, police force, or basic health) as long as it runs smoothly. If it does not function properly, however, privatize and get rid of rules protecting the monopoly.

• In the West in the past few decades, we have overstressed rights and neglected duties of citizens, including immigrants. Authority—even as practiced in essential professions by nurses, doctors, train drivers, etc.—has become a dirty word. Thus, we have created a moral vacuum that no technology is able to solve.

• Decide whether you want criminals to have the same privacy as decent citizens. Decide whether you help criminals or punish them. Any techno system follows a basic moral value.

• Celebrate heroes in workplaces. Successful innovation is not about policy, it is about enthusiastic people. We should reward these people.

• If criminality is bothering you, change the balance between criminal law and civil law. Criminal law is about punishing people *after* the crime. A combination of civil law and technology makes it possible to *prevent* crimes from happening.

• Delete all organizational stimulants for fraud, such as if the law forbids an insurance company to kick someone out of basic health insurance although he has committed fraud.

• In wealth, we tend to accept enormous amounts of fraud. We just raise the premiums since it costs so much energy to go for the criminals. Ask yourself if that is still a valid option in times of economic decline.

Tactical Policy, Techno Trends

• Combine and reduce rules. Stop making any new rules.

• Create a smart knowledge infrastructure. Reduce all government passes into one self-service card. Accelerate the creation of authentic registrations like addresses, companies, etc. Create knowledge systems and Web services instead of Web sites. Create and use only open standards for data and preferably open source for software.

• Forbid governments to ask the citizen any data that is already available (ask once, use many). Create transactions portals for this purpose.

• If you have severe congestion problems: create forms of high-quality virtual mobility. Technology enables the reduction of physical mobility. It is a highly valued export product as well.

• Create intelligent financial systems, especially if you are troubled by the ethics of Enron and the like. Intelligent money knows its owner and destination and as such will prevent most of the current financial fraud.

• Get rid of the doctor-centered logistics in public health care and create patient-centered health logistics. Use knowledge health systems.

• Use the real-time information provided by sensors in products, trees, buildings, and roads to prevent environmental disasters from happening.

• Buzzword in the next 10 years: *chain* (chain services, chain cooperation, shared services). All-time buzzword: *customer*.

• Monitor Japanese schoolgirls and English schoolboys carefully. Children's behavior is significant to your policy making.

[Editor's Note: A full version of this article appears in the July-August 2004 issue of *The Futurist*. This article is an edited version of the presentation the author held on September 18, 2003, in Estonia for the 37th congress of the worldwide e-government platform ICA, for government representatives from 26 countries.]

HEALTH CHALLENGES

EMERGING DISEASES: NEW THREATS FROM AN OLD NEMESIS

by

Tyler A. Kokjohn, Kimball E. Cooper, and Laszlo Kerecsen

CHANGE AS DISEASE OPPORTUNITY

Scientific advances and modern medicine have doubled human life expectancy over the last century (Roher et al., 2003). We are accustomed to equate change with progress and anticipate as routine continued advances in medicine and health. Success against infectious disease has instilled a false sense of security and masks a little-appreciated countertrend; despite a future projected to include stunning health enhancements, changing food consumption patterns, travel and migration, economic interactions, military campaigns, aging populations, even modern medical practices sometimes create novel, potentially disastrous health threats (Palumbi, 2001). Change is inevitable as humans continue to alter their environment and living patterns, and indeed there seems little question that the pace of change itself will accelerate to inevitably create more unanticipated disease opportunities.

Predicting before the fact disease emergence as a consequence of any specific change may be difficult or impossible. For example, providing clean drinking water has saved untold numbers from premature deaths due to typhoid fever, cholera, and other water-borne diseases. An unanticipated result of improved water supplies was the emergence of large-scale poliomyelitis epidemics around the beginning of the twentieth century (Davis et al., 1980; Joklik et al., 1992; Volk et al., 1996). Poliomyelitis, a disease that leaves some of its victims with permanent, asymmetric flaccid paralysis, was known to medicine before these epidemics began and was named "infantile paralysis." Prior to the advent of generally available poliovirus-free water, most individuals were infected during infancy, the period when they were least likely to become paralyzed. Improved living standards meant that many escaped typical early infection with this pathogen. Unfortunately, these individuals remained susceptible to poliovirus infection and, because the infections now occurred at older age, were more likely to end up paralyzed. In effect, improved living standards delayed the time of poliovirus infection to ages that were more vulnerable to paralysis and unwittingly set the stage for large-

Tyler A. Kokjohn *is associate professor of microbiology at Midwestern University, Arizona College of Osteopathic Medicine, in Glendale, Arizona. He may be contacted at tkokjo@midwestern.edu.* **Kimball E. Cooper** *is associate professor of biomedical sciences at Midwestern University, Arizona College of Osteopathic Medicine, in Glendale, Arizona. He may be contacted at kcoope@midwestern.edu.* **Laszlo Kerecsen** *is professor of pharmacology at Midwestern University, Arizona College of Osteopathic Medicine, in Glendale, Arizona. He may be contacted at lkerec@mid western.edu.*

scale disease epidemics. While poliomyelitis is now prevented through vaccination and a worldwide eradication effort has driven the disease-causing forms of this virus to near extinction, the history of its epidemic emergence is instructive.

While poliomyelitis was a relatively slowly developing threat to human health, deadly change-linked disease has struck with blinding speed. In 1978 toxic shock syndrome appeared among young women and swiftly killed many of its victims. Retrospective investigations revealed that the use of super absorbent tampons had allowed the causative microbe, *Staphylococcus aureus*, to establish a local infection that produced exceptionally high bloodstream levels of the deadly toxic shock toxin (Salyers and Whitt, 1994). Since the recognition of the underlying basis for this disease and appropriate changes in tampon use to avoid it, the incidence of toxic shock syndrome caused by *S. aureus* infection has decreased.

BATTLING ADAPTABLE ENEMIES

While the cardinal signs and symptoms of some infectious diseases have been recognized for centuries, the nature and extent of the threat they pose has not necessarily remained as constant. Somewhat over a century ago scarlet fever, a complication of an infection with the "strep throat" bacterium *Streptococcus pyogenes*, was a common childhood disease in the United States and Europe (Salyers and Whitt, 1994; Volk et al., 1996). Scarlet fever once had mortality rates of ca. 30%, yet only a few decades later, the same disease killed in less than 3% of total cases (Volk et al., 1996). This virulence change cannot be linked completely to changes in environmental conditions and occurred well before modern antibiotics were introduced, suggesting that unknown change(s) in the intrinsic virulence of *S. pyogenes* was an underlying factor. New whole-genome sequencing analyses have confirmed that some distinct disease-causing strains of this species differ in the virulence factor (disease-causing) genes they possess (Banks et al., 2002). While such strain-specific genetic differences were anticipated, the recognition that a substantial proportion of these disease-linked genes were actually components of viruses peacefully harbored in the bacterial genomes was an unexpected revelation. This observation suggests that under the right circumstances bacterium and virus coexist to in effect combine forces to create a stronger pathogen. Viruses sometimes move from one host bacterium to another, and these constant genetic exchanges and rearrangements probably contribute to the differing disease-causing potentials noted in this species. This unexpected pathogenic partnership between *S. pyogenes* and its viruses means that a long-recognized disease agent has the ability to acquire and rearrange new genes rapidly and thus adapt to novel conditions such as the human use of antibiotics. Bacterial gene exchange is frequent, and several methods in addition to virus infections are known to allow these rapid evolutionary changes. In some instances, genes move between entirely different species, making bacteria and viruses the most genetically flexible creations known. This enormous genetic adaptability suggests that, while many pathogens can be controlled, it is never safe to assume that they can be vanquished completely. The general and steady rise in bacterial pathogen resistance confirms that even the most potent antibiotics can be overcome and suggests that novel control strategies may be essential in the near term.

Influenza, one of the greatest and most adaptable human killers, is largely ignored and accepted as the occasional winter season nuisance. Influenza pandemics, large-scale disease outbreaks extending across the entire world, occur often, but are not predictable. These viruses possess a segmented genome, meaning that genetic exchange between different virus strains is comparatively easy and frequent (Wuethrich, 2003). These genome segment exchanges, termed antigenic shifts, favor the emergence of new virus strains to which virtually no one is immune. Typically most dangerous to older and debilitated individuals (Joklik et al., 1992), the type A influenza viruses exhibit vast intrinsic differences in disease pattern and lethality. In 1918, the deadliest influenza epidemic in human history struck and left millions dead (Reid and Taubenberger, 2003). This influenza strain, known as the "Spanish flu" or "Swine flu," was unique in its ability to kill its victims directly and swiftly. Additional unusual aspects peculiar to this virus were the facts that fatal infections were concentrated primarily in young adults (Davis et al., 1980) and that the heaviest portion of the epidemic occurred in the fall, months earlier than normal. While influenza vaccines are available, a sudden reappearance of this influenza virus would present an enormous public health challenge and probably strain national vaccine production capability far beyond capacity (Abbot and Pearson, 2004).

It is important to recognize that influenza presents a constant threat even if another exotic killer strain like that of 1918 never appears. Influenza viruses infect a wide variety of animals, including birds and pigs, and this fact also contributes to its potential to cause devastating human epidemics. Humans exploit birds such as chickens as food sources, meaning that extensive human contact with influenza reservoir species is unavoidable. Raising large numbers of animals in close quarters is becoming common business practice, and other stress-causing aspects of mass-scale production methods may enhance the probability for new deadly influenza strain development. The recent appearance and spread of "bird flu" across Asian poultry populations has raised concerns that a devastating new human influenza pandemic is imminent. This particular influenza virus has never circulated widely in human populations, meaning that most individuals will be highly susceptible to it. Should the bird flu virus evolve to a form that readily infects humans, widespread loss of life is predicted (Abbot and Pearson, 2004).

Exploited as important and affordable mass-scale food sources, pigs and birds such as chickens harbor a diverse influenza virus population and may actually be the critical link to their evolution into dangerous human pandemic strains (Wuethrich, 2003). Even if pigs and birds were eliminated as food items or vaccinated against all known influenza viruses, there is no guarantee that such drastic measures would halt all future human influenza outbreaks, nor would they ensure humans were safe from emerging diseases. Zoonotic pathogens, agents capable of afflicting both animals and humans, are well known to medicine and considered by some authorities to represent the greatest share of presently emerging human diseases (Woolhouse, 2002). Acquired immunodeficiency syndrome (AIDS) and the human immunodeficiency virus (HIV) were unknown prior to 1981, but only a few years after the initial recognition of unusual respiratory disease deaths among young gay men (Prusiner, 2002) came the recognition that a new and dangerous infectious agent had entered human populations. There is now no question that AIDS will be recognized as one of the greatest human pandemics of history. HIV-1 may have first entered human populations decades ago as a consequence of traditional hunting practices in which wild animals, including primates, are hunted and exploited as diet-supplementing meat sources. HIV-1 is structurally similar to primate viruses, and this suggests that African hunters were accidentally infected through contact with virus-infected animal blood as bush meat was prepared for consumption (Hahn et al., 2000). If this hypothesis is true, AIDS joins diseases such as plague, tularemia, and rabies that are caused by animal pathogens quite capable of infecting humans under the proper circumstances to cause devastating disease.

Because wild animal populations act as disease reservoirs and in principle many zoonotic agents remain unknown to medicine, control at the source is, frankly, impossible. Given inexorable human population growth and expansion into new regions, emergence of both recognized and entirely novel zoonotic diseases would seem to be inevitable (Woolhouse, 2002). Severe acute respiratory syndrome (SARS), a sudden-onset respiratory disease with a high case fatality rate, emerged in 2002 in the People's Republic of China and rapidly produced over 800 confirmed deaths across the world. Caused by a new coronavirus (Rota et al., 2003) thought to be harbored by civet cats and other animals (Guan et al., 2003), this explosive SARS emergence is just a recent example of this zoonotic disease potential.

MEDICINE AS PROBLEM SOLUTION AND SOURCE

Consequence is the inevitable companion to change, and medicine is certainly no exception to this rule. The benefits accruing from medicine have been enormous, but it must be recognized that the ultimate result of medical interventions is the creation of a new human population with perhaps a propensity to express new and unexpected disease patterns (Roher et al., 2003). Medical practices sometimes mitigate a problem while actually creating debilitated patients more susceptible to infectious disease. Organs and tissues are now routinely transplanted, but in order to control rejection, recipient immune systems are curbed, thereby creating opportunities for infections. Cancer therapies often render patients more susceptible to infections. HIV-infected persons live longer thanks to new virus-suppressive drug regimens. In effect, medical success has created a cadre of individuals susceptible to novel and not-so-novel pathogens. Under some conditions, immune-compromised individuals may foster disease agent emergence. In addition, invasive procedures such as blood transfusion and organ transplantation have the potential to disseminate widely diverse and incurable viral disease agents such as HIV, hepatitis viruses, West Nile virus, and cytomegalovirus. The situation is clearly complex, but can be summed up neatly: Despite impressive medical advances, and sometimes because of them, infectious disease will continue to pose a risk to humans. Employing advanced medical procedures may actually foster further problems by creating susceptible patient pools or directly transmitting pathogens. Indeed, the move toward economic "globalization" in which foods, products, and people traverse the planet with unprece-dented speed and ease, are potential contributing and accelerating factors (Woolhouse, 2002), and the predicted aging of world popula-tions adds an additional complication. Together, these conditions may produce an under-considered and unwelcome future counter-trend to hoped-for enhancements in human health and projected life-span extensions.

DEFENDING AGAINST THE UNKNOWN

Paralytic poliomyelitis and toxic shock syndrome resulted from changes that initially seemed to pose little risk of disease. Spectacular medical advances have created a subpopulation of immune-compro-mised persons. Improvements in living conditions have led to a crowded world with more elderly individuals. Even political changes such as the dissolution of the former Soviet Union and regime-change-prompted prisoner release have fostered the spread of drug-resistant tuberculosis. Because the connection is so remote, few of these changes would have stimulated much concern over their global health effects implications.

While changes initiated by humans often emanate through a desire to improve conditions, recognizing that these alterations may also present novel opportunities for human adversaries is disturbing. Because change is self-stimulating and accelerating, and it is impossible to anticipate fully the disease consequences for any given action, the situation may appear unmanageable. The critical step is to note that change is almost inevitably associated with some degree of adverse outcome and recognize that disease promotion is an under-appreciated, but general, risk linked to a broad array of changes. Recognizing this reality sets the stage to detect problems and develop potential mitigation strategies (Table 1).

TABLE 1 - NEAR-TERM ACTIONS TO ENSURE THE LONG-TERM PUBLIC HEALTH

• Upgrade the existing national disease-surveillance capacity.
• Develop the capacity to detect the emergence of insidious diseases.
• Produce influenza vaccines before massive epidemics appear and/or accelerate efforts to develop and implement novel vaccine production methods.
• Stockpile antiviral drugs such as Tamiflu as a hedge against near-term sudden influenza pandemic.
• Support antibiotic discovery research that exploits untapped biodiversity of bacteria, protozoa, and viruses.

How may societies be safeguarded against unknown infectious adversaries emerging from new reservoirs or are spawned by new situations of our own unwitting creation? Recent events have forced governments to consider strategies to detect, contain, and eradicate disease resulting from intentional biological agent attacks. The existing medical surveillance system, the National Notifiable Diseases Surveillance System, is inadequate for this task and will require update, upgrade, and expansion. It is important to recognize at the outset that a data collection/analysis system developed to meet military and civil defense needs might also serve to improve security against the threat posed by emerging infectious diseases and to plan accordingly.

Internet communications, database searching with high-speed computers and algorithms, and large-scale data-mining techniques could be combined to create a powerful disease outbreak detection capability. A data repository synthesizing information from a variety of sources—clinician office and emergency room reports; school and other organization absence reports; prescription and over-the-counter drug sales; agricultural, veterinary medical, and environmental reports such as unusual animal deaths—could be scrutinized continuously for unusual events. In effect, this system would become "total information awareness" for the public-health field.

It is vital to consider that some emerging diseases could be insidious and reveal themselves slowly, perhaps indirectly, and over long time frames. For example, AIDS, the end stage of typically years-long HIV infection, was first noted as an unexpected cluster of rare skin cancers and opportunistic infections. A new disease emerging slowly over a wide area could conceivably escape early detection. For this reason, future analytic systems strategies need to be broad in perspective in terms of both the parameters and time scales examined.

Whether attempting to combat terrorism or stave off natural epidemics, assuming a global perspective is vital. The World Health Organization (WHO) has ongoing efforts to identify and respond to the threat of a range of diseases, including influenza. Only a fraction of the influenza viruses isolated worldwide are fully characterized, and the limited extent of reliable surveillance may impair the recognition of the early stages of pandemic influenza emergence. Influenza vaccine production requires months and accurate anticipation of the dominant virus strains, so this WHO global surveillance program fills a critical need. New rapid screening technology may allow for the reporting of more, and more accurate, epidemiological data on viruses circulating worldwide, and automated genomic sequencing could allow for the complete characterization of a greater fraction of influenza isolates. Both will require investments in equipment and personnel training. In addition to improving surveillance capacity, it is possible to stockpile anti-influenza drugs such as Tamiflu and produce vaccines to potential pandemic influenza strains like bird flu before large numbers of human cases appear (Abbott and Pearson, 2004). Given the proven global nature posed by the influenza threat, it seems in the direct national interest to ensure that the WHO has resources to accomplish these tasks.

Often great effort is expended to project the implications of plans prior to their implementation. Experience suggests that some changes may have significant and wholly unpredictable human health implications that classic risk-assessment methods simply cannot reveal. Recognizing that future infectious disease threats will emerge at unpredictable times, emanate from unexpected sources, and sometimes involve novel pathogens leads to a realization that extensive and continuous monitoring efforts will be vital to safeguard the future public health.

REFERENCES

Abbott, A., and H. Pearson. "Fear of Human Pandemic Grows as Bird Flu Sweeps through Asia," *Nature*, 427 (2004), 472-473.

Banks, D.J., S.B. Beres, and J.M. Musser. "The Fundamental Contribution of Phages to GAS Evolution, Genome Diversification and Strain Emergence," *Trends in Microbiology*, 10(11) (2204), 515-521.

Davis, B.D., R. Dulbecco, H.N. Eisen, H.S. Ginsberg. *Microbiology*,

3rd Edition (New York: Harper & Row, 1980).

Guan, Y., et al. "Isolation and Characterization of Viruses Related to the SARS Coroavirus from Animals in Southern China," *Science*, 302 (2003), 276-278.

Hahn, B.H., G.M. Shaw, K.M. De Cock, and P.M. Sharp. "AIDS as a Zoonosis: Scientific and Public Health Implications," *Science*, 287 (2000), 607-614.

Joklik, W.K., H.P. Willett, D.B. Amos, C.M. Wilfert. *Zinsser Microbiology*, 20th Edition (Norwalk, CT: Appleton & Lange, 1992).

Palumbi, S.R. "Humans as the World's Greatest Evolutionary Force," *Science*, 293 (2001), 1786-1790.

Prusiner, S.B. "Discovering the Cause of AIDS," *Science* 298 (2002), 1726-1727.

Reid, A.H., and J.K. Taubenberger. "The Origin of the 1918 Pandemic Influenza: A Continuing Enigma," *J. Gen. Virol.*, 84(9) (2003), 2285-2292.

Roher, A.E., et al. "Circle of Willis Atherosclerosis is a Risk Factor for Sporadic Alzheimer's Disease," *Arterioscler. Thromb. Vasc. Biol.*, 23(11) (2003), 2055-2062.

Rota, P.A., et al. "Characterization of a Novel Coronavirus Associated with Severe Acute Respiratory Syndrome," *Science*, 300 (2003), 1394-1399.

Salyers, Abigail A., and Dixie D. Whitt. "Bacterial Pathogenesis. A Molecular Approach" (Washington, D.C.: American Society for Microbiology, 1994).

Volk, W.A., B.M. Gebhardt, M.-L. Hammarskjöld, R.J. Kadner. *Essentials of Medical Microbiology*, 5th Edition (New York: Lippincott-Raven, 1996).

Woolhouse, M.E.J. "Population Biology of Emerging and Re-Emerging Pathogens," *Trends in Microbiology*, 10(10) (2002), Suppl.: S5-S7.

Wuethrich, B. "Chasing the Fickle Swine Flu," *Science*, 299 (2003), 1502-1505.

THE AMERICAN DRUG ABUSE EPIDEMIC: POLICY FAILURES, BETTER APPROACHES, SOCIETAL BARRIERS

by

Donald B. Louria and Amiram Sheffet

For the last 50 years, illicit use of mind-altering drugs has plagued all parts of American society. It spread progressively from 1950 to the mid-1970s. Since then, little has changed, despite massive efforts and expenditure of huge amounts of money to mitigate it. New fads have appeared and faded, use of specific drugs has increased somewhat or decreased somewhat; but, overall, the chronic use of drugs such as heroin and cocaine is largely unchanged—a persistent societal problem that refuses to go away.

Our approach has been threefold—reduce supply, incarcerate users and sellers, and "treat" users. These approaches have failed to solve our drug problem for the last 50 years and will fail for the next 50 or 100 years.

Reducing supply. That will not succeed so long as there is continuing demand for the drugs by young people and so long as these people are willing to pay a lot of money for those drugs, thus creating huge profits. If the billion-dollar campaign to wipe out the cocaine supply from Colombia were to succeed (it won't), another source of supply would crop up. The same is true of heroin. Cut off one supply route, say, in Mexico, and another will develop through the Caribbean immediately. And then there are clandestine laboratories manufacturing drugs like Ecstasy.

There are also unexpected events that boost production. In Afghanistan, the vicious Taliban reduced opium production by about 80%. After their removal from power, subsistence farmers in rural Afghanistan, impoverished even more than usual by constant war and an implacable drought, found that they needed to cultivate opium to survive, and within one year, Afghanistan opium production increased dramatically. Reducing supply is still worthwhile—you can win individual battles, but you cannot win the war so long as demand is strong.

Incarceration. We continue to throw nonviolent users and small-time drug sellers into prison for extended periods. That is stupid, cruel, and unproductive. They account for more than 20% of our jail and prison population, and that is a major reason our jail and prison population now exceeds 2 million people—at a cost of $20,000 or more per person per year. Building more prisons is not the answer to our drug problem. New York State is among the worst. I (DBL)

Donald B. Louria *is professor and chair emeritus, Department of Preventive Medicine and Community Health, New Jersey Medical School, Newark, New Jersey. He may be contacted at louriado@umdnj.edu.* Amiram Sheffet *is an associate professor, Department of Preventive Medicine and Community Health, New Jersey Medical School, Newark, New Jersey. He may be contacted at sheffeam@umdnj.edu.*

was the president of Governor Nelson Rockefeller's Drug Abuse Control Commission and supposedly his top adviser on drugs. He spent $500 million on rehabilitation efforts. When that failed, in frustration and desperation, without adequate consultation, he enacted the draconian lock-them-up laws that are still in place in New York State. Nelson Rockefeller was an intelligent, compassionate pragmatist. Had he remained governor he would have rescinded those cruel laws decades ago. The prolonged incarceration of non-violent users and small-time sellers (supporting their own habits) is a disgrace that tarnishes any claims of accomplishments by governors and legislators in New York State over the last three decades.

Incarceration is not the answer or even an intelligent approach to the drug problem—except for major sellers and suppliers and violent drug offenders who ought to be given long prison sentences.

Treatment. That is the current rage. But it is largely an inadequate solution. Most heroin or cocaine users are not motivated to enter drug rehabilitation. For those who enter long-term residential program (LTRs), a modality designed for individuals with more severe drug abuse problems who are also more likely to have alcohol and criminal justice problems, improvement is dependent on strength of motivation and duration in treatment.

Length of time spent in treatment has been one of the most reliable predictors of post-treatment outcomes.[1, 2, 3] Usually, 12 or more months of treatment are required to complete treatment. It is estimated that less than 20% of the patients stay in LTR for 12 months or longer.[2, 4] It has also been reported that significant improvement is shown by patients who stay in LTR for three months or longer. However, less than 50% stay in LTR for more than three months, and average length of stay is even shorter for patients with cocaine dependence or alcohol dependence.

For the motivated abusers who enter LTR, drug use and criminal behavior one year post-treatment drop substantially and employment status improves. For example, in one analysis, drug injection during the past year dropped from 17% to 5% (daily use, 10% to 2%).[1] Any cocaine-crack use fell from 82% to 39% (daily use, 39% to 11%), and heroin use dropped from 19% to 7% (daily use, 10% to 2%). Also, daily alcohol use fell from 23% to 12%, arrests and jail dropped from 53% to 32% and 77% to 37% respectively, and part- or full-time employment rose from 54% to 68%. Yet, full recovery cannot be determined because of lack of long-term follow-up.

So, treatment may benefit half or fewer of the heroin and cocaine users who are motivated enough to seek treatment. Retention rates in LTR may be better among those under legal pressures (court orders),[5] but differences are not substantial. Treatment regimens in LTRs are quite severe and disciplined. There is no reason to believe that compelling "treatment" will succeed for arrested users who are not motivated to undergo treatment and rehabilitation.

We need good treatment and rehabilitation programs, and we

desperately need post-treatment support by social workers, coun-
selors, etc. Good programs deserve public and private financial
support. But treatment is *not* the answer to our drug problem—it can
help, but it is not *the* answer.

These three "solutions" have been supplemented in the last
decade by a novel "preventive" approach, mandatory urine testing
of students and workers to detect what amounts to sub-clinical drug
use.

Urine testing has to be viewed in light of the Fourth Amendment
and the progressive encroachment on privacy condoned by the
Supreme Court.[6]

The Constitution of the United States does not guarantee privacy,
nor do any amendments to the Constitution. However, the Fourth
Amendment embodies language that has been used to protect certain
aspects of individual privacy. That amendment states "the rights of
the people to be secure in their persons, houses, papers and effects
against *unreasonable* searches and seizures shall not be violated and
no warrants shall be issued but upon probable cause, supported by
oath or affirmation and particularly describing the place to be
searched and the persons or things to be seized."

Starting in the 1960s, a series of federal and state court decisions
subordinated Fourth Amendment privacy rights of individuals to the
perceived needs of the society. To do so, in part, requires circumvent-
ing the warrant provision requiring "probable cause," a phrase that
legally profoundly restricts invasion of individual privacy. Circum-
vention has been accomplished in three ways. First, the court would
declare that obtaining warrants in certain circumstances was
impractical or was not required; *therefore*, probable cause was not
required. Second, the court would decide probable cause was too
restrictive and not required. Third, and most important, the court
focused on the word "unreasonable," concluded the search in
question was reasonable and, consequently, did not need probable
cause. These interpretations are critical to the progressive encroachment on individual privacy that has taken place in the last 40 years.

In point of fact, the Fourth Amendment separates "unreasonable
searches" from "probable cause" and in no way suggests that
concluding a search is reasonable somehow lessens the need for
demonstrating probable cause.

At first, the reasonableness criterion was applied to inspections
or searches of buildings or dwellings. Then, it was expanded to cover
luggage searches at airports, use of metal detectors when entering
courthouses, stopping cars at checkpoints near the US–Mexico
border, and stopping automobiles to test for sobriety if there was
reasonable suspicion the driver was intoxicated.

In 1989, two landmark Supreme Court decisions (*National Treasury
Employees Union v. Von Raab*, 489 US 656; *Skinner v. Railway Labor
Executives' Association*, 489 US 602) moved from external searches to
invasive body searches by testing of body fluids (blood or urine) or

exhaled breath.

Although limited in scope, these decisions have been widely interpreted as providing the legal underpinning for widespread work site testing for drug use.

In *Skinner v. Railway Labor Executives' Association*, the Supreme Court upheld regulations promulgated by the Federal Railroad Administration that required railroad companies to conduct blood and urine tests of railroad employees involved in accidents resulting in death, injury, or property damage, and authorized railroads to conduct breath or urine tests when an employee violated certain rules, or a supervisor had a reasonable suspicion to believe an employee's acts or omissions contributed to a reportable accident or incident. The regulations also permitted railroad companies to require breath tests when a supervisor had a reasonable suspicion that an employee was under the influence of alcohol at work.

In *National Treasury Employees Union v. Von Raab*, the Supreme Court upheld the United States Customs Service regulations requiring drug tests of any United States Customs Service employee who sought transfer or promotion into a position that directly involved the interdiction of illegal drugs, required the carrying of a firearm, or placed the employee in a position to have access to "classified material." In both cases, the drugs for which blood or urine were being tested included illegal and prescription drugs.

In the *Von Raab* decision, the Supreme Court entered a new area of body searches. Based, in part, on that decision, employers have initiated drug-testing programs with the expectation that the overwhelming majority of those tested will be test-negative. Thus, we are progressively shifting from testing for drug use in situations in which a positive is anticipated to widespread random testing by invasive techniques (body fluid analyses) in situations in which the data indicate at least 80%, usually more than 90% or 95%, of those persons selected for testing will have negative test results.

Testing for alcohol intoxication has been legally condoned since the *Schmerber v. California* decision in the 1960s, but testing was carried out only if there was a reasonable suspicion that the individual was under the influence. In 1990, the Supreme Court permitted suspicionless law enforcement alcohol sobriety checkpoints in the *Michigan Department of State Police v. Stitz* decision.

Each encroachment on privacy has been a harbinger of further encroachments.

For those urging mandatory urine testing for junior and senior high school athletes, the premise was simple. Do unannounced mandatory urine analysis of athletes to detect use of marijuana, cocaine, heroin, etc., in the middle schools and the high schools and it will go a long way to controlling substance abuse. The athletes were singled out with rationales that ranged from safety to being good role models, with the notion that, if athletes reduced their drug use, the rest of the school body would follow. That notion was used to justify coercive invasion of students' privacy.

There were real consequences for positive findings, including forced counseling and dismissal from the team. Refusal to participate resulted in the student being prevented from participating in athletic activities.

This action is diametrically opposed to what those of us involved in drug abuse policy and prevention have consistently recommended, namely that the best antidote to illicit drug use is providing extracurricular activities that students find exciting and interesting so they are not bored and thrust into drug-using peer groups. We have argued that those committed to sports or other extracurricular activities are less likely to get deeply involved in the drug scene and, more likely, if they do use illicit drugs, to use them on a less frequent basis (transient experimentation).

The mandatory testing program for student athletes was started in Vernonia, Oregon. The school board of that community, reacting to teachers' and administrators' perceptions of increased marijuana and stimulant use, approved a policy in 1989 of testing urine specimens of student athletes in grades 7 to 12. No study was carried out on actual prevalence of drug use. Requiring students to undergo urine tests in order to be allowed to play was challenged in court, eventually reaching the Supreme Court, which, in 1995, handed down an extraordinary decision.

The following is part of the decision written by Justice Antonin Scalia: "Legitimate privacy expectations are even less with regard to student athletes. School sports are not for the bashful. They require 'suiting up' before each practice or event, and showering and changing afterwards. Public school locker rooms, the usual sites for these activities, are not notable for the privacy they afford. The locker rooms in Vernonia are typical: no individual dressing rooms are provided; shower heads are lined up along a wall, unseparated by any sort of partition or curtain; not even all the toilet stalls have doors."[7]

Because students who participate in sports are allegedly not "bashful" and shower together, they have, according to Scalia, reduced expectations of privacy and it was, therefore, all right to demand they provide urine samples under the watchful eyes of "discrete micturition observers." Taking communal showers according to six members of our Supreme Court was enough to say that these athletes did not deserve the privacy protection of the Fourth Amendment to our Constitution! I (DBL) have dubbed that decision "the communal shower decision."

In 2002, a second Supreme Court decision expanded testing to cheerleaders, band, choir, and other extracurricular activities. Justice Clarence Thomas wrote for the majority:

In any event, students who participate in competitive extracurricular activities voluntarily subject themselves to many of the same intrusions of their privacy as do athletes. Some of these clubs and activities require occasional off-campus travel and communal undress.[8]

The logic is mind-boggling. You cannot be a bashful athlete, according to the Supreme Court, and if anyone goes to an athletic club and takes a communal shower, he or she forfeits the limited protection to privacy our forefathers provided in the Fourth Amendment.

The Supreme Court and approving school administrators were not concerned about the consequences of false positives (just eat a poppy muffin and you can get a false positive). They did not even demand that surveys be done first to determine whether there really was a significant problem of regular use of illicit drugs (rather than transient experimentation).

The schools that opted for invasive urine tests first picked on the students who chose to participate in sports and other extracurricular activities rather than the nonparticipants who would actually be more likely to have the uncommitted time to engage in regular illicit drug use.

Aside from the ethical issues of selecting only students in sports or other extracurricular activities (the ones less likely to use illicit drugs extensively), and the absence of probable cause, the obvious question is whether coercive testing does any good. It certainly does nothing but harm for those students who are misidentified by false positive tests.

Two studies are worth noting, both published in 2003.[9, 10] In one, a group from Oregon Health and Science University got schools to initiate a mandatory drug testing program and compared their drug use with "control" schools.[9] Drug use was analyzed by questionnaires at the beginning and end of the school year. The questionnaires for athletes were *not* anonymous; those for non-athletes were anonymous. Obviously, in a school with a mandatory drug testing program, a nonanonymous questionnaire is likely to produce a reluctance to admit drug use in the follow-up questionnaire. The authors concluded that random drug testing reduced drug use, but not alcohol use, but the program also increased negative attitudes towards the school and counterproductive attitudes towards drug use. Furthermore, *new* use of illicit drugs during the school year actually *increased* among athletes in the school with urine testing. As was predictable, the nonathletes in both schools used a lot more drugs than the athletes.

In the other study, investigators from the University of Michigan (considered to be the best group in the country for evaluating student drug use) reported that 18% of schools carried out mandatory testing for student drug use. Among the eighth, tenth, and twelfth graders they studied with questionnaires in a national sample, there was no evidence that mandatory drug testing affected the frequency of student marijuana use or use of other illicit drugs among athletes or the rest of the student body.[10]

Picking on athletes and others participating in extracurricular activities focuses on the wrong group, and, in the absence of probable cause, it is an unethical invasion of privacy. In most schools, it was instituted without proper studies or concern for the severity of the drug problem. There is inadequate evidence of its effectiveness, and it can ruin lives because of false positives and the consequences of overreacting to transient experimentation. Some schools have done questionnaires before starting mandatory testing programs and report a decline after the program was started; but, given the fluctuations in the drug scene from year to year, those questionnaire results cannot be interpreted unless the same questionnaires are given to control schools where the testing was not initiated. Furthermore, the questionnaires have to be able to detect shifts to new drug fads. These criteria are virtually never met.

The mandatory urine tests for students actually followed similar testing at the work site, sometimes as a condition of employment, sometimes as a surveillance mechanism. Tens of millions of Americans now undergo mandatory urine testing at the work site. The rationales for testing in the workplace, even in the absence of an accident or reasonable suspicion, have been:

1. To protect the safety of the workplace. Drug users, it was said, caused more accidents.

2. To increase productivity. It was alleged drug users are less productive and have a much higher absenteeism rate.

3. To help the drug-using employee seek assistance and thereby improve his or her health.

4. To improve the overall work-site morale.

5. To be in conformity with state and federal laws about drug use.

It should be clear that the overwhelming majority of those detected in random drug testing programs will not be addicts or heavy users or drug-dependent persons. They will be recreational users or regular users who are having no demonstrable effects from the drug use. Furthermore, the tests can pick up use well away from the work site. A person using cocaine on Saturday at home will likely still have a positive test the following Tuesday or Wednesday. For marijuana, it is a much longer interval; have a few joints on a weekend and the urine is likely to show marijuana metabolites (and give a positive test result) two to four weeks later. Interestingly, most of the companies that were so determined to have extensive urine testing for illicit drugs, including heroin, morphine, cocaine, crack, amphetamines, barbiturates, and LSD, were not interested in extensive blood or breath analyzer tests for, by far, the most abused drug—alcohol.

Let us look at the assumptions on which suspicionless drug testing is usually based:

1. *Increased productivity, decreased absenteeism.* The data are limited, uncertain, and unconvincing.[11, 12, 13] It is not clear at all that the type of drug use detected in a suspicionless search has anything to do with productivity, absenteeism, employment duration, or promotions. That is counterintuitive. You would think it would be easy to show that drug users are less productive. That is not the case. Of course, this excludes the obvious drunkards or drug addicts. It refers to drug users who are detected only by the urine test. At present, they seem to be as productive and be promoted as frequently as non-drug users.

2. *Promotion of individual health.* Here again, there are no adequate data. If someone is addicted or habituated, detection can, indeed, promote health, but those situations are subsumed under the rubric of testing for reasonable suspicion or probable cause. There is no evidence that those users detected by suspicionless searches are any less healthy than their peers, colleagues, or fellow employees.

3. *Safety.* Even in the absence of good epidemiological data for any drug except alcohol, common sense and the alcohol data justify random drug testing of certain groups (airplane pilots, train motormen, those with hands-on responsibility for nuclear weapons), but there are actually no data that would justify random drug testing of all employees for safety reasons. Occasionally, there are spectacular cases, but there is no evidence that random drug testing will make a workplace safer.

4. *Detection of users who can then be provided with assistance.* The term assistance is often deliberately unexplicated. In other cases, it is defined as referral for treatment. There are treatments for heroin addiction and some heavy cocaine users that help some motivated individuals. But there is no known effective "treatment" for the recreational user of any drug, and there is not even predictably effective treatment for heavier uses of marijuana, amphetamines, or LSD. That fact is almost always ignored.

In sum, the assumptions underpinning drug testing policy are shaky and are inadequately supported by convergent epidemiological evidence.

False positives are a big issue, but loss of privacy is an even bigger issue. The urine test not only picks up drug use days or even weeks prior to the test, but also will show prescription or over-the-counter drugs, medication-taking the individual may not wish to be known to people working for his or her employers. He/she may feel disturbed, even outraged, at having to "explain" use of prescription or over-the-counter medications to employer representatives. Possibly that information could affect promotions or employment, even if supposedly confidential. It is hard to convince employees (and a lot of other people) that employers would not be given the results of or find out about positive tests. Besides, if a person testing positive has to go to an employee assistance program for disposition, counseling, etc., those visits to employee assistance programs cannot be kept secret.

Urine drug testing makes your life a lot less private. In future years, the testing technologies will result in detection of ever smaller amounts of any drug the individual has taken, and will be able to detect use for longer periods after a given drug has been taken. That, in turn, means a further invasion of privacy because it increases the likelihood of detecting use far away from the work site—during vacations, for example—or of prescription or over-the-counter medications taken a substantial time before the test. Even more important, testing of body fluids for drugs, an invasive procedure, can provide the milieu in which even greater invasions of privacy will occur.

A major problem in regard to coping with drug use is our insistence on viewing it with simplistic, linear thinking. That has been true with both mandatory urine testing and incarceration.

Major drug problem → jail more people for longer time → (hopefully) reduction in severity of drug problem

Major drug problem → test urine of students, or at workplace → (hopefully) decreased drug use

The linear approach has also been used in regard to reducing supply and dependence on the supposed effectiveness of treatment.

Simple solutions to complex problems usually fail. The drug scene is complex, and to have any realistic chance of approaching it effectively requires holistic, systems thinking.

The accompanying diagram (Figure 1) is a systems approach to this vexing problem. The systems diagram includes a large number of individual and societal variables and their interrelationships that will determine the nature and severity of the drug scene. Included are leverage points indicating areas or actions that could potentially change the entire system. In theory, every variable or determinant is, to a greater or lesser extent, modifiable and could, therefore, alter the system in a beneficial fashion. The leverage points indicate those variables or determinants that seem to be most susceptible to change and suggest that there are potentially much more effective approaches to abuse of illicit or mind-altering drugs than our present largely futile actions. We propose investing in true prevention.

FIGURE 1 - A SYSTEMS (HOLISTIC) APPROACH TO TEENAGE OR YOUNG ADULT ILLICIT DRUG USE

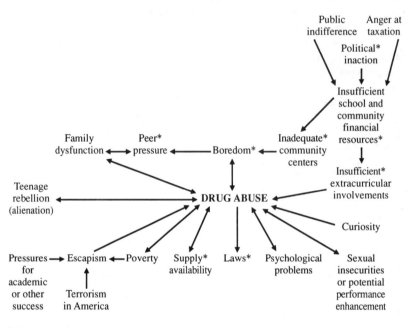

* Leverage points

Why do young people use illicit mind-altering drugs? There are many reasons. Probably the top three are curiosity, pleasure, and peer-group pressure. It is hardly surprising that curiosity heads the list. A biblical phrase goes "a man should live if only to satisfy his curiosity." Equally unsurprising is pleasure seeking; we are, after all, a hedonistic society focused on both pleasure and instant gratification. Peer groups have an extraordinary influence, for good or bad, on the fragile egos of adolescents seeking acceptance.

The best way to prevent commitment to the drug scene is to create positive peer pressure by having young people involved in activities that make them feel good about themselves and, at the same time, avoid boredom. Boredom is an invitation to involvement in the drug scene. As Shakespeare noted in *Antony and Cleopatra*, "ten thousand harms, more than the ills I know, my idleness doth hatch." The highest juvenile crime period is between the end of school and dinner time—a period in which boredom and bad peer-group pressure dominate.

The proposed remedy is to provide a wide variety of extracurricular activities that should be an intrinsic part of the educational program of every junior high school and high school and should be mandatory unless there is a valid excuse. All sorts of activities should be encouraged so that each young person can find something that he/she finds interesting and fulfilling. If that is done, it will not prevent experimentation with drugs such as marijuana, but it will markedly reduce serious involvement in the drug scene, and it will create constructive peer groups.

We have known this for 40 years. One of us (DBL) emphasized it in books and articles written in the late 1960s and early 1970s.[14, 15] Despite that knowledge, what have we done as a society in the last three decades? Counterproductively, we have progressively reduced funding for extracurricular activities in our schools, a move that is catastrophic in regard to the drug scene and promotes the influence of unconstructive peer groups.

I (DBL) remember well, in the 1970s, being asked to address a parent-faculty-student gathering at a suburban high school. The subject was how to cope with their substantial drug problem. The auditorium was jam packed. As the principal and I were walking towards the podium, he said "it is unfortunate that this week we were informed we could expect a 50% cut in our funding for extracurricular activities."

I stopped walking, turned to him, and replied, "It's not your fault, but why am I here? Given that funding decision, there is nothing I can say about lessening drug use that will be particularly useful."

Everybody shares the blame—politicians, school boards, members of communities who regularly vote down school budgets, school administrators who have not formulated adequate plans and have not been effective advocates for extracurricular programs. All these individuals and groups decry the drug scene, but then take actions that promote it. That is sheer stupidity. Parents, too, have a responsibility to find interesting, constructive activities that occupy their children. But the major preventive societal action we could take would be to establish extensive extracurricular activities that provide plenty of individual choice, fund them adequately, and then make individual involvement mandatory.

Reducing supply, laws and incarceration, and voluntary and involuntary treatment can help keep the drug scene from getting worse, but cannot provide a solution to this persistent societal malady. Getting young people involved in extracurricular activities that will help protect them against serious involvement in the drug scene is no panacea—nothing is—but it could have a major impact. It does take thought, careful planning, and commitment of resources, but if we are not willing as a society to make such a commitment, then we ought to stop complaining about the severity of the drug scene.

We offer this approach as an antidote to involvement in the drug scene, but there are no guarantees. Although the evidence indicates that those involved in extracurricular activities are less likely to be committed to the drug scene, it could be that self-selection into extracurricular activities identifies those who would be less involved in the drug scene, even if they were not involved in the extracurricular activities. It is, therefore, necessary to test this approach (in essence a hypothesis) by annual *anonymous* questionnaires about transient experimental use, occasional use of less-dangerous drugs, and more-serious or extensive involvement in the drug scene. These questionnaires should be conducted in all middle schools and high schools in similar fashion to the national surveys conducted by investigators at the University of Michigan.

There are many who continue to believe that "educating" students about the perils of drug use is an effective strategy. That has never been adequately documented. Such efforts could be useful, but should never be conducted unless accompanied by careful evaluation by validated questionnaires administered before, immediately after, and then repeatedly in annual follow-ups.

As implied throughout this paper, it is imperative that we stop regarding illicit drug use in monolithic fashion. In our thinking and approaches, it is critical to separate drugs with greater potential for more-serious physical or mental harm (e.g., heroin, cocaine, LSD) from those with far less potential (e.g., marijuana). Similarly, for most drugs, more-extensive involvement must be distinguished from ephemeral experimental or recreational use.

Although offering alternatives to the drug scene and avoiding boredom could, hopefully, profoundly reduce the severity of the drug scene, there is no action that will totally prevent substantial use of mind-altering drugs for nonmedical purposes. In large part, our inability to diminish the abuse of narcotics, stimulants, and mind-altering drugs to an irreducible minimum is rooted in the nature of our society. Professor Pitrim Sorokin of Harvard University pointed out in a prescient 1945 book, *The Crisis of Our Age*, that Western society has gone through multiple culture cycles he designated as ideational (religiously dominated), idealistic, and sensate.[16] The advent of sensate predominance presaged a dramatic restructuring of the society, in each cycle a return to an ideational era. Western society has now been in a progressive sensate phase for several centuries. In a sensate society, the dominant values are those that appeal to the senses and that make drug use and abuse not only appealing, but virtually irresistible. As we have moved further along in our sensate focus, there has been increasing attention to sexuality and sexual performance. In a society mesmerized by celebrity, film, and television sexuality creating the mirage of unfailing spectacular sexual performance and with a pharmacologic cornucopia, it is hardly surprising that sexual enhancement prescription, over-the-counter, and Internet drugs are among the best sellers. In that situation, illicit drugs (as well as alcohol) will be used extensively not only to reduce inhibitions or allegedly enhance sexual performance, but also, increasingly, to escape from physical sexual involvement. The latter should not be ignored. One way to avoid sexual intimacy is to withdraw into what amounts to a protected shell by use of a variety of pharmacologic agents, including marijuana, opiates, hallucinogens, sedatives, and even alcohol. Lacking adequate epidemiological studies, the extent of such withdrawal is currently unknown. With a concatenation of drug-use-promoting variables—a sensate society, a focus on sexual performance, promotion of sexual enhancement, and ready availability of mind-altering drugs—it is impossible to reduce demand enough to completely avoid a thriving drug scene.

The behavior of our society fosters drug use by example and promotion. The famed physician Sir William Osler noted that "man has an inborn craving for medicine.... The desire to take medicine is one feature which distinguishes man, the animal, from his fellow creatures." We take a gallimaufry of medicines for any slight illness, pain, or discomfort. Much of the prescription medicine taking is unnecessary, and that is even more true for nonprescription agents and herbs or other substances designated as alternative or complementary, for many of which there is inadequate evidence supporting the claims.

La Rouchefoucauld noted, "There is nothing so infectious as example." It should not surprise us that the extensive use by adults of unnecessary medications and a plethora of unproven agents to improve physical or mental well-being, including the massive use of legal mind-altering agents for relaxation, sedation, or emotional support, would encourage use by young people of illegal or legal drugs to "relax" them, or for "mind expansion" or sexual enhancement, or for pure hedonism.

The promotion of prescription and over-the-counter agents through television and other media with direct-to-the-consumer advertising may be good business, but urging the public to "ask your physician" about a variety of pharmacological agents has a major downside (aside from excessive prescribing), and that is promotion of the notion that drugs solve all problems and invariably make people feel better. In that environment, any substance that offers the hope of making people feel good or at least better will be used; drug abuse follows ineluctably.

The epidemic of performance-enhancing drugs by athletes only exacerbates the problem. If athletes can take performance-enhancing drugs, why shouldn't nonathletes take pleasure-enhancing drugs?

There are other variables that are difficult to control that promote drug use. We take comfort from the fact that "only" about 12% of the population live in poverty (some 36 million people), but the poverty level is set so artificially low that, if given a quality of life adjustment, the true figure is at least doubled. That guarantees a large number of young people living in urban and suburban environments who are susceptible to drug entrepreneurs because of frustration, anger, envy, or as a way of escaping an unpleasant environment.

In sum, primary prevention by offering alternatives to the drug scene can help enormously in mitigating the severity of the drug scene and in increasing the ratio of ephemeral or minor use to committed, regular, intensive use. Treatment options can help a bit. But a significant portion of the drug scene is rooted in our sensate, hedonistic society. So long as hedonism is the dominant motif and is not placed in perspective, the use of illicit and mind-altering drugs will persist as a major problem.

Additionally, two ticking time bombs in regard to drug abuse are festering major societal problems and the threat of close-to-home terrorism. If critical societal problems persist unchecked, they may threaten perceptions of meliorism. Meliorism is the ability to solve our problems by the dint of our own efforts. If major societal problems are treated with insouciance and get progressively worse, there will come a time when one or more problems will appear to many, validly or not, to be beyond solution or significant mitigation. In such a scenario, young people are likely to lose faith in the future, to no longer believe we are a meliorist society. Problems that would fit that category of threatening the viability of the global society would include population growth beyond a certain as yet undefined level, the consequences of and the inevitability of significant global warming, the likelihood of nuclear holocaust, and the occurrence of multiple sequential epidemics with resistant emerging and re-emerging microorganisms (dwarfing the HIV/AIDS epidemic). Each of these problems could have such catastrophic effects on the society that young people, persuaded we are no longer a meliorist global society, could lose confidence in their future and, as a result, turn increasingly to the pleasures of today, including the hedonism and escapism of regular, and often heavy, use of legal and illegal mind-altering drugs.

The threat of terrorism—nuclear or biological—could spur the same retreat into hedonism and escapist drug use. We are already subjected to multiple, repeated warnings of potential terrorist acts on American soil. If a few events with conventional weapons (bombs) do occur, the threat of worse attacks with deadlier weapons of mass destruction is likely to imbue many with a gnawing and persisting anxiety that will be accompanied by attempts to cope with the generated fears. For many, part of the coping mechanisms may well be the use of alcohol and other mind-altering drugs.

Futurists create scenarios for the future, some overly optimistic, some overly pessimistic, some realistic. Here is one particularly mordant one for the year 2050. There are 50% more people on Planet Earth (9.5 billion), the planet is a few degrees warmer, and these two determinants (population size, warming) have created hundreds of millions of refugees and internally displaced people, often herded together into unhygienic refugee camps that are breeding grounds for severe epidemics that rapidly spread around the world—a world already savaged by nuclear and biologic terrorist acts and terrorized by the potential of self-replicating nanotechnology weapons. That may be an overly bleak scenario, but it is possible, and if anything like it occurred, huge numbers of people, given the opportunity, would elect to retreat into a drug-induced solipsistic cocoon. A second scenario for the not-too-distant future relates global warming to terrorism and, thence, to drug use (see Figure 2). The scenario again shows the usefulness of a systems approach; without it, it is much less likely that linkages will be considered. Without an appreciation of the linkages and their consequences, necessary preventive or remedial actions are less likely to be undertaken. Fortunately, those scenarios do not have to be, but it will require conscientious efforts and thoughtful leadership to avoid a scenario that, to some extent, resembles the worst-case scenarios we have depicted.

FIGURE 2 - THE GLOBAL WARMING—TERRORISM—DRUG USE SCENARIO

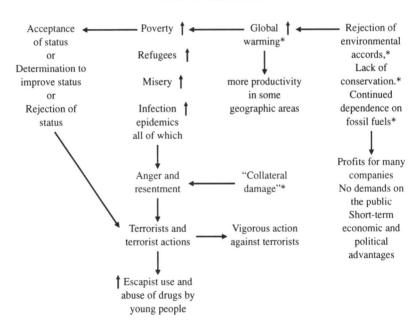

* Leverage points

To some, the linkage between the consequences of population growth or global warming with drug use will appear to be, at best, an exaggeration. It is not. The linkage is through loss of perception of meliorism and loss of faith in the future. If young people no longer believe there is much of a future, if they believe that one or more of our major societal problems has become insoluble, in our already sensate and hedonistic society, they may well turn to legal and illegal mind-altering drugs for pleasure and escapism in numbers and percentages that are far higher than found currently.

There are three obvious possibilities in regard to the use of mind-altering drugs for nonmedical hedonistic purposes; the drug scene can get worse, get better, or stay the same. For the past 50 years, our attempts to mitigate it have failed, and our policies have either been ill-considered or ineffective. The prospects for the future are not encouraging if we continue on the same paths. It seems to us there are some sensible steps that we have outlined in this essay.

To summarize, we should:

1. View current use of legal and illegal mind-altering drugs in a systems context.

2. Offer young people real alternatives to the drug scene—and carefully evaluate the effectiveness of those alternatives once implemented.

3. Examine the future of the drug scene with a systems approach and by delineating potential scenarios. Then, by focusing on leverage points (such as preventing some of the global warming) and moving towards reasonably attractive scenarios, we may be able to avoid the worst-case scenarios and even reduce the severity of our current problem.

4. Consider what steps we can take in our sensate, hedonism-driven society to alter the milieu in which abuse of mind-altering pharmacological agents seems almost a natural extension of the behaviors that dominate the society.

The abuse of mind-altering drugs is not immutable. We had better figure out how to make the situation better before it gets a lot worse.

NOTES

1. D.D. Simpson, G.W. Joe, and B.S. Brown. "Treatment Retention and Follow-Up Outcomes in the Drug Abuse Treatment Outcome Study (DATOS)," *Psychology of Addictive Behaviors*, Vol. 11 (1997), 294-307.
2. A.M. Sheffet, M.A. Quinones, K. Doyle, M.A. Lavenhar, and D.B. Louria. "Assessment of Treatment Outcomes in a Drug Abuse Rehabilitation Network," *The American Journal of Drug and Alcohol*

Abuse, Vol. 7, No. 2 (1980), 141-173.

3. W.S. Condelli and R.L. Hubbard. "Relationship Between Time Spent in Treatment and Client Outcomes from Therapeutic Communities," *Journal of Substance Abuse Treatment*, Vol. 11 (1994), 25-33.

4. D.D. Simpson, G.W. Joe, K.M. Broome, M.L. Hiller, K. Knight, G.A. Rowan-Szal. "Program Diversity and Treatment Retention Rates in the Drug Abuse Treatment Outcome Study (DATOS)," *Psychology of Addictive Behaviors*, Vol. 11 (1997), 279-293.

5. W.S. Condelli. "External Pressure and Retention in a Therapeutic Community," *International Journal of Therapeutic Communities*, Vol. 10, No. 4 (1989) 21-33.

6. C.M. Cornish and D.B. Louria. "Employment Drug Testing, Preventive Searches and the Future of Privacy," *William and Mary Law Review*, Vol. 33 (1991-1992), 95-125.

7. *Vernonia School District 47J v. Acton* (94-590). (1995) 515 US 646.

8. *Board of Education of Independent School District No. 92 of Pottawatomie County v. Earles* (01-332). (2002) 536 US 822.

9. L. Goldberg, D.L. Elliot, D.P. MacKinnon, et al. (2003) "Drug Testing Athletes to Prevent Substance Abuse: Background and Pilot Study Results of the SATURN (Student Athlete Testing Using Random Notification) Study," *Journal of Adolescent Health*, Vol. 32 (2003), 16-25.

10. R. Yamaguchi, L.D. Johnston, P.M. O'Malley. "Relationship Between Student Illicit Drug Use and School Drug-Testing Policies," *Journal of School Health*, Vol. 73 (2003), 159-164.

11. C. Zwerling, J. Ryan, E.J. Orav. "The Efficacy of Pre-employment Drug Screening for Marijuana and Cocaine in Predicting Employment Outcome," *Journal of American Medical Association*, Vol. 264 (1990), 2639-2643.

12. D.C. Parish. "Relation of Pre-Employment Drug Testing to Employment Status: A One-Year Follow-Up," *Journal of General Internal Medicine*, Vol. 4 (1998), 44-47.

13. J.P. Morgan. "The 'Scientific' Justification for Urine Drug Testing," *University of Kansas Law Review*, Vol. 36 (1998), 683-397.

14. D.B. Louria. *The Drug Scene* (New York: McGraw-Hill, 1968).

15. D.B. Louria. *Overcoming Drugs* (New York: McGraw-Hill, 1971).

16. P.A. Sorokin. *The Crisis of Our Age* (New York: E.P. Dutton and Co. Inc., 1945).

RENEWED IMPORTANCE OF A
SPACE MISSION

USING THE RESOURCES OF SPACE TO PROVIDE EMPLOYMENT AND PROSPERITY ON EARTH

by

Lester Kuhl

CURRENT SITUATION

President Bush announced earlier this year that the United States would go to Mars. Such announcements have been made before. The "first" Bush declared a Mars program in 1989, but enthusiasm lasted only until scientists determined the cost to be $400 billion ($600 billion today) for the program. In the current announcement the total funding for the program was not discussed, but an increase in NASA's budget of $1 billion was made over the next five years, and NASA was told to reprogram $5 billion from existing projects. NASA responded to the funding reprogramming as it has in the past by announcing the cancellation of the Hubble telescope, one of their major successes—a tried and true approach by NASA to get more money from Congress rather than to refocus the agency to accomplish a new major project. This "business as usual" approach taken by NASA is what concerns the people who seriously think planetary exploration can be the next wave after information technology. It can be argued that NASA and its contractors have the best experience and scientific know-how in the Western hemisphere, if not the world, for space projects, but their approach to any project is locked in the 1960s. Because of the lack of management flexibility at NASA, there is a concern that it would not be a good candidate to lead the Mars project. The international space station, which started out as an $8 billion project in 1984 and today is up to $100 million, is nowhere near completion or meeting its stated mission. NASA does not have a good track record to manage a mission of the size and duration that will be required to place people on Mars.

Down the street from the White House is the Cato Institute, a libertarian think tank. In March of 2001 the institute sponsored a conference on "Space: The Free Market Frontier" to look at a market approach to open space. The results of the conference were published in a book of the same name. The conference covered all aspects of applying the free market to space projects and is a good source document on various approaches.

Some areas covered:[1]

> 1. NASA's domination of the space effort is recognized by everyone. Several of the papers in various ways demonstrate NASA's organizational problems. The concept of NASA's centers of excellence is great on the technical side, but it is disastrous on the economical/political side because the semi-

Lester Kuhl *is a graduate engineer with experience in design and project management. He may be contacted at earth2mars@erols.com.*

autonomous centers end up competing for funds. In addition, the change of priorities by various administrations, and Congress, guarantees that NASA will not be able to keep "focused" for a long-range space- development program.

2. Several different approaches that were used to kick start early aviation were discussed for the possible use in the advancement of space development. Some may be usable in the space area, like the awarding of prize money for certain achievements. The problem with comparing the early aviation model with present space development is that, in the period before the First World War, small advancements were made by offering prizes for achieving various goals. But the war provided the major incentive for aircraft development, and after the war the excess equipment and many excess pilots willing to fly the aircraft continued the "push."

3. Many of the barriers to space are not physical but bureaucratic. Various papers outline the current supposedly streamlined approach to the licensing of commercial launches, but the results are anything but streamlined. Today it can be a mindboggling exercise that can add costs and delays to a commercial launch. One of the contestants for the Cheap Access to Space prize missed the contest's launch window because of delayed paperwork. The launch approval cycle is a major reason to look at alternate methods for the current initial launch methodology.

4. The private property rights of the use of space are discussed, and although there are several limitations set out by international treaties on how space can be used by nations, none of the exclusions should preclude the use of any economical instrument that is developed to support the development of space.

In summary, the conference highlighted that in today's space market the primary return on investment in space is in communication satellites. But even these free-market advocates could not come up with a practical, realistic, market-driven approach to finance viable space development in the current financial environment.

In Colorado, Robert Zubrin and the Mars Society are working on the "Mars Direct" approach, an exploration that would take a crew of four to Mars.[2] The plan is similar to the one used in the exploration of Antarctica. Pre-propositioned supplies would be remotely positioned in space and on Mars awaiting the crew—a thoughtful approach if your objective is the exploration of Mars and you are willing to take some risk. The approach does not provide help in the short or medium time frame towards the commercialization of space.

There is no doubt that all these organizations and people want to open space for exploration and commerce, but where NASA, the free traders, and the Mars Society go wrong is trying to make the mission the product. As we know from the exploration of the New World by the Europeans, it takes a while before profits are made on new territories.

The current approach by the scientific community to solicit interest in space exploration as a "research project" is shortsighted and counterproductive. The major technical issues of the project have long been solved, but the financial issue, which involves the use of a nation's resources for a "nonproductive" effort of space development, has yet to be defined. The exploration/commercialism of space can be a positive economic venture, thereby making it a positive political venture. The venture can be used to generate jobs and not be thought of as one that is competing for resources of other national priorities. With this approach, the exploration of space takes on a whole new meaning.

THE PRODUCT

Instead of trying to finance a mission to the moon or to Mars, what is required is the creation of a planetary or space transportation system. As a transportation system the entity/product would have assets, and its mission would be to move supplies and personnel to and from Earth, the moon, Mars, and the asteroid belt. Because an organization would have assets that could be amortized over a long period, the cost charged per pound launched could be lowered considerably. The transportation system would be like the railroad systems throughout the world. For the remainder of the paper we will call this transportation system the Mars Transportation System (MTS) with the understanding that the "parts" developed can be used to deliver cargo and personnel to the moon, Mars, or asteroids.

A Mars Transportation System (MTS)

American engineers have traditionally approached the design of spacecraft, whether communication satellites, weather satellites or manned vehicles, the same—make them as multipurpose as possible. They have continued to break the engineers' unwritten design postulate of keep it simple stupid (KISS). The Russians have long used the KISS approach, designing two or three satellites to do what one of our satellites does, and by keeping the design simple they usually get their three working in orbit while we are struggling with our one satellite. Granted, if you gave "points" for elegance in design we would win hands down, but if you are judged on practicality, the Russian designs would have the edge. This complex design approach has flowed into the manned satellite program. The reason this approach has developed is that it is easier to "sell" Congress a program for a single entity than a program made up of a series of parts like a space transportation system. The space shuttle is a good example. Designed to handle both cargo and humans, it is not very good at either. If it had been designed as a cargo ship, fewer precautions would be needed on launching, the cost to lift cargo to orbit would be lower, and more launches per year could be accomplished. This high cost of putting cargo into space is one of the major problems hampering commercial space usage. If the shuttle had been designed to carry humans, more safety precautions (such as ejection capsules) could have been designed into the vehicle. We need to develop a space transportation system that is made up of simple maintainable vehicles, each designed to do its job, not one all-encompassing vehicle.

The first step in the design of the MTS is to plan a new approach to the initial launch that makes space launches as routine as air travel, taking off from a standard runway and returning. This basic change is a key design and physiological change that will help bring space travel to the marketplace. The taking off of a spacecraft should be similar to the departure of an aircraft or a ship—a routine activity, not an event. This change would help de-mystify the space business, taking it from science to commerce.

Next part of the MTS is vehicles to move cargo and humans from low obit to Earth Terminus Station (ETS). A point yet to be determined somewhere between the geosynchronous point (22,000 miles) and the Lagrange point (200,000 miles) where the Earth-to-Mars train will depart. A tug-type vehicle would pick up the cargo modules from low orbit and move them to Earth terminus. Implied here is some type of container or module that would be outfitted for cargo or habitat, would attach to the launch vehicle, and eventually would be attached to the planetary train vehicle. Envision a box car or shipping container that can be transported to the surface of the moon or Mars and used for storage or living. At ETS the launch engines would be disconnected from the containers and the containers would be attached to the vehicle that would move them from ETS to Mars Terminus (MT) or to the moon if you like. The engines used for lifting the containers into the low Earth orbit would be returned to Earth for reuse. A human transfer vehicle would also be required. The ETS and MT are envisioned as a series of cargo modules outfitted for habitation.

The "train" would consist of a frame with a power supply and propulsion engines to which living and cargo modules would be attached.

At Mars Terminus the containers/modules that were being transferred to the surface would be attached to landing vehicles while the humans would transfer to a shuttle to be taken to Mars Port. Mars Port would end the space flight but would be the "hub" of the Mars Planet Transportation System (MPTS). Going out from Mars Port would be the radii of the MPTS; periodically, tracks/roads would connect the radii. The system would start as a series of roads and advance to whatever was required.

The MTS would be made up of many space vehicles (12 to 15), each with its own simple mission, as opposed to one complicated "do-all" vehicle. None of the parts of the MTS stresses current technology capability; the overall project is "doable" today. The MTS is not for the exploration of Mars but providing a transportation system to and in space. We have outlined the equipment required for a transportation system; we now need a way to finance the building of the system.

The use of the system would be by governments, corporations, universities, and individuals, which would lease the equipment to carry cargo and personnel to Mars (or wherever). The financing of the use of the system for a project or expedition would be like any other expedition or project today on Earth. Since the MTS could amortize itself over 100 years (or more) a rate schedule that would be affordable to individual missions could be provided because each mission does not have to justify the total cost of the system. Once the transportation system is fully operational the charge to use it would pay for the operation and maintenance of the system plus the original debt and the debt service. Such an approach will allow commercial opportunities for space ventures to be explored by the market.

A FINANCIAL MODEL

With a product to finance, what is required is a financial vehicle that can be used to put the MTS in place. Are there existing financial models that can be used to finance the expedition and colonization of the moon or Mars?

One model would be the one used to find new trade routes. In the past, merchants and countries would back expeditions to the Far East and later expeditions to the New World looking for treasure. This model requires that there is something at the destination that is of value to you so a cost/return analysis can be made. Currently there is no such commodity on any extraterrestrial body.

A popular model is the early aviation one, where prize money was offered for some advancement in aviation. The current prize, called X Prize, is offered for a space vehicle capable of take off and return twice in two weeks and reach low orbit with a crew of three— a first step but a long way to interplanetary space travel.

Another model that could be used is some type of a land grant model, where in exchange for building a transportation system an organization would be assured of government support for using a portion of the moon or Mars for a set time period. Current treaties state that nations cannot claim territory but go on to say that territory can be used for commercial activities. This is very close to a long-term lease, like the British had in Hong Kong. Some arrangement could be worked out with the international community, especially if we limit the size of the area claimed and acknowledge that it would be returned to the international community sometime in the future.

Some form of a limited land use grant might provide the positive cash flow towards space travel. The land ("use of") could be used as collateral for the venture.

A PROPOSED FINANCIAL MODEL

The will to establish a space presence is the issue that must be considered since a majority of Americans react to the colonization of Mars as interesting science fiction or at least a low-priority goal. Few people are receptive to proposals for a manned mission to Mars. A forecast by George Washington University of 85 emerging technologies placed manned flights to Mars in the time frame of 2037.[3] An approach must be taken so that space utilization is seen as a win/win situation. The premise is if the project will create wealth and significant jobs then it will be politically desirable.

A project of this size will involve all segments of the economy and provide economic stimulus for many years. The key is to provide financing of a long-term project without the problems of current deficit spending. A new financial model is needed for the planetary venture.

Can a financial model be developed that would use the assets of Mars as collateral and be accepted by the public?

Picture a circle with a radius of 400 miles on the surface of Mars, which represents the Mars colony. Divide the circle into 60 sectors with one sector belonging to each state and the other 10 sectors reserved for the federal government. In the center imagine an area for the Mars Port. Each of these 10 degree of radii would be used by each state as collateral for their part in the construction of the transportation system. Each state's area would be over 5 million acres of land. For this model the value of this land will be based on what it would be worth in 100 years. The exact total value of "funds available" is the function of the radius and the value set per acre; the time in the future payback is made so the total amount can be adjusted. We can send the accountants off to come up with the ideal number. But let us assume the following. If in 100 years an acre of Martian land is worth $10,000, each state now has assets worth over $600 billion. Each state would use the future value of the Martian land today to back the establishment of the Mars Transportation System (MTS). To this point what is being proposed is little different from selling land in Florida. We need to translate the money sitting on Mars 100 years in the future to something of value on Earth today.

Stock could be sold in the company with a 100-year payback. If it is assumed that each acre is worth $10,000, in 100 years the value of the 400-mile radius circle would be worth more than $3 trillion. If it requires $1 to $2 trillion to put the system in place, that would allow only $1 trillion for debt service—not a good rate of return. You could extend the radius of land leased until you got a reasonable rate of return, but that would decrease the future value per acre. The problem with this model is the debt service.

Can a model be developed where the debt service is not a problem? The approach should account for the interest and at the same time help the project win wide popular acceptance. Instead of selling stock in Mars land at a future value, a financial instrument could be created that would be used as currency to pay for the MTS project. This slight modification to the normal stock approach would help eliminate the long-range debt-service problem and provide immediate return on the investment to the nation. To make the venture even more acceptable, it is proposed that the spending of this currency be directed towards real assets that will contribute to a nation's wealth. We would get the value of our investment up front (think of this as the interest on the value of the land). For this exercise assume the four areas in which the currency could be used by the consumer to purchase items. They are health, education, home mortgage, and anything to support the project.

The proposed financial instrument would have different characteristics depending on the maturity and the holder of the instrument. In the near term (first 10 years after issue), the instrument would be used as payment for services to individuals working on the project but could only be used by the individual to purchase a limited set of products. The individual employees could use the instrument to pay for education, medical expenses (insurance or treatment), or for their personal home. The products purchased would directly or indirectly add to the assets of the nation. The organizations (health or education) from which these services or products were bought could only use the financial instrument for physical assets in their line of endeavor. The financial instrument (vouchers) could also be used for buildings and equipment in the MTS program by businesses engaged in the project. Contractors who successfully win bids for the various parts of the MTS would use the MTS vouchers to purchase supplies and labor for the project. If hard cash was required, businesses and/or states could finance the additional money requirements using tax credits, issuing company stock, etc.

The object is to use the Mars Financial Instrument to add to the nation's assets through the well-being of the people and to increase the physical assets of a nation. Banks would accept the financial instrument as cash for the first 10 years and could turn the instruments into the Treasury for funds or keep them in their portfolios. The Mars Financial Instrument would end up in banks as payment for loans or with individuals as investments for future generations. In 100 years the Financial Instrument, no matter if in private or commercial hands would become stock in the MTS.

By taking the 100-year time frame, the MTS can be amortized to the point that it is financially viable. If the total MTS cost is $1 trillion, you have $10 billion a year to pay on the principal. The operation and maintenance costs will be another $2 billion to $3 billion a year. If you use the concept of building the nation's assets as the interest payment, the interest is paid up front and there are no interest payments. The cost of the planetary transportation system is $12 billion a year. As a comparison, NASA's current budget is $15.5 billion a year and the shuttle program is 40% of the budget or $6.2 billion a year.[4] For two shuttle programs we could go to the moon, Mars, and the asteroid belt whenever we like.

If the Mars Transportation System Project is successful, the individuals will have provided their progeny with a sizable inheritance and the banks can convert "Financial Instrument" to stock for a profit. If the project is not successful, the government can extend the 100 years for conversion to stock or allow the banks to forgive the bonds over time.

The above suggested financial approach is provided as a start towards looking for positive ways to pay for the development of space. It may not be a wholly practical or optimum approach of getting the benefits from the exploration of the planets. That is why it is proposed that the economic/financial community develop new economic approaches. The economic/financial community needs to be encouraged to develop a methodology and/or a financial instrument that addresses the intellectual value of a nation as an asset and one that can fund long-range projects. There are several ways this could occur. The economic/financial community could accept the challenge and sponsor the development of an approach, private organizations can offer a prize for an approach, Congress can form a commission to call leading economic/financial personnel together to work on the problem, or the president could issue an executive order to call a group together. The first step in a creditable movement from Earth is to develop an acceptable financial instrument for long-range projects that does not jeopardize short-range economics. We have the scientific intellect that can get us to the planets, but we have not developed the intellect to pay for the process other than using outdated financial methodologies.

WHY NOW

A successful space program will require the acceptance of the general public, not just the scientists and former "Trekkies." As the world attempts to become more integrated, there is more indication that the United States is heading toward long-term financial problems. The population is getting older, causing Social Security concerns and the need for better health benefits. There is the need to change some of our infrastructure to protect us from long-term terrorism threats. There is the shift of high-pay manufacturing and white-collar jobs to other nations, requiring a better and more dynamic education system.

Given the right financial vehicle, this is an opportunity where the space program could energize the national economy and position the nation as a leader in space. By using the vouchers earned on MTS, people could pay for their or their children's education. The education community could use the vouchers for the building and equipping of schools, thus freeing funds for paying educators. By providing funds for more medical facilities and equipment, the MTS could make overall health costs more affordable.

This effort could also assist in keeping technical skills in the United States. One thing that caught most economists off guard in the free trade/outsourcing area was the Internet, which allowed for the loss of mid-level jobs like accounting and engineering. Involving the states in the MTS project would provide incentive for their support by assuring them that they could control the work that would be accomplished in their state.

A second level of problems created by outsourcing that is often ignored by economists because they are looking at the job and not the person doing the job is the individual's capabilities and likes. Many people have skills and creative abilities that use their minds and hands. When farming was replaced by manufacturing it was not a great leap for people to go from working on a farm to working with their hands in manufacturing. But as we have seen, going from manufacturing to information jobs is a greater leap, and some people end up in areas where the pay may or may not be equal to manufacturing. Building a space transportation system will help maintain a hands-on, highly technical manufacturing capability in the nation.

Given the transportation system and the financial model, there are several ways we could proceed with the building of the MTS. It could be broken up in pieces and put out for bid as a normal large project. A slightly different approach would be to involve the states, letting each state develop methods to do a part of the project using the state's universities and businesses to design and manufacture a part of the project. This would allow each state to develop technology for the space industry and would allow the states to assure, if they want, that the jobs the industry develops stay in the state. This would provide jobs plus help the states' education and health areas. With 50 different models, many useful methods would be developed that could be applied to other areas of endeavor. The opportunities are limited only by our imagination and initiative.

SUMMARY

An integrated space transportation model needs to be designed. A financial model that allows for a long-term payback needs to be developed and accepted by the financial community. Finally, the nation needs to be energized to the project, perhaps by having state involvement.

This may be rocket science, but working with the political,

academic, and commercial segments of the nation at all levels, local, state and national, establishment of a viable planetary transportation system is a sound political and economic venture that we as a nation may want to embrace to open the doors to a new area of endeavor for the nation.

NOTES

1. For a more detailed discussion on the conference and the subjects below see Edward L. Hudgins, *Space: The Free-Market Frontier* (Washington, DC: Cato Institute, 2002).

2. Robert Zubrin, with Richard Wagner, *The Case for Mars* (New York: The Free Press, 1996).

3. "Emerging Technologies: What's Ahead for 2001-2030" by William E. Halal, Michael D. Kull and Ann Leffmann, *The Futurist*, November-December 1997, 20-28.

4. "Mission to Mars," by Thomas, Cray, Hylton, Liston, Roston, Sikora, Bird and Forney, *Time*, January 24, 2004, 42-50.

RECREATIONAL FUTURES

THE FUTURE OF SPORT

by

Robin Gunston

INTRODUCTION

In preparation for my participation last year at the ACE-Arena international sports conference held in Greece, involving 800 people from over 160 countries, my mind was asking that perennial question all futurists grapple with constantly, "Why?" In my case the questions were these:

> "Why was a poor country with a long heritage of Olympic tradition getting itself into substantial long-term debt by hosting the 2004 Olympics?"

> "Why are we seeing enormous worldwide growth in people watching sport and at the same time growing obesity and non-participation by younger people?"

> "Why has sport replaced traditional religions in some countries?"

> "Why has sport attracted and even become big business?"

This line of questioning led me to contacting a number of futurists in different countries who have encouraged me to examine the future of sport. This paper is therefore an overview and is not intended to be exhaustive in the true sense of classical futures studies. My desire is that it may lend itself to many such studies that will aid us in creating a new future for sport that regains some of its ancient meaning and purpose.

A POTTED HISTORY OF SPORT

The Council of Europe defined sport as "all forms of physical activity, which through casual or organized participation, aim at expressing or improving physical fitness and mental well being, forming social relationships or obtaining results in competition at all levels." This is a good test to put to any new future of sport.

The Ancient Olympics, which commenced in Olympia in 776 BC, are often hailed as the true historical roots of competitive sport, especially of amateurism. Crowther[1] writes, "Visiting the Olympic Games was a popular activity in the ancient world but one which was full of danger and hardship for those travelling either by land or by sea, even with the benefit of the sacred truce. At Olympia itself the treatment of both athletes and spectators was harsh. Food, water

Robin Gunston *is chairperson of the New Zealand Futures Trust Inc. in Wellington, New Zealand. He may be contacted at robing@busdevclub.co.nz.*

and accommodation were at a premium and the sporting facilities were poor. Visitors endured such primitive conditions for various reasons including the concept of victory, the religious experience, the spectacle itself, the opportunities for trade and meeting people and the cultural, educational and aesthetic ideals." The Games at Olympia, which were only one of four in Ancient Greece, were part of the whole development system of a democratic nation seeking to balance its education system around knowledge, culture, religion, and physical agility. Competitors in these events were well known, often political figures or military leaders who competed as much for raising awareness of their fitness for other more important tasks as for the glory it personally brought them. Prizes, though, were few unless one highly valued rotting celery or a laurel leaf!

Religious influences have always been associated with much of early sports' development. Each of the Pan-Hellenic Games was dedicated to a god or goddess, with its accompanying rituals usually being sexually driven, which may account for some of the antics that reportedly goes on in modern Olympic villages! In the early 19th century it was often the Church that became the instigator of organized events in a community or in its schools, especially as working hours gave people more time to indulge in other leisure activities. Yet it was in AD 393 that a Christian Emperor, Theodisius, finally put a stop to the Ancient Olympic Games on the grounds that it was a pagan religious festival. One might wonder, what he would think of the modern spectacle?

Sports have also been influenced by the type of work performed at various points in history. Armies and navies up until modern times needed people with high levels of fitness and strength, and their training manuals record the playing of team games as well as regimented physical exercise.

Sports have been a social class separator, in which a few were the exclusive rights of nobles and kings. Both real tennis and horse racing started within royal circles many centuries ago, and motor racing could only ever be indulged in by those with considerable wealth. Even today polo is mainly associated with wealth and royalty in its playing nations.

Amateur team sports started to surface in an organized way in the 19th century, often following on from their introduction at English public schools and universities or their counterparts in other developing countries. The rules of Rugby Football were first adopted in 1848, and the Football Association came into being in 1863, although it had almost self-destructed by 1867.

Professionalism is still a "dirty" word in some modern sports, yet it has been a topic of discussion from whenever sports were played in a serious way. In ancient times villages might pay for their champion to attend a Games because of the glory it might bring them; in Victorian English society it was considered "unsporting" to pay a gentleman but acceptable to provide a financial incentive for someone from a lower social class to play for one's club, often as a compensation for lost wages. Leadership in professionalism has often come from those players from outside of the area where the sport is governed; e.g., the Australian tennis players Rod Laver and Ken Rosewall led the way for professionalism to come to dominate virtually all elite areas of sport today. Peter Williams[2] comments, "As rugby union's development in the late 20th century brought it to resemble other professional team sports, the Rugby Football Union remained steadfast in retaining the game's officially amateur status. There was a critical period in which a combination of events set in motion forces for change the authorities would be unable to contain. This turning point in the sport's recent history caused the RFU to defend its increasingly isolated position against three separate, though related, pressure groups: the senior English clubs, the national team and the progressive elements on the International Rugby Board."

Major events have been the most significant change on the 20th century sporting landscape. Beyond the Olympics, major spectator sports have moved to a system of World Cups for their events, often on a four-yearly cycle. These are mass-marketed spectaculars where the sport is sometimes incidental to everything else that goes on around it. Devoted fans spend vast amounts of money to go on overseas tours built around their team's games in the tournament interlaced with other forms of tourism to the host country. Unfortunately this is sometimes accompanied by undesirable behavior, which taints the sporting event itself.

Wars and politics seem to have an inextricable link with sport, perhaps stemming from George Orwell's quotation that sport is "war minus the shooting." Events such as the Moscow Olympics boycott of 1980, the Springbok tour to New Zealand of 1981, and the soccer war between El Salvador and Honduras following a World Cup (which claimed over 5,000 lives) come readily to mind, but a closer examination of many such events back through history shows that sport was sometimes deliberately used as a tool of imperialism by many nations. Today, the importance of sport is often recognized at a transnational level by the visits of the head of the IOC, which take on the full paraphernalia of state visits.

CURRENT TRENDS

As futurists we want to document and analyze the key trends that we perceive may lead to different possible future end states for sport. The key ones that I believe will have the most impact and uncertainty are:

Sport as Entertainment

In their essay "Australian Sport in a Postmodern Age,"[3] Bob

Stewart and Aaron Smith show that sport has been transformed by the process of postmodernization. "The process began in the late 1960s when Australian sport threw away many of its moralistic pretensions and repressive formality, and locked itself into the corporate world. By the 1990s, a number of professional sport leagues had emerged as amateurism lost its snobbish appeal and sport went about building its commercial value. Corporate signage saturated the major venues, and players were marketed as celebrities. Excitement, speed, the 'quick grab,' and sensory bombardment became the defining features of the spectator experience. Spectacular and dramatic contests became just as important as skill and aesthetic display. Fans increasingly narrowed their attention span, but were no longer bound by a parochial tribalism. They took on multiple identities that could shift from an elite European soccer team one week, to a suburban Brisbane rugby team the next. At the same time, branding and image making were used to re-position leagues and major events, and attract fans and corporate supporters. Moreover, the television programmer became the final arbiter on how the game should be scheduled and played. The Sydney 2000 Olympic Games convincingly demonstrates that Australian sport has become a chaotic mix of ancient ritual, traditional athletic contests, slickly marketed and customized leisure experiences, and ultra-professional sports that combine complex strategy with Hollywood-style showmanship."

Sir Dennis Follows, chairman of the British Olympic Association, said as far back as 1983, "We have now reached a stage where sport at top level has become almost completely show business with everything that one associates with show biz; the cult of the individual, high salaries, the desire to present a game as a spec-tacle—with more money, less sportsmanship, more emphasis on winning. All this has come about through television."

The trend has continued with some of the largest TV audiences ever recorded being for sports events. A recent scan of cable TV channels in the USA showed viewers in one state having 27 sports channels to choose from, covering some "sports" that one wonders who the audience might possibly be!

Yet can this trend go on for ever? Both ESPN and NBC stated over 10 years ago that their networks no longer had any "must see" events, including the Olympics, which only survives financially on such revenue as well as the sponsorship of companies like McDon-ald's. Many sports bodies, participants, and viewers are also starting to resent the intrusion of the TV scheduler and advertisers into the flow of the game.

Team Versus Individual

An emerging trend which seems set to continue is the demise of team sports and the ascendance of the individual sport. This trend seems closely associated with changes to work/life balance and the culture of individualism so apparent in most of Generation X.

Team sports rely heavily, in the amateur phases, on the volunteer based club management and coach. Long-term volunteerism is in rapid decline in most areas of modern society, and the financial strains of operating sports clubs is a major contributor to this. In many developed countries schools no longer form the basis for sports developments, as teaching pressures force teachers out of extra duties, but the community is unable to pick this up because of its lack of resources. There would not appear to be any driving forces on the horizon that will change this trend.

The modern worker too is forced to balance his or her participation in organized sports with the demands of the workplace and home life. With the demise of the standard office/factory working day and the trend towards multiple jobs there is little ability to commit to a regular training schedule for a team sport. Thus the serious fitness addict or sporting person is turning more and more to individual pursuits—triathlons, marathons, the personal fitness regimen at the gym, Ironman competitions, etc., to achieve his or her prowess. It should be noted that such events are also a lot harder to attract TV or paying viewers to.

Ownership of Clubs

The majority of team sports in professional leagues e.g., baseball, basketball, soccer and rugby—are becoming franchised business operations whose ownership takes on many shapes and forms. Baseball took an early lead in this with clubs being owned by a business and employing players on salaries. Clubs regularly change hands for colossal sums and sometimes the entire team changes cities as the new owners are based elsewhere and want their team under their control. Recently, a Russian bought Chelsea FC and a New Zealand businessman bought the premier Rugby League team.

Business owners, however much they may like a sport or a club, want one thing above all else—a better than normal rate of return on their investment. Inevitably, this trend will create demands on coaches and players that, like the infamous Chicago White Sox "game throwing" incident of 1919 in the World Series, or the Indian cricket gambling controversy over the last few years, will eventually result in the true essence of sport being lost because of the need to win at all costs.

Terrorism

One normally perceives terrorism to be more of a wild card than a trend as it usually seeks publicity about a cause from capturing the public interest by staging a dramatic event, e.g., the Munich Olympic siege. Now, however, modern terrorism is seen as an international movement, constantly with us, seemingly inspired by hatred for all things Western/American, which disturbingly leads to trends that over time we could see infiltrating sport at all levels. The modern terrorist worldview sees the future in a different way and is prepared to take time to accomplish its ends, planning for events yet to take place many years hence. Today, there may already be selected athletes and sportspersons being trained not only to excel at the highest levels but also to be able to completely disrupt major events in the years to come. Imagine a winning World Cup team clutching the Jules Rimet trophy and blowing themselves up with it on the podium!

Designer Drugs and Sportspeople

The trend for sportspeople to enhance their performance through substances is not a modern one. Records of the Ancient Games show athletes selectively feeding on herbs for many weeks before such major events.

It was not until 1969 that robust analytical techniques were used for drug detection in sports, and since then both coaches and pharmaceutical interests have been trying to find drugs that get around the testing regimen. When testers catch up, athletes inevitably end up losing—their records, their medals, their sponsorships, and their reputations.

In 2003, a new human gene was discovered—the so called "speed gene" in people from East Africa, and geneticists hailed the day when a purpose-built athlete could be cloned! Perhaps the first speed baby is already with us.

A 2004 announcement from the American Association for the Advancement of Science shows how far this trend in enhancement has come. "Combining genetic manipulation and weight training in rats yields leg muscles that are bigger and stronger than the muscles of rats exposed to just one of these two muscle-building techniques, according to a new study. These findings will frame a discussion at the 2004 AAAS Annual Meeting on potential uses of genetic enhancement in competitive sports, from the perspective of athletic organizations, athletes, scientists, and ethicists."

High-Technology Equipment

Technology trends worldwide indicate that we are approaching a convergence in technologies that will soon see completely new forms of artificial intelligence based machinery taking over areas of human activity within the next 20 years.

Sport is no exception to this high-tech world. One can go to the local sports store and plug oneself into a machine that will fit each individual foot with a designer sports shoe for the particular sport and the particular performance enhancement one requires to perform better. At the golf range the computerized swing analyzer will tell you what shaft length is required, what club head and what ball gives one the greatest distance. In athletics, specially designed field event equipment has been known to give one athlete over a meter in distance over his competitor by tuning the characteristics of the athlete and the stadium together. In motor sport and America's Cup yacht racing technologists sit amidst a vast array of computerized analysis systems taking race data, analyzing it, and sending it back to the driver or helmsman to make minute corrections that might win them the race. It may not be long before a humanoid robot sits in the driving seat of a Formula One car and the champion driver sits under the grandstand or in an apartment at a beach in another country driving the car remotely. The only time the fans or officials will suspect the difference is when the champagne flows and the robot shorts out!

The Sports Industry

Sport is no longer a way of life, it is BIG business. As far back as 1959 a survey of 20 sports in the USA showed an expenditure of $18 billion. A similar report from the United Kingdom on the economic impact of sport found it accounted for 367,000 jobs, and the industry was bigger than the agricultural, chemical, and motor industries.

Over a 20-year period there has been a 10,000% increase in sports sponsorship, affecting every possible sport imaginable—even sheep shearing! Most professional sports cannot afford to operate without guaranteed TV rights payments and commercial sponsorship. Even at the amateur level, club finances are reliant on the local sportswear store to provide the kit, and the local butcher or hardware store may have its name adorning the shirts or the goalposts.

Will this trend continue? It is believed by many different commentators that we have reached a point of discursion. As the economic, environmental, and social results of business are being equated in the minds of ethical investors, many large businesses are finding it difficult to account for the benefits that such sponsorship actually brings in the marketplace, especially where the sport supported or a major team has a poor reputation in some way. Our local sports stadium has had many corporate boxes standing empty since its inception, and New Zealand lost some of the game hosting rights for the last Rugby World Cup mainly because of arguments between the IRB and stadium sponsors over advertising. In Australia, almost an entire rugby team has been recently accused of pack rape—if convicted one will not be able to see their sponsor distance themselves fast enough!

Without sponsors there will be no teams or individual superstar sportspeople; without teams there will be no leagues; without leagues there will be no major competitions; without major competitions there will be no sports TV, no merchandising, no corporate boxes; and thus it goes on.

So what will the future of sport be?

Drivers of Change

The drivers of change in sport, particularly those associated with business and professionalism, appear to have seriously undermined the entire value of sport to society.

Sport has become a career and an enterprise that appears to have lost much of its original values base and its idealism, at the behest of power brokers within governments, business, and modern-day society.

To examine where sport is heading we need to identify the key drivers of change. There are five that would appear to be fundamental to understanding where sports as we know it may move to in the future:

- Work and leisure—the loss of a clear definition between the two is creating a change to the types of sports played.

- Instant society—the drive for instant entertainment is placing high demands on sportspeople and the industry.

- Mogulism—the drive by media companies to own our allegiance to their ideas and businesses to their products and services is dictating more control of sporting performance and behavior.

- Transnational politics—as sports bodies, e.g., IOC, ICC, IRB, become neo-political entities they are controlling key aspects of the destiny and sovereignty of sporting nations through their decisions.

- Religious vacuum—the loss of a conscience and core values in society due to the waning influence of the church creates a spiritual vacuum into which sports may fall and take its place.

SOME POSSIBLE FUTURE SCENARIOS FOR SPORT

From these drivers of change four possible future long term scenarios appear to emerge:

Religiosport, where major sport has replaced conventional religion and become a self-perpetuating entity with its shrines (stadiums), costumes (strips), its services (games/events), its rituals (chants and songs), its High Priests (the Beckhams and Lomus), and its fanatical demands on fan loyalty and fiefdom.[4] It has established and encourages a set of values that promote selfishness and anti-social behaviors and it actively condones violence against rival sects (teams). In places some governments have put a ban in place on its activities, limiting the rights of the followers.

Machosport is a future where individual sportspeople are the instant popular idols of the time, feasted and fêted wherever they go, promoted by the entire media circus, and displayed as being the ideal of modern man or woman. In this scenario, knowing about the sport is incidental to knowing about the person. It is increasingly associated with the worst forms of idolatry and leads to individuals losing their human rights and respect. Supporters form fan clubs for individuals instead of participating in the sport. As their heroes get older they pass, with their "sport," out of existence.

Technosport is the scenario alluded to in the trends above when reaching top performance is everything and ethics counts for nothing. At this stage the sport exists and is managed entirely by large businesses which appoint the sports administration body and control all aspects of the sport's development, rules, competitions, etc. The individual player, coach, or manager is only a pawn in winning at all costs, the crown being a better promoted product, or the adulation for creating higher value teams than someone else has. In this scenario only two international sports eventually remain—soccer and basketball, with most nations only having one team.

Valuesport is the scenario driven in a large part by a necessary response to the wild card events of the 200x Olympiad where the action of global terrorists and the impossibility of funding the event due to a last minute pullout of the biggest media empire in the world over naming rights, meant the cancellation of the Olympics and the end of the Modern Games. In this and most other scenarios, health specialists, trying to cope with the vastly increased death rates stemming from obesity and lack of fitness, have lobbied governments for a return to a different style of sports participation at all levels of society. Advertising is no longer permitted to be linked to sports, and all teams participating in healthy competition are backed by their community supported by additional local taxes on unhealthy products such as alcohol, certain drugs, and tobacco.

A NEW EMERGING FUTURE—GLOBAL COMMUNITY GAMES

A rational person can see that to benefit the future of our societies "Valuesport" is a preferred scenario, but how could we turn everything around now and not wait for the eventuation of any of the other possible scenarios?

The key is in the building up of underlying values that must be recreated to support the future participation in sport because of the vast void of values we have at present. These values have to be continually reinforced through many avenues, including a more sensitive media, to ensure that sport does not get captured by other interests, as history has shown us has already occurred.

Fortunately this work has already begun, quietly without fanfare. For the past four years an international group of sportspeople and community workers have been collaborating and bringing about such a change. It all started with the dream of a Spanish woman many years ago and has now built into a self-perpetuating, collaborative volunteer force worldwide who are using a simple experiential learning model used with sports and games and values derived from Bible stories, to get people of all ages involved in improving their physical, moral, and spiritual health. Many sporting champions have also lent their support to the program by appearing at some of the Opening and Closing Ceremonies of KidsGames, TeenGames, EdgeGames and FamilyGames[5] to encourage people of all ages to reach their goals. Some of these events have been the largest sporting events ever held in their cities or countries.

Therefore the largest sports "event" of lasting value in 2004 will not be the Athens Olympic Games. It will be something much grander, the continuing building of a values-based movement committed to ensuring that sport has a real future—*Global Community Games*.

REFERENCES

Coe, Sebastian, David Teasdale, and David Wickham. *More Than a Game*, BBC Books, 1992.

NOTES

1. Nigel Crowther, "Visiting the Olympic Games in Ancient Greece: Travel and Conditions for Athletes and Spectators," *Journal of History of Sport*.
2. Peter Williams, "Battle Lines on Three Fronts: The RFU and the Lost War Against Professionalism," *Journal of History of Sport*.
3. Bob Stewart and Aaron Smith, "Australian Sport in a Postmodern Age," *Journal of History of Sport*.
4. Ian Harris, *The Dominion Post*, Wellington, New Zealand, November 22, 2003.
5. www.globalcommunitygames.com.

PHILOSOPHICAL INSIGHTS/VALUES

FUTURE LIFE-FORMS AMONG POSTHUMANS

by

José Luis Cordeiro

Popular culture is abuzz with new terminology. Genetic engineering. Cyborgs. Artificial intelligence. Consciousness (mind) uploading. Nanotechnology. Singularity. Transhumanism. Posthumanism. In particularly, the terms "transhuman" and "posthuman" seem to be gaining more and more currency with each passing year—especially in the media and academia and among the techno-intelligentsia.

Yet, as futurists make these grand prognostications, do we really know what's in store for *Homo sapiens*? Just *how* will we "improve" ourselves? What do we really mean when we refer to the posthuman physical condition? Just *what*, exactly, is the grand potential for intelligent life? What does advanced intelligence look like?

The world is moving fast towards a fourth wave (following the terminology of US futurist Alvin Toffler) in which humans will become transhumans, and then posthumans, thanks to the multiple and simultaneous advances of technology. We could redesign ourselves in any number of ways, and we have to examine radical scenarios for the evolution of the human species. Such a transcendental change has been described by some experts as analogous to when apes evolved into humans.

TRANSHUMANISM

As the possibility for conscious human redesign has emerged, so too has a philosophical movement that considers the implications. This approach to future-oriented thinking, known as transhumanism, works on the premise that the human species does not represent the end of human evolution but, rather, its beginning (see, for example, www.transhumanism.org). Transhumanism is an interdisciplinary approach to understanding and evaluating the possibilities for overcoming biological limitations through scientific progress. Ultimately, transhumanists hope to see technological opportunities expanded for people, so that they may live longer and healthier lives and enhance their intellectual, physical, and emotional capacities.

Transhumanism emphasizes that we have the potential not just to "be" but to "become." Not only can we use rational means to improve the human condition and the external world; we can also use them to improve ourselves, the human organism. And we are not limited only to the methods, such as education, which humanism (its philosophical precursor) normally espouses. Rather, transhumanists

José Luis Cordeiro *is co-founder of the Venezuelan Transhumanist Association, director of the Venezuelan chapter of the Club of Rome, and director of the Venezuelan node of the Millennium Project, Caracas, Venezuela. He may be contacted at jose@cordeiro.org.*

argue, we will have the means that will eventually enable us to move beyond what most would describe as human.

Transhumanists believe that, through the accelerating pace of technological development and scientific understanding, we are entering a whole new stage in the history of the sapient species. Advances in artificial intelligence, robotics, bioengineering, cloning, cryonics, nanotechnology, new energies, mind uploading, dietary restriction, "designer babies," cyborgs, molecular chemistry, telecommunications, space exploration, virtual reality, life extension and immortality will lead to substantial physical and mental augmentation, possibly converging at a "singularity" point.

The historical human desire to transcend bodily and mental limitations is deeply intertwined with a human fascination with new knowledge, which might be both inspiring and frightening. How these technologies are used could fundamentally change the ways in which our society functions and raises crucial questions about our identities and moral status as human beings.

ADVANCING TECHNOLOGIES, ADVANCING POSSIBILITIES

New developments in science and technology are occurring so fast that some might begin to overwhelm our capacities to adapt to change. Personal computers did not exist 30 years ago, cell phones did not exist 20 years ago, and the Internet (actually, the World Wide Web, www) did not exist 10 years ago. What will come in the next 10 years? And in the next 20 years? And beyond that? The British-born engineer and science-fiction writer Arthur C. Clarke claimed that "people tend to overestimate the short-term impact of new technologies and to underestimate the long-term impact."

In the biological sciences, similar achievements have been made since the discovery of the DNA structure in 1953, including new medicines, bioengineering, and cloning technologies. In 2002 a living creature—polio virus—was assembled piece by piece with several biochemicals by US scientists J. Cello, A. Pauli, and E. Wimmer in the New York State University. Cryonics and nanotechnology, for example, were also totally unknown just a few decades ago. Indeed, Clark said many years ago that "any sufficiently advanced technology is undistinguishable from magic."

The pace of change is not only very fast but it is also accelerating. Some experts, like US engineer Ray Kurzweil, even talk about a coming "singularity" where artificial intelligence and artificial life-forms will overtake human intelligence and human life in the coming decades. Slow biological evolution seems to be approaching fast a dead end: Our species will continue changing, not through the old and slow biological evolution but through the new and fast technological evolution.

Today many boundaries are blurring. Boundaries between birth and death, between virtual and real, between morality and immorality, between truth and falsity, between inner and outer worlds, between me and "non" me, between life and "non" life, even between natural and "non" natural. What is life? What is death? What is "non" life? What is natural life? What is "non" natural life? What is artificial life?

These are all deep questions for a new deep world of trans-humanism and subsequent posthumanism. The answers are compli-cated, and they might be so difficult for us to comprehend as many of our current problems might seem to monkeys, or even to ants. British writer H.G. Wells said it very well about a hundred years ago: "All that the human mind has ever accomplished is but the dream before the awakening."

MANY NEW EMERGING SPECIES

If we believe that biological evolution has reached a limit, what will come next? Finnish engineer Pentti Malaska tried to answer this question in 1997 during a speech in Brisbane, Australia, while he was president of the World Futures Studies Federation (WFSF). He talked about human-made non-human generations in the pipeline of evolution. Malaska described two major kinds of species (carbon-based humies and silicon/information-based high techies, as a rough simplification) and four minor kinds of global persona sapiens, as can be seen below:

FIGURE 1 - SPECIES OF GLOBAL PERSONNA SAPIENS

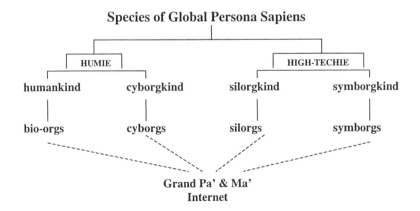

In such a posthuman world beings of other kinds, different from us (bio-orgs of *Homo sapiens*), may well be within the bounds of human invention. Malaska defined the other intelligent and conscious beings as:

- Bio-orgs or *Homo sapiens*—a protein-coded bio-organism in the earthly infrastructure as their "natural" surrounding.

• Cyborgs—a cybernetic organism—a combination of techniques and human biology mainly for the earthly infrastructure and the near space.

• Silorgs—a silicon organism—a humanlike non-human, fashioned by coding artificial DNA onto silicon compounds with ammonium as a solvent and aimed basically for outer space infrastructure.

• Symborgs—a symbolic organism—self-reflective, self-reproducing, self-conscious, "living programs" within the Internet as their "natural" infrastructure with advanced interface functions with the other species.

According to Malaska, Cyborgs of Cyborgkind, Silorgs of Silorgkind, and Symborgs of Symborgkind are "gestating, waiting to be brought to life." Finally, there is the Grand Pa'&Ma' Internet—a global mind with superior intelligence and wisdom. This Grand Pa'&Ma' Internet could be a Quantum Global Brain.

Australian economist Paul Wildman, also an active member of the WFSF, further talks about terrestrial and non-terrestrial Forms Of Life (FOL). Wildman uses the concept "borg" in its historical and generic sense to identify a "Bionic" (i.e., human made) "ORGanism," and defines five such terrestrial FOL borgs:

• Orgoborgs—organic FOL, including "traditional" Humborgs (like *Homo sapiens*) and new and hybrid bioengineered Bioborgs.

• GEborgs—Genetically Engineered FOL.

• Cyborgs—human/machine composite FOL.

• Symborgs—symbolical and symbological FOL, including Conscious/External (such as cultures and corporations) and Unconscious/Internal (such as myths and archetypes) FOL.

• Technoborgs—technological FOL, including Exoskeletalborgs (with an external insect-like skeleton) and Siliborgs (silicon-based FOL).

According to Wildman, some of these new FOL already exist in a technical sense, since 12% of the current US population could be considered incipient "cyborgs" that use electronic pacemakers, artificial joints, drug implant systems, implanted corneal lenses, artificial skin, etc. All the previous FOL are our creations and will be populating our world and remaking us genetically and mechanically and thereby changing our consciousness forever.

Wildman also briefly described four other non-terrestrial FOL. They are Macrorgs (macrocosmic FOL), MVorgs (Micro Vita—microscopic FOL), ETorgs (Extra-Terrestrial FOL), and Psyorgs (psychic FOL). Obviously, these exotic FOL depend very much on what definition of life is being used; but several unknown or not yet created intelligent and conscious entities will definitely pass the test of being "alive" and will satisfy most criteria under several concepts of "life."

Other authors have written about even more life-forms in a possible posthuman future, from the very physical to the very ethereal. A simple classification between carbon-based and silicon-based organisms seems like a good place to start. Such a concise system allows us to incorporate not just humans but also several types of robots, cyborgs, and symborgs (including different logical entities, both physical and nonphysical).

INTO THE FUTURE

US futurists Jerome Glenn and Theodore Gordon review possible scenarios for humanity in the year 3000 in the *State of the Future 2000* published by the Millennium Project (of the American Council for the United Nations University). They reviewed six scenarios with the following names:

1. Still Alive at 3000.
2. End of Humanity and the Rise of the Phoenix.
3. It's About Time.
4. The Great Divides.
5. The Rise and Fall of the Robot Empire.
6. ETI Disappoints After Nine Centuries.

These fascinating scenarios include frightening possibilities like the collapse of the human civilization and intriguing comments about the expansion of different forms of intelligent life to the rest of the universe. The scenarios were developed through a two-round questionnaire sent to a special panel selected by the Millennium Project nodes and the Foundation For the Future (FFF). Several factors were considered (from, for example, a global ethical system to the ability to destroy humanity) and their trajectory over the next 100, 500, and 1,000 years, with special attention to "unexpected" consequences.

The FFF is also doing some important work on the future evolution of humankind through its Humanity 3000 seminars and the preparation of its television series *The Next Thousand Years*, which is expected to be broadcast in 2006 with biannual program updates thereafter.

While the opportunities and possibilities for the future are mindboggling, the risks and threats to life itself are also very real. World-renowned scientists like Albert Einstein and Robert Oppenheimer were once deeply concerned about the perils of a nuclear holocaust, which we have managed to escape from so far. Those were the days of the Cold War, but many of those concerns are reappearing now with the rise of global crime and terrorism.

There is always the possibility of a complete collapse due to global warming, a new Ice Age, an asteroid collision, or major gamma-ray bursts, among many real threats to civilization. Several science-fiction works and the scientific literature also cite other existential threats to humankind, like the development of a non-friendly artificial intelligence or the "gray goo" effect caused by nanobots spreading out without any control. All these challenges have to be seriously considered by both current and future sentient life-forms in order to survive and thrive. In fact, UK scientist Stephen Hawking has warned that we need to consider moving to space if we want to avoid the extinction of human knowledge.

New technologies certainly bring new risks. On the one hand, US scientist Bill Joy wrote a controversial article, "Why the Future Doesn't Need Us," where he worries about robotics, genetic engineering, and nanotechnology. His answer is to relinquish and stop the development of these new technologies. On the other hand, US engineer K. Eric Drexler, usually called the "father" of nanotechnology, argues just the opposite: In order to avoid the problems of emerging technologies, we have to do more research and understand them better.

The debate is open, but one thing is certain: Humanity has always advanced thanks to science and technology. In fact, what makes humans different from other animals is the development of different technologies. This has been true since the very early prehistoric times when fire, the wheel, agriculture, and primitive writing first appeared on the face of our planet.

MORAL IMPLICATIONS

While humanity will undoubtedly express itself in a number of different incarnations, it will subsequently give birth to an entirely new form of life: artificial intelligence. The future will be populated by several different forms of intelligent life, and humanity is already attempting to reconcile the implications, particularly those in the moral realm.

The word "robot" was created in 1921 by the Czech playwright Karel Capek in his book *R.U.R.: Rossum's Universal Robots*. It was immortalized in 1950 by Russian-American scientist and writer Isaac Asimov in his book *I, Robot*, where he created the Three Laws of Robotics:

1. A robot may not injure a human being, or, through inaction,

allow a human being to come to harm.

2. A robot must obey orders given it by human beings except where such orders would conflict with the First Law.

3. A robot must protect its own existence as long as such protection does not conflict with the First or Second Law.

Asimov eventually improved his system and extrapolated the Zeroth Law: A robot may not injure humanity or, through inaction, allow humanity to come to harm. He also modified the other Three Laws accordingly.

On a separate front, US futurist Phil McNally and Pakistani-born futurist Sohail Inayatullah wrote *The Rights of Robots* in 1987, and US feminist Donna Haraway published *A Cyborg Manifesto* in 1991. Both are important documents that defend robots and cyborgs on their own right. These concepts imply a continuum based on previous ideas concerning animal and human rights.

US robotics expert Hans Moravec wrote two books about robots and our/their future: *Mind Children* in 1988 and *Robot* in 1998. Moravec argues that robots will be our rightful descendants, and he explains several ways to "upload" a mind into a robot. Similarly, US scientist Marvin Minsky, one of the fathers of artificial intelligence at MIT, wrote his very famous 1994 article "Will Robots the Earth?" in *Scientific American,* where he concludes: "Yes, but they will be our children. We owe our minds to the deaths and lives of all the creatures that were ever engaged in the struggle called Evolution. Our job is to see that all this work shall not end up in meaningless waste."

More recently, UK cybernetics professor Kevin Warwick has been implanting his own body with several microchip devices and published in 2003 a book titled *I, Cyborg* explaining his experiments. Warwick is a cybernetics pioneer who claims that "I was born human. But this was an accident of fate—a condition merely of time and place. I believe it's something we have the power to change.... The future is out there; I am eager to see what it holds. I want to do something with my life: I want to be a cyborg."

As these authors and thinkers suggest, we need to start preparing ourselves for the coming robot and artificial-intelligence realities. To ease the transition into a posthuman condition, we must ready ourselves for the distinct possibility that Earth will be inherited by not one, but several forms of highly intelligent and sentient life-forms.

THE HUMAN SEED

The human body is a good beginning, but we can certainly improve it, upgrade it, and transcend it. Biological evolution through natural selection might be ending, but technological evolution is only accelerating now. Technology, which started to exhibit some dominance over biological processes for the first time some 100,000 years ago, is finally overtaking biology as the science of life.

As US fuzzy logic theorist Bart Kosko has said: "Biology is not destiny. It was never more than tendency. It was just nature's first quick and dirty way to compute with meat. Chips are destiny." And photo-qubits might come soon after standard silicon-based chips, but even that is only an intermediate means for eternal intelligent life in the universe.

Humans are the first species that is conscious of its own evolution and limitations, and humans will eventually transcend these constraints to become posthumans. It might be a rapid process like caterpillars becoming butterflies, as opposed to the slow evolutionary passage from apes to humans. Future intelligent life-forms might not even resemble human beings at all, and carbon-based organisms will mix with a plethora of other organisms. These posthumans will depend not only on carbon-based systems but also on silicon and other "platforms" that might be more convenient for different environments, like outer space.

Eventually, all these new sentient life-forms might be connected to become a global brain, a large interplanetary brain, and even a larger intergalactic brain. The ultimate scientific, religious, and philosophical queries will continue to be tackled by these posthuman life-forms. Intelligence will keep on evolving and will try to answer the old-age questions of life, the universe, and everything.

In order to become permanent rational "demiurgi" of the known universe of space and time, it is vital to be aware that even more important than to create is not to destroy. With ethics and wisdom, humans will become posthumans, as US science-fiction writer David Zindell suggested:

"What is a human being, then?"
"A seed."
"A...seed?"
"An acorn that is unafraid to destroy itself in growing into a tree."

REFERENCES

Asimov, Isaac. *I, Robot*. (New York: Bantam Books [1950] 1994).

British Telecom. *Technology Timeline*. (London: British Telecom, 2002), www.btexact.com/white_papers/downloads/WP P106.pdf.

Capek, Karel. *R.U.R.* (New York: Dover [1921] 2001).

Clarke, Arthur C. *Profiles of the Future: An Inquiry into the Limits of the Possible* (New York: Henry Holt and Company, 1984 [revised]).

Cordeiro, José Luis. *Benesuela vs. Venezuela: El Combate Educativo del Siglo* (Caracas: Cedice, 1998), www.cordeiro.org.

Drexler, K. Eric. *Engines of Creation* (New York: Anchor Books, 1987), www.foresight.org/EOC.

Foundation For the Future. *The Next Thousand Years* (Bellevue, Washington: Foundation For the Future, 2002), www.futurefoun dation.org/documents/nty_projdesc.pdf

Glenn, Jerome, and Theodore Gordon. *State of the Future 2000: At the Millennium* (Washington, D.C.: Millennium Project, 2000), www.StateOfTheFuture.org.

Haraway, Donna. "A Cyborg Manifesto," *Simians, Cyborgs and Women: The Reinvention of Nature* (New York: Routledge, 1991), www.stanford.edu/dept/HPS/Haraway/CyborgManifesto.html.

Hawking, Stephen. *The Theory of Everything: The Origin and Fate of the Universe* (New York: New Millennium Press, 2002).

Inayatullah, Sohail. "Science, Civilization and Global Ethics: Can We Understand the Next 1000 Years?" *Journal of Futures Studies*, Vol. 5, No. 2, November 2000 (Taipei, Taiwan: Tamkang University, 2000).

Joy, Bill. "Why the Future Doesn't Need Us," *Wired*, April 2000. www.wired.com/wired/archive/8.04/joy.html

Kurian, George T., and Graham T.T. Molitor. *Encyclopedia of the Future* (New York: Macmillan, 1996).

Kurzweil, Raymond. *The Age of Spiritual Machines* (New York: Penguin Books, 1999), www.kurzweilai.net.

Malaska, Pentti. "Inventing Futures," Opening Address: WFSF XV World Conference. Brisbane, Australia: World Futures Studies Federation, 1997.

McNally, Phil, and Sohail Inayatullah. "Rights of Robots," *Futures*, Vol. 20, No. 2 (1988), 119-136, www.metafuture.org/Articles/TheRightsofRobots.htm.

Minsky, Marvin. "Will Robots Inherit the Earth?" *Scientific American*, October 1994, www.ai.mit.edu/people/minsky/papers/sciam.inherit.txt.

_____. *The Society of Mind* (New York: Simon and Schuster, 1987).

Moravec, Hans. *Robot: Mere Machine to Transcendent Mind* (Oxford: Oxford University Press, 1998), www.frc.ri.cmu.edu/~hpm/book97.

_____. *Mind Children* (Boston: Harvard University Press, 1988).

Paul, Gregory S., and Earl Cox. *Beyond Humanity: Cyberevolution and Future Minds* (Hingham, Massachusetts: Charles River Media, 1996).

Pearson, Ian. *Atlas of the Future* (New York: Macmillan, 1998).

Regis, Edward. *Great Mambo Chicken and the Transhuman Condition: Science Slightly over the Edge* (New York: Perseus Publishing, 1991).

Toffler, Alvin, and Heidi Toffler. *Creating a New Civilization: The Politics of the Third Wave* (Atlanta: Turner Publishing Inc., 1995).

Warwick, Kevin. *I, Cyborg* (London: Garnder's, 2003).

Wells, H.G. "The Discovery of the Future," *Nature*, 65 (1902), www.geocities.com/yokelcraig/hgwells1.html.

Wildman, Paul. *Life Futures: An Initial Taxonomy of Terrestrial and Non Terrestrial Forms of Life* (Brisbane, Australia: Metafuture), www.metafuture.org/articlesbycolleagues.htm.

World Transhumanist Association. *The Transhumanist Declaration* (New York: World Transhumanist Association, 2002), www.transhumanism.org/declaration.htm.

Zindell, David. *The Broken God* (New York: Acacia Press, 1994).

CREATIVITY, INNOVATION, AND VISIONARY THINKING: BECOMING ALL YOU CAN BECOME

by

Lynn Elen Burton

Be who you are and say what you want, because those who
mind don't matter and those who matter don't mind.
—Theodor Geisel, aka Dr. Seuss

Some people think that visionary thinkers and creative geniuses
are born extraordinary. Others believe that they are made. And each
and every one of us has the power to learn from these exceptional
individuals and exploit our own unique potentials to become
extraordinary in our own right.

In her book, *Breakthrough Creativity* (2001), Lynne Levesque uses
the Myers Briggs Type Indicator (MBTI), a personal preference tool
based on Carl Jung's eight ways of knowing, to show the unique
snowflake nature of individuals. She claims that relative to gathering
and remembering information, the great men Charles Darwin and
Claude Monet likely used the senses of touch, sight, smell, sound
and taste, or the MBTI Sensation Perceiving Function (S). In contrast,
Walt Disney and Albert Einstein probably used a sixth sense to
generate their "off-the-wall" creative ideas and far-reaching visions
for the future, or the MBTI Intuition Perceiving Function (N).

To sort, organize, and prioritize, Buckminster Fuller and Frank
Lloyd Wright probably preferred the Thinking (T) approach, for the
MBTI Judging Function. They would come to conclusions using logic,
objective reasoning, models, and systems. Conversely, Levesque
(2001) says that Mahatma Gandhi and Eleanor Roosevelt probably
used a values-based Feeling (F) approach to get people to work
together to achieve creative solutions to their problems.

Based on the Myers Briggs Type Indicator results, Levesque
(2002) identifies eight creative types. The above MBTI Perceiving and
Judging Functions are coupled with either Extraverted Attitude (E)
or Introverted Attitude (I) to determine the eight categories. The
creativity of the extravert draws energy from interacting with others,
whereas the creative results for the introvert are uniquely his/her
own.

According to Levesque (2001), the first creative type, the *Adventurer* (ES), is a skilled improviser while the *Navigator* (IS), the other
Sensing type, is a thoughtful adapter. Similarly, the *Explorer* (EN)
type pulsates with possibilities while the *Visionary* (IN) type has far-
reaching insights. The *Pilot* (ET) uses analytical strategies while the
Inventor (IT) shifts to new paradigms. And finally, the *Harmonizer*
(EF) seeks human solutions while the *Poet* (IF) seeks those that are

Lynn Elen Burton *is an associate professor of futures studies in the Department
of Humanities at Simon Fraser University in Vancouver, British Columbia, Canada.
She may be contacted at leburton@sfu.edu.*

values-based.

The *Adventurers* (Extraverted Sensing) are spontaneous, expressive people with vivid imaginations. But they also have a sharp eye for detail, shapes, colors, and textures. From what we know about him, we might speculate that Steven Spielberg is an *Adventurer.*

> Imagination is the key to our future.
> —*Adventurer* Steven Spielberg

Conversely, the *Navigator* (Introverted Sensing), Nobel Prize winner Linus Pauling, uses careful observation to guide his actions.

> I console myself with the thought that although they [other physicists] may be smarter and may be deeper thinkers than I am, I have broader interests than they have.
> —*Navigator* Linus Pauling

By breaking new ground and going beyond limits in pursuit of their creative ambitions, the Beatles show themselves as *Explorers* (Extraverted iNtuitive). Typically, *Explorers* posit new ideas, bring novel meanings, and create alternative and far-reaching solutions in many fields of endeavor. Few would challenge that the Beatles revolutionized modern music. They imported unconventional techniques and applied them to unconventional music.[1]

> But it does move.
> —*Explorer* Galileo after recanting that the earth moves around the sun

By substituting the Introverted Attitude for that of the Extravert, the *Visionary* (Introverted iNtuitive) attains significant insight into many future possibilities. For example, in addition to his magnificent artistic talent, Leonardo da Vinci foresaw parachutes, cannons, missiles, and submarines. This type also challenges society to be self-critical and to prepare for the challenges ahead. As he created and critiqued, *Visionary* Aldous Huxley viewed the dangers of scientific progress independent of morality.

The *Pilot* (Extraverted Thinking) has high personal standards and excels in analyzing trends and problems. This type is goal oriented and acts in accordance with his/her principles. Writer Ayn Rand and industrial philanthropist Andrew Carnegie might be examples of this creative type.

> Happiness is that state of consciousness which proceeds from the achievement of one's own values.
> —*Pilot* Ayn Rand

The *Inventor* (Introverted Thinking), on the other hand, uses careful, detached analysis to see how the world works. Nietzsche, Arthur C. Clarke, and physicist Stephen Hawking have created their own unique perspectives and models of how the world does and should work.

> My goal is simple. It is complete understanding of the universe, why it is the way it is and why it exists at all.
> —*Inventor* Stephen Hawking

Harmonizers (Extraverted Feeling), like Aung San Suu Kyi of Burma, Mahatma Gandhi, and Martin Luther King Jr., dedicate their lives to solving human problems and seeking justice.

> Injustice anywhere is a threat to justice everywhere.... We must learn to live together as brothers or perish as fools.
> —*Harmonizer* Martin Luther King Jr.

And the last creative type identified by Levesque (2001), the *Poet* (Introverted Feeling), reflects on life to make the "right" decisions. Dedicated to helping others, the *Poet's* personal values guide their actions and motivate their prescriptions for change.

> I am not a political figure, nor do I want to be one; but I come with my heart.
> —*Poet* Diana, Princess of Wales

Just like the snowflake, no two of us are exactly alike in every single way. We differ in our genetic makeup, intelligence, personality, education, and experience. But also, just like the snowflake, many snowflakes together can make a great difference. Depending on where we fall, we can block the streets, wreak havoc on humanity's diurnal existence, or we can beautify the earth and make it a better place to live. Either as individuals or in the complementary strengths of groups, we have the opportunity to learn from extraordinary people.

> You are only given a little spark of madness. You mustn't lose it.
> —Robin Williams

But what are the lessons that we can learn from extraordinary people? Professor Howard Gardner in *Creativity & Leadership: Making the Mind Extraordinary* (1998) observes that "creative people are creative regularly: creativity is a way of life, rather than a 'single great idea.'" They are always raising issues and asking questions. They are usually creative within a particular domain, although there are some exceptions. According to Gardner, the idea of excellence in a specific domain "is a marked departure from the IQ point of view."

Creativity is also culture specific. If society thinks it is creative, it is.

Through his studies of extraordinary people, Gardner rejects the notion that there is such a thing as "creativity in general." He believes that creators have different kinds of intelligences, much like the Theory of Multiple Intelligences. With the notable exception of prodigies, Gardner believes that extraordinary individuals are "made" not "born."

> Genius is 1% inspiration and 99% perspiration.
>
> —Thomas Edison

From his observations, Gardner believes the making of an extraordinary person requires framing, reflection, and leveraging. With reference to this, visionaries learn very early in life to "frame" their failures and the blocks that they encounter. Instead of giving up, they strive to learn lessons and achieve a greater understanding of their circumstances. Exceptional people tend to ignore failure by asking, "what can I learn from this?" and, "how can I turn this obstacle into an opportunity?" Going deeper and deeper into the same hole doesn't usually find the treasure. According to Edward De Bono (1992), new holes (ways of thinking) are often required.

> I have not failed; I've just found 10,000 ways that didn't work.... If we did all of the things we are capable of doing, we would literally astound ourselves.
>
> —Thomas Edison

Exceptional people frame their circumstances by being persistent, looking for opportunities, and demonstrating strength of conviction. They are often self-made, embrace paradox, are concerned about progress, and overcome difficulties. They demonstrate courage, determination, and self-motivation.

The current Dalai Lama is another visionary who demonstrates a remarkable capacity to "frame" the significant events that have altered both his life and the lives of others. For example, when driven out of his Tibetan homeland, he turned the exile into an opportunity. In December 1989, he was awarded the Nobel Peace Prize for his efforts. Today his message of peace and non-violence extends to all areas of the world.

> In the struggle between forces of war, violence and oppression on the one hand, and peace, reason, and freedom on the other, the latter are gaining the upper hand.
>
> —Dalai Lama, 2003

Another determinant of success that Gardner notes in his observations is the capacity of "visionaries" to reflect not only on where they have been but also on where they are going. If there are problems they adjust rudder. Many extraordinary people seem to be in a constant dialectic with their work, projects, or sets of projects. They do not proceed on blind faith but constantly confirm and re-confirm where it is they want to go, and how they plan to get there.

In reflecting, exceptional people often choose to go against the norm, such as advocating for peace in wartime. They are divergent thinkers, consider alternative perspectives, and often engage in creative problem solving. Exceptional people tend to be "workahol-ics" with significant output. They often broaden their perspectives through travel and teaching. As well, while they set high standards for themselves, they tend to expect the same from others, sometimes resulting in political actions.

> I could never convince the financiers that Disneyland was feasible because dreams offer too little collateral.[2]
>
> —Walt Disney

This, however, did not stop Disney. He believed in and doggedly pursued his dreams to make them reality. Likewise, without Orville's conviction that "human flight is both practical and possible,"[3] and the complementary support from his brother Wilbur, we would not now be celebrating 100 years of human flight.

Similar to Orville Wright's circumstances, in addition to framing and reflecting, Howard Gardner (1998) claims that extraordinary people need to "leverage" their strengths and supplement their weaknesses. This assumes that not all people are equally adept at all things and they need to find their niche(s). Extraordinary people do not lament this, but rather find their competitive advantage and push as hard as they can in this direction. They recognize and develop their talent(s). They demonstrate clarity of thought and discipline. They are innovators and often have huge influence, even after death. They are often multi-talented, prolific, visionary, and communicate their ideas in persuasive and unique fashion(s).

In leveraging, these extraordinary people find other people with talent to complement the areas in which they are weak. This is where a perceived deficit can be lessened by the talent of someone else in a creative team. Although Wolfgang Amadeus Mozart lived most of his life in poverty, he managed to leverage his tremendous musical talent to become one of the world's greatest composers. As well, Oprah Winfrey overcame immense childhood and racial disad-vantage, to leverage her exceptional communications ability and become a leading talk-show host and modern social icon. Indeed, her show "has remained the number one talk show for 17 consecutive seasons.... It is seen by an estimated 23 million viewers a week in the United States and is broadcast internationally in 109 countries, and is the highest-rated talk show in television history."[4]

In contrast, however, there are exceptions to the leveraging rule. Two notable exceptions are Gene Roddenberry, the creator of *Star*

Trek, and the great Renaissance man himself, Leonardo da Vinci. While Gene Roddenberry had faith in his own abilities, others surely regarded him as "foolish" when he left a secure pilot's job to pursue his interests as a screenwriter. Likewise, rather than focus on his "main" talent, Leonardo frequently left his canvas to embark on uncharted territory. He ventured into such diverse fields as aerodynamics, anatomy, botany, geology, hydrodynamics, and optics.[5]

In *How to Think Like Leonardo da Vinci,* author Michael Gelb identifies "Seven Steps to Genius Every Day." (1998) Gelb expands upon the eclecticism that personifies the Renaissance man. Da Vinci's creative genius was a rare admixture of creative and technical expertise, vision, and hard work, held together by the following:

Questionaire: Questing, an insatiable curiosity about life.
Dimostrazione: Testing knowledge through experience.
Sensazione: Continually refining through the senses.
Sfumato: Embracing ambiguity, paradox, and uncertainty.
Arte/Scienza: Balancing art and science, logic and imagination.
Connessione: Recognizing and appreciating the interconnectedness of all things.

Edward De Bono (1992) further says that serious creativity requires strong motivation—call it Leonardo's curiosity, if you would like. It also requires the attitudes of challenge (why do we do it this way?), possibility (are there alternatives?), provocation (this may be a crazy idea, but...), focus (what are we really trying to do here?), and creativity (belief that futures thinking can make a difference). Much like Michael Michalko (1998), De Bono also proposes a number of creative thinking techniques to support creative thinking productively, rather than reproductively.

In closing, research for and in the Simon Fraser University Futures Studies course, "Creativity, Innovation, and Visionary Thinking" (2002-2003) leads to the following conclusions. A "visionary," "creative genius," or "exceptional person" can have the power to help change the world. This power can be developed. It requires great awareness of one's individual talents and passion—the fire within and the drive to overcome obstacles.

"Visionaries" need to focus on what they want to do. They need to know what they excel at and be driven to realize their potential. Leonardo called it "curiosity." Exceptional people generally focus their curiosity. They often have mentors, are passionate, and practice, practice, practice.

Dreams are all but useless without reflective action. Creative geniuses work hard to both increase their knowledge and skills, and to pursue their visions. One cannot succeed if one does not try. Exceptional people are risk takers and do not fear ridicule. They define and maintain their uniqueness.

Both success and failure are seen as learning opportunities.

Exceptional people frame these experiences to increase future chances of success. They recognize their own shortcomings and draw strength from others without those deficits.

> If I have seen further, it is by standing on the shoulders of giants.
>
> —Isaac Newton

And finally, exceptional people harness their imaginations and create future scenarios, alternatives, and inventions. Creative inspiration comes from finding a perspective that no one else has taken, acting on your newly found knowledge, and then seeing the contribution that your efforts make to the betterment of humanity.

> May the force be with you!
>
> —George Lucas

REFERENCES

De Bono, Edward. *Sur Petition.* (New York: Harper Collins, 1992).

Gardner, Howard. *Creativity and Leadership: Making the Mind Extraordinary.* BCLC/Into the Classroom Media, 1998.

Gleb, Michael J. *How to Think Like Leonardo da Vinci: Seven Steps to Genius Everyday.* (New York: Dell Publishing, 1998).

Hart, Michael. *A View from the Year 3000–A Ranking of the 100 Most Influential People of All Time.* (Crofton, MD: Poseidon Press, 1999).

Imagination. ToInspire.com. Oct. 27, 2003. www.toinspire.com/quotes.

Levesque, Lynne. *Breakthrough Creativity.* (Palo Alto, CA: Davies-Black Publishing, 2001).

Michalko, Michael. "Thinking Like a Genius: Eight Strategies Used by the Super Creative, from Aristotle and Leonardo to Einstein and Edison," *The Futurist*, World Future Society, Bethesda, MD (May 1998).

My Favorite Quotes. Quotes. Nov. 14, 2003. www.grmhpetition.org/quotes.html.

The Nobel Lecture. Dalailama.com. Nov. 16, 2003. www.dalailama.com/html/nobel.html.

NOTES

1. It is interesting to note that, in two classes of Humanities course 381, "Creativity, Innovation, and Visionary Thinking" at Simon Fraser University, more than 80% of the students in the course were *Explorers* (Levesque, 2001) in their results from the Myers Briggs Type Indicator. This suggests a "chicken and the egg" type of

research question.

2. Imagination. ToInspire.com. Oct. 27, 2003. www.toinspire.com/quotes.asp?catid+22.

3. Inventing the Airplane. Wright Brothers Airplane Co. Oct. 17, 2003. www.first-to-fly.com/History/Wright/%20Story/inventin.htm.

4. Oprah Winfrey Biography. Oprah.com. November 20, 2003. www.oprah.com/about/press/about_press_bio.jhtml.

5. Leonardo da Vinci: Renaissance Man, Scientist. Museum of Science. November 2, 2003. www.mos.org/leonardo/scientist.html.

THE MATERIAL CULTURE OF HAPPINESS

by

Francesco Morace and Tiziana Traldi

Any field of knowledge, from religion, psychology, and economics to popular culture, has produced vast literature on happiness and on how to find the "magic formula" that increases individual and public well-being. Yet happiness seems, for most of us, something impossible to grasp, something that is just transitory, intangible, and certainly hardly possible to study following scientific venues.

However, the last decade has witnessed a new generation of studies on happiness from popular culture and, in particular, from the academic world that has made the study of happiness a proper field of knowledge. Like other social sciences, happiness is now "taught" in university programs and has a proper journal, called the *Journal of Happiness Studies*, edited by Ruut Veenhoven, professor of social conditions for human happiness at the Erasmus University in Rotterdam. Veenhoven believes that the conditions of happiness can be systematically collected and analyzed and that happiness can become a new fascinating discipline. Veenhoven argues that, as happiness research takes off, it will be possible to establish risk levels, individualize therapies, and give people proper "cures" in order to maximize well-being. As he claims, "We should be able to show what kind of lifestyle suits what kind of person." (*New Scientist*, April 10, 2003, p. 42.)

This idea seems to be positively confirmed by some recent "bibles" of happiness, like Stefan Klein's *The Happiness Formula* in which it is described as something achievable through learning and discipline. Klein argues that the secret is to teach your brain "how to see happiness" in day-to-day life. He also states that happiness has to be found individually and that "there is no one happiness formula but as many as the living people on the earth." Dalai Lama's *The Art of Happiness* follows the same idea. According to Lama, happiness is a discipline whose secrets need to be individually learned and applied to life. Seligman himself, the father of positive psychology and author of *Authentic Happiness* (2003), holds courses of happiness focusing on ways in which people can learn to see the positive side of our everyday life experiences. Interest in happiness also comes from the biological field in which some scholars, following a more positivist philosophy, contend that 50% of our happiness is genetically determined; it is written in a person's DNA at birth. The hereditary nature of happiness then mixes with our personality and, for the remaining 50%, people can positively influence the achievement of happy feelings and intentions (David Lykken, University of Minnesota).

Francesco Morace *is president of the Future Concept Lab, Milan, Italy.* Tiziana Traldi *is an associate at the Future Concept Lab, Milan, Italy. They may be contacted at labgroup@tin.it.*

What seems even more important, however, is that, out of the melting pot of the happiness stories, experts and politicians have started taking this data into account in virtue of a strong need for searching levels of well-being departing from pure economic principles. Hamilton's recent book *Growth Festish* (2003) can be seen as yet more evidence that the politics of today is in need of a change. Hamilton talks specifically of the unbridled pursuit of economic growth and its negative effects on society, effects so often ignored by political decision makers and mainstream economists who are unwilling to acknowledge the empirical evidence. One of the most significant observations, also confirmed by many surveys and statistics, is that in industrialized nations the average happiness has virtually remained constant since the end the Second World War, despite the significant increase of the individual level of income.

Economists like Richard Easterlin, Daniel Kahnemann (Nobel 2002), and Clive Hamilton write on happiness as a new perspective, a new way to raise the right questions that are primarily relevant to people. A possible positive reaction to all the talks on happiness comes from the British government, which has made a first attempt to take this data into consideration. The Cabinet Office has held a string of seminars on people's life satisfaction that is not based on the annual income only. The Prime Minister's Strategy Unit has published a paper recommending that policies that might increase people's happiness. The focus is on the quality of the public service and the sense of public security.

Happiness has also attracted the world of marketing and consumption. The underlying principle of the so-called "happy consumption" and "happy products" is not just a new form of hedonism but it can bring a tangible quality and innovation in product making using happiness as a new research venue. Future Concept Lab (FCL), as a research institute and as a group of sociologists and researchers who believe that happiness studies can make a significant impact in the world of consumption and public service, has carried out the first part of a cross-cultural study called "The Material Culture of Happiness." The basis of this independent research study aims to hear people's voice on happiness and identify the material basis that help people to construct and reinforce their day-to-day well-being. Our study therefore concentrates on "tangible happiness," on its daily expressions, its artifacts, its objects, products, places, people, etc.

For the occasion of "WorldFuture 2004," FCL will therefore illustrate this research program that provides an insight on day-to-day happiness experienced in eight European countries namely Spain, France, the United Kingdom, Italy, the Netherlands, Germany, Finland, and Russia. The research focuses on the material forms, images, and places that young adults (14-22) and mature adults (55-70) recognize as meaningful to the building of their day-to-day well-being.

The research has been carried out by employing a cocktail of in-depth methodologies that combine psychological methods and with qualitative fieldwork. Respondents have been asked to fill in a photo diary for a period of several days and taking photos to the "objects of their happiness," people, places, products, etc. Diaries have been followed by in-depth interviews with the respondents on the basis of ad hoc designed discussion guides that took into consideration people's cultural backgrounds, lifestage, and the content of the diary.

The result is a collection of 1,200 stories of happiness reported in people's own words and through visuals, symbols, and drawings. The result is the analysis of some key happiness trends divided by age, cultural difference, and specific areas of interest like, for example, Domesticity, Leisure and Consumption, Daily Responsibility, Relationship with the City, Nature, etc. For this reason the evidence we will be presenting at the World Future Society 2004 conference is, in our opinion, relevant for the academics but primarily for private sector companies themselves.

REFERENCES

Hamilton, C. *Growth Fetish* (UK: Pluto Press, 2003).

Lama, D. *The Art of Happiness* (UK: Coronet, Hodder & Stoughton, 1988).

New Scientist, April 10, 2003, 40-44.

Seligman, M. *Authentic Happiness: Using the New Positive Psychology to Realize Your Potential for Lasting Fulfillment*, (NY: Free Press, 2002).

INTERNET REFERENCE

www.number-10.gov.uk/su/ls/paper.pdf

TRIBE, EMPIRE, OR GLOBAL COMMONWEALTH?

by

W. Warren Wagar

THE CENTRALITY OF GOVERNANCE

The greatest question confronting the human race in the 21st century is not whether climate change will devastate our economies, or whether the progress of technology can avert impending shortfalls in the supply of energy, or whether international terrorism will require the creation of garrison states, or whether the globalization of capitalism will succeed or fail in expanding the wealth of all nations. In the final reckoning, what really matters is our response to the oldest of purely human challenges: how we choose, as tribes, as peoples, as the far-flung interdependent family of humankind, to govern ourselves.

Choose well, and all the other questions baffling us today could be answered readily. An appropriately governed world could prevent or cope with global warming, adopt alternative energy technologies or adjust to lower levels of energy consumption, eradicate the deep systemic causes of terrorism, trim or abolish megacorporate exploitation in the broad public interest, and solve many other pressing problems. The power of wise governance to improve the quality of life has been amply demonstrated in many countries in many ways throughout history, even if its full potential has yet to be realized anywhere.

Choose poorly, however, and the 21st century may be our last.

JIHAD VS. McWORLD

Our choices, at first blush, may seem quite limited. Especially since the appearance of Benjamin R. Barber's remarkable book *Jihad vs. McWorld* (1995) it has been a commonplace of political discourse to identify two sharply opposed and well-nigh irresistible forces at work in the post-Cold War world. One is centrifugal, the other centripetal. "Jihad" comprises all those movements fiercely determined to achieve full independence from the culture and politics of modernity through a militant reassertion of traditional tribal identities. "McWorld" denotes the thrust of international capital, from its chief strongholds in Western Europe, North America, and East Asia, to transform the whole world into a single marketplace with a single ideology and way of life. Both, Barber rightly fears, are antipathetic to the cause of democracy.

Some conservatives in the West, most notably Samuel P. Huntington, prefer to see Jihad as part of a larger "clash of civilizations,"

W. Warren Wagar *is a Distinguished Teaching Professor Emeritus at Binghamton University, SUNY, in Binghamton, New York. He may be contacted at wwagar@ binghamton.edu.*

which they invite their fellow Westerners to join as doughty contestants, not to engulf others but to preserve intact their own heritage. Expanding Barber's concept of McWorld, liberals warn of a sinister plot, hatched by henchmen in the administration of George W. Bush, to create an "American empire," a new world order in which the United States polices the planet to make it safe, not for democracy, but for McDonald's and Exxon.

Which, then, will it be in this new century? A balkanized world of hundreds of sovereign tribes each jealously guarding its sacred patrimony or a vast global shopping mall managed by a consortium of profiteering corporate giants under the protective shield of one or more capitalist superpowers?

Or should we cast Barber's dichotomy in a different light? Perhaps Jihad is actually just an ill-humored trope for the legitimate aspirations of peoples to lead their own lives as they choose, free from imperialism both political and cultural. Once all peoples enjoy self-determination, they will cease to quarrel and the Earth will be at peace. Or perhaps McWorld is a disparaging term for something quite noble and rational, a future in which the pursuit of prosperity replaces the lethal contests of politics, and (albeit for entirely different reasons) the Earth will also be at peace.

Nonsense. Let me cut to the chase. Whether one paints a sad or a happy face on these two great forces dominating contemporary history, I cannot believe that if and when we reach the 22nd century either one will be in charge of human destiny. Both will continue their malevolent competition for decades to come, with fortune favoring first one and then the other, but they will have exhausted their relevance well before the 21st century expires. Both are in fact excellent formulas for planetary disaster.

Not that self-determination of peoples or globalization of the economy are, in and of themselves, disastrous objectives. Within limits and under the appropriate circumstances they might be highly desirable objectives. All other things being equal, Palestinians and Israelis should not oppress one another, and the good folk of Shanghai should have the right to dine on the Colonel's fried chicken.

But all other things are not equal. In an interdependent world rife with disparities and asymmetries, no tribe acting unilaterally can or should determine its own fate. In an interdependent world of finite resources and masses yearning for social justice, globalization on market principles is neither sustainable nor fair. Jihad and McWorld not only fight one another, each gravely impeding the progress of its adversary, but together they ensure that human civilization will soon implode. Given the weaponry of mass destruction available to modern armed forces, the near-imminent disappearance of adequate supplies of fresh water and arable land and essential minerals including fossil fuels, the likelihood of major global climate disruption, the widening gap between rich and poor within and among nations, and the political and economic instability menacing the future of whole continents, Jihad and McWorld are helpless to save themselves, let alone civilization.

They are helpless because of what they are. The central mission of Jihad is to secure the greatest possible advantage for one's own tribe, whether it be Hutus or Tutsi in Burundi, Basques or Castilians in Spain, Hindus or Muslims in Gujarat. For numerous reasons, what is best for one tribe may be bad or even intolerable for its neighbors. Indelible facts of history, geography, and culture intercede time and again to make compromise difficult or even impossible. In time a durable modus vivendi may evolve, as has already happened in Scandinavia and may be happening in other parts of Western Europe, but there are few comparable examples in history. Meanwhile, wars and civil wars in the name of tribalism continue to cost the lives of millions and could someday pulverize our fragile world order.

McWorld, too, is helpless to save us. Its engine is the relentless search for profit through maximizing production and sales and minimizing the costs of both, above all the costs of labor. As Karl Marx himself testified long ago, no system of relations of production in world history has proven capable of generating material wealth in such abundance as capitalism. But it is not a sustainable system in the long term, because it concentrates too much of its wealth in the hands of the few, who cannot consume it all, and places demands on the carrying capacity of the Earth that it cannot meet. Producing all that we can produce this year in the expectation of producing still more next year, and so on throughout eternity, calls to mind the fate of Goethe's (and Walt Disney's) Sorcerer's Apprentice. It is certifiably insane, even if purchasing power were equal for all, which market logic ensures can never happen.

THE SANE ALTERNATIVE

The manifest alternative to the multiple doomsdays of Jihad and McWorld is a democratically regulated system of global governance in which all tribes yield their sovereignty and all multinational corporations surrender their capital to overarching common authorities. The founder of modern futures studies, H.G. Wells, made this imperative clear in a prophetic career that spanned more than 50 years. Everything that has happened since he died in 1946 serves to confirm the wisdom and sanity of his vision.

But there is a serious problem with Wells's vision. Translating it from words on paper to the real world, no matter how doomed that real world may be, seems utterly and incontestably impossible.

On most days of the week, I find myself fearing that it not only *seems* impossible. Perhaps, indeed, it *is* impossible. As we enter the 21st century, the tribes of humankind are more clamorous than ever in their demands for self-determination, no matter at whose expense, and the multinational corporations together with their suborned confederates in national governments are more capable than ever of herding us all willy-nilly into their global marketplace even if we arrive with purses almost empty and cupboards almost bare.

AMERICAN EMPIRE

Do other practicable choices exist? Can we do better?

One imaginable alternative much in the news today is the plan ascribed to the aforementioned henchmen of George W. Bush to make this a second "American Century" by thwarting the rise of rival superpowers, tirelessly safeguarding the interests of American-based corporations everywhere, and, in effect, creating a world empire. The empire they have in mind is more than vaguely reminiscent of Adolf Hitler's design for a German-led New Order in Europe or Matsuoka Yosuke's project of a Greater East Asian Co-Prosperity Sphere. It may also deserve comparison with the recently dissolved bloc of so-called Communist nations headed and dominated by the Soviet Union of Joseph Stalin and his immediate successors.

To be sure, the use of the term "empire" in this context is somewhat misleading. Traditionally an empire is a state consisting of a large number of territories under a single sovereign authority, usually an "emperor." Most of these subject territories have lost their independence through defeat in war. The United States assembled such an empire in the 19th century by purchasing lands already conquered by others (Spain, France, and Russia) and by successful wars against Mexico, Spain, and various Amerindian nations. Its presidents did not choose to become known as emperors, but they might just as well have done so.

Today, however, the phrase "American Empire" refers to a much more diffuse political and economic entity, formed not by acquisition of territory but by the assertion of hegemonic or preponderant power over the affairs of others, thanks to the enormous size of the American economy and the unmatched strength of its armed forces. Because the "others" include virtually every state and people on Earth, this American Empire is, by design, a world empire. It intervenes wherever and whenever it pleases, militarily if need be, to safeguard its vital national interests and to prevent at all costs the rise of any polity capable of challenging its authority, regionally or globally. Just as Hitler envisaged a system of quasi-independent fascist powers in the thrall of Berlin, just as Japan dreamed of an East Asia bent to the will of Tokyo, and just as Moscow controlled without literally absorbing the smaller members of the Warsaw Pact, so the American Empire is conceived as a confederacy—or "coalition"—of nations subservient on all key issues to Washington. Nations that foolishly fail to collaborate suffer ostracism and banishment from the banquet table.

The unprovoked war in 2003 against Iraq is often cited as the first great example of the American Empire at work, but earlier wars against Panama (1989) and Afghanistan (2001) may qualify as well. Although at this writing the outcome of the 2004 national elections in the United States is unknown, there is no reason to believe that a change in administrations in Washington would make any serious difference in the conduct of American foreign policy. Administrations led by the Democratic party initiated almost all of America's wars in the 20th century, and a great many Democrats in the US Congress have voted in support of the military actions taken by Republican presidents, including the invasion of Iraq in 2003, and in that case also including most of the impenitent seekers of the Democratic presidential nomination in 2004, such as senators John Kerry, John Edwards, and Joseph Lieberman, not to mention the Democratic heiress apparent, Senator Hillary Rodham Clinton.

But never mind whether the American Empire has behaved righteously or unrighteously. Can it help provide the kind of global governance that would advance the security and welfare of humankind and protect the biosphere from further ravages?

Obviously not. And for two reasons. In the first place, the mission of the American Empire is to serve American national interests, which can be perceived, and often will be perceived, as diametrically opposed to the interests of the rest of our species. Americans comprise a tribe, no longer based on race, religion, and ethnicity (white Protestant Anglo-Saxondom as in the original 13 colonies), but still a tribe, molded by history and a uniquely hybrid culture, with no warrant to speak and act for humankind. What Americans do abroad is done on no authority but their own. They do not enjoy the consent of the governed of other lands, they are not lawfully deputized to run the world, and their record as promoters of global social justice and environmental health is appalling.

But let us be charitable. Let us imagine that future Americans somehow become the best of Good Samaritans, reaching out to help everyone from the sheer benevolence of their hearts. Could they save civilization if they really wanted to? The answer is no, and for another but equally obvious reason. Americans may boast the world's largest economy at this point in time and also the world's mightiest army, navy, and air force, but their vaunted greatness rests on slender foundations. They now have only 4.6% of the world's population, 7.2% of its land, and 21.9% of its annual gross income. Their share of the world's population and annual gross income is certain to shrink as the years go by.

Even if it did not, how long could one-twentieth of the Earth's people with one-fifth of its wealth retain hegemonic power, especially if this one-twentieth were compelled to squander trillions of dollars every few years on overseas exploits necessary to preserve an ultimately worthless hegemony? As Paul Kennedy has shown in *The Rise and Fall of the Great Powers* (1987), every "great power" in recent centuries has declined because of imperial overreach, and the United

States is already well advanced on the same perilous path to bankruptcy.

THE CONDOMINIUM OF THE RICH

Another option is for the United States to join with other affluent nations in setting up what I have called a "condominium of the rich." In this scenario, anticipated to some extent in the coalitions that waged the 1991 war in the Persian Gulf against Iraq and mounted the 1995 NATO intervention in Bosnia, there would be no American Empire as such, but rather a pact among the leading countries of Europe, North America, and East Asia to divide the planet into spheres of influence or domination. Under this pact the designated powers would be held responsible for maintaining stability in their part of the world, and might also, if necessary, invite the assistance of signatories responsible for other parts. The signatories would further collaborate in regulating international commerce, protecting the environment, and suppressing terrorism.

How all this might work out is detailed in the early chapters of my own *A Short History of the Future* (1989, 1999). It would require a substantial enlargement and modernization of the armed forces of selected European and East Asian countries, something they are not currently prepared to fund, but times change. Certainly they have the technological and industrial capacity to bring their forces up to American standards.

But it is doubtful that a condominium of the rich would do much to slow the plundering and deterioration of our terrestrial biosphere. The high costs of policing the world might, in the long run, prove just as ruinous financially to several nations as to one. Acute differences of opinion arising from the conflicting national interests of the signatories might shatter the pact and dissolve the whole system, just as the "Concert of Europe" fell apart less than a decade after Waterloo. While it lasted, moreover, the condominium would exploit and disempower the peoples of Latin America, Africa, the Middle East, and South Asia, who would surely struggle against it with all the resources at their command.

REVISING THE UNITED NATIONS

Loyalists of the United Nations, for their part, argue that the best way to advance the human cause in the 21st century is to revise and strengthen its Charter, converting the UN into a true global security system. A more powerful and activist UN would surely enjoy more legitimacy than the American Empire or the condominium of the rich. But as long as it remains an assemblage of diplomats appointed by sovereign member governments with no popular mandate and no authority to tax, its resolutions and its work can be sabotaged at any time by nations unwilling to cooperate; and it is almost inconceivable that the member governments of the UN would agree to amend the Charter to allow popular election of delegates or require their citizens to pay taxes directly to the world body. The UN is designed as a forum for national governments, not as a government in its own right, much less a sovereign state.

It is also in its present form and in any likely future form a profoundly undemocratic institution, awarding the same franchise to governments with only thousands of citizens as to governments with hundreds of millions. A resolution could pass in the General Assembly if the ambassadors of the 96 smallest countries, totaling less than 4% of the world's people, voted in favor and the ambassadors of all the others voted against. Even the Security Council, as currently constituted, is something of a joke, refusing to grant permanent membership to major countries such as Germany, Japan, Brazil, India, and Indonesia, while still conferring on any current permanent member the right to veto resolutions approved by all the rest.

GLOBAL DEMOCRACY

I conclude that, if we are serious about wanting to give our grandchildren a 22nd century, we will acknowledge the imperative of moving forward with all possible speed from the international anarchy of the early 21st century to a world government with full sovereignty, a democratically elected parliament and executive authority, a constitution, an array of courts with both original and appellate binding jurisdiction, a monopoly of armed force, the power to mundialize (i.e., transfer to global public ownership) any and all private corporations, and the stewardship of the planetary environment. Nothing less will do.

Will this be a federal or a unitary world government? Will it follow the examples of such federal republics as the United States, Mexico, Brazil, and Germany, or the equally successful examples of unitary government furnished by the United Kingdom, France, Italy, and Japan? I lean to the second alternative, but either one might work well, and I take notice that most advocates of world government strongly prefer the first. In either system ultimate sovereignty would reside in the whole and not in local or regional authorities.

What I cannot accept are the often repeated arguments that the world is too big for a global governance system or, if such a system did prove feasible, it would have to be a despotism. Direct town-meeting democracy with all citizens fully participating around the clock is clearly beyond our reach at this time, although the physicist Eduard Prugovecki has plausibly foreseen technological breakthroughs that would allow citizens to make group decisions by computer-assisted polling. But even the less desirable strategies of electoral and representative democracy in place today in many countries worldwide provide a rough model for what can happen on a planetary scale. If polyglot multicultural countries with nearly 300 million people (the United States) or more than 1 billion people (India) can make democracy work, however imperfectly, why not the whole Earth? The difference in scale is not a difference in substance.

But we need to return to the vexatious question of feasibility. How can we get from here to there? If present-day regimes are unwilling even to strengthen the United Nations, who in her/his right mind would venture to forecast that they will someday choose to supplant themselves altogether?

I am in my right mind, and I do not so venture. Futurists must not substitute wishful thinking for the sober assessment of odds. Present-day regimes and others like them in days soon to come will almost certainly not take such radical steps. Nor, even in the most democratic of nations, are mass electorates attracted to this vision of world governance. I doubt if more than one voter in a thousand would cast a "yes" ballot in a referendum to transfer the sovereignty of her/his country to a world government. We find ourselves in a damnable quandary. What is possible will not work, and what will work is not possible.

Be this as it may, human civilization is fast approaching a point of no return with scant chance of redemption. The bare outlines of an answer to our dilemmas may be visible in the efforts of Green parties and the World Federalist Movement, and in the good work of the World Social Forum launched recently in Brazil, but measured against the might of the powers-that-be such achievements do not loom large. H.G. Wells's concept of a revolutionary Open Conspiracy to bypass national governments (discussed in an earlier conference volume of the World Future Society), or my own suggestion of a World Party, would be worth trying out, but so far they have provoked little interest.

With reluctance I suspect that our best hope is to wait until the present-day world order generates a crisis so deep and pervasive that the necessity of thoroughgoing structural transformation becomes obvious to almost everyone, prompting the spontaneous rise of future Open Conspiracies and World Parties.

If, for just one example, rapid climate change triggered by fossil fuel combustion drastically reduces rainfall in major Asian grain-producing nations, at just the time when headlong industrialization has slashed their agricultural output and the depletion of aquifers has forced agribusiness in the American Midwest to resort to less productive dryland farming, the world may be confronted with widespread famine and intolerably high food prices in the 2020s. Compound this disaster with the radical chilling of the Atlantic seaboard of the United States and much of Western Europe caused by the melting of polar ice and the resulting deflection of the Gulf Stream, and you have the makings of the mother of all economic depressions. Such a crisis could change hundreds of millions of minds and inspire an appropriate political response. At least there would be no more talk of "business as usual."

In *A Short History of the Future* the repugnant midwife of creative transformation is a third world war wiping out most of the world's people and invalidating both Jihad and McWorld decisively. In place of anarchy, chaos, and measureless suffering arises a new kind of polity known simply as the Commonwealth, a democratic governance system for the whole planet that renders all the historically rebuked states of the past obsolete and remakes the world. I do not contend that such a Commonwealth could emerge only out of the ashes of a global cataclysm, and it is doubtful even that it would. More likely the survivors would be reduced to medieval or Bronze Age poverty and isolation. But my objective was to underscore the gravity of the human predicament.

Meanwhile, there may still be time to turn our collective lives around. No one can prove conclusively that our time has run out. All the same, the doomsday clock ticks and ticks and ticks. When will our slumbering, distracted species rouse itself and begin the long march to global union and democracy? This is, indeed, the greatest question confronting humankind in the 21st century.

REFERENCES

Bacevich, A.J. *American Empire: The Realities and Consequences of U.S. Diplomacy* (Cambridge, MA: Harvard University Press, 2002).

Barber, Benjamin R. *Jihad vs. McWorld: How Globalism and Tribalism Are Reshaping the World* (New York: Times Books, 1995).

Huntington, Samuel P. *The Clash of Civilizations and the Remaking of World Order* (New York: Simon & Schuster, 1996).

Kennedy, Paul. *The Rise and Fall of the Great Powers: Economic Change and Military Conflict from 1500 to 2000* (New York: Random House, 1987).

Prugovecki, Eduard. *Memoirs of the Future: A Futuristic Novel* (Notre Dame, IN: Cross Cultural Publications, 2001).

Wagar, W. Warren. *A Short History of the Future* [1989] (Chicago: University of Chicago Press, 1999), 3rd Edition.

Wagar, W. Warren. "Utopias, Futures, and H.G. Wells's Open Conspiracy," *Frontiers of the 21st Century: Prelude to the New Millennium*, ed. Howard F. Didsbury Jr. (Bethesda, MD: World Future Society, 1999), 141-147.

Wells, H.G. *The Open Conspiracy: H.G. Wells on World Revolution*, ed. W. Warren Wagar (Westport, CT: Praeger, 2002).

EVOLVING FUTURE CONSCIOUSNESS THROUGH THE PURSUIT OF VIRTUE

by

Thomas Lombardo and Jonathan Richter

INTRODUCTION

According to many social commentators and psychologists, our modern high-tech, fast-paced world is becoming increasingly frenzied and fragmented. In a time when we possess more financial wealth, material goods, and technological conveniences than ever before, we suffer from chronic stress and anxiety, information and choice overload, a decrease in perceived happiness, feelings of loss of control, deterioration in interpersonal trust and connectivity, and an epidemic of escalating depression. Of special significance, there are various writers who believe that our conscious sense of the future is narrowing and weakening. We are becoming lost and forlorn in an overpowering present. What is going wrong, and more importantly, what can we do about it?

In this paper, we examine the chaotic and disruptive aspects of our contemporary society, identify its key features, and outline a constructive approach for addressing these problems and improving the quality of our lives and mental well-being. This approach proposes that happiness, purpose, and meaning in life, as well as a strong sense of future consciousness, are created through the exercise of a core set of character virtues.

THE PROBLEM: A WORLD OF PANDEMONIUM, SPEED, EGOCENTRICITY, CONSUMERISM, AND NIHILISM

There are several central themes that run through many critical commentaries on contemporary society. These main disruptive features of contemporary society work against future consciousness and purpose, meaning, and happiness in life.

PRESENTISM

In a time when it is critical to think about the future, given the rapid changes occurring around us, we increasingly focus on the present, having lost touch with both the heritage of our past and our sense of direction into tomorrow.

Thomas Lombardo *is professor and faculty chair of psychology and integrated studies at Rio Salado College, Tempe, Arizona. He may be contacted at tlombardo1@cox.net.* **Jonathan Richter** *is assistant professor, The College of Education and Graduate Programs, Montana State University-Northern, and president of The Foundation for Consciousness of the Future, Havre, Montana. He may be contacted at richterj@msun.edu.*

Immediate Gratification in a "Hedonistic Society"

One main inspiration for writing this paper is Howard F. Didsbury Jr.'s article "The Death of the Future in a Hedonistic Society." Didsbury claims that human concerns and human consciousness are narrowing in focus toward the immediate gratification of needs. He believes that a "hedonism of the present"—a life of pleasure for the moment—supported and increasingly reinforced by modern technology and its conveniences, is diminishing our sense of the future and the importance we place on it.[1]

Didsbury's description of our modern lifestyle and mind-set brings to mind the classic brain self-stimulation experiments of the 1950s.[2] Through the use of electrodes placed in one of the "pleasure centers" of the septal-hypothalamic regions of the brain, rats could receive immediate electrical stimulation to these regions for pressing a bar in a Skinner box. In this experiment rats often repeatedly and furiously pressed the bar for thousands of times until physical exhaustion and sometimes death resulted. The rats behaved as if nothing mattered but the next jolt of electricity and pleasure to their brains. They became compulsively addicted, and paradoxically, though they ostensibly had complete control over when they would feel pleasure, they ended up losing all self-control and were totally overpowered by the technology of immediate and effortless pleasure. The analogy to our times is that we live in "pleasure boxes" stimulating our pleasure centers through the use of multifarious, efficient, and convenient technologies that give us immediate gratification. We are "pressing the bars of technology" to the point of exhaustion in total disregard of the consequences, that is, the future.

A complete hedonism of the present generates temporal chaos in our lives. We simply live for the pleasure of the moment with no sense of overall direction, for there is no need to think ahead and no need to remember. There is no sense of connection among the lived moments of our lives. There is no sense of long-term effort since all we have to do is press the bar, push the button, or hit the key.

Neil Postman, in his book *Amusing Ourselves to Death*, warned that we were becoming addicted to our pleasures. He saw Huxley's vision of the future in *Brave New World* as coming true. There is no need to think about anything, including the future, if pleasure can be obtained effortlessly in a moment.[3]

The Cult of the Present

Not only is a technology of immediate gratification reinforcing presentism, so is our ontology. The historian Robert Nisbet argues that it is the "Cult of the Present"—the view that the present is all we have and that the present is of central importance—that is undermining the idea of progress into the future.[4] We focus on the here and now as opposed to where we might be going.

The argument is often presented that it is only the present that is real—that the past no longer exists and the future, by definition, is yet to be.[5] Our lives are lived in the present, so the argument goes. So why pay any attention to what isn't real? Why should we think about past or future?

The "Cult of the Present" undermines the future in an insidious way by particularly undermining the value of the past. If we believe that mostly everything of importance has recently been created or discovered, then the past will seem unimportant and primitive. If the past is negated, then a sense of direction is also destroyed. We have no sense of how what exists has been built upon the past. Nisbet argues this point when he asserts that the modern concept of progress involves the idea of cumulative growth into the future built upon accomplishments of the past. Progress is a trend across time, encompassing past, present, and future. If we demean the past we lose our sense of direction into the future.

Speed, Uncertainty, and the Narrowing of the Temporal Horizon

Peter Russell argues that the increasing speed of change and consequent growing uncertainty of the future is pushing the human mind more toward the present. The faster things change, the more uncertain the future becomes.[6] Uncertainty brings fear and fear engenders paralysis in the present.

Accelerative change contributes to presentism. Stephen Bertman, coining the term "hyperculture" to refer to the increasingly fast paced modern world, has argued that our sense of both past and future is diminishing. We have to stay so focused on what is happening right now that we don't have the time or attention to consider either the past or the future. Consequently, an awareness and sense of connection to both the past and the future have diminished.[7]

James Gleick similarly states that our attention span is narrowing due to the speed, compression, and incessant shifting and changing of messages and information surrounding us.[8] More is squeezed into less and less. As Gleick states, "we live in the buzz." Our moments of attention are disconnected and jump about from one item to the next. There is no sense of sustained long-term attention—we suffer from a collective attention deficit disorder.

Relativism, Nihilism, and the Loss of Purpose and Direction

According to many writers, with the rise of postmodernism and philosophical relativism, which are critical of any claims to absolute truth or value, we don't have any acceptable grand narrative we can legitimately feel certain and secure about. There is no single credible view or authority regarding the purpose and direction for all humanity. This may be seen as either good or bad, depending on one's perspective.[9]

Critiques of the Western idea of progress have undermined our secular sense of a positive direction for human society. Similarly during the Enlightenment, earlier critiques of Western religious views of progress and the future undermined a spiritual sense of direction in the West. Science and reason, creations of the Enlightenment, undercut all mythic and religious views around the world. Yet in turn, science and reason have been challenged as definitive and singular authorities. As globalization has spread across the globe, all cultures and peoples have been exposed to numerous alternative views of reality, meaning, and purpose. Local cultures, once secure in their particular visions of life, are now invaded with multiple perspectives and philosophies that challenge their authority.

If one view is perhaps as good as the next, then there is no convincing way to go or secure choice to make. There are no apodictic or universal criteria for evaluation or decision making. We are left without a viable sense of direction amidst a plethora of varied ideas and choices.[10] Even though there are many possibilities for a new story for humanity, none of these new stories has yet captured the allegiance of the bulk of humanity. There is, in fact, incessant and ongoing conflict and disputation among the promoters of such stories and philosophies.[11] To quote a line from Walter Truett Anderson, if there are "Four Different Ways to be Absolutely Right," then what in fact is right, especially if these different viewpoints are conflicting and contradictory?[12]

If the future is uncertain and we cannot even agree on which path or possibilities are preferable, then adopting a philosophy of nihilism is a natural consequence. Hope becomes meaningless, for we don't know what to hope for. Why not simply focus on the present, on immediate pleasure, on "just looking out for number one"? Let us play our fiddles and stimulate our brains with our technological "joy sticks" while Rome burns.

SPEED AND OVERLOAD

Living in a Buzz—on the Go—in Accelerative Change

Since Alvin Toffler published *Future Shock*, the idea that many aspects of our world are undergoing accelerative change has become an extremely influential and accepted description of our times.[13] Toffler spoke of the "death of permanence," where jobs, friends, spouses, homes, belongings, and everything else that gives human life stability have become unstable, transient, disposable, and exchangeable. The exponential curve of growth and change has become the most pervasive icon of our times.

As Gleick has described in his book *Faster: The Acceleration of Just About Everything*, modern humans are obsessed with time, speed, and efficiency. We compress more information and more activities into shorter and shorter units of time. We manage and schedule time in innumerable ways, including time to relax. We measure time with increasing precision and find ways to "save" time. We squeeze more productivity into our lives. In the process of managing, coordinating, measuring, and accounting for our time, we have become enslaved to it. We are in a race with the clock and chained to it.[14] We live in the "Age of Velocity"—our lives a blur on the Minkowskian tapestry of existence.

As noted earlier, various writers believe that increasing speed and rate of change narrows human consciousness to the present. It also amplifies the feelings of chaos and loss of control. We do not have time to put the pieces together and we feel swept away by the rush of life.

The philosophy of accelerative change is supported by contemporary interpretations of modern cosmology and evolution. Both Ray Kurzweil and Hans Moravec, for example, argue that the informational complexity of life and mind has been exponentially increasing throughout the history of the earth, reflecting a cosmological trend of accelerative growth of complexity throughout the universe. They foresee this trend as continuing in the future.[15] Following the logic of this argument, there will come a time in the not so distant future when the pace of change and the growth of complexity will become so great that typical human minds will no longer be able to comprehend it. We will pass through what Vernor Vinge calls the technological "Singularity," where only techno-enhanced or artificial intelligence minds will be able to understand and keep up with it.[16]

Ambient Engulfment, Bombardment, and Overload in Choices and Information

We are engulfed and inundated with information and choices. Not only is the speed of data transmission—of chunks of information—increasing, but we are literally surrounded by multiple channels of input. We go into a lounge or restaurant and there are multiple TVs showing different channels, there's music playing, lights flashing and streaming about, and people talking on their cell phones. The grocery store is not much different. For that matter, our homes are also on information overload. The ambient stimulus array is a cacophony of different voices, images, and competing data flows.

Advertising is pervasive and insidious. Commercials must be short, dramatic, and to the point, allowing more commercials and ads to be compressed into periods of time. Further, with visual displays (TVs, computer screens, electronic billboards) becoming more pervasive, multiple sources of information can be placed in the same perceptual space—bombarding us from every direction in our field of view.

Our lives are similar in chaotic structure. Multitasking has become a way of life. We make countless lists lest we forget something. Instead of focusing, we jump back and forth between multiple tasks, messages, and agendas. Our lives are filled with competing demands and unending distractions. We drive our cars, wait in lines, and go for walks with our cell phones and CD headsets, perpetually engaged and distracted by the noise in our heads.

Recently Barry Schwartz, in his book *The Paradox of Choice: Why More Is Less*, argues that we are overloaded with choices.[17] Information overload is connected to choice overload. The more TV channels that are available, the more potential choices there are. The more books to read, the more choices there are. Although offering more choices presumably gives us more freedom and more pathways for self-development and self-expression, if there are too many options, everything becomes a blur, which generates confusion and behavioral paralysis. Coupled with the loss of any secure and certain criteria for making choices and decisions, we simply flounder in a sea of plenty.

Too much of everything backfires. Based on George Miller's classic psychological paper on memory and attention, it appears that humans may not be able to intelligently handle more than seven (plus or minus two) distinct items of information at the same time.[18] We cannot hold in our mind and intelligently think about 500 different courses we can take at college, 500 different brands of cereal to choose from, or 500 different career paths to pursue in our lives.

There are of course reactions to information and choice overload, which include the simplicity movement, running back to nature, and curling up in some form of authoritarian fundamentalism. But there are problems with all these solutions. Running back to nature seems regressive (and paradoxical since often we take our cell phones, SUVs, and laptops along with us). As Gleick points out, we are overloaded with simplicity solutions. Also the simplicity movement seems yet another commodification of something that used to be free. Fundamentalism is closed-minded and dogmatic and often leads to militancy and violent conflict, which in turn brings more chaos and disruption to our lives.

CHAOS

Chaos can be defined as a lack of coherence, pattern, connection, or relationship among events, entities, or items of information.

Disconnected, Trivialized, and Perpetually Shifting Information Flow

Neil Postman argued 20 years ago that the disconnected and perpetually shifting information flow presented in the media, and especially on TV, is undermining sustained dialogue and extended human attention span.[19] Chunks of information (commercials, advertisements, news items, e-mails, etc.) are coming at us without any overall pattern or direction. We hear about a bombing in the Middle East, a new brand of cereal, the baseball scores, debates on cloning and same-sex marriages, entertainment specials on TV tonight, and the election of a new Pope in quick succession without any meaningful transitions. All items are given equal billing, from deodorants to death. All data are equalized—reduced to bits, numbers, time slots, and short moments of notoriety and importance.

Mental Pandemonium and the Fragmented Self

Not only is chaos and disconnectedness a pervasive feature in our lives and in our social reality, but our very minds and selves—our presumed psychological core—are supposedly not of one piece. Walter Truett Anderson, among others, has argued that the theory that the human self is a singular, centralized and constant psychological reality—an idea derived from modern Western thought—is both historically dated and empirically mistaken.[20] The postmodern self is many voices, many roles, and many personae, often shifting and transforming depending upon the circumstances. The psychologist Sherry Turkle has proposed a similar thesis regarding the nature of the self on the Internet where people can experiment with different personal identities. Who is to say which is the real self?[21] Arguments are presented from psychology that the undercurrents of the human mind are actually a plurality of voices and selves—a "pandemonium" as Daniel Dennett describes it—and that the sense of an organized and singular self is a social and psychological construction, or fiction, that gives us an illusory sense of stability and security.[22]

Our selves are becoming more multifarious as our lives and world become more complex and chaotic. Just as cultural and religious worldviews once provided a sense of order and stability for human societies, the idea of a stable self provided order and meaning to our individual lives. Both sources of order have been challenged and undercut.

Out of Control, Stress, and Reveling in Chaos

In his highly influential book *Out of Control*, Kevin Kelly argued that we must give up the Newtonian and rationalist ideal of attempting to control life. Life, the world around us, the future, and even ourselves—none of it can be controlled. There are no central command stations. There is interaction among multiplicities and resultant levels of chaos. The hierarchical model of control is passé— we live in a world of networks, distributed power, swarm or hive minds, and inherent unpredictability.[23] We should stop trying to impose order on a world that squirms and wiggles about and has many minds of its own.

As a general philosophical and cultural phenomenon, there has been an increasing emphasis on the concept of chaos and its integral and necessary importance in the workings of nature.[24] Supposedly, we should understand the role of chaos and live with it, and even revel in chaos. There are advocates of "creative disorder" who believe that chaos and disorder supports flexibility, freedom, creativity, and individuality.[25]

Generally, though, stress occurs when people no longer feel in control of their lives. In a chaotic world that is bombarding us with too many different things from too many different directions, coming and going too quickly, we often feel that we don't know where we are going and that we don't have command of the steering wheel. Stress and anxiety frequently follow.

Individuals do show differences, though, in their perception of control in their lives and the value they place on such control. There is significant individual variability in reactions to stress and un-controllable change.[26] On a continuum, people may see themselves as being more in control of their lives (internal locus of control) or as people whose lives are more influenced by external factors (external locus of control). Having a sense of internal locus of control is correlated with psychological well-being.[27]

Yet just as feelings of lack of control often generate negative psychological states of stress and anxiety, people find the experience of disorder unpleasant and depressing. According to the psychologist Mihaly Csikszentmihalyi, people find work where they are engaged in purposeful tasks more satisfying than free time and aimless activities.[28] At the extreme end of the continuum, chaos totally unleashed in the human mind is tantamount to psychosis.

MONETIZATION, COMMODIFICATION, AND CONSUMERISM

People in modern society not only have their basic survival needs more than satisfied, but have more wealth, possessions, and purchasing power than at any previous period in history; yet they do not feel any happier and in fact exhibit more depression.[29] Once basic survival needs are met, money can't buy you happiness. In fact, being excessively motivated to increase one's material wealth comes with a cost. What is wrong with a monetary philosophy of life—why doesn't it work?

Commodification is becoming an increasingly pervasive para-digm. Everything in life is being turned into a product with a mone-tary value that can be purchased for a price. Monetary worth has become the common denominator for everything of value and acquires a psychological and social power that ends up negating or minimizing the value of other things in life. To use psychological terminology, money has become a universal secondary reinforcer, associated with all possible primary reinforcers. As a universal secondary reinforcer it is always perceived as a necessary means to all ends, and in fact, often becomes the perceived end itself. We no longer pray for wisdom, friendship, or kindness; we pray to get rich. Many of us have become firmly convinced that if we had enough money we would be happy, though the evidence clearly indicates otherwise. All in all, money has become God—we worship the "golden cow."

Second, because everything is reducible to a "product that can be purchased" there is no sense of effort or self-initiative directly associated with identifiable things of value. Rather, identifiable things of value are bought. If a person has enough money, presumably everything of value can be obtained. Value is not the result of a doing—it is the result of a buying. Further, because modern technologies invariably require money to purchase or use, the more we become dependent on technologies to accomplish our goals or give us pleasure in life, the more we become dependent on money.

Third, since things of value are purchased with money (as opposed to earned with effort or even bestowed on us as gifts of God), we are reduced to the role of consumers or customers, rather than creators and contributors. We become takers who are filled with needs rather than givers who have something to offer to the world.

Finally, since money is the means to all ends, and everything is a product to be purchased, future consciousness is undercut. What is of value does not require long-term effort or thinking—it simply requires bucks in your pocket.

The historian Peter Watson has commented, we are all "doing too well to do good."[30] Acquiring and maintaining material plentitude and financial wealth is a full-time job. Our fast-paced life, our stress, our individual isolation, and our focus on the demands of the present to a great degree revolve around advancing our careers and generating a good income. Our plentitude comes with a price.

EGOCENTRICITY, INDIVIDUALISM, AND NARCISSISM

The psychologist Martin Seligman has argued that there has been too much emphasis on the individual—that our philosophy of life has become too self-centered.[31] Seligman contends that one main cause of increasing depression is excessive expectations for the self. Excessive expectations produce frustration, anger, and disappointment later in life and consequently depression.

In the last few decades, our popular culture has witnessed the self-actualization, human potential, self-esteem, and human diversity movements, all of which focus on the self and human uniqueness. We have been told that we are unique, special, and deserving of all life has to offer. We are not told that humans have numerous common biological, psychological, and social qualities, though the scientific evidence strongly supports a high degree of "human universality" and invariant "human nature."[32]

Excessive individualism produces social disconnectedness and consequent social chaos. As various writers have argued, relative to the past, there has been a loss of community and social coherence in our modern society.[33] We are all "bowling alone."[34] We live in our individualized pleasure boxes. We have fortified ourselves in gated communities and SUVs.

Walter Truett Anderson has recently argued that our strong sense of individualized and egocentric identity is our deepest social problem. We all want and cling to all kinds of identity labels. We are all taught to respect each other's identities. There is a great deal of positive reinforcement in our society for developing one's individual self and being egocentric. Yet there is, and in fact has been throughout history, immense and incomparable violence committed in the name of personal, cultural, national, and religious identity. For Anderson, our contemporary culture wars are actually identity wars.[35] Advocates of cultural pluralism and human diversity often sound egocentric and confrontational and, hence, self-contradictory.

Egocentricity and extreme individualism generate social fragmentation not only through confrontation and self-centeredness, but through social apathy and perfunctory tolerance. We live in an era of postmodernism and philosophical relativism. There are presumably no universal systems of truth and value. Truth and value have become subjective and culturally relative. Hence, in a true liberal fashion, no one presumably has the right or privileged vantage point to judge anyone else. We unquestioningly accept multiple points of view and ways of life because what is subjective, individual, and unique has become our philosophical absolute. Each person and each culture simply "does their own thing." This produces total disconnectedness.

Extreme individualism, though, backfires. We are all told that we are unique, and we all end up conforming to this social-psychological absolute. We are a plethora of special egos. If we are all special, no one is special. If we are all right, no one is right. Our individual selves would vanish without constructive interaction, dialogue, and mutual evaluation. We are open systems and reciprocally interdependent—we cannot stand alone. Excessive individualism is scientifically and philosophically flawed.

There is one other apparent paradox associated with our egocentric and individualist society. Although we pride ourselves on our individuality, we feel increasingly impotent to effect real change. People feel helpless in the face of the powerful corporate, cultural, and government forces that seem to determine the pattern and direction of events. There was a belief once that humans could solve the problems of the world. Now, though, we have become nihilistic and uncertain about what the future will bring. Feeling helpless is a defining feature of depression.[36]

If people feel that they cannot effect change, they are more likely to retreat into their isolated worlds. They are also more likely to look for pleasure in the technological conveniences and material products the society of plentitude provides for them—that is, people end up being pacified and addicted to the very forces that rob them of an authentic sense of happiness and accomplishment. No wonder we are increasingly depressed.

SUMMARY AND CONCLUSION

There are many interconnected reasons why people in modern society are stressed out, depressed, too present focused, and not very happy. For Didsbury, we are addicted to short-term pleasures delivered through technology. According to Gleick and Bertman, we are obsessed and captured by speed. Some writers focus on excessive materialism, consumerism, and individualism as the primary causes.[37] Anderson highlights our ego-centered way of thinking. The Integral Culture movement, aside from identifying materialism as an important cause, emphasizes a multifaceted loss of connection in modern society among ourselves, with nature, and with the cosmos as a whole.[38] Neil Postman sees our society as a technological realization of *Brave New World*. Our values are increasingly defined by technology and media—communication technology fragments our consciousness and dialogue into disconnected and trivialized bits of entertainment and information. We are "preoccupied with some equivalent of the feelies, the orgy porgy, and the centrifugal bumblepuppy."[39]

Nihilism is another disturbing feature of modern society. If there is no credible image for tomorrow, this leads to hopelessness and a loss of optimism. Nihilism generates depression, which motivates people to seek short-term pleasures to counteract the depression. Increased depression, though, creates a narrowing of temporal consciousness. Depression is also connected with perceived helplessness. Not only is the future dark and uncertain, but we can't do anything about it.

If we do hear upbeat visions of the future, they often highlight the very things that seem to be making us stressed and unhappy. We are asked to adapt to and revel in chaos, in the accelerating development of technology and human life, in unpredictability, and our special little egos.

THE SOLUTION: THE PURSUIT OF VIRTUE

Character Virtues and Universal Values

Our central hypothesis is that our psychological and social reality can be significantly improved through a focused exercise and development of a core set of character virtues.

The idea that the "good life" can be achieved through the

internalization of character virtues goes back at least as far as Aristotle. For Aristotle, a life of virtue not only creates happiness in the individual but equally contributes to the well-being of the community.[40] Virtues are not simply self-centered or self-serving. Further, for Aristotle happiness is not the same as pleasure. Pleasure is a good feeling; happiness is an accomplishment, a form of excellence, and a way of life. Happiness is not achieved through practicing a "hedonism of the present."

Virtues are connected with values, in that a virtue is a value lived and internalized into the character of a person. If truth is a value, honesty and forthrightness are the corresponding virtues.

As noted earlier, our contemporary world has been strongly influenced by postmodernism and cultural relativism. The argument has been repeatedly made that values are relative and different across cultures. In spite of its popular appeal, this argument is probably wrong. Based on a lifelong survey of different cultures, the futurist Wendell Bell contends that all human societies share the common values of human life and health, knowledge, truth and evaluation itself. (All cultures believe in the value of values.) Further, there are many other almost universal values, including justice, peace, loyalty, courage, friendliness, trust, self-realization, and autonomy.[41] Rushworth Kidder also argues that there is a high degree of global consensus on human values. He interviewed a set of culturally diverse people, each respected by their peers for their ethical thinking and behavior. The following eight common values emerged from the interviews: love, truthfulness, fairness, freedom, unity, tolerance, responsibility, and respect for life.[42] Note that there is significant overlap between the two lists.

In a more general vein, the anthropologist Donald Brown has compiled a vast list, numbering into the hundreds, of "human universals" across all cultures. This list includes social conventions, modes of behavior, conceptual distinctions, and values.[43] The postmodernist emphasis on relativism and subjectivism appears clearly contradicted by Brown's research. We seem to have been misled by the propaganda of extreme individualism. As a species, we think and behave in very similar ways, and part of this commonality is in our values.

One of the most interesting surveys of common human values has been conducted by Martin Seligman and his associates.[44] What is particularly important about his research is that it surveyed key values not just across cultures but across human history. A large selection of influential writings from different cultures and different historical periods was identified and presented to a group of investigators for review. According to Seligman, six fundamental virtues across all cultures and historical time periods emerged from this review. The six virtues and subcategories are:

- *Wisdom* (curiosity, love of learning, judgment, ingenuity, social

intelligence, and perspective).
- *Courage* (valor, perseverance, and integrity).
- *Love and Humanity* (kindness, generosity, nurturance, and the capacity to love and be loved).
- *Temperance* (modesty, humility, self-control, prudence, and caution).
- *Justice* (good citizenship, fairness, loyalty, teamwork, and humane leadership).
- *Transcendence* (appreciation of beauty, gratitude, hope, spirituality, forgiveness, humor, and zest).

Seligman's argument is that *authentic happiness* is built upon the exercise and development of these character virtues. Sounding very Aristotelian, Seligman believes that authentic happiness is a relatively enduring quality and is not necessarily associated with short-term pleasure at all. Momentary pleasures tend to diminish quickly, for people adapt to the frequent experience of a repeatable pleasure. Character virtues, on the other hand, require effort and challenges. Hence, authentic happiness is something that must be worked at, and the pathway involves an ethical growth in the individual.

For Seligman, meaning and purpose in life involve both the development of character virtues and the identification with some reality or goal "beyond oneself." The virtues serve a "transcendent reality" rather than just being self-serving. Consequently, extreme individualism works against finding meaning and purpose. Interestingly, "transcendence" is one of the primary character virtues listed. In many ways, transcendence is anathema to our modern emphasis on the ego, self-gratification, and subjectivism—there is something beyond our private realities that needs to become our center of gravity and our standard of truth and value. It should also be noted that since purpose in life requires transcendence, a future-oriented mind-set involves practicing the virtue of transcendence. Extreme individualism and egocentricity work against future consciousness.

We are going to take Seligman's theory of authentic happiness as one major starting point for our approach to modern life. Virtue leads to happiness and purpose. We also contend that there is a set of relatively universal human virtues that provide some common criteria for leading the good life.

ARTICULATING A LIFE NARRATIVE BASED ON CHARACTER VIRTUES

Our second main proposal consists of two connected parts. First, we should conceptualize our existence and our temporal consciousness in terms of the narrative or the story. Second, we should use character virtues as the central theme or motif in our life narrative.

People cognitively represent their personal identities as "narratives" or "stories." To use an expression of Antonio Damasio, we understand and describe ourselves in terms of an "autobiographical self." The object of self-consciousness is not a static thing but an unfolding story.[45] Our self-narratives change over time depending on new experiences and new interpretations. Also, people often have multiple stories they tell themselves about themselves—even contradictory ones. Self-narratives can be a mixed bag of positive or negative, tragic, comical, or self-elevating elements. Human societies or cultures also conceptualize identity in terms of stories or narratives with a distinctive heritage, collective myths, dramas, heroes and villains, and usually visions for the future.

The narrative is the most appropriate and valuable way to conceptualize the future. A narrative for the future does not just identify a goal or vision, which is a frozen "idea" in time. A narrative is a story that extends in time—it is a process rather than a state. A life narrative usually entails the identification of challenges and problems to address. Narratives have drama and are filled with emotional color. Narratives also usually involve multiple characters, both supportive and adversarial, who will have an effect upon our lives. Our future will not unfold in a social vacuum. These various aspects of a narrative make it a realistic way to conceptualize the future.

Using the narrative as a mental framework for self-description, we need to rediscover our heritage and past, if we have forgotten or forsaken it. In order to expand our temporal consciousness, we need to reintegrate our past into our sense of identity. We need to emphasize accomplishments and important events that are connected with the development of virtues.

Just as our past needs to be framed in terms of the achievement and expression of virtues, our future narrative should also center on character virtues. How does one live a life dedicated to the development of wisdom, temperance, or transcendence? We should be motivated toward realizing such virtues.

One important benefit in centering on character virtues in the articulation of a life narrative is that it takes the focus off of the self. Life becomes the realization of virtues, rather than an expression of self-aggrandizement. Depressed and anxious people are more self-absorbed than happy people, and given the excessive self-centeredness of our times, it is important to find a way to conceptualize our lives that is not so egocentric.

THE SIX KEY VIRTUES FOR THE FUTURE

Now we wish to propose and describe six key virtues for the future. This list derives from the lists created by Bell, Kidder, Brown, and Seligman, as well as other sources. Special consideration is given to what seem to be our most glaring contemporary problems and what virtues we especially need for the future. The six proposed virtues are:

- Self-Efficacy and Self-Responsibility.
- Order, Integration, and Direction.
- Courage, Faith, and Freedom.
- Wisdom and the Love of Thinking.
- Reciprocity and Balance.
- Evolution and Transcendence.

SELF-EFFICACY AND SELF-RESPONSIBILITY

Achieving authentic happiness is first and foremost an accomplishment. It requires effort, rather than being something that can be purchased, or something that can be produced through momentary pleasures. Developing character virtues requires self-effort and produces a sense of accomplishment. Hence, a prime virtue that is required for the exercise and development of all other virtues is self-responsibility. What is good in life is achieved rather than bestowed upon us.

Through the accomplishment of goals, one strengthens one's sense of self-efficacy. Without self-accomplishment there is no sense of self-efficacy. Perceived self-efficacy is the degree to which one sees oneself as capable of accomplishing goals.[46] People show different degrees of "self-efficacy." A person with low self-efficacy believes he is relatively powerless with respect to the future, whereas a person with high self-efficacy believes he has a high level of control or influence on the future. High self-efficacy is the opposite of perceived helplessness and counteracts the experience of depression.

A critical belief connected with the idea of self-efficacy is that you can transform your life for the better. Behind this belief is a set of key assumptions. You are assuming that the future is not determined by uncontrollable forces. You are also assuming that you are not trapped by the past. Additionally, you are assuming that you have the power through self-initiative and the exercise of various capacities to significantly influence the future. Also, this belief is framed as a "possibility" rather than a certainty. Framing it as a possibility engenders effort—if it were framed as a certainty there would be no reason or need to think you had to make an effort. Further, it is framed as an ideal. The future is not seen as a result of causes but of choices and effort to realize ideals. The future is described as prescriptive and idealistic, rather than deterministic. What is it that we hope to achieve? What can we achieve? Values rather than causes determine the future.

Framing the future in this manner also supports the need for courage in the face of the future, another one of the character virtues to be described below. One does not need courage if the future is secure, certain, dependent on others, or determined by external factors.

ORDER, INTEGRATION, AND DIRECTION

If one of our key social and psychological problems is chaos and disconnectedness, then it stands to reason that what we need is more order and integration in both our lives and our minds. Although chaos and disorder have been connected in popular contemporary philosophy with freedom and creativity, the exact opposite is frequently the case. Chaos tends to produce feelings of lack of control, helplessness, confusion, and stagnation. It is our argument that mental discipline is a central character virtue that is critically important for the future and that it facilitates creativity and the evolution of order.

Csikszentmihalyi, who has studied the psychology of creativity extensively, believes that we need more order in our minds.[47] He argues that there is a strong dimension of chaos in the typical human mind. In spite of what people may believe, we do not control what we think about very well. Typically our thoughts and feelings jump around as if they had a will of their own. If given free time, humans tend to become unhappy, disordered, and unproductive. Surprisingly, people tend to find work more satisfying than free time. When we focus our minds we feel better. Csikszentmihalyi thinks that we need to consciously structure our minds more, a task he believes is definitely within our power. If we do not attempt to bring order to our minds, we degenerate into mental entropy and chaos, which is depressing and psychologically unpleasant. Mental order leads to increased happiness and productivity.

If Csikszentmihalyi addresses the need for increased mental order, the Integral Culture movement (which includes writers such as Barbara Marx Hubbard, Riane Eisler, and Hazel Henderson) highlights the need for increased social, ecological, and cosmic order and integration. In opposition to the dualist and individualist philosophies of traditional Western thinking, which separated everything, advocates of the Integral Culture movement assert that we need to reconnect with each other, reconnect the sexes, reconnect with nature and our "Mother Earth," and reconnect with the cosmos. A philosophy of love is central to their message, and love entails a coming together of the many pieces of our highly fragmented human reality.[48]

Another key feature to psychological order is meaning and purpose in life. Meaning and purpose entail some sense of direction and some core set of values and themes that define the sense and significance of one's life. Meaning and purpose integrate—that is, bring order to—life. The pieces are fitted together and a direction is defined. Meaning and purpose in particular enhance future consciousness. We see and articulate a direction to our lives.

We propose that it is the exercise of a set of virtues that gives meaning and purpose to life. Virtues give meaning—what is the significance of doing something—and virtues give direction—life is the development of these virtues. Anchoring one's life to virtues provides order amidst the chaos and flux. Living a life dedicated to virtue is a way to practice and realize the specific virtue of mental order and discipline.

Virtues are a particularly good way to conceptualize meaning and purpose. Virtues provide for an idealistic or preferable order and direction; they put the individual in the driver's seat regarding the value of his or her life, and they contribute to the well-being of both the individual and society as a whole. Finally, following Aristotle and Seligman, ordering one's life around virtues brings happiness. Centering one's meaning and purpose around the acquisition of wealth, power, fame, or momentary pleasures does not seem to bring happiness.

In the pursuit of increasing mental order we also need to resurrect the value of linear thinking. Linear thinking has been excessively criticized over the last few decades, being associated with rationalist and closed-minded thinking, but to go to the opposite extreme of horizontal or free-associative thinking leads to a psychotic and disorganized state of mind. Without linear thinking we would not be able to create any focused or directional line of behavior. Sequential and goal-directed behavior, planning, history and narrative, causal thinking, and logical thought all require linear thinking. Purpose and direction by definition imply linearity. Linearity creates continuity in our lives. If we are to recreate some viable notion of progress we need to articulate some sense of positive linear direction extending out of the past into the future. Without a belief in progress, we will remain stuck in feelings of hopelessness and depression. A belief in progressive linearity is critical to happiness.

One final theme relevant the development of order is the reconnecting of the past, present, and future. We need to integrate our sense of the overall temporal structure of reality. Our contemporary temporal consciousness, being focused on the present, is fragmented. To move out of the chaos of the here-and-now it is critical to integrate past, present, and future. We have already noted, following Nisbet and his study of progress, that broadening our sense of history is actually supportive of future consciousness, and gives us a sense of linearity and development. As Leonard Shlain argues, "To understand and change the present condition of our species, we must gain insight into the past. If we do not, we cannot exert a lasting influence on the future."[49]

COURAGE, FAITH, AND FREEDOM

Courage and freedom appear as core virtues and values in the lists of Seligman and Kidder. We suggest that these two ideals are psychologically connected and, further, that faith is related to both factors, thus forming a triad or character cluster.

Courage, faith, and freedom are connected with the theme of the future as possibilities. As argued earlier, it is important to view the future as possibilities. Seeing the future as deterministic or teleological certainties disempowers us. Unless the future is possibilities there is no real freedom of choice and no real self-determination. Believing in a predestined or deterministic future may give us a sense of security, but we must transcend this need if we are to live the future as possibilities. Hence, living in a future of possibilities where there is real freedom of choice requires courage. There would be no need for courage if one felt secure and safe. Similarly, faith is required in a world of uncertainty. Although people often state that they have faith and are certain or convinced of whatever beliefs they profess to have faith in, true faith only exists if one isn't certain. Faith is believing when you aren't certain—faith, in fact, requires courage.

Faith is often opposed to reason, as if to live a life of faith meant to forsake reason (and also empirical evidence). In fact, faith can be seen as believing in spite of what reason and evidence may indicate, yet this concept of faith turns it into a state of being closed-minded, unrealistic, and even mad. What we mean by faith, though, is simply believing in something even though one realizes one isn't certain. Faith is not arrogant but humble. Neither reason nor empirical evidence can provide absolute certainty and proof for our beliefs. It is unreasonable to expect certainty. Almost all our beliefs about the world, including our scientific ones, are contingent. Having faith is realizing and living with this uncertainty. Faith requires courage and not being overpowered by our fears.

Although freedom is often listed as a central ideal that most people around the world profess to highly value, freedom is, in fact, a frightening thing to many of us. As Eric Fromm argued years ago, people find many ways to "escape from freedom."[50] Freedom entails choice and self-responsibility. Expressing our freedom of choice and self-determination involves moving beyond the securities of authority, conformity, and dependency on others.

There are many ways in which we can be constrained by reality, but these constraints actually provide for security and safety. Our culture, our religious beliefs, and even our self-defined sense of who we are, are all factors that give us identity but constrain us to a particular way of being, thinking, and living.[51] As Anderson argues, the Western theory of a unique, single, and constant ego may in fact be a self-imposed limitation on our nature—in a world of excessive individualism we may not really be that free.[52]

True freedom means that any of these constraints can be altered or abandoned through choice and action. If we are free then we embody possibilities. As with courage and faith, freedom entails overcoming our fears and our very human need for security.

Approaching the future with faith, courage, and freedom means that we don't simply adapt to, conform to, or accept the prophecies and predictions we hear about the future. There are different ways the future could unfold, and these different possibilities provide the arena of choice for us. We need to become open and realize that through self-initiative we can guide which future is realized.

WISDOM AND THE LOVE OF THINKING

The love and practice of good thinking is a virtue. Good thinking is a proactive mental activity—it is something accomplished, as with all the other virtues. It requires self-initiation, effort, and practice. It also brings self-control and self-discipline to the mind; hence it serves the virtue of mental order. It contributes to the overall excellence of life and counteracts some of the most basic problems of our contemporary world.

Good thinking, as with other virtues, is a skill that can be enhanced, and, as with any skill, it involves standards, ideals, and values. The qualities of good thinking have been extensively addressed within the Critical Thinking movement. As its advocates have argued, there are "universal standards" for good thinking.[53] Although there are significant individual differences in how people think, good thinking, like human values in general, is not as subjective and variable as contemporary relativistic philosophy would have us believe. As Jacob Needleman stated, "It is good to be open-minded but not so open that your brains fall out."

Critical thinking has been defined as the opposite of egocentric thinking. Critical thinking involves the capacity to entertain and evaluate, according to rational standards, alternative points of view. Egocentric thinking is seeing things from only one point of view.[54] Egocentricity involves being exclusively concerned with satisfying one's own personal desires and goals and protecting and justifying one's own beliefs. Egocentric thinking is biased and prejudicial. Since one of the central mental qualities associated with the chaos and disconnectedness of our times is egocentrism, we should adopt a form of thinking that explicitly challenges this mode of viewing reality. Critical thinking is the antidote to egocentricity.

Critical thinking also serves human freedom, for it brings flexibility and openness to the human mind. Being trapped in an egocentric mode of thinking constrains the individual to one point of view. It is interesting then that a virtue that brings self-control and order also brings freedom.

Given the vast array of different voices, philosophies, and cultures a globalizing society brings to the individual, it is essential that people develop the capacity to sort through and evaluate all these different points of view. How do we bring order to the chaos? How do we decide which ideas are worthwhile and which ideas are not? Advocates of critical thinking suggest that the standards they have outlined provide a way to evaluate and decide amidst the noise.

Lest the critical thinking perspective be accused of adopting a form of dogmatism in advocating for certain standards of thought and cognition over others, it should be mentioned that one common description of critical thinking is simply "thinking about thinking." Dogmatism has the feature of leaving various assumptions unquestioned—it is not self-reflective. Good critical thinkers evaluate their own mode and standards of thinking—they are explicitly non-dogmatic. Hence, critical thinking raises self-consciousness, which is another way it benefits freedom. The critical thinker is more aware and less trapped by his or her own ego and assumptions.

Closely connected with the idea of critical thinking is the theory of *reflective thinking*. Reflective thinking is moving beyond absolutism and relativism. Patricia King and Karen Kitchener describe three developmental stages of thinking and judgment making. Stage one is absolutist thinking: It is true and right because some identified authority says so. Absolutist thinking is highly egocentric and dogmatic. This mode of thought is the mind of a child. Stage two is relativist thinking: All ideas are equal because there are many different possible points of view on a topic. This mode of thought produces thoughtless tolerance, disconnectedness, and indecisiveness. Stage three is reflective thinking, which is identifying the most convincing position among many alternatives based on evidence and reasoning without the need to be absolutely certain.[55] Reflective thinking achieves a balance between, or, perhaps more accurately, a transcendence of, closed-minded absolutism and noncommittal relativism.

Utilizing critical and reflective thinking involves assessing alternatives and making thoughtful commitments, decisions, and choices without the security of definitive answers. It means acknowledging and living with uncertainty. It also means not being paralyzed by fear. It is courageous thinking. It is the ideal mode of thinking for the future in that it thrives in a world of mystery and possibilities rather than certainties.

A devotion to critical thinking facilitates the growth of wisdom, one of the six key virtues in Seligman's list. Seligman includes "curiosity, love of learning, judgment, and perspective" as subcategories of this virtue, and all of these character qualities are distinctive traits of the ideal critical thinker.[56] Wisdom is a quality that transcends mere information or knowledge. Wisdom implies a deep understanding of reality and the application of that understanding to life. One could even say that wisdom is a process and a capacity as much as a body of content. Wisdom is also connected with a love of thinking. There is an affective and passionate dimension to critical thinkers. As a virtue, wisdom is not simply a skill but a passion.

Sadly in our society today, we are drowning in information and devoid of wisdom. The ongoing corruption of education is a case in point. Knowledge is broken down into modules and sold for a price. Further, in spite of various and continued efforts to transform education, it is still primarily concerned with learning facts and specialized skills. Integrative and interdisciplinary programs, which would facilitate the development of wisdom, flounder, whereas programs that promise job advancement and focus on isolated areas of expertise flourish. Neither students nor schools profess any interest in the development of wisdom. Given the presumed accelerative growth of information and knowledge, it would benefit us to strongly support educational programs that promise to pull the pieces together and apply this integrative knowledge to the problems and challenges of the world as well as our own personal lives. Wisdom is power and ordered knowledge. Data glut is chaos and generates impotence.

A NEW CONCEPTUAL FRAMEWORK OF THINKING— EVOLUTION AND RECIPROCITY

A common argument among many futurists and visionaries is that we need a new way of thinking to live and thrive in the future. Many of these arguments focus on critiques of Newtonian, Industrial Age, and Western Enlightenment thinking and propose some type of evolutionary, ecological, and pluralistic mind-set to take its place.[57] The old way of thinking is seen as too linear, analytic, static, rationalistic, and hierarchical. The proposed new way of thinking is more horizontal, holistic, dynamic, intuitive, and network-like. Interestingly, this new way of thinking is similar to "feminine" and "non-Western" thinking, whereas the old way of thinking is associated with Western males.[58]

The problem with such critiques is that they tend to throw the baby out with the bathwater and consequently all of the stereotypical Western male cognitive and psychological traits have been unfairly and one-sidedly undermined. As noted earlier, we would be lost without linear thinking, and, to pick another example, without analytic thought, logic and science would go out the window and life would be reduced to a chaotic blur.

So what type of conceptual scheme best captures the full breadth of human experience and thinking and provides a constructive and viable mind-set for the future? Based on a review of many contemporary proposals we suggest that two key ideas emerge, which are evolution and reciprocity. These two ideas form the core of the last two character virtues we describe.

RECIPROCITY AND BALANCE

Reciprocity

We use the term "reciprocity" to mean distinct but interdependent. The dictionary definition of reciprocity highlights the idea of mutual exchange. An open-systems view describes nature as reciprocal systems. The whole idea of ecology is built on the notion of reciprocity—of mutual dependency of life forms forming an integrated whole.[59] A philosophy of reciprocity views reality in terms of complementarities and balance. The Chinese Yin-Yang exemplifies this perspective. Many concepts of justice and fairness derive from the idea of reciprocity. The expressions "An eye for an eye," "Do unto others," and "You scratch my back" all describe reciprocities. Reciprocity is a key principle underlying the idea of partnerships.[60] One could argue that all evolution, natural and man-made, involves the creation of new reciprocities. All evolution is reciprocal evolution, or as Harold Morowitz states, "All evolution is co-evolution."[61]

At the most basic level, integrating the idea of reciprocity into one's philosophy and behavior means acknowledging one's inter-dependency with the rest of humanity, with nature, with the cosmos, and even with technology. It means giving up the mistaken notion of extreme individualism—that each of us is a separate self-contained entity.

Reciprocity and Creating Resonant Environments

The person and the environment form a reciprocity.[62] The person and the environment mutually affect and determine each other. To use an expression coined by the psychologist Albert Bandura, there is "reciprocal determinism" between the person and the environment.[63] We are neither passive victims nor totally in control. What happens in our lives is an interaction effect.

Given this fundamental reciprocity, the level of future conscious-ness a person is able to develop and maintain is integrally connected with the environment. People at times can maintain a strong future orientation in spite of an impoverished present-centered environ-ment, but generally speaking, environmental conditions and opportunities strongly impact a person's state of mind.

Based on the notion of reciprocal determinism, people can influence and in fact change their environment. Consequently, it is important to identify, seek out, nurture, and create *resonant environ-ments* that support future consciousness. Many of the critiques of our contemporary lifestyle cited above put the blame on environmental factors that deteriorate extended consciousness, purpose, and mental order. Hence, it is critical to realize that evolving meaning, purpose, and future consciousness cannot take place in a vacuum—it is not something done alone. One must find reciprocal exchanges and mutual support with others. One must integrate the inner self with community and others. One must go beyond the self-defined ego and find a context in which to thrive.

Expanding future consciousness is not something that is instan-taneously achieved; it is a growing and open-ended process. Similarly, resonant environments need to be cultivated and devel-oped, as does one's mode of interaction with these environments.

Future consciousness and resonant environments reciprocally evolve.

Engaging a resonant environment should produce challenges and surprises. A resonant environment is not something one completely controls. There is a degree of uncertainty in that the environment contributes to the unfolding of events. A resonant environment that facilitates the development of future consciousness stretches the mind-set and capacities of an individual. An environment that simply responds to the wishes and actions of an individual without challenge or effort (our rats in Skinner boxes) does not enhance future consciousness. Hence, resonant environments that support the development of any of the virtues we have described must create a challenge for the individual.

Finding the Tao—Finding Balance

Reciprocity also means seeking and creating balance in life. We should become attuned to the Tao—the balancing of Yin and Yang. This is the practice of temperance, another of Seligman's key virtues. Balance allows one to maintain self-control and order. One can become a slave to any value or goal if it is carried to an extreme. It is important to balance logic with intuition, reason with emotion, and the quest for certainty with faith. It is important to balance work and focused activities with play and rest.

One important example of balance is that we should acknowledge that there are two reciprocal forms of thinking, both of which have value and validity. These two forms of thinking, circular and linear, holistic and analytical, capture the variability that is seen between female and male thinking, Western and non-Western thinking, and left versus right cerebral functioning.[64] In a true global society in the future, East and West, women and men, artist and scientist, all need to be seen as having an essential and valuable place and contribution.

Balance and interdependency are tied together in the idea of reciprocity, as they are connected in the Taoist Yin-Yang. Each polarity requires the other for its full realization—one cannot suppress half of the human equation in pursuit of some extremist dream.

In our fast-paced, frantic world, it is also important that there is disengagement, acceptance, and stillness in life. One needs to stop and assess reality. One needs time to reflect and to feel oneself. One needs to be alone. One needs to accept and stop pushing all the time. Burn-out, exhaustion, excessive stress, and general psychological mania all result from too much focused doing and not enough disengagement, inner peace, and tranquility.

One of the most important themes in contemporary science is the interdependency of order and chaos.[65] The psychologist Maureen O'Hara has developed a theory of human personality that addresses the issue of finding a balance of order and chaos in our lives.[66] According to O'Hara, there are three fundamental ways of dealing with change—defensive, psychotic, and growth responsive. The defensive response is "anxiety repressed"; the psychotic response is "anxiety unleashed"; and the growth response is "anxiety contained and transformed." She refers to the growth-oriented self as a "transformative self."

According to O'Hara, the defensive reaction emphasizes the need for excessive order and involves efforts to simplify reality. It produces rigidity, conformity, addiction, dependency on authority, lack of creativity, and feelings of apathy and depression. It is the psychological source of absolutism, fundamentalism, the retreat into the security and stability of the past, and the desire for excessive control.

The psychotic reaction produces excessive psychological chaos. It involves withdrawal and a retreat into fantasy, a lack of psychological coherence, mania, psychic pain, and a collapse of any boundaries between the self and others. It is the source of extreme subjectivism, fragmentation, and deterioration in any standards.

For O'Hara, the transformative reaction involves flexibility, creativity, integration, balance, openness, interconnectedness, expansive consciousness, a synthesis of the rational and intuitive, a tolerance for ambiguity, a balance of cooperation and competition, empathy, and joy. The transformative reaction generates psychological and social evolution and involves a synthesis and balance of chaos and order.

Notice that many of these psychological features correspond to the type of character we have described in our outline of fundamental virtues for the future and that many of the features of the defensive and psychotic personality types correspond to negative aspects of contemporary society as we have described it. Neither the defensive nor the psychotic reaction generates psychological growth.

O'Hara believes that the most adaptive and functional self for a society that is both pluralistic and changing is the transformative self. She contends that appropriate social systems and cultures are needed to support a transformative self. In our terminology, the evolution of future consciousness requires resonant environments. According to O'Hara, neither contemporary Western nor Eastern culture provides such social support for a transformative self. In support of her claim, we would point out that social and psychological research indicates that Eastern cultures are holistic, conformist, and "right brain," whereas Western cultures are analytic, individualistic, and "left brain."[67] We need a culture that is more balanced and brings together in mutual support the strengths of the West and the East.

EVOLUTION AND TRANSCENDENCE

The last key character virtue that Seligman identifies is transcendence—the capacity to go beyond the individual self and find meaning and purpose in something greater than oneself. We propose that this virtue be coupled with the idea of evolution. Evolution also entails a sense of beyondness, particularly regarding time and the present. From an evolutionary perspective, we have a sense that we are moving toward something in the future that transcends the present. It may seem strange that we are bringing together these two ideas, since transcendence has a strong spiritual connotation, whereas evolution is a scientific and naturalistic idea. The idea of evolution, though, was greatly inspired by earlier Western religious views that saw time as linear and progressive.[68]

As noted, evolution is a pivotal idea in proposals for a new way of thinking about reality. Our past intellectual heritage, in both the East and the West, has identified the most elevated aspects of reality as eternal, unchanging, and permanent. God was changeless, and the scientific laws of nature were presumably constant and fixed. Yet, as the last few centuries have demonstrated at many levels and from many perspectives, it is entirely unrealistic to view reality as static, permanent, and secure. Life is fluid, transforming, and to a degree uncertain. Evolution provides a scientifically grounded theoretical framework for understanding the history and dynamics of all of nature, including humanity and the cosmos.[69] The history of evolution also clearly shows that the growth of complexity, though involving an irreducible dimension of creativity and novelty, is built upon the past, rather than being a rejection or jettison of the past.[70]

It is our contention that our fast-paced contemporary society exhibits a lot of change and very little significant evolution. There is a great deal of chaos and many defensive counterreactions that are either regressive or static. As a remedy, we advocate for a philosophy and ethics of evolution and growth. Practicing the virtue of evolution and transcendence involves the pursuit of progressive development through the exercise of all the important virtues. Following O'Hara, and a philosophy of reciprocity, evolution requires balance and synthesis and not the mad pursuit of extremes and domination over nature and others. Evolution involves the creation of new order that incorporates the best of the past but also transcends the past.

Developing Optimism and Combating Pessimism

According to Seligman, one of the key subcategories of transcendence is hope and optimism. Seligman, who has studied the attitudes of optimism and pessimism extensively, argues that the belief that one can positively affect the future is critical to optimistic thinking. Optimism involves a strong sense of self-efficacy. He defines optimism as a way of thinking involving the beliefs that misfortunes are relatively short-lived, limited in their effect, and due to external circumstances. Pessimists, on the other hand, not only have negative images about the future, they believe that they cannot positively affect any change in what is to come. They believe that they are doomed to failure. They feel hopeless and helpless. Seligman defines pessimism as involving the beliefs that misfortunes have long-term and pervasive effects and are the fault of the individual. Following a cognitive theory of motivation and emotion, Seligman contends that depression is primarily due to pessimistic thinking.

Both optimism and pessimism are self-fulfilling prophecies. Consequently, each mode of thinking gets reinforced since it tends to lead to the very results it anticipates. Seligman sees optimism and pessimism as "habits of thought," which obey the laws of reinforcement. Based upon a great deal of accumulated experimental evidence, he believes these habits of thought can be changed through relearning, education, and training.[71]

Optimism, though, can be either realistic or unrealistic. According to Noelle Nelson, another researcher, fear of the future leads to inaction and negative emotional states. But to uncritically think the future will be wonderful is unrealistic and will invariably lead to frustration and disappointment. Nelson, instead, argues that a "winner" belief about the future involves acknowledging both the negative and positive possibilities of tomorrow and believing that we have some power and choice in determining which possibilities are realized. Hence, perceiving the risks, but also seeing that one has some control over what will come to pass, generates good mental health. Conversely, Nelson argues that believing that external forces beyond our control determine the future, or that the future is set, generates apathy and other negative emotional states.[72]

From Nelson's analysis, and Seligman would concur on many of these points, realistic optimism involves critical and reflective thinking about the future, seeing the future as possibilities and taking responsibility for which possibilities are realized. It requires courage and faith in the face of acknowledged risk, and in general produces more happiness than misery and depression. Further, we would add, and Seligman would concur again, that realistic optimism expands future consciousness, whereas pessimism and depression close down the human mind to the future. Why think where there is no hope? Believing in the possibility and value of evolution gives us hope.

Flow and Cultivating an "Evolving Self"

Csikszentmihalyi presents a theory of mental health that specifically highlights the concepts of evolution and transcendence. His theory of the "evolving self" emphasizes the need to transcend the egocentric constraints within us.[73] He believes we have the inherent capacity to see beyond the limits of our present condition and transcend them. Csikszentmihalyi argues for a new type of self in the future—one that does not identify with or accept the selfish needs of genes (the body), culture, or the ego. He believes that the ego was created when humans first distinguished their minds as something distinct and separate from the body. The future self—an evolving self—should identify with something beyond itself. He thinks that achieving this transcendent state requires a strong element of mental control. We need to learn to believe in freedom and self-determination.

According to Csikszentmihalyi, the key to an evolving self is the experience of flow. Flow is a state of consciousness to be cultivated within life. He describes the flow experience as involving both clear goals and feedback—an open system of interaction between the self and the environment. Within flow experiences, the skills match the challenge; a balance is achieved between the person's abilities and the difficulty of the task with just enough tension. There is a "one-pointedness" of mind and a merging of thought and action. There is a sense of potential control, not complete control, though, or else the activity becomes boring. Further, there is a loss of self-consciousness and a feeling of self-transcendence. There is an altered sense of time and a feeling that the activity is worth doing for its own sake.

The experience of flow in life continues if we keep finding new challenges. Flow requires novelty. According to Csikszentmihalyi, it is the engine of evolution. When flow is absent, people turn to self-destructive and other negative actions.

Csikszentmihalyi presents a theory of *transcenders*, of people who pursue the experience of flow. They search for increasing complexity in their own consciousness. They enjoy a life of developing skills, meeting challenges, being part of the evolutionary process, and moving to higher levels of harmonious complexity. Transcenders are evolving selves.

He describes the ideal self of the future as recapitulating the ideals of the past and as encompassing a balance and synthesis of the opposite traits within us. He sees this ideal evolving self as a cosmic self that identifies and integrates with all humanity, nature, and the universe. He describes the growth of this new type of self as dialectical, between differentiation and integration, and inner and outer concerns. The evolving self grows through increasing uniqueness and through increasing integration and transcendence. The evolving self is original yet systematic, independent yet responsible, intuitive yet rational. It possesses pride, yet it is concerned with others. It is a self that "flows" and "transcends" its own boundaries. It is an evolving narrative that is moving with a sense of adventure and purpose. It is open to the world and to its own inner workings.

Cosmic Evolution, Enlightenment, God, and Mystery

It is important to develop a global and cosmic view of the future and integrate one's life narrative into it. We need openness to something higher, something beyond the self. One must let go of the inner defined self and of past habits and ways of thinking. We need to move beyond a self-centered point of view. Placing one's life narrative in transcendent context gives one's life purpose and meaning.[74] The state of enlightenment, whether spiritual or secular, according to Walter Truett Anderson, involves connecting with the Oneness of it all.[75] For biologist John Stewart, identifying with cosmic evolution is the highest form of adaptation. We see ourselves as participatory in the grand cosmic process of evolution and are centrally motivated to contribute to this process.[76]

Whether one believes in natural cosmic evolution or God, or some synthesis of the two ideas, it is critical for our growth to acknowledge the mystery of existence. If we believe we have all the answers, we cannot experience transcendence and we cannot grow. We are closed within a self-defined egocentric universe. God must be an open definition—a real transcendence. Transcendence is not a form of security. Transcendence, whether secular or spiritual, requires faith and courage.

CONCLUSION

We conclude this paper with a quotation from Spinoza. He is one of those giants of the past on whose shoulders we should stand. Spinoza argued that we should view ourselves through the "eyes of eternity"—that is, humans should see themselves in a cosmic context. He also believed that the key to happiness was through ethics and virtue, a philosophy and psychology we clearly also endorse. Spinoza was also a paragon of reason, yet equally a person of courage, passion, and humility.[77] Though he lived long before the emergence of the modern theory of evolution, he was indeed an evolving self. He is the pristine synthesis, in thought and action, of the ideals of the Western Enlightenment. And finally, he was a truly independent soul, a person of self-determination. And thus, on this theme, we end with his closing words to *The Ethics*, "If the way which I have pointed out...seems exceedingly hard, it may nevertheless be discovered.... How would it be possible, if salvation were ready to our hand, and could without great labor be found, that it should be by almost all men neglected? But all things excellent are as difficult as they are rare."[78] Let us hope that perhaps we can evolve to the point where our modern salvation, though undoubtedly difficult and challenging, will not be a rare and infrequent achievement among us.

NOTES

1. Howard F. Didsbury Jr. "The Death of the Future in a Hedonistic Society," ed. H.F. Didsbury Jr., *Frontiers of the 21st Century: Prelude to the New Millennium* (Bethesda, MD: World Future Society, 1999).
2. J. Olds and P. Milner, "Positive Reinforcement Produced by Electrical Stimulation of the Septal Area and Other Regions of the Rat Brain," *Journal of Comparative and Physiological Psychology*, Vol. 47, 417-427.

3. Neil Postman, *Amusing Ourselves to Death: Public Discourse in the Age of Show Business* (New York: Penguin Books, 1985).

4. Robert Nisbet, *History of the Idea of Progress* (New Brunswick: Transaction Publishers, 1994).

5. Edward Cornish, "How We Can Anticipate the Future," *The Futurist*, Vol. 35, No. 4, July-August 2001.

6. Peter Russell, *The White Hole in Time: Our Future Evolution and the Meaning of Now* (New York: HarperCollins, 1992).

7. Stephen Bertman, "Cultural Amnesia: A Threat to Our Future," *The Futurist*, Vol. 35, No. 1, January-February 2001.

8. James Gleick, *Faster: The Acceleration of Just About Everything* (New York: Pantheon Books, 1999).

9. Steven Best and Douglas Kellner, *The Postmodern Turn* (New York: The Guilford Press, 1997).

10. Francis Fukuyama, *The End of History and the Last Man* (New York: The Free Press, 1992).

11. Steven Best and Douglas Kellner, 1997.

12. Walter Truett Anderson, "Four Different Ways to be Absolutely Right," ed. W.T. Anderson, *The Truth About the Truth: De-Confusing and Re-Constructing the Postmodern World* (New York: G.P. Putnam's Sons, 1995).

13. Alvin Toffler, *Future Shock* (New York: Bantam, 1971).

14. James Gleick, 1999.

15. Ray Kurzweil, *The Age of Spiritual Machines: When Computers Exceed Human Intelligence* (New York: Penguin Books, 1999); Hans Moravec, *Robot: Mere Machine to Transcendent Mind* (Oxford: Oxford University Press, 1999).

16. Vernor Vinge, "The Coming Technological Singularity: How to Survive in the Post-Human Era," *Vision-21: Interdisciplinary Science and Engineering in the Era of Cyberspace NASA-CP-10129*, 1993, or see www.ugcs.caltech.edu/~phoenix/vinge/vinge-sing.html.

17. Barry Schwartz, *The Paradox of Choice: Why More Is Less* (New York: Ecco, 2004).

18. George Miller, "The Magical Number Seven, Plus or Minus Two: Some Limits on Our Capacity for Processing Information," *Psychological Review*, Vol. 63, 81-97.

19. Neil Postman, 1985.

20. Walter Truett Anderson, *The Future of the Self* (New York: Putnam, 1997); Walter Truett Anderson, *The Next Enlightenment: Integrating East and West in a New Vision of Human Evolution* (New York: St. Martin's Press, 2003).

21. Sherry Turkle, *Life on the Screen: Identity in the Age of the Internet* (New York: Simon and Schuster, 1995).

22. Daniel C. Dennett, *Consciousness Explained* (Boston: Little, Brown, and Co., 1991).

23. Kevin Kelly, *Out of Control: The Rise of Neo-Biological Civilization* (Reading, MA: Addison-Wesley, 1994).

24. Ilya Prigogine and Isabelle Stengers, *Order Out of Chaos: Man's New Dialogue with Nature* (New York: Bantam, 1984); James Gleick, *Chaos: Making a New Science* (New York: Viking, 1987); Sally Goerner, *Chaos and the Evolving Ecological Universe* (Luxembourg: Gordon and Breach, 1994).

25. Rudy Rucker, R.U. Sirius, and Mu Queen, *Mondo 2000* (New York: Harper Collins, 1992).

26. Carole Wade and Carol Tarvis, *Psychology*, 7th Edition (Upper Saddle River, NJ: Prentice Hall, 2003), Chapter 15.

27. Julian Rotter, "Internal Versus External Control of Reinforcement: A Case Study of a Variable," *American Psychologist*, Vol. 45, 1990.

28. Mihaly Csikszentmihalyi, *The Evolving Self: A Psychology for the Third Millennium* (Harper Collins, 1993).

29. Stephen Moore and Julian Simon, *It's Getting Better All the Time: 100 Greatest Trends of the Last 100 Years* (Washington, D.C.: Cato Institute, 2000); Gregg Easterbrook, *The Progress Paradox: How Life Gets Better While People Feel Worse* (New York: Random House, 2003).

30. Peter Watson, *The Modern Mind: An Intellectual History of the 20th Century* (New York: HarperCollins Perennial, 2001).

31. Martin Seligman, *Learned Optimism: How to Change Your Mind and Your Life* (New York: Pocket Books, 1998).

32. Donald Brown, *Human Universals* (New York: McGraw-Hill, 1991); Steven Pinker, *The Blank Slate: The Modern Denial of Human Nature* (New York: Penguin Books, 2002).

33. Francis Fukuyama, *The Great Disruption: Human Nature and the Reconstitution of Social Order* (New York: The Free Press, 1999); Dinesh D'Souza, *The Virtue of Prosperity: Finding Values in an Age of Techno-Affluence* (New York: The Free Press, 2000).

34. Robert Putnam, *Bowling Alone: The Collapse and Revival of American Community* (New York: Touchstone, 2000).

35. Walter Truett Anderson, 2003.

36. Martin Seligman, 1998.

37. Martin Seligman, 1998; Martin Seligman, *Authentic Happiness: Using the New Positive Psychology to Realize Your Potential for Lasting Fulfillment* (New York: The Free Press, 2002); Gregg Easterbrook, Gregg, 2003.

38. Foundation for Global Community, www.globalcommunity.org/; Jon Spayde, "The New Renaissance," *Utne Reader*, February, 1998.

39. Neil Postman, *Technopoly: The Surrender of Culture to Technology* (New York: Vintage Books, 1992); Neil Postman, 1985.

40. Robert Solomon, *The Big Questions: A Short Introduction to Philosophy*, 6th Edition (Orlando, Florida: Harcourt College Publishers, 2002), Chapter 8.

41. Wendell Bell, "Values," *Encyclopedia of the Future*, eds. George Thomas Kurian and Graham T.T. Molitor (New York: Simon and Schuster Macmillan, 1996).

42. Rushworth M. Kidder, "Universal Human Values: Finding an Ethical Common Ground," *The Futurist*, Vol. 28, No. 8, July-August 1994.

43. Donald Brown, 1991; Steven Pinker, 2002, pp. 435-439; Human Universals, condor.depaul.edu/~mfiddler/hyphen/humunivers.htm.

44. Martin Seligman, 2002.

45. Antonio Damasio, *The Feeling of What Happens: Body and Emotion in the Making of Consciousness* (Harcourt Brace, 1999).

46. Albert Bandura, "Human Agency in Social Cognitive Theory," *American Psychologist*, Vol. 44, 1989; B.R. Hergenhahn and Matthew Olson, *An Introduction to Theories of Personality*, 6th Edition (Upper Saddle River, NJ: Prentice Hall, 2003), Chapter 11.

47. Mihaly Csikszentmihalyi, 1993.

48. Foundation for Global Community, www.globalcommunity.org/; Jon Spayde, 1998.

49. Leonard Shlain, 2003.

50. Erich Fromm, *Escape from Freedom* (New York: Avon Books, 1941).

51. Mihaly Csikszentmihalyi, 1993.

52. Walter Truett Anderson, 2003; Morris Berman, *The Twilight of American Culture* (New York: W.W. Norton, 2000).

53. Universal Intellectual Standards, www.criticalthinking.org/University/unistan.html.

54. Critical Thinking Consortium, www.criticalthinking.org/humanmind.html.

55. Patricia King and Karen Kitchener, *Developing Reflective Judgment: Understanding and Promoting Intellectual Growth and Critical Thinking in Adolescents and Adults* (San Francisco: Jossey-Bass, 1994).

56. Insight Assessment, www.insightassessment.com/dex.html.

57. Sally Goerner, 1994; Steven Best and Douglas Kellner, 1997.

58. Richard Nisbett, *The Geography of Thought: How Asians and Westerners Think Differently...and Why* (New York: The Free Press, 2003); Leonard Shlain, *The Alphabet Versus the Goddess: The Conflict Between Word and Image* (New York: Penguin Arkana, 1998).

59. Elisabet Sahtouris, *EarthDance: Living Systems in Evolution* (Lincoln, Nebraska: IUniverse Press, 2000).

60. Riane Eisler, *Sacred Pleasure: Sex, Myth, and the Politics of the Body* (San Francisco: HarperCollins, 1995).

61. Harold Morowitz, *The Emergence of Everything: How the World Became Complex* (Oxford: Oxford University Press, 2002); Robert Wright, *Nonzero: The Logic of Human Destiny* (New York: Pantheon Books, 2000); Howard Bloom, *Global Brain: The Evolution of Mass Mind from the Big Bang to the 21st Century* (New York: John Wiley and Sons, Inc., 2000).

62. Thomas Lombardo, *The Reciprocity of Perceiver and Environment: The Evolution of James J. Gibson's Ecological Psychology* (Hillsdale, NJ: Lawrence Erlbaum Associates, 1987).

63. B.R. Hergenhahn and Matthew Olson, 2003, Chapter 11.

64. Richard Nisbett, 2003.

65. Ilya Prigogine and Isabelle Stengers, 1984; Sally Goerner, 1994; Stuart Kauffman, "Order for Free," ed. John Brockman, *The Third Culture* (New York: Touchstone, 1995).

66. Maureen O'Hara, "Future Mind: Three Scenarios for a Psychological Future," World Future Society Conference Presentation, 1999.

67. Richard Nisbett, 2003; Harry Triandis, *Individualism and Collectivism* (Boulder, CO: Westview Press, 1995).

68. Robert Nisbet, 1994.

69. Barbara Marx Hubbard, *Conscious Evolution: Awakening the Power of Our Social Potential* (Novato, CA: New World Library, 1998).

70. Harold Morowitz, 2002; Paul Davies, *The Cosmic Blueprint: New Discoveries in Nature's Creative Ability to Order the Universe* (New York: Simon and Schuster, 1988).

71. Martin Seligman, 1998.

72. Noelle Nelson, "Beliefs About the Future," *The Futurist*, Vol. 34, No. 1, January-February 2000.

73. Mihaly Csikszentmihalyi, 1993.

74. Martin Seligman, 2002.

75. Walter Truett Anderson, 2003.

76. John Stewart, 2000.

77. Antonio Damasio, *Looking for Spinoza: Joy, Sorrow, and the Feeling Brain* (Orlando, FL: Harcourt, Inc., 2003).

78. Benedict de Spinoza, *On the Improvement of the Understanding: The Ethics Correspondence* (New York: Dover Publications, 1955).

THE COMING CONFLICT BETWEEN SCIENCE AND SPIRIT

by

William E. Halal

Rushing advances in neuroscience, computer power, and artificial intelligence are approaching the ability to model human behavior with remarkable precision. Extend these gains a bit and it's easy to envision a scientific revolution that automates human intelligence. Even now, scientists claim they will soon explain away consciousness and free will.

Meanwhile, the Information Age is driving an explosion of heightened awareness, global crises demanding broader perspectives, and growth in authentic forms of spirituality. All this suggests a rise of "human spirit" that may swell into a "spiritual revolution" paralleling the scientific revolution above.

It is tempting to think these two great trends could converge in time. But for the foreseeable future, they seem to be propelling us into the maws of a great conflict now shaping up between Science and Spirit. Are we humans simply a biological system for processing information? Or is there something about life and humanity that transcends sheer knowledge?

THE SCIENTIFIC REVOLUTION IN CONSCIOUSNESS

The traditional model of human behavior formulated long ago by Rene Descartes has served as a foil against which scientists have argued for centuries. Descartes proposed a theory commonly called "dualism," which states that behavior consists of two different types. "Simple" behaviors are deterministic in that an environmental stimulus automatically produces a response (touching a hot stove), while "complex" behaviors are unpredictable because they involve higher-order issues that Descartes attributed to "the soul." Well, you can imagine how the second category rankles scientists, and many neuroscientists are hard at work demonstrating that complex behavior can be effectively explained.

A prominent perspective draws on probability theory, Bayesian statistics, economics, game theory, behavioral ecology, and the Nash Equilibrium that won John Nash a Nobel Prize. This view claims that any organism can be accurately modeled as a decision maker driven by Darwinian logic to find optimal solutions to complex problems involving uncertainty.

A wonderful example is offered by studies of how ducks respond to uncertainty in their feeding. D.G.C. Harper at Cambridge University observed the results of two people positioned 20 meters apart at

William E. Halal *is professor of management at George Washington University, Washington D.C., and project director of the* GW Forecast. *He may be contacted at halal@gwu.edu.*

the edge of the lake throwing breadballs to feed ducks. One throws breadballs weighing 2 grams every five seconds while the other throws the same breadballs every 10 seconds. Using game theory and the Nash Equilibrium, the optimal location is calculated to define how each duck can maximize its catch. It turns out that this optimal solution occurs when two-thirds of the ducks place themselves near the researcher throwing breadballs every five seconds and one-third near the one throwing every 10 seconds.

Results showed an uncanny approximation to this optimal solution. Within 60 seconds, two-thirds of the ducks moved to the spot where food was dropped every five seconds and one-third went to where they were fed every 10 seconds. This outcome was obtained automatically as each duck maintained a one-third/two-thirds ratio of its time in each area, illustrating that the overall solution derives from an aggregation of individual ducks pursuing the logic of this payoff matrix. Furthermore, when the relative size of the breadballs and their frequency was changed, the ducks immediately repositioned themselves in accordance with the theory.

Other experiments involving monkeys, birds, and mice bear out the same conclusions. In the words of neuroscientist Paul Glincher: "Animals come remarkably closer to achieving optimal solutions."[1] This is a great advance in our understanding of behavior and it has an intuitive appeal. Animals may not process mathematical calculations, but they instinctively judge the likelihood of obtaining various sources of food and they adjust their behavior to maximize the chance of success. The same could possibly be shown for sex and other common behaviors. Glincher concludes, "Mind ... simply does not figure in the equation."

LIFE BEYOND RATIONALITY

My reservation about this line of thought is that it cannot be extended to include *all* behavior. To most people, the above claim amounts to a *reducio ad absurdum.* It is one thing to observe animals responding to offers of food, and quite another when aware human beings struggle with issues involving love, family, community, fear, patriotism, religion, joy, sadness, art, humor, hatred, meaning, purpose, and all the other woes that flesh is heir to. Indeed, the theory itself points to this same dichotomy. Scientists view animals as decision makers but they focus on outward behavior while ignoring the myriad phenomena taking place inside the decision maker's mind—the likelihood that some sort of "post-rational," "transcendent," "integrated," or "spiritual" domain may exert an even greater influence.[2]

The life of John Nash himself, who contributed the central concept of Game Theory Equilibrium, attests to the central role of consciousness and free will. As his story is told in the movie *A Beautiful Mind,* Nash was incapacitated for years by paranoid delusions. Through sheer will and against psychiatric advice, he finally mustered up the conviction to learn that he could ignore these delusional impulses, and thereby regained control of his behavior.

Most thinking adults are preoccupied with such subjective matters that defy logic because they transcend sheer information and knowledge. The crucial actions of life—succeeding in a career, keeping a marriage alive, raising children, etc.—require drawing on the inner strength, wisdom, and willpower of a person, self, or soul. After all, somebody is acting as a decision maker. Try telling executives, lovers, parents, the devout, and other normal people that their behavior is purely an automatic response to environmental stimuli and you are likely to get a blank stare. To most people there is no need for proof—the domain of consciousness, will, and human spirit is self-evident.

A GREAT SOCIAL EXPERIMENT IS UNDER WAY

This question about the nature of consciousness defines one of the central debates of our time. Scientists increasingly have been studying consciousness because the exploding power of computers and artificial intelligence point directly to this mysterious phenomenon we take for granted.[3] The consensus today is that computer power should match that of the human brain about 2020, setting the stage for a grand test of a paramount scientific question: "Is there is a substantial difference between human intelligence and machine intelligence?" IBM's Deep Blue computer is now tied with chess master Garry Kasparov, and Kasparov admits that it's only a question of time until he is surpassed.

The issue is more than brute computer power, however. The real issue revolves around the possibility that humans—and other life forms—possess some form of awareness, willpower, or other such abilities that transcend information. It could be thought of as a "spiritual Turing test"—can we demonstrate the existence of human spirit?

Not surprisingly, scientists are largely united in thinking there is no such "Ghost in the Machine." The guiding hypothesis is that consciousness is an "emergent" phenomenon, arising automatically out of the functioning of the brain and body, and thus behavior is determined by physical causes. Consider the work of a few well-known authorities:[4]

- Benjamin Libet, a University of California physiologist, has provoked great attention by finding that there is a one-third second delay between the time an act is initiated in the brain and the time the subject reports a decision to initiate the act, suggesting that decisions are a mere afterthought.

- Other studies show that stimulating sections of the brain with magnets strongly influences actions, confirming the strong role of brain circuitry and impulses.

• Neuroscientists have identified regions of the brain that are active during intense meditation, suggesting that religious experience is a neural phenomenon.

• The above types of work have been replicated and are widely interpreted to dispel the role of free will. For instance, the New York Academy of Sciences recently held a conference titled "From Soul to Brain."

• Nobel laureate Francis Crick, co-discoverer of the DNA helix, claims, "You, your joys, and your sorrows, your sense of personal identity and free will, are in fact no more than the behavior of a vast assembly of nerve cells and their associated molecules."

• Microsoft Chairman Bill Gates goes even further: "There's nothing unique in human intelligence that can't be replicated by machines."

• Pulitzer Prize winning scientist Edward Wilson contends, "Scientific knowledge holds that religious experience is entirely neurobiological."

The other possibility is also disruptive. As human thought becomes increasingly automated, we could just as easily bump against the limits of technology. After all, previous forms of automation have shown similar patterns. When factories were automated it was feared that the loss of jobs would produce rampant unemployment, but the reverse occurred and better jobs became plentiful. What we have learned is that, as automation eliminates routine tasks that can be relegated to machines, this frees people to focus on more complex, creative tasks that can only be handled by humans. I suspect the same will prove true for the automation of human thought.

Computers may master routine thought, but they are not likely to master higher-level thought, forcing us to recognize that there truly is a transcendent dimension underlying life. The most powerful, the most intelligent information system may never simulate this uncharted domain of values, choice, intuition, creativity, emotion, willpower, and other subjective qualities associated distinctively with human spirit. I can vividly imagine us complaining as we correct dumb mistakes of robots. We are likely to treat them as backward children.

If this limit exists, science may mature to recognize the unique power of human spirit and its implications. David Chalmers, a philosopher at the University of Arizona, thinks "We are likely to discover that consciousness is a fundamental property of the universe, like space, time, and gravity."[5] Consider the evidence on the spiritual side of this cosmic debate:[6]

- Hundreds of medical studies demonstrate the powerful influence of beliefs on health. The well-known placebo effect is so strong that medical trials all control for it. In fact, a mere sugar pill can be more effective that the best medications in relieving depression.

- People who practice religion have been shown to be healthier. Studies show that those with religious beliefs, who attend church regularly, and have friends are far less likely to suffer heart disease and depression, and they live longer.

- Rupert Sheldrake, a physical scientist, has conducted experiments that suggest "morphogenetic" energy fields influence learning, they allow people to sense being stared at, and alert dogs when their masters are coming home.

- Maharishi University faculty have published dozens of studies in scientific journals demonstrating a link between meditation and social order. The number of people involved seems to be inversely correlated with crime, violence, and other social statistics.

- Untold numbers of people who have been clinically dead and returned to life all relate the same spiritual experiences of being welcomed by their deceased loved ones and religious figures like Christ. Afterward, they have no fear of death.

- A medical study found that having people pray for patients had a positive impact statistically—even though the patients were unaware they were being prayed for.

- All societies throughout history have been organized around some type of belief system. Even in high-tech America, surveys consistently show that around 90% of Americans believe in a God with whom they talk and pray.

STAY TUNED FOR THE ANSWER

Whether the scientific or spiritual explanations are correct is impossible to say at this point. The scientific view is likely in time to demonstrate that huge hunks of human behavior can be modeled as rational, deterministic systems, possibly leading to another historic revolution. Much as Galileo shattered conviction in an Earth-centered universe and Darwin dispelled the distinction between humans and animals, the neuroscience revolution is even now challenging deeply held beliefs about will, awareness, and other qualities attributed to spirit and soul. Without the foundation of free will that underlies society, how could we punish crime? Reward the successful? Aspire to betterment?

But press scientists to explain how consciousness arises from the brain and you will be disappointed. I've made a point of following the literature in this field, and I am impressed with how vacuous the explanations are. The most plausible theories hold that consciousness is the brain's electromagnetic field interacting with its own circuitry, or it's an aggregation of the sea of memes populating civilization.[7]

In the end, it may be easier to accept the possibility that some form of spiritual energy permeates the universe than to accept the convoluted explanations scientists propose. How, exactly, can the brain produce consciousness? Where is the evidence that subjective experiences can be replicated by machines? In short, science is doing a wonderful job of explaining the mechanics of behavior, but it shows no understanding of that inner spirit that drives behavior. Daniel Batson, a University of Kansas psychologist, put it best: "To say that the brain produces religion is like saying a piano produces music."[8]

This academic dilemma is rather similar to current theories that attempt to explain why our universe is so perfectly hospitable to life. Rather than accept the mere possibility of some divine power or intelligence, science now posits a "multiverse" in which our universe happens to be suited to life, while billions of others remain sterile. Physicist Charles Townes highlights how bizarre this theory is: "The speculation that there exist billions of invisible, parallel universes would be laughed out of town if it came from a religious text."[9]

Either way, we are in for a fascinating learning experience during the next 20 years or so as computer power and our ability to model human intelligence matures. Will life be dominated by artificial intelligence systems or the divine spark of life? Perhaps we will witness a synthesis of these two poles. Stay tuned.

[Editor's Note: Portions of this paper first appeared in *On the Horizon*, Vol. 11, No. 4 (2003).]

NOTES

1. Marcus Anthony, "Integrated Intelligence," *Journal of Futures Studies*, Vol. 8, No. 2, 2002.
2. Paul Glincher, *Decisions, Uncertainty, and the Brain: The Science of Neuroeconomics* (MIT Press, 2003).
3. William E. Halal, "The Intelligent Internet," *The Futurist*, Vol. 38, No. 2 (March-April 2004).

4. Carey Goldberg, "A Question of Will," *Boston Globe* (10/15/02), "In Search of the Buy Button," *Forbes.com* (Sept. 1, 2003), William E. Halal, "Beyond Knowledge" (A Working Paper).

5. Shankar Vedantam, "A New Thinking Emerges About Consciousness," *Washington Post*, May 20, 2002.

6. Halal, "Beyond Knowledge," Op. Cit.

7. Jeffrey Benner, "Consciousness Based on Wireless?" *Wired News*, May 21, 2002.

8. Shankar Vedantam, "Tracing the Synapses of Spirituality," *Washington Post*, June 17, 2001.

9. Gregg Easterbrook, "The New Convergence," *Wired*, December 2002.

REFECTIONS ON TEACHING ABOUT UTOPIAS: OH, WHAT A LIFT THAT PHANTOM OFFERS!

by

Arthur B. Shostak

Progress is the realization of utopias.

—Oscar Wilde

If sociologists, as key and strategic allies of futuristics, are soon to improve our contribution to the concept of utopia, a proud and distinctive contribution that dates back to Comte and nowadays features the seminal work of Daniel Bell, W. Warren Wagar, Rosabeth Moss Kanter, and Wendell Bell, among many others, we could begin by improving our teaching of the subject.

I propose to make a straightforward case for new attention to utopias. In this way we may help ensure the emergence soon of zesty new 21st-century counterparts of D. Bell, Wagar, Kanter, and W. Bell, acolytes convinced, to paraphrase a thought of Wilde's about England, that sociology will never be civilized until it has added Utopia to its domains.

My case argues, first, that the costly neglect of utopias which characterizes the basic textbook scene is unwarranted. Second, that undergraduate students need academic attention to utopias. Third, that many fine new teaching aids are available. And finally, that we should share advice drawn on our own classroom experiences helping young adults profit from this extraordinary topic.

TEXTBOOK BLACKOUT

Search in the indices of major new introductory texts and you will find nary a reference to one of the key subjects that animated the discipline's founders, Comte and Saint Simon. Typical are three books whose year 2001 copyright attests to their modernity—*Sociology*, by James M. Henslin; *In Conflict and Order*, by D. Stanley Eitzen and Maxine B. Zinn; and *Sociology*, by Thomas J. Sullivan.

Why this neglect? Lacking interview data, I can only speculate that some basic text writers (and editors) may be captive to one or more of four costly errors—each of which I would briefly challenge.

Some such sociologists may think the concept passé, a misperception refuted, however, by the seemingly endless call for vision (a major characteristic of all utopian designs) from high-minded politicians (especially in an election year), media pundits, corporate consultants, clergy, and others whose role it is to sound the needs of the public.

Still other negligent text writers may fear a contagion effect. That is, they may fear young readers will associate the "U" word—

Arthur B. Shostak *is a retired professor of sociology from Drexel University, Philadelphia, Pennsylvania. He may be contacted at shostaka@drexel.edu.*

utopia—with the stigmatized "S" word—*socialism*—much to the detriment of their book's adoption and re-order rate. To be sure, narrow-minded critics of utopian thinking like to represent socialism as "the most influential utopian idea of the 19th and 20th centuries ... [one] which has failed everywhere."[1]

But this misperception is refuted by scholars who help us distinguish among different types of socialism (democratic versus totalitarian, etc.), and thereby help redeem both worthy concepts— utopia and socialism—from malevolent slander.[2]

A third plausible explanation has certain writers wary of utopia's alleged provincialism, oppressive conformity, and haughty intolerance of deviation. These sociologists associate utopias only with "an uncomplicated warm nest from which all the noise of the real world is excluded."[3] But this rampant misperception, like that cited above concerning socialism, ignores the existence of many and varied utopian blueprints, only a few of which resemble small self-righteous and self-centered communities.

Finally, some of the textbook blackout may reflect a most revealing absence of anything valuable to say. That is, as a recent leader of the American Psychological Association ruefully noted in his 1998 Presidential Address, "Social Science now finds itself in almost total darkness about the qualities that make life most worth living."[4] Our texts, in short, may only mirror a serious imbalance in our sociological work, with far more attention being paid to pathologies than to sources of strength and fulfillment.

CURRENT COLLEGIANS

To judge very cautiously from new survey data, the cohort we have at present on campus would seem in great need of exposure to utopian thinking—pro and con.

Consider, for example, data from the 34th UCLA Annual Survey of incoming students (261,217 students at 462 institutions). These young adults continue "to avoid a commitment to social activism— particularly in terms of race relations, the environment, and 'helping others' who are in difficulty."[5] The percent who said they wanted to "help promote racial understanding" reached its lowest level since 1986. Similarly, the percent feeling it was important to "influence social values" also reached a low since 1986.[6] Interest in becoming a community leader waned from previous years, even as new highs were reported in levels of personal stress.

Materialism, however, gets quite a play: In October 1999, a professor at Montana State University wrote ruefully in the *New York Times* of students on that campus "sleek with optimism [about] the productive world that surely will await them. They save little, spend much, use their credit cards as if they were enchanted lamps... they no more expect economic calamity in their lifetimes than they worry that buboes will suddenly appear in their armpits." He admitted to envy, to wishing he could share their insouciance. But he made a point in closing of noting that he "feared for them ... [since] innocence and hope are fragile shields against the implacability of fate."[7]

Intent on probing this alleged "innocence and hope," I recently polled 35 students in a winter 2000 course about what they imagined life would be like in 2010. Their materialism and seeming optimism not withstanding, only 10% thought the world would then be a better place, with 65% uncertain. While 42% thought Americans like themselves would be better off, another 29% feared otherwise. As many as 52% thought the danger of nuclear war would be more severe, with only 13% disagreeing. And three out of four expected our natural resources would be worse off in 2010, a harrowing expectation with which only 16% disagreed.

Assuming my very cautious, or even gloomy, students are broadly typical—and widely scattered colleagues with whom I have discussed this vexing matter bolster that notion—a lack by young adults of an invigorating vision of a better future would seem a major hazard to the well-being of us all. At least one response worth serious consideration would have us deliberately increase the attention we pay in sociology courses to utopian material.

AVAILABLE AIDS

Happily, a profusion of good new teaching aids can help any sociologist eager to get on with it. Thanks to the Millennium Fever only now subsiding, relevant materials about utopian matters are more plentiful than ever.

Outstanding in this regard is *Century's End*, by Hillel Schwartz, a wise and humane survey of how we have met calendar endings from ancient times forward. ("It were best...to take the year 2000 not as a summing up, but as a summons.")[8] A 1997 collection of original essays, *The Year 2000*, also merits special attention. ("...2000 suggests much about potential ultimate human endings and God's agency in creating new forms.... The real question about 2000 is what follows?")[9]

Where utopias per se are concerned, you cannot do better than Wendell Bell's treatment of same in his two-volume work, *Foundations of Futures Studies*.[10] Far less friendly but no less valuable is a January 2000 magazine article by an eminent physicist intent on exposing the perils lurking behind five major types of popular utopian blueprints: "We had better watch out for people selling these utopias: each of these visions abandons one or more of the grand causes—equality, liberty, and the quality of life and work—that motivated the best utopian ideas of the past."[11]

A bold and immediately controversial book recently published, *NonZero*, sounds like "must" reading for any seriously concerned with utopian questions. Its author, Robert Wright, argues that game theory explains both natural and human history—on indefinitely into the future. He believes an ongoing "win-win" dynamic assures the continued growth of complexity in both scope and depth, a scenario likely to cheer otherwise cautious utopians.[12]

ADVICE FROM THE TRENCHES

Having incorporated utopian material into all of my sociology courses for the past 42 years (as of my retirement in 2003), I would like to close this deliberately brief paper with three pieces of pointed advice.

First, I recommend extensive use in class of one's own explorations of utopian projects. I tell students about my research trips in the early 1970s to the British Garden Cities and New Towns. I discuss my consulting work in the late 1970s for HUD, field work that had me assessing the innovations developers were required by HUD to introduce into America's Planned Communities. I review my involvement with urban communes and Hippie homesteads. I show slides I took during a visit in the mid-1980s to Solari's Archology building site in Arizona. And I talk about my seven research visits since 1971 to Israeli kibbutzim.

Nowadays I emphasize my ongoing effort to help labor unions enlarge their vision of themselves, especially as this involves utilizing the awesome potential of computers and telecommunications—a key ingredient in new formulas for utopian gains.[13] Here, as with all of my classroom processing of my own experiences, I strive to tell the whole story, warts and all, the better to underline how complex and challenging are real-world efforts at utopia-building.

Second, I recommend tracing linkages between classic utopias of old and their modern adaptations. I call attention, for example, to Edward Bellamy's remarkably popular 1888 fictional state-socialist utopia, set in 2000CE.[14] Then I trace its link to an ongoing effort around America (as in Ithaca, New York) to substitute a barter system—one only made possible by modern computers—for a capitalist cash economy. Bellamy's barter idea floundered in the late 1800s for being too complicated, a challenge easily handled today by conventional spreadsheets.

Third, I recommend finding and sticking with utopian literature that "speaks" to today's collegian. Outstanding here is a novel I have used since its 1975 publication in nearly every sociology course I have taught since then. *Ecotopia*, authored by Ernest Callenbach, raises consciousness about what might go into a total system overhaul. It offers a thorough plan for an ecologically sound, democratic, creative, and liberated society, a plan that stirs some of the best utopian dialogue I have known in class over four decades.[15] Where magazines are concerned, issues of *The Futurist* magazine win accolades from students open to fresh possibilities. Its graphics, wide range of topics, and clear copy make it a sound aid to utopian thinking.[16] Similarly, a young publication, *YES! A Journal of Positive Futures*, stands out with its positive air, its case studies of successes, and its unabashedly utopian air.[17]

SUMMARY

In a very insightful assessment of our times, Andrew Delbanco identifies the absence of utopianism as the "root of our modern melancholy. We live in an age of unprecedented wealth, but in the realm of narrative and symbol, we are deprived. And so the ache for meaning goes unrelieved."[18] Utopian thought—and action—offer some relief.

Many of us were attracted originally to sociology by its seeming ability to help us get beyond the limits we had set for ourselves. Utopian thought has that same attraction, that same potential—provided we do our very best with it.

At present we in sociology make far less of utopian reasoning than is good for any of us—or for futuristics and the future. A small but valuable start at reform would have us do much more in our texts and classrooms alike.

[Editor's Note: This paper was first presented at the American Sociological Association session, "Utopian Reasoning and the Future," held in Washington, D.C. in August 2000.]

NOTES

1. Steven Weinberg, "Five and a Half Utopias," *The Atlantic Monthly*, January 2000, 108.
2. See, for example, *Whose Millennium? Theirs or Ours?* (New York: Monthly Review Press, 1999).
3. W. Warren Wagar, *The City of Man* (Baltimore, MD: Penguin, 1967 ed.), 14.
4. Martin Seligman as quoted in "Why Do People Benefit from Unfounded Optimism?" by Terence Monmancey, *Philadelphia Inquirer*, January 24, 2000, C-1.
5. Leo Reisberg, "Student Stress is Rising, Especially Among Women," *The Chronicle of Higher Education*, January 28, 2000, A-52.
6. Jodi Wilgoren, "More than Ever, First-Year Students Feeling the Stress of College," *New York Times*, January 24, 2000, A-18.
7. T.H. Watkins, "The Boom Generation," *New York Times*, October 8, 1999, A-31.
8. Hillel Schwartz, *Century's End* (New York: Doubleday, 1990).
9. Charles B. Strozier and Michael Flynn, eds., *The Year 2000* (New York: New York University Press, 1997).

10. Wendell Bell, *Foundations of Future Studies* (New Brunswick, NJ: Transaction Press, 1997), Volumes 1, 2. See also Ian Tod and Michael Wheeler, *Utopia* (New York: Harmony Books, 1978).

11. Steve Weinberg, "Five and a Half Utopias," *The Atlantic Monthly*, op. cit.

12. Robert Wright, *NonZero: The Logic of Human Destiny* (New York: Pantheon, 2000).

13. Arthur B. Shostak, *CyberUnion: Empowering Labor through Computer Technology* (Armonk, NY: M.E. Sharpe, 1999).

14. Edward Bellamy, *Looking Backward* (Cambridge, MA: Harvard University Press, 1967 ed.).

15. Ernest Callenbach, *Ecotopia* (New York: Bantam, 1977 ed.). See also Maius de Geus, *Ecological Utopias: Envisioning the Sustainable Society* (Concord, MA: Paul & Company, 1999).

16. Available from the World Future Society, 7910 Woodmont Ave., Suite 450, Bethesda, MD 20814 (1-800-989-8274), or at major bookstores.

17. Available from *YES!*, P.O. Box 10818, Bainbridge Island, WA 98110 (1-800-937-4451), or at major bookstores.

18. Andrew Delbanco, *The Real American Dream* (Cambridge, MA: Harvard University Press, 1999) 107.

SUSTAINABLE DEVELOPMENT

NEW PARADIGMS IN WORLD TRADE AND THE GLOBAL ECONOMY

by

Hazel Henderson

Thank you for the honor of addressing this important gathering. SEBRAE represents many of the key values for building more equitable, sustainable futures in Brazil and Latin America: entrepreneurship, leadership in local development, innovation in both social and technical spheres, social responsibility, and best practices in management of small and medium size enterprises, which are the engines at the heart of robust, home-grown, domestic economies. Today, economists are reassessing their fashionable strategies of export-led national GDP-growth—in the face of a crisis-ridden world economy in need of repair and rebalancing. The traditional economic theories that produced today's economic globalization are discredited—as are many of its international financial institutions—the International Monetary Fund (IMF), the World Bank and the World Trade Organization (WTO).

President Luiz Inacio Lula da Silva has emerged as a world leader in pointing to healthier, alternative paths toward sustainable economies, at local, national, regional, and global levels. Brazil's leadership in forming the Group of 21 (now 22) developing nations opened a new era in world trade at the Cancun WTO meeting. Brazil's view since prevailed in the April 2004 WTO ruling on the illegality of US cotton subsidies. No longer will narrowly calculated trade rules and negotiations trump fairness, higher human values, and goals. Brazil's business community also articulated at Cancun the new model of socially responsible business management. Ricardo Young Silva of the Instituto Ethos de Empresas e Responsabilidade Social, called for these higher standards of social and economic performance to be incorporated, along with full cost prices and life-cycle costing, into WTO rules and accounting practices. The new economics and indicators of sustainable human development and quality-of-life are beginning to call into question the traditional GNP-growth model. The social costs, waste, and ecological destruction of this obsolete model are now self-evident. The first international conference of world-class statistical experts on these expanded national accounts, ICONS, convened in Curitiba, October 26-29, 2003. Brazil's leaders in these new statistics of sustainability showcased their groundbreaking work.

The obsolete neoliberal model applied to world trade drove World Bank advice, which led developing countries to focus on short-term export-led growth and resulted in many of today's glutted markets in commodities, from coffee to computer chips. Such short-

Hazel Henderson *author, futurist, evolutionary economist, founded Ethical Marketplace Media (www.ethicalmarketplace.com) and with the Calvert Group, the Calvert-Henderson Quality of Life Indicators, updated at Calvert-Henderson.com.*

term strategies, often with tax holidays, export platforms, and reliance on cheap labor, minimum regulations, and all the other Washington Consensus policies, have led to today's global "race to the bottom." In Mexico, some 300 manufacturing plants have moved to China in the past two years.[1] China will soon overtake Mexico as the second largest US trading partner after Canada. China's labor costs, combined with today's undervalued renminbe (rmb), are about one quarter of those in Mexico. One cannot blame China, since some two-thirds of all China's exports to the USA are by US corporations.[2] The longer-term structural focus needed in Mexico must address general education and the skill levels of its workforce to retain its back-office paperwork businesses (still second only to India). Even deeper is the issue that only 1% of inputs to Mexico's export manufacturing plants are produced in Mexico and little tech transfer occurs in this typical world-trading pattern. Thus, many developing countries, including those like Mexico, in the top tier, are vulnerable to powerful global market rule-makers, corporations, investors, and currency speculators they cannot control.

Brazil's new leadership is addressing these global forces and Washington Consensus rule-makers and their resulting unfair outcomes: wider poverty gaps, subsidies to producers in powerful OECD countries, and perverse rules on tariffs, intellectual property and financial services. The new Group of 22 has opened the door to a long struggle between powerful countries, corporations, and financial interests versus more numerous, weaker developing countries, smaller and medium-sized enterprises, labor unions, and civil society worldwide. These new global dynamics will be driven by electronic networks and mass media and the world's newest superpower: global public opinion. Here also, Brazil is in the lead. The World Social Forum not only made Porto Alegre into a well-known center of alternative global thinking to rival the Davos-based World Economic Forum—but also another worldwide tourist destination in Brazil. The World Social Forum is typical of 21st century civil society organization: electronically networked, Internet-based, virtual, flexible, with a widely distributed leadership and knowledge base. Similar organizational forms account for the movement criticizing President George W. Bush in the US 2004 election campaign, led by Dr. Howard Dean, which raised millions of dollars more than any other official Democratic candidate—via the Internet.

These global forces provide the current context for Latin America and Brazil. The WTO responded to Brazil's challenge, while the IMF is still discredited as too aligned with global creditors and banks. The World Bank is still in the messy process of trying to change its paradigms. The USA will continue its divide-and-conquer strategies, making bilateral trade pacts and other deals to assist in Iraq reconstruction and reversing the return to warlordism in Afghanistan and opium poppy exports, which now comprise 50% of GDP.[3]

Awareness grows about how the neoliberal world trade paradigm increases the power and wealth of powerful countries and corporations. Regional integration strategies, including MERCOSUR, become more attractive for developing countries—including, eventually, a common currency to increase Latin American trade independent of US dollar, euro, and sterling reserves.

A stronger MERCOSUR and Latin American integration could advance entrepreneurship and new businesses based on local currency loans and venture capital. This strategy could also enhance domestic business-to-business trade and help grow more robust, homegrown, consumer-driven economies based on total productivity of all factors. While world trade wars are likely to last for many years, regional, national, and local trade can flourish under new agreements, policies, and strategies. The September 2003 two-day retreat at the Fundacao Dom Cabral (FDC) held by the Economic and Social Council and chaired by Minister Tarso Genro envisioned a bright future for Brazil in 2020, including continuing robust exports to the world.

Some 200 participants from business, labor, and civil society developed scenarios around the shared goal of sustainable development. The "VISION BRAZIL 2020" that was reported looks back from the year 2020 and views the achievements that produced this preferred future scenario:

> We are a nation of 210 million people reigned by peace and wide access to work. In the last 16 years we have presented significant improvements in the income share, in the rich and poor gap, in balanced geographical occupation, in access to education, culture and health.
>
> We are a nation without misery in which education is a priority. A country in which there is a high life expectancy, oriented by sustainable development.
>
> We are a country which is able to develop widely accessible technologies.
>
> We are a nation with more safety, more justice and with an increasing feeling of social responsibility.
>
> Today, our human relations are based on the respect of the elderly and children; we have more time with our families, we are guided by confidence and ethics in our commitments. Equal opportunities are provided and we are recognized in the world by our culture of peace.
>
> We are widely perceived in the global scenario as a country that has taken a leadership role in the Latin American continent, due to solidarity, full and sovereign international integration.
>
> We are the biggest and better benchmarked in the world production of food, based on a sustainable agriculture that conciliates different forms of production organizations. There

are no land conflicts. Twenty to 30 million people live in "rural towns" producing with more added value.

We utilize our environment assets with preserving actions. Alternative energies are applied. Our cities are clean, non-polluted, with more green spaces accessible to the whole population.

Science & Technology research efforts interrelate the private and the public sectors. Small businesses have assured access to the most advanced technologies.

Our participatory and collaborative culture has favored innovation and competitiveness of our products, as well as a Brazilian management style that is internationally appreciated.

Every Brazilian is a citizen. The public interest prevails over the private interests. The State is controlled by society. The political representation is legitimate and the public administration is guided by morality and effectiveness.

The participants also articulated the goals and values behind the fundamentals of the vision:

- Education as a value—with priority in the government budget.
- Commitment with a healthy, joyful, and happy life.
- Democracy and the national unity and peace.
- Pride of being Brazilian—self-esteem.
- Miscegenation and ability to live with differences, large ethnic and cultural diversity.
- Creativity, flexibility and intelligence.
- The national unity.
- Entrepreneurship, cooperation, and solidarity.
- Assurance of opportunities, compromises, and detachment.
- The creation of favorable conditions for the effective participation of citizens.

Also described were the challenges:

- Paradigm shifts in the economy.
- Full employment policies.
- Political, agriculture, administrative, judicial, labor, and tax reforms.
- Eradication of child and slave labor and illiteracy.
- Rational utilization of natural resources.
- Development of citizenship and fight against corruption.
- Development efforts concentrated in the government, private enterprise and NGOs.
- Dissemination of good news to the whole society, by reducing the dark side of the media.
- Acceptance and assumption that Brazilians act with their hearts.

- Incentive to youth to embrace public missions.
- Incentive to micro and small business.

Many of the necessary policies to create this prosperous, globally competitive, educated, equitable, healthy Brazil—leading the world in international cooperation and peaceful sustainable development—require the paradigm shift now widely acknowledged and discussed in Brazil. I expect Brazil will exert ever more influence in global affairs, including taking its place as a permanent member of an enlarged United Nations Security Council. As I have outlined (see my "New Opportunities for the United Nations," www.hazelhenderson.com, click on Editorials) the debacle in Iraq and the US need for UN allies now acknowledged by President Bush, will provide impetus for many UN reforms, including expanding the Security Council and ending the veto. Brazil, India, and other new permanent members can help achieve more pragmatic and harmonious negotiations and outcomes. Issuing bonds, together with other financing mechanisms, including user fees for commercial exploitation of global commons, currency exchange taxes, etc., can reduce overreliance on the USA and membership dues.

Brazil can help reshape the WTO and limit its rule making to trade in goods—with full-cost pricing and corrected GDP statistics. Separate agreements and regimes are needed for financial services, foreign direct and portfolio investment, currency trading, intellectual property, patents, research and development and other global securities rule making for a "global securities and exchange commission." Indeed, such new global financial architecture has been discussed for over a decade by groups including IOSCO (the International Organization of Securities Commissions) and the OECD, whose ill-fated Multilateral Agreement on Investment was rightly defeated by global NGO opposition. Currency trading is the most urgent target for global regulation. (Over 90% of $1.5 trillion of daily trading is speculation.) (See my *Beyond Globalization* [1999], Editora Cultrix, Sao Paulo, 2003.)

There are several viable methods of regulating currency exchange, which do not require laborious international agreements to prevent such trading moving to offshore havens. This evasion has been made less likely by the OECD's blacklisting of such havens for money-laundering and illegal transfers to terrorist groups. The screen-based Foreign Exchange Transaction Reporting System (FXTRS) I designed with my partner, Alan F. Kay (founder of AutEx, the first computerized securities trading system, now owned by Thomson Financial) is also described in my *Beyond Globalization*. Royalties from this fully transparent, best practices, patented currency exchange will be donated to the United Nations. This system is designed to protect currencies from speculative bear raids and employs a below 1% fee structure acceptable to currency traders since it creates better-regulated and informed trading conditions. Not surprisingly, China may be the first country eventually to launch its currency with such a "state-of-the-art" system.

Meanwhile, the daily avalanche of currencies sloshing around the planet continues to destabilize national macroeconomic policy making in even the most democratic and well-managed countries. Today's currency markets are not efficient, but driven by psychology, rumors, herd behavior, and financial mass media from Reuters and Bloomberg to CNN, CNBC and Globo. In 21st century global warfare and markets, currencies are now the weapon of choice. The US dollar has lost over 25% of value against the euro (as I predicted in 2001). The US dollar may fall further as it becomes less tenable for the United States to continue being the "locomotive" of global GDP growth.

The United States is the world's largest debtor and has flooded the world with paper dollars in exchange for the world's goods. Continuing on this path will expand the US trade deficit from its current 5% of GDP to 6% and 7%—until the dollar adjusts downward. But this will make imported goods too expensive for US consumers to buy in past quantities. Thus, US Treasury Secretary John Snow's pleas to Japan and China to allow their currencies to appreciate. China's central bank may checkmate such pleas by also tying its rmb to a basket of other reserve-quality currencies. Today, the US dollar is no longer the world's only reserve currency—being edged out by the euro (which now accounts for 35% of all global reserves and trade), with sterling and other hard currencies in the mix. This will eventually lead to a more stable, diversified "basket" of global reserve currencies, including the Japanese yen and China's rmb—as well, I expect, as a MERCOSUR common currency.

Now is the time to rethink the future of sustainable world trade—and trade *within* countries and regions. Some important principles of such a new world trading regime include:

- Adherence to all United Nations principles, treaties, and conventions on human rights, labor standards, and environmental protection, including the UN Global Compact on good corporate citizenship and accountability.

- A well-regulated, transparent, democratic, global financial architecture, including reforming the international financial institutions.

- Ending corruption.

- Ending relocation practices based on tax giveaways and other forms of tax competition already illegal under WTO rules.

- Calculating all traded goods and negotiations in full-cost prices.

• Truly level playing fields on subsidies.

• Correcting GDP per capita based economic growth measures as agreed in Rio de Janeiro in *Agenda 21* (1992)—to include social, human, and environmental assets and costs.

• Correcting stock and bond markets' evaluations of country risk ratings to include such broader statistics and similarly correcting their capital asset pricing models (CAPM).

As these corrections and emerging statistical paradigms and corporate accounting changes (i.e., "triple bottom line," economic, social, and environmental measures of corporate performance; see www.gri.org) take over from today's obsolete methodologies, world trading patterns will be steered gradually toward sustainability. Economic measures of "efficiency" will at last align with true physical efficiency, measured in thermodynamics.

Today's goods that are subsidized by below full cost pricing, social costs born by taxpayers, environmental costs born by others or future generations and also by direct government subsidies and protectionism, will tend to disappear from international trade. Much of today's trade is simply entropic, e.g., container loads of identical cars, crossing each other on the world's oceans in energy-gulping planes and ships. Correct full-cost prices would reveal these goods as uncompetitive with those produced and consumed in domestic markets. Most basic goods are produced efficiently in most countries at lower costs while providing local employment.

Exports and imports will be limited to unique goods and commodities, where each country offers true comparative (not competitive) advantage. Thus, the original world trade theories of Ricardo were based on such natural niches and comparative capabilities and advantages—essentially cooperative strategies. Today's knee-jerk competition of "market fundamentalism" and global economic warfare between countries will tend to disappear. Goods, including agricultural commodities, will tend to be traded regionally, domestically, and locally—particularly perishable foods whose optimal nutritional value is in freshness. Some agricultural food products will remain in global trade—from grains, tea, coffee, soybeans, etc., as well as unique foods, such as Brazilian fruits and nuts. However, many countries will reserve the right to protect domestic food supplies on grounds of national security (to prevent TNCs from monopolizing supplies) or health (e.g., non GMO-foods, hormone-free meats, etc.)—accepting reciprocal measures of other trading partners.

My views on agricultural products in world trade can be summarized by my experience with a major food multinational in the early 1980s. This company asked me to do an evaluation for their product line (mostly based on corn) and their corporate strategy for the future. I agreed. My evaluation was almost totally negative. They were taking a highly nutritious crop, corn, and actually subtracting from its nutritional value with heavy processing into highly advertised dried soups and other packaged foods, syrups, and even ethanol fuel additives. Their top-heavy centralized US-based management of divisions in 90 countries impeded feedback on local knowledge, markets, and culture, while their ethanol production was purely entropic—driven by tax subsidies. My verdict: shut the operations down and re-deploy the assets into more sustainable products of higher nutritional value, partnering with local producers while lowering costs of transport, packaging, and advertising. The good news? The management still invited me to present my report to their conference with their 90 country managers in a two-hour discussion in roundtables. The two different paradigms: the *company's* based on traditional market economics and trade strategies—*mine* on thermodynamics, human nutrition, and new measures of corporate performance and macro-indicators of quality-of-life. Big companies can listen—but the bad news was that little change occurred.

In a new sustainable world trade system, trade would gradually dematerialize from standardized, similar goods toward unique goods and raw materials, for example, the global anti-virus software company Trend Micro Inc. founded in Taiwan by entrepreneur Steve Chang.[4] Trade in services would grow much larger under precisely crafted agreements: on tech transfer, patents, science and technology, and intellectual property, so as to rebalance power and knowledge between North and South. It is much more efficient to trade "recipes" than cakes and cookies, for example, the software of clean technologies and design rather than the hardware and machines themselves. This emphasizes the importance of tech-transfer, license agreements, joint ventures geared toward building local content and skill levels. The Chinese are masters at creating these kinds of joint ventures with global companies: no tech-transfer, no deal! This is the best kind of foreign direct investment. Brazil can also drive equally tough bargains with investors and global corporations due to its huge domestic market and its immense wealth: social, cultural, human, and ecological. As I have documented, using new indicators of sustainability and quality of life, per capita, Brazilians are amongst the richest people on Earth.

World trade in good design, better ideas, cultural goods (such as Brazil's music, art, literature, TV shows, dance, etc.) will allow the human family to celebrate and savor our magnificent diversity. Local cuisines, fashions, style, architecture, urban design, and other unique contributions of the "cultural DNA" of all nations enrich us all. Social innovations are the highest form of world enrichment, like democracy, great literature, agrarian reform (the foundation of China's new prosperity), education policies (such as Brazil's bolsa escola, now being copied elsewhere), urban planning, such as pioneered by Curitiba, Internet-linked civil society and the World Social Forum, and most of all cultures of peace. Such intangible exports are often of the highest added value enhancing national prestige. Today, countries recognize the value of such intangible, attractive, image building, e.g., "cool Britannia" and the USA's image of "the American Way of Life" (now much discredited).

Accountants are still learning how to value intangibles, brands, from Coca Cola to the World Wildlife Fund panda, as well as knowledge and intellectual property, the key factors of production in our 21st century information societies. For example, Britain has earned millions from exporting eccentricity (i.e., the Beatles, the Spice Girls, crazy fashions, etc.), while Holland's unique comparative advantage has been its special knowledge of how to reclaim and defend land areas from the sea and floods. Brazil is already adept at these kinds of high-value intangible exports, which also augment the value of tourism. Some of the socially innovative policies, such as Participatory Budgets, pioneered by the city of Porto Alegre, could be offered under license to other cities worldwide.

Most importantly, how can we turn the millions excluded from today's globalization into healthy, educated, productive citizens? By broadening our analyses and statistics and including the world's unpaid, undocumented informal sectors, where people are self-employed, build their own homes, grow their own food in traditional livelihoods. In Brazil's informal sectors lie untapped skills and entrepreneurship, such as the People's Banking groups in Belem and many other citizen-based movements being documented in Brasilia by IPEA (Instituto de Pesquisa Economica Applicada). They know the huge potential of barter networks, both based in neighborhoods and wider electronic trading systems. World barter by transnational corporations and governments is over $1 trillion annually. Throughout history, there have always been two ways that humans transact: (1) pure exchange (barter) and sharing for mutual aid and (2) using money. Any time money systems break down, people recreate barter and local scrip, or people's money No poverty-reduction strategy can be successful without barter and full participation of productive, unpaid, informal sectors. They seek deeper dialogue with SEBRAE— whose members they admire and seek to emulate. They know much about the need for economic reform in Brazil—to reduce interest rates and create robust financial networks for local credit, micro finance, and enterprises. The time is right for all these changes in Brazil's new democracy.

We all know that there are at least three better ways to check inflation than by inflicting high interest rates across the whole economy. First, bank reserve requirements can be raised as needed, beyond the 8% mandated by the Bank for International Settlements. The Chinese have taken this course. Second, margin requirements on stock exchanges can be raised to reduce speculative borrowing to buy stocks and bonds. Third, a robust national network of credit unions such as in the USA can compete with commercial banks. Local depositors can deposit their paychecks in local credit unions to provide lending funds for local entrepreneurs. Local venture capital clubs can be connected in secure electronic networks with start-up companies. This will overcome the image of Brazil as a destination for hot money and speculators and make it more welcoming for investors such as myself.

As the global economy grows into greater global interdependence, we can track the driving forces accelerating change. Technologically, we are moving in to the Age of Light. Traditional macroeconomic management is failing because interactions between all global players are increasing exponentially. Industrial sectors are restructuring. A new type of economy is emerging in many industrial societies.

Development models are still in disarray. My own model sees development as the evolution of human societies' understanding of three basic resources, matter, energy, and information, and the substitution patterns toward greater thermodynamic[5] (not economic) efficiency. Thus, a society's key resource is information and the extent to which its culture educates and nurtures its human and social capital and applies its knowledge base to managing its material and energy resources. An example is the evolution of fossil-fuel technologies (based on advancing knowledge) since 1850 from solids and liquids to gases. The deeper transition to the solar age of renewable resources is still hampered by transnational corporations dominating energy systems, fossil fuels, nuclear power, high-tech weapons systems. Industrialization methods are still applied inappropriately to agribusiness and genetic engineering of living organisms, chemicals, pharmaceuticals, transportation and communications technologies, mass media, and networks. Today's forms of globalization have been designed by TNCs, with support of the government bodies—local, national, regional, and international—over which TNCs exert major influences.

As we explore the emerging global playing field we see many great opportunities for human development, greater shared global prosperity, and enough good and necessary jobs to employ every able-bodied man and woman on our planet. Global polling, using the best scientific sampling, North, South, East, and West, confirms the emergence of the new superpower: global public opinion (see for example, Globescan, London and Toronto, Canada). Poll after poll confirms that ordinary people in over 60 countries want more education, health, cleaner environments, access to credit, better technologies, and opportunities. Too often, their governments buy weapons and lead them into wars.

Rio de Janeiro hosted the formation of the Earth Council in 1992. After 10 years of effort by NGOs worldwide, the Earth Charter was launched at the Peace Palace in The Hague, Netherlands. This Charter of 16 principles of human responsibilities—for each other, our families, our communities, our countries, all species, and the planet's living biosphere—has been hailed as the most important new soft law since the Universal Declaration of Human Rights (www. earthcharter.org). Towns and cities worldwide, as well as companies, including my partner, The Calvert Group, have adopted the Earth Charter. Brazil is recognized worldwide as a culture that fosters such social innovations, including the concepts and operationalizing of sustainable development and new indicators to measure true prosperity and quality of life.

[Editor's Note: The following remarks—with some relevant updates—are from the Plenary Session for the SEBRAE conference entitled, "Beyond Globalization—Foreign Trade Sustainability, a Social Responsibility Conference," held October 20, 2003, in Vitoria, Espirito Santo, Brazil.]

REFERENCES

Henderson, H. *Beyond Globalization*, Kumarian Press, 1999.

Henderson, H. *Building a Win-Win World: Life Beyond Global Economic Warfare*, Berrett-Kohler, 1996.

Henderson, H. *Transcending Economics*, Editora Cultrix, Sao Paulo (1991); US edition, *Paradigms in Progress*, Berrett-Kohler, 1995.

NOTES

1. *PODER* and *The Economist*, Miami, September 2003, p. 63
2. *Business Week*, October 6, 2003, 40.
3. *The Economist*, August 16, 2003, 35-37.
4. *Business Week*, September 22, 2003, 68.
5. My late friend Nicholas Georgescu-Roegen, *The Entropy Law and the Economic Process* (Harvard University Press, 1971) grounded erroneous economic theories of "productivity" and "efficiency" in thermodynamics following British chemist, Frederick Soddy, who shared a Nobel Prize with E. Rutherford for the discovery of isotopes.

THE FUTURE OF SUSTAINABLE DEVELOPMENT: A EUROPEAN PERSPECTIVE

by

Ruth Kelly, Lorcan Sirr, and John Ratcliffe

THE CONTEXT

The World Commission on Environment and Development (WCED) report, *Our Common Future*, is credited with having popularized the concept of sustainable development (Brundtland Commission, 1987). The report identifies three leading interconnected principles, briefly summarized as follows: environmental efficiency, inter- and intragenerational social justice, and participation in decision making (Jansen, 2003). It emphasized that environmental problems cannot be considered in isolation from others, such as poverty and social disintegration. However, the concept itself has a longer lineage. In Stockholm, 1972, the UN held the first ever Conference on the Human Environment, which attracted worldwide attention to the dangers of, *inter alia*, pollution, exhaustion of natural resources, and desertification (Rist, 1997). The publication of the Club of Rome report *Limits to Growth* in 1972 highlighted the consequences of exceeding the carrying capacity of the natural environment (Meadows, 1972). The report allowed the emphasis to change from local pollution to the use (and misuse) of resources in a global context (Blutstein, 2003) and also redirected attention towards possible global futures.

In the years following the 1972 Stockholm Conference, the scientific consensus on the occurrence of ecological imbalances has become more focused, coming to the conclusion that the damage inflicted by human activities on the environment render these activities unsustainable (Ekins and Jacobs, 1995). This subsequently created the need for a new worldview to serve as a basis for global consensus, which eventually led to the sustainable development concept. Over the past decade the concept has expanded to include the simultaneous consideration of economic growth, environmental protection, and social equity in planning and decision making (Schmidheiney, 1992). Policy integration, particularly in relation to the integration of environmental issues into other areas of policy, has been a key area of interest at the European level for some time (Geerlings and Stead, 2003). Indeed, the publication of the *European Union Sustainable Development Strategy* in 2001 represented a distinct

Ruth Kelly *is a postdoctoral research scholar at the Futures Academy, Department of the Built Environment, Dublin Institute of Technology, Dublin, Ireland. She may be contacted at ruth.kelly@dit.ie.* **Lorcan Sirr** *is head of the Futures Academy, Department of the Built Environment, Dublin Institute of Technology, Dublin, Ireland. He may be contacted at lorcan.sirr@dit.ie.* **John Ratcliffe** *is director of the Futures Academy, Department of the Built Environment, Dublin Institute of Technology, Dublin, Ireland. He may be contacted at john.ratcliffe@dit.ie.*

movement towards more integrated, participatory, and holistic strategies. This is discussed in further detail later in the paper.

In 1997, there were over 300 published definitions of sustainable development, the products of diverse worldviews and competing vested interests (EEA, 1997). No doubt this number has since increased. There is no commonly accepted single definition of the concept (Haughton and Hunter, 1994), and in the third decade since the publication of *Our Common Future*, sustainable development remains a concept intuitively understood by many but still very difficult to express in tangible or operational terms (Lele, 1991).

Fundamentally, sustainable development represents a transformation in both the way society approaches growth and the attendant stress that growth places on the environment. However, sustainable development is considered an oxymoron by some: The idea of "development" implies continued economic growth, while "sustainable" implies that constraints must be applied. Similarly, distinct development trajectories in different countries suggest that no single strategy, however sustainable, will apply equally in all countries (Alberti and Susskind, 1996). Couch and Dennemann (2000) argue that there is an ambivalent attitude to sustainable development and a constant attempt to reinterpret and compromise the concept to support the aims of economic development. Patterns of resource use are influenced by each nation's society, environment, and economy. This has resulted in different paradigms that are based on "weak" and "strong" sustainability principles. With strong sustainability there is little if any consideration of the financial costs of attaining this state of development. It is coterminous with what some call ecological sustainability and the focus is primarily on the environment (Bell and Morse, 1999). The strong paradigm is also associated with a robust approach to community and social issues, including equity and active participation (Pearce, 1993). Weak sustainability considers the costs of achieving sustainable development (financial or otherwise) and is typically based on cost benefit analysis (CBA), which inevitably involves trade-offs between environmental, social, and economic development. Essentially, the main difference between weak and strong sustainability is the degree to which substitutability between different forms of capital is considered (Figge and Hahn, 2004). The most frequently cited definition of the concept is that which emerged from *Our Common Future*: Sustainable development is "development which meets the needs of the present without compromising the ability of future generations to meet their own needs" (Brundtland Commission, 1987). This definition is based on an ethical imperative of equity within and between generations and implies sustaining the natural life-support systems on the planet, while extending to all the opportunity to improve quality of life (Hediger, 2000). Although the definition is powerful and appeals strongly to the responsibility of the present generation, it is not obvious how sustainable development might be achieved (Vollenbroek, 2002). At its core, sustainable development addresses three major concerns:

1. The need to arrest environmental degradation and ecological imbalance.

2. The need to avoid impoverishment of future generations.

3. The need for equity in the quality of life among present-day populations (Redclift, 1987).

In other words, sustainable development encompasses not only environmental protection, but also economic development, social cohesion, and quality of life. The paradigm of sustainable development inherently but not explicitly embraces futures thinking. Almost all published definitions of the concept, whether based on weak or strong sustainability principles, refer to both present and future generations and are generally motivated by a real concern for the long-term well-being of humanity (Kelly et al., 2004). However, the potential to apply futures thinking in order to move towards a more sustainable society is yet to be elaborated and advanced at a global level. The following sections describe current efforts at the European level to translate sustainable development rhetoric into strategic planning, and also examine the possible benefits of utilizing futures thinking to achieve sustainable development for present and future generations.

SUSTAINABLE DEVELOPMENT IN EUROPE

The immediate outcome of *Our Common Future* was the United Nations Conference on Environment and Development (UNCED), held in Rio de Janeiro in 1992. This conference represented the culmination of negotiations to bring about a coherent framework for the global application of sustainable development (McClaren and Bosworth, 1994). Participating countries endorsed *Agenda 21*, a blueprint that was intended to set out an international program of action for achieving sustainable development into the 21st century. Chapter 28 of *Agenda 21* (Local Agenda 21) emphasized the role of local authorities and called upon them to develop local strategies for sustainable development (Dooris, 1999). Local Agenda 21 involves community-based conceptualization and implementation of sustainable development. It has precipitated extensive action for sustainable development at the level of the municipality (Selman, 1998) mainly because it encourages a more proactive role and requires stakeholders to explore wider implications of their lifestyles while promoting collective responsibility for actions (Mehta, 1996). The Charter of European Cities and Towns *Towards Sustainability* (Åalborg Charter) is regarded as the European version of Local

Agenda 21 (Mega, 2000). By signing the Charter, local authorities commit themselves to the development and implementation of comprehensive, long-term strategic action plans for sustainable development, notably through Local Agenda 21 processes (Payne and Löffler, 1999).

The Treaty for European Union (Maastricht Treaty) came into force in 1993, the same year as the Fifth Environmental Action Program. The Program focused on the central theme of sustainable development and demanded the development of meaningful CBA methodologies in respect to policy measures that impinge on natural stock (Bräuer, 2003). It was a definite illustration of the move towards integration, calling for priority to be given to, *inter alia*: sustainable management of natural resources, integrated pollution control and prevention of waste, reduction in the consumption of nonrenewable energy, and improved public health and safety (Ziegler, 1996). Another milestone in the advancement of sustainable development at the EU level was the Sustainable Cities Project launched by the Urban Environment Expert Group and the European Commission in 1993, which identified mechanisms needed to pursue sustainable development, not only in cities, but at all levels of the urban settlement hierarchy (Directorate General Environment, Nuclear Safety and Civil Protection, 1996). This development was significant given that the development of Europe's cities and towns and the relations among them constitute one of the most important driving forces for the future of Europe (Rotmans et al., 2000).

At the EU level, two significant developments following the publication of *Agenda 21* included the UN World Conference on Social Development (The Social Summit) held in Copenhagen, 1995, and Habitat II (The City Summit) held in Istanbul, 1996. Both conferences addressed many contemporary problems, including homelessness, crime, unemployment, poverty, waste disposal, traffic congestion, and underfunded services. Habitat II adopted a world-wide plan of action, the *Programme for Habitat*, and a statement on human settlements by the heads of state and government known as the Istanbul Declaration (Bindé, 1997). More recently, the Economic Commission for Europe regional ministerial meeting for the World Summit on Sustainable Development in Johannesburg, South Africa, in 2002, recognized that the EU has a major role to play in global efforts to achieve sustainable development. In pursuit of Europe's commitment to sustainable development, there are ongoing efforts at the regional, subregional, and transregional levels, including, *inter alia*, the Environment for Europe process; the fifth Economic Commission for Europe ministerial conference, held in Kiev in May 2003, and the work of the Organization for Economic Cooperation and Development on sustainable development (United Nations, 2002). In 1999 the Helsinki European Council invited the European Commission to "prepare a proposal for a long-term strategy dovetail-ing policies for economically, socially, and ecologically sustainable development" in time for the Gothenburg European Council in June 2001. The *European Union Sustainable Development Strategy* was adopted by the Commission on 15 May 2001. The sixth Environmental Action Programme *Environment 2010: Our Future, Our Choice* (2002) may be seen as the environmental component on which the EU sustainable development strategy is based, and, in addition, the strategy requires that social, economic, as well as environmental considerations are integrated into policy making (Feldmann et al., 2001).

However, in spite of these developments, sustainable development remains an ambiguous and intangible concept, compounded by the lack of a global consensus as to how this level of development might be achieved, or indeed what it is. One of the most problematic aspects of sustainable development is its breadth, combined with the abstract nature of the concept. Various "in house" approaches to advance the realization of sustainable development adopted by industry, organizations, and governments alike include, for example, development of environmental management systems (EMS); "green housekeeping" measures or environmental and social charters or mission statements. Efforts to "externalize" sustainable development include, *inter alia*, development of corporate social responsibility (CSR) strategies, development of sustainability indicators, and establishment of effective participatory and consultative networks with representatives from local government, interest groups, and the general public.

The issues of stewardship and the sustainability of natural resources, enhanced social cohesion, and economic development cannot be neglected if we want to preserve and enhance the well-being and quality of life of future generations (Wright and Lund, 2000). However, the application of futures thinking as a means to move towards sustainable development is still in its infancy at the European level, although it is becoming increasingly recognized as a valuable tool to contribute to our understanding of the driving forces which propel change in a dynamic, complex, and uncertain environment. Indeed, the nebulous nature of the sustainable development paradigm attaches new sources of conflict and uncertainty to strategically planning for the future. Sustainable development operates over the long run, into a future whose details are incapable of prediction (Rotmans et al., 2000). The multiplicity of driving forces that shape the future, their heterogeneity and interactions, and consequently their outcomes, are quite unforeseeable (Enserink, 2000). Although the future cannot be predicted, it can be anticipated. Therefore, the need to develop new mechanisms to envision and prepare for the future is gaining greater impetus (Puglisi and Marvin, 2002). Consequently, the growing field of "futures thinking" is evolving as a means to help governments, policy makers, industry, and businesses alike to think, talk, plan, and act cognitively and imaginatively in pursuit of a more sustainable society.

FUTURES THINKING FOR SUSTAINABLE DEVELOPMENT

This section does not attempt to make a comprehensive review of the literature that deals with futures thinking. The more limited objective is to review the generic futures field and its potential to advance sustainable development in Europe.

According to Bell (2001) the publication of *The Limits to Growth* marked a period of accomplishment not just in highlighting the dangers of exceeding the carrying capacity of natural ecosystems but also in the futures field. *Limits*, for example, encouraged long-term thinking, focused on holistic approaches and integrated strategies, showed how to develop quantitative scenarios of possible futures, showed how current choices and policy decisions could affect the future, and influenced millions of people worldwide to think about the well-being of future generations. However, futures thinking has a much longer ancestry. According to Malaska (2001), "futures thinking" can be traced back over 2 million years ago to our ancestors who invented tool manufacture and learned how to satisfy their present needs as well as developing an awareness of the possibilities of these new technologies for their future. Since then, awareness of the future, as well as the past and present, has been central to the evolution of human mind pattern involved in everyday thinking and life experience.

The umbrella term *futures thinking* embraces futures study, futures research, and prospective study. Another term that has recently evolved is "futurology," which may be regarded as the scientifically disciplined mode of "futures thinking" (Masini, 1998). Given the restricted nature of the text, all that is possible here is a brief note on each. In general, futures studies may simply mean an exploration of what might happen and what we might want to become. The statement that futures studies is a "field" or a "discipline" is made as an assertion, often with the undocumented addition that it is a "growing field" (Marien, 2002). Futures studies focus on the world 15 to 50 years from now; focus on the degree of change; describe alternative, possible, and preferable futures rather than single predictions; and utilize both qualitative and quantitative method-ologies. In the last few decades futures studies has made important progress in theory, methodology, and applications, but according to Aligica (2003), it is yet to make a convincing case to gain epis-temological legitimacy outside its own field. However, there is substantial evidence that futures studies today is an identifiable collective, intellectual activity, with its own distinctive features. Such evidence ranges from futures organizations, peer-reviewed journals and periodicals, international conferences, university futures courses, and futures consulting groups (Bell, 2002). Although futures studies is increasingly being incorporated into university-based programs,

Glenn and Gordon (1999) believe that public education or social marketing for public awareness of the need for futures thinking is crucial. Indeed, the aim of incorporating futures thinking into general education is not mere futurist chauvinism, but comes from the belief that futures studies has important contributions to make to long-term human well-being (Cole and Masini, 2001). Similarly, education, community involvement, consultation, and participation are essential to the advancement of sustainable development. The importance of education can be traced back to the 1980 *World Conservation Strategy*, published by the World Conservation Union (IUCN), which "first redirected the goals of environmental education towards what it referred to as education for sustainable development" (Tilbury, 1995).

Futures research, in contrast, means the use of techniques to identify systematically the consequences of policy options and to identify alternative futures with policy implications for decision makers. Futures research investigates trends in order to help anticipate and influence possible outcomes in the years ahead. Changes in complex and uncertain environments require futures research approaches that combine knowledge of many different fields, both quantitative and qualitative (Fontela, 2003). The prospective process through scenario development essentially entails the development of scenarios of desirable future states as a foundation for strategic action (Dreborg, 1996). Scenarios are hypothetical sequences of events, through which possible future developments are made visible (Gausemeier et al., 1998). Developed by Herman Kahn in cooperation with Anthony J. Wiener, scenarios have the potential of being a less rigorous and more open method of exploring the future. They are, according to Wegener (1993), "perhaps the only method to identify 'corridors' of relevant and feasible futures within a universe of possible ones." Systematic development of future scenarios involves identifying key driving forces of change and their different possible interactions, then selecting combinations of driver issues and trends on which to build scenarios. In practice, the driving forces of change are identified by continuous monitoring through horizon or environmental scanning, in-depth interviews with acknowledged experts, targeted questionnaire surveys (Delphi surveys, for example), and brainstorming workshops at the start of the prospective process. Driving forces are typically characterized under the "six sector approach" and include economy, society, environment, governance, technology, and demography. Since the identification of driving forces in a large-scale scenario exercise may lead to the surfacing of hundreds of ideas, the next step is to cluster issues and trends and determining relatedness in order to bring manageability without reduction and elimination (Cairns et al., 2002). In identifying key drivers of change, MacKay and McKiernan (2003) warn, there is a tendency to rely excessively on hindsight when analyzing past trends and issues. Consequently, the driving forces from the past that have been identified to shape change in the future may be overestimated and mis-clarified. This can dilute foresight ability and the plausibility and desirability of future scenarios.

According to List (2003), an assumption inherent in most scenario planning has been that "we" have a shared present, which arises from "our" shared past. From this present, the futures and visions outlined in the various scenarios branch out (see Figure 1).

FIGURE 1 - DECISION MAKING AND MANY FUTURES (KAIVO-OJA ET AL., 2004)

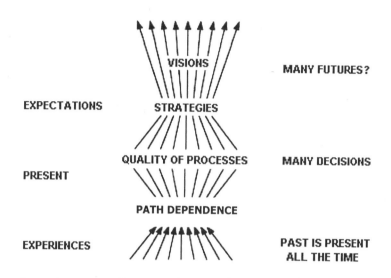

Scenarios generally come in two forms: exploratory and normative. Exploratory scenarios depict self-consistent future worlds that would emerge from the present through credible cause, effect, and feedback developments and reach an end-point that seems plausible. Normative scenarios, on the other hand, represent desirable future worlds (Ratcliffe, 2003). Effective scenario planning functions as a collective thinking exercise. Consequently, "brainstorming," participation, and consultation are essential to the scenario development process. Scenarios have the potential to translate expert knowledge and opinion into a format accessible also to non-experts and ordinary members of the public and so have the potential to stimulate debate between the expert community and the public.

Prospective (or "la prospective") through scenarios is not only an exploratory approach, but also a normative one in that it concludes by describing a single preferred future. Prospective emphasizes the importance of long-range and alternative thinking in strategic decision-making processes (Godet, 2000). The "prospective" approach is becoming more popularly applied across Europe in a variety of strategic settings. In the francophone context, from whence it originates, the prospective refers to a much wider exploration and much longer time horizon than conventional strategic planning. It comprises, moreover, not only the study of the future and an evaluation of alternative outcomes against given policy decisions, but also the will to influence the future and shape it according to an organization's or society's wishes. Prospective through scenarios offers an opportunity to think "preactively" (understanding) and "proactively" (influencing) to develop more innovative and creative strategies towards sustainable development.

TOWARDS THE FUTURE: RECENT DEVELOPMENTS AT THE EU LEVEL

The notion that Europe at the start of the third millennium is facing many complex and uncertain environmental and socio-economic changes is gaining widespread acknowledgement. In 1997 the Forward Studies Unit of the European Commission launched a project, *Scenarios Europe 2010*, with the objective of producing a set of coherent and thought-provoking visions of the future of Europe. Through a process of participation, consultation, and structured "brainstorming," the background knowledge and emerging ideas of the participants were drawn together into a global project. The project, which took two years to complete, was aimed at fostering a "futures" ethos inside the Commission. The resulting scenarios, which were essentially qualitative in nature, present a range of plausible, internally coherent scenarios of the future of Europe to which no probability is attached (Forward Studies Unit, 1999).

Europe has generally had a strong foundation in the world of futures thinking, concepts, and methods. Yet, in much of Europe, futures research is too weak, funding too short, and the next generation of futurists is in danger of disappearing. Responding to this challenge, the European Economic Interest Group (EEIG) euroProspective was formally established in 2001 by the futures studies research center proGective (France) and the Jules Destrée Institute (Wallonia, Belgium). The EEIG brings together two public members (Futures Studies Center, Budapest University of Economic Sciences, Hungary, and the Futures Academy, Dublin Institute of Technology, Ireland), and five private members: Z-punkt GmbH, Germany; Periscopi, Spain; Scenarios + Vision, France; the Jules Destrée Institute, Wallonia; and proGective, France. The main activities of euroProspective include (Goux Baudiment, 2004):

- The exchange of information about futures thinking and research, especially through the management and co-ordination of a multilingual Web site.

- Promotion of existing high-quality foresight and prospective practices, both for the human values they carry and for the rigor of their methods.

- Organization of a strong and permanent network between European and non-European futurists (academics and professionals).

A key focus point of euroProspective is the implementation of futures-oriented projects in the areas of sustainable development, modernization of the public and private organizations, public policies, geopolitical stakes, non-governmental organizations (NGOs) management and innovations (Goux Baudiment, 2004).

The creation of The Futures Academy at the Dublin Institute of Technology, Ireland, for the first time in Ireland furnishes Irish public and private sectors with expertise and networks within which to develop and instigate future-proofing in their own disciplines and industries towards sustainable development. Application of futures thinking to move towards sustainable development is a focal point of research carried out at the Academy.

The main aims and objectives of the Futures Academy include:

- Building a network of people from diverse backgrounds who have a commitment towards futures.

- Testing policies directed towards evolving a sustainable future.

- Making a significant contribution to advancing sustainable development.

- Identifying "key predictors of change" that might impact on the sustainable development of the environment.

The Academy is currently involved in a European project to contribute to sustainable urban development in large urban distressed areas (LUDA). The LUDA project aimed at improving the quality of life in such areas, tackles problems such as:

- Uneconomic use of resources and narrow options for development.

- High level of political pressure to make rapid improvements to the quality of life.

- Lack of the knowledge about the phenomenon of large urban distressed areas.

- Large urban areas suffering environmental, economic, and social distress.

The project brings together six cities as well as nongovernmental organizations from eight different European countries (including an accession state) in an interdisciplinary way. Furthermore, it provides a platform for a broader discussion with other cities, research institutions, and civic organizations in working towards a more sustainable future in distressed urban areas.

A significant milestone in the application of futures thinking to advance sustainable development is the upcoming conference "Towards Sustainable Futures: Tools and Strategies" to be held in Tampere, Finland, June 2004. The conference, organized by the Turku School of Economics and Business Administration, Finland Futures Research Center, with Finland Futures Academy, is aimed at both researchers and corporate representatives. The aim of the multidisciplinary conference is to bring together those interested in sustainable development and futures-oriented research. New perspectives and methods for measuring sustainable development and creating strategies will be examined and the conference will also cast a look into how sustainability aspects are actually taken into consideration in corporations (Internet reference 1).

CONCLUSION

At the beginning of the third millennium, we find ourselves overwhelmed by complexities and uncertainties unprecedented in human history. As Peter Senge states, "Today, mankind has the capacity to produce far more information than anyone can absorb, to foster far greater interdependency than anyone can manage, and to accelerate change far faster than anyone's ability to keep pace" (Senge, 1990). The concept of sustainable development evolved as a means of tackling these unprecedented changes in environmental quality, economic development, and social structure in order to meet the needs of both present and future generations.

However, it is becoming increasingly evident that a clear blueprint for achieving sustainable development cannot be given and certainly not one that applies equally in all countries. The only major point of general agreement is that sustainable development means different things to different people (Gustavson et al., 1999). What is considered sustainable is to a great extent subject to personal and societal preferences with respect to economic development, environmental quality, assessment of (future) technological possibilities, and the attitude towards risks and uncertainty (Dellink et al., 1999). It has been suggested that if sustainability work does nothing more than challenge assumptions and presumptions it may be that it is doing enough, for "people use their ideas about the future to direct their actions in the present" (Internet reference 2). A common element inherent in almost all definitions of sustainable development is concern for the well-being of future generations. However, the potential to link futures thinking to advance sustainability is constantly evolving. Futures thinking represents an innovative, imaginative, and creative vehicle for attempting to deal with the multifaceted nature of the concept. If we are to robustly address sustainable development, scenarios of the future must encompass long-term time horizons including the development of strategic contingency planning to cope with what the future might be. We must also acknowledge that there will be surprises or scenario-spoiling "wild cards" of low possibility futures and that the passing of time may knock probabilities off course (Saunders, 2002). As Boyle et al. (2000) point out, we should be thinking about sustainable futures in four principal ways:

1. Their psychological and experiential aspects.
2. Their cultural, symbolic, and ideological aspects.
3. Their objective physical, behavioral, and material (including biological) aspects.
4. Their socio-political, ecological, and economic aspects.

In an age of anxiety and a period of transition when institutions and industries of all kinds crave an insight into the future, we must learn from social, technological, environmental, economic, and political changes of the past and present, but be disrespectful enough to adapt and consciously design the future before us as best we can.

At the European level, the advancement of futures thinking has made rapid progress in recent years, in particular given the establishment of a Forward Studies Unit at the European Commission, the establishment of EEIG euroProspective, and the development of a range of futures scenarios for Europe. Despite these developments, there is still a need to explicitly address and integrate futures thinking into strategic planning for sustainable development. Although not the only means available to us to strategically progress sustainable development, futures thinking has the potential to contribute to improving overall socio-economic well-being of present and future generations in Europe, and in maintaining the integrity of the ecological systems on which all life and production depends.

REFERENCES

Alberti, M., and L. Susskind. "Managing Urban Sustainability: An Introduction to the Special Issue," *Environmental Impact Assessment Review*, Vol. 16, No. 4-6 (1996), 213-221.

Aligica, P.D. "The Challenge of the Future and the Institutionalization of Interdisciplinarity: Notes of Herman Kahn's Legacy," *Futures*, Vol. 36, No. 1 (2003), 67-83.

Bell, S., and S. Morse. *Sustainability Indicators: Measuring the Immeasurable* (London: Earthscan, 1999).

Bell, W. "Futures Studies Comes of Age: Twenty-Five Years After the Limits to Growth," *Futures*, Vol. 33 (2001), 63–76.

Bell, W. "A Community of Futurists and the State of the Futures Field," *Futures*, Vol. 34 (2002), 235–247.

Bindé, J. "The City Summit: The Lessons of Istanbul," *Futures*, Vol. 29, No. 3 (1997), 213-227.

Blutstein, R. "A Forgotten Pioneer of Sustainability," *Journal of Cleaner Production*, Vol. 11 (2003), 339–341.

Boyle, G., C. Thomas, and D. Wield. "Beyond Single Vision," *Futures*, Vol. 32 (2000), 221–228.

Bräuer, I. "Money as an Indicator: To Make Use of Economic Evaluation for Biodiversity Conservation," *Agriculture, Ecosystems & Environment*, Vol. 98, Issues 1-3 (2003), 483-491.

Brundtland Commission. *Our Common Future* (Oxford: World Commission on Environment and Development, University Press, 1987).

Cairns, G., G. Wright, R. Bradfield, K. Van der Heijden, and G. Burt. "Exploring E-Government Futures through the Application of Scenario Planning," *Technological Forecasting and Social Change*, Vol. 5538 (2002), 1–22.

Cole, S., and E. Masini. "Limits beyond the Millennium: A Retroprospective on the Limits to Growth," *Futures*, Vol. 33 (2001), 1–5.

Couch, C., and A. Dennemann. "Urban Regeneration and Sustainable Development in Britain: The Example of the Liverpool Ropewalks Partnership," *Cities*, Vol. 17, No. 2 (2000), 137-147.

Dellink, R., M. Bennis, and H. Verbruggen. "Sustainable Economic Structures," *Ecological Economics*, Vol. 29 (1999), 141–154.

Directorate General Environment, Nuclear Safety and Civil Protection. *European Sustainable Cities Report* (Luxembourg: Official Publications of the European Communities, 1996).

Dooris, M. "Healthy Cities and Local Agenda 21: The UK Experience, Challenges for the New Millennium," *Health Promotion International*, Vol. 14, No. 4 (1999), 365-375.

Dreborg, K.H. "Essence of Backcasting," *Futures*, Vol. 28, No. 9 (1996), 813-828.

EEA. *Towards Sustainable Development for Local Authorities: Approaches, Experiences and Sources* (Copenhagan: European Environmental Agency, 1997).

Ekins, P., and M. Jacobs. "Environmental Sustainability and the Growth of GDP Conditions for Compatibility," *The North, the South and Sustainable Development*, eds. A. Glyn and V. Baskar (Tokyo: United Nations University Press, 1995), 9-46.

Enserink, B. "Building Scenarios for the University," *International Transactions in Operational Research*, Vol. 7 (2000), 569-583.

Feldmann, L., M. Vanderhaegen, and C. Pirotte. "The EU's SEA Directive: Status and Links to Integration and Sustainable Development," *Environmental Impact Assessment Review*, Vol. 21 (2001), 203-222.

Figge, F., and T. Hahn. "Sustainable Value Added: Measuring Corporate Contributions to Sustainability beyond Eco-Efficiency," *Ecological Economics*, Vol. 48 (2004), 173–187.

Fontela, E. "The Future Societal Bill: Methodological Alternatives," *Futures,* Vol. 35 (2003), 1027–1040.

Forward Studies Unit. *Scenarios Europe 2010* (Brussels: European Commission, 1999).

Gausemeier, J., A. Fink, and O. Schalke. "Scenario Management: An Approach to Develop Future Potentials," *Technological Forecasting and Social Change,* Vol. 59, No. 2 (1998), 111-130.

Geerlings, H., and D. Stead. "The Integration of Land Use Planning, Transport and Environment in European Policy and Research," *Transport Policy,* Vol. 10 (2000), 187–196.

Glenn, J.C., and T.J. Gordon. "The Millennium Project: Issues and Opportunities for the Future," *Technological Forecasting and Social Change,* Vol. 61, No. 2 (1999), 97–208.

Godet, M. "The Art of Scenarios and Strategic Planning: Tools and Pitfalls," *Technological Forecasting and Social Change,* Vol. 65, No. 1 (2000), 3-22.

Goux Baudiment, F. *Together, Let's Further Futures Intelligence* (Paris: EuroProspective Network Partnership, 2002).

Goux Baudiment, F. "The EEIG EuroProspective: Implementing Futures Thinking on European Scale," *Futures,* Vol. 36 (2004), 131–135.

Gustavson, K.R., S.C. Lonergan, and H.J. Ruitenbeek. "Selection and Modelling of Sustainable Development Indicators: A Case Study of the Fraser River Basin," *Ecological Economics,* Vol. 28, No. 1 (1999), 117-132.

Haughton, G., and C. Hunter. *Sustainable Cities* (London: Kingsley Publishers, 1994).

Hediger, W. "Sustainable Development and Social Welfare," *Ecological Economics,* Vol. 32, No. 3 (2000), 481-492.

Jansen, L. "The Challenge of Sustainable Development," *Journal of Cleaner Production,* Vol. 11 (2003), 231–245.

Kaivo-oja, J., T. Katko, and O. Seppälä. "Seeking Convergence between History and Futures Research," *Futures,* in press, 2004.

Kelly, R., L. Sirr, and J. Ratcliffe. "Futures Thinking to Achieve Sustainable Development at Local Level in Ireland," *Foresight-The Journal of Future Studies, Strategic Thinking and Policy,* in press, 2004.

Lele, S. "Sustainable Development: A Critical Review," *World Development,* Vol. 19, No. 6 (1991), 607-621.

List, D. "Multiple Pasts, Converging Presents, and Alternative Futures," *Futures,* Vol. 36, No. 1 (2003), 23-43.

MacKay, R.B., and P. McKiernan. "The Role of Hindsight in Foresight: Refining Strategic Reasoning," *Futures,* Vol. 36, No. 2 (2003), 161-179

Malaska, P. "A Futures Research Outline of a Post-Modern Idea of Progress," *Futures,* Vol. 33, Issues 3-4 (2001), 225-243.

Marien, M. "Futures Studies in the 21st Century: A Reality-Based View," *Futures,* Vol. 34 (2002), 261–281.

Masini, E. *Futures Research and Sociological Analysis,* A draft of discussion. The XIV World Congress of Sociology, The International Sociological Association, RC07 Futures Research, July 16–August 1, 1998.

McClaren, D., and T. Bosworth. *Planning for the Planet: Sustainable Development Policies for Local Strategic Planning* (London: Friends of the Earth, 1994).

Meadows, D. *The Limits to Growth: A Report for the Club of Rome's Project on the Predicament of Mankind* (London: Earth Island Ltd., 1972).

Mebratu, D. "Sustainability and Sustainable Development," *Environmental Impact Assessment Review*, Vol. 18, No. 6 (1998), 493-520.

Mega, V. "Cities Inventing the Civilisation of Sustainability: An Odyssey in the Urban Archipelago of the European Union," *Cities*, Vol. 1, No. 3 (2000), 227-236.

Mehta, P. "Local Agenda 21: Practical Experiences and Emerging Issues from the South," *Environmental Impact Assessment Review*, Vol. 16, No. 4-6 (1996), 309-320.

Payne, A., and P. Löffler. "The Åalborg Charter: Cities and Towns on the Move Towards Sustainability," *Naturopa, Local and Regional Authorities and the Environment*, Vol. 89 (1999) 4.

Pearce, D. *Blueprint 3: Measuring Sustainable Development* (London: Earthscan, 1993).

Puglisi, M., and S. Marvin. "Developing Urban and Regional Foresight: Exploring Capacities and Identifying Needs in the North West," *Futures*, Vol. 34, No. 8 (2002), 761-777.

Ratcliffe, J. *Imagineering for Construction: Using a Prospective Process through Scenario Thinking for Strategic Planning and Management in the Construction Industry* (Dublin: Futures Academy, Dublin Institute of Technology, 2003).

Redclift, M. *Sustainable Development: Exploring the Contradictions* (London: Routledge, 1987).

Rist, G. *The History of Development: From Western Origins to Global Faith* (London: Zed Books, 1997).

Rotmans, J., M. Van Asselt, and P. Vellinga. "An Integrated Planning Tool for Sustainable Cities," *Environmental Impact Assessment Review*, Vol. 20 (2000), 265–276.

Schmidheiney, S. *Changing Course: A Global Business Perspective on Development and the Environment* (Cambridge, MA: MIT Press, 1992).

Selman, P. "Local Agenda 21: Substance or Spin," *Journal of Environmental Planning and Management*, Vol. 14, No. 5 (1998), 533-553.

Senge, P.M. *The Fifth Discipline: The Art and Practice of the Learning Organizations* (New York: Doubleday, 1990).

Tilbury, D. "Environmental Education for Sustainability: Defining the New Focus of Environmental Education in the 1990s," *Environmental Education Research*, Vol. 1, No. 2 (1995), 195-212.

United Nations, *Report of the World Summit on Sustainable Development*, Johannesburg, South Africa, August 26–September 4, 2002.

Vollenbroek, F.A. "Sustainable Development and the Challenge of Innovation," *Journal of Cleaner Production*, Vol. 10 (2002), 215–223.

Wegener, M. *How Useful are Scenarios? A New (Old) Approach in Transport Planning*, The Dutch Transportation Planning Research Colloquium, Limits to Transportation Planning, Rotterdam, 1993.

Wright, S., and D. Lund. "Gray and Green: Stewardship and Sustainability in an Aging Society," *Journal of Aging Studies*, Vol. 14, No. 3 (2000), 229-249.

Ziegler, A.R. *Trade and Environmental Law in the European Community*, (Oxford: Clarendon Press, 1996).

INTERNET REFERENCES

www.tukkk.fi/tutu/conference2004/
www.soc.hawaii.edu/future/syllabi/polsci171.html

THE CULTURE OF GROWTH AND THE CULTURE OF LIMITS

by

Richard D. Lamm

The opposite of a correct statement is a false statement; the opposite of a profound truth may well be another profound truth.

—Niels Bohr (1885-1962)

Humankind can seldom resist dividing aspects of life and human events into two opposing positions. "Black or White" or "all or nothing." "Either you're with me or you're against me" is part of our vernacular and thinking.

One has to be careful, of course, not to overuse these stark divisions. Truths overlap, reality is seldom simple and the color of truth is usually gray. But as C.P. Snow has shown us in *The Two Cultures and a Second Look: An Expanding Version of the Two Cultures and the Scientific Revolution*, it is still useful to make a point by delineating contrasting viewpoints. Even when the exercise is exaggerated, which it often is, the concept is immensely useful. Like a contrasting agent in radiology, the very starkness helps clarify. We often cannot appreciate the full nuances of a problem without a contrast, often in the form of parables, metaphors, and simplifications.

Snow contrasted the differences between the world of science and the world of letters and went on to observe, "Between the two a gulf of mutual incomprehension...sometimes hostility and dislike, but most of all lack of understanding."

This same "two cultures" metaphor is useful to spotlight what I consider a new chasm of "mutual incomprehension"—the culture of growth and the culture of limits. Are resources finite or infinite? Can we solve the problems of growth with more growth? Will existing mechanisms and institutions (including capitalism) be sufficient and successful for the next 200 years as they have been for the last 200 years? There is the culture of growth, which denies limits, and the culture of limits, which seeks to adapt to those limits.

Aldo Leopold saw a similar conflict in writing about his "land ethic":

One of the anomalies of modern ecolog[ical thought] is that it is the creation of two groups, each of which seems barely aware of the existence of the other. The one studies the human community, almost as if it were a separate entity, and calls its finding sociology, economics and history. The other

Richard D. Lamm *is former governor of Colorado and director of the Center for Public Policy and Contemporary Issues at the University of Denver, Denver, Colorado. He may be contactd at rlamm@du.edu.*

studies the plant and animal community and comfortably relegates the hodgepodge of politics to "liberal arts." The inevitable fusion of these two lines of thought will, perhaps, constitute the outstanding advance of the present century (*Sand County Almanac*).

Most of human experience is on the side of both the population and economic growth culture. The world of growth has succeeded brilliantly. It allowed survival in a harsh world. It has brought health, wealth, increased life expectancy, leisure, and—most important—freedom. Growth has approached the status of a religion. Sociologist Peter Berger points out:

> Development is not just a goal of rational action in the economic, political and social spheres. It is also, and very deeply, the focus of redemptive hopes and expectations. In an important sense, development is a religious category. Even for those living on the most precarious margins of existence, development is not just a matter of improved material conditions; it is at least also a vision of redemptive transformation.

But even in our religious fervor we must ask, "can it last?" Is this a sustainable vision? Is this the *permanent* secret to success for societies?

The other culture believes that, for all our genius, we cannot escape ecological limits. This viewpoint holds that we must modify and in some cases reverse mores and cultures that have worked well and under which we have prospered for hundreds of years. They assert that we can delay but not totally avoid the consequences of our infinite demands on a finite earth. They argue that a very fundamental new world has emerged, a set of circumstances which is as important as the industrial or agricultural revolution. It is to change the world of growth into the world of sustainability.

Some would say that this is merely an extension of Snow's two cultures. But the stakes are much higher in the limits/growth dichotomy because they go to the basic assumptions of our civilization. As philosopher Herschel Elliott warns, "We can disagree on the right way to live and use resources, but we cannot avoid the collective consequences of wrong ways." Has economic growth and population growth become more problem than solution? Is the ecosystem a hurdle or a barrier? What is our vision of the future and how do we organize the economy and social systems of the future? Can "Yankee ingenuity" and a "can do" culture solve growth-related problems as it has solved so many others, or do we have to change our basic operating assumptions and culture?

One of the human dilemmas is that we often see the world not as it is, but as we think it is. Columnist and thinker Walter Lipp-mann warned: "At the core of every moral code, there is a picture of human nature, a map of the universe and a version of history...." Our economy, our ethical standards, our moral standards depend on the mental map we have of the world. Author Thomas Sowell points out that people have very different visions of how the world works. "Visions are foundations on which theories are built," and Sowell observes that most of us have mental maps of the world in our minds which do much to control our viewpoints. Sowell divides them into "constrained" and "unconstrained."

These visions often arise from fundamentally different premises, says Sowell. Visions are like maps that guide us through the tangle of bewildering complexities. Like maps, visions must leave out many concrete features in order to enable us to focus on a few key paths to our goal. Visions are indispensable, but dangerous—precisely to the extent that we confuse them with reality itself. Visions paint with a broad brush. What has been deliberately neglected in our vision may not turn out to be negligible in its effect on the results.

> The great evils of the world (war, poverty and crime) are seen in completely different terms by those with constrained and unconstrained visions. If human options are not inherently constrained, then the presence of such repugnant and disas-trous phenomena virtually cry out for explanation—and for solutions. But if the limitation on passions of man himself are at the heart of this painful phenomena, then what requires explanation are the ways in which they have been avoided or minimized (*Conflict of Visions*).

Are there limits in the physical world, or are those "limits" only limitations of our vision, creativity, technology, and ingenuity? Are there limits to human development in the physical world around us, or only in our minds? Can the mental map that Western Civilization has formed in our minds and human expectations be achieved in the physical world we live in? Is the past a guide to the future or a "moral trap" that keeps us from recognizing that we are approaching carrying capacity? Could we end up being victims of our past successes because they have given us the wrong mental map?

> Believers in unconstrained visions seek the special causes of war, poverty and crime. Believers in the constrained view seek the special causes of peace, wealth and law-abiding society. In the unconstrained vision, there is no tractable reason for social evils; therefore, no reason they cannot be solved with sufficient moral commitment. In the constrained vision, whatever the artifices or strategies are strained or ameliorated inherent human evils will themselves have cost, some in the form of other social ills created by the civilizing

institutions so that all that is possible is a prudent tradeoff (*Conflict of Visions*).

This reasoning fits perfectly into the dichotomy between the culture of growth and the culture of limits. The jury's still out—neither side can claim victory, but the world is presently developing and increasing population and standards of living, so the presumption should be with the growth vision. That is not something we should easily give up. The culture of growth has served us well. However, it is not the end of the argument, for, as Huxley reminds us, "Facts do not cease to exist just because they are ignored."

One of the great challenges of history is to know when a new world or new paradigm has emerged. It is my passionate belief that economic theories cannot be at variance with ecological reality. Our economic system must adapt to our ecological system, or at a minimum our economic system cannot destroy our ecological system. We are, perhaps understandably, blinded by our past successes and those successes make it all the harder to change those policies to meet the new realities. We cannot assume that the practices and policies of the last 100 years will be applicable for the next 100 years. "Success" in societies is not a permanent state but a permanent challenge. Remember the dictum: "Nothing fails like success."

Is additional population growth and economic growth an asset or a liability? Can science delay or avoid the consequences of finiteness (limits)? Is science and technology a cure or could it be part of the disease itself? Is technology and ingenuity a solution or does it buy us some time? The larger ecosystem is likely totally indifferent to whether we get the answers to these questions right. Natural ecosystems are never altruistic. Millions have died in the past—the just and the unjust—due to the impact of nature (the ecosystem).

The assumptions that undergird our whole society incorporate infinite resources. We confidently feel that there are no limits that cannot be overcome. But are these assumptions correct or in error? Public policy and most of our institutions, as presently structured, assume unlimited resources, infinite wealth creation capacity, and no ecological limits. The resulting society is vastly different from a society which assumes environmental and ecological limits.

I think the future can be better planned for by confronting limits to the best of our ability and heeding the warning that infinite growth cannot take place in a finite world. The fact that we have been so successful in pushing back those limits does not dissuade me from believing that those limits are real. "All modern day curves lead to disaster," warns former French President Valery Giscard d'Estaing. (Population, consumption, environmental destruction.) Human civilizations are presently living on the upper shoulders of some incredibly steep geometric curves. We have used more resources since 1950 than in the million years preceding 1950. We experience more change in a year than our grandparents did in a lifetime.

Yesterday's solutions have a nasty habit of becoming today's problems.

Evidence increasingly shows that something is fundamentally wrong with the growth paradigm. Our globe is warming, our rain forests are shrinking, our icecaps are melting, our coral is dying, our fisheries are depleting, our deserts are encroaching, our water is under more and more demand. I suspect these to be the early warning signs of a world approaching its carrying capacity. We cannot call upon human ingenuity, science, and technology to develop new solutions to all these new challenges. We must instead change our mental map of the world, our culture, and our economy.

I suggest we need not better scientists and technicians but better poets and prophets. We have to modify ourselves and our lifestyles. We are unlikely to be the first species in the world to be exempt from limits.

This writer has been impressed by a scholar named Herschel Elliott who has taken similar reasoning and applied it trying to change all "human centered ethics." Our hubris notwithstanding, he suggests we ultimately must live within a limited and increasingly fragile ecosystem. Elliott doubts that growth can ultimately solve growth-related problems; we must move to sustainability. "It is extremely improbable that human ingenuity could devise a system that would be as stable and secure as the one which nature has already designed. The new human system would be unlikely to function for more than a few ticks of geological time."

He questions whether "a priori, human centered ethics" are sustainable in a finite ecosystem. He postulates that no ethical system or value system can be valid if it cumulatively destroys the ecosystem of which it is a part.

Elliott points out that, however laudatory and well meaning in human terms, we can't give priority to humans over every other living thing.

When the man-made biosystem fails because of some ethical misconception about how human beings ought to live in the world, it will be irrelevant that Christians, Muslims and Jews had believed that the true morality was revealed to man in the eternal world of God. It will be beside the point that professionals in ethics and philosophy had used the demands of conscience, the self-evident truths of reason, their theories of justice or the logical inferences from moral language to justify their moral convictions about how human beings ought to live and act.

I fear that Elliott is right. We cannot avoid the collective consequences of wrong ways. The ecosystem has little use for our elegantly reasoned ethical systems. To be valid, a thought pattern must be sustainable. "...The fact is that if the practice of a mistaken conception of ethics should ever allow the world's life-support system to break down, nature's experiment with Homo sapiens would be over. "If living by a system of ethics should make human life physically impossible, that ethics is absurd."

CONCLUSION

We must reconcile our thinking and culture to the ecological system that surrounds us. No matter how attractive and elegantly reasoned is the world built up in our unconstrained vision, it ultimately must fit within the reality of the physical world. As Elliott points out:

> The culture of growth which drives the ethical, political, economic thinking in the Western nations, confuses the two domains (mental world and physical world). It assumes the open-ended, infinite expansion which is possible in the mental-cultural domain is also possible in the physical world.

But I fear that it is not. If these fears are valid, the ultimate dichotomy will be between our mental map of the future being largely an extrapolation of the past, and a new mental model requiring profound cultural and economic change to align human activity to the realistic limits of our ecosystem.

Peter Russell in his book *Waking Up in Time* gives us a powerful metaphor to ponder. Describing a scene from a Zola novel he says:

> While a train full of soldiers on the way to war is rushing downhill, the driver and fireman are fighting. The fireman insists on stoking the engine and the driver is trying to stop him. As they tussle, one grabs the other by the throat and together they tumble off the engine, leaving the trainload of drinking and singing soldiers hurtling through the night, totally unaware of what has happened. And there the book ends!

Is humanity on a similar course?

OPPORTUNITIES AND CHALLENGES OF THE FUTURE TRANSAMAZONIC CONNECTIONS IN SOUTH AMERICA: WHAT COULD ONE EXPECT?

by

Michael Edgard Ridia

INTRODUCTION

In the next years, the highways that connect the Atlantic and the Pacific oceans through the Amazon forest will be completed. The Amazon forest is the biggest tropical forest in the world. It has an area of 5.5 million km² and occupies territory in many countries in South America: Brazil, Peru, Venezuela, Ecuador, Colombia, and Bolivia. In general terms, it has more than 30,000 species of plants and 2,500 species of trees. At present, it has lost more than 13% of the original forest due to colonization. However, these "colonists" live in urban centers, leaving the natives in the faraway regions. The current access to the Amazon area is very difficult because of inadequate highways. This has a direct influence on transport costs when people want to take advantage of the region's natural resources.

The Amazon nations, in particular Brazil and Peru, will integrate their connecting roads. This will facilitate the existence of diverse transamazonic roads that connect the Brazilian Amazon with the Pacific Ocean. This situation does not have precedent in contemporary history in any region of the world. Therefore, a vision of the future is essential in order to assure sustainable development.

The first aim of this paper is to analyze the future viability of using ports in the Pacific Ocean for trade between the interior Brazilian regions and the Asia Pacific Zone, instead of using the Panama Canal. Most of the load to be transported between Amazonic Brazil and the Pacific basin will be done by the route that allows competitiveness to the owner of the load. It is necessary to highlight not only the "strategic position" of the ports in the Pacific Ocean, but to analyze the unitary cost (monetary value per unit of weight) for the different alternative routes. In this approach, some origin-destination points will be selected inside Brazil, which would be: Manaos-Itacoatiara and Porto Velho. In Asia, the origin-destination point would be Shanghai. In the case of the routes through ports of Western South America, the author will estimate the complete cost of the route, including all the multimodal connections. Another factor to study will be the value of the load, as well as the influence of the economic scale principle, the time of journey, and the load asymmetry.

The second objective of this paper is to describe the impact of highways on the Amazon forest. There will be an increased develop-

Michael Edgard Ridia *is an industrial engineer and independent consultant in Lima, Peru. He may be contacted at mridia@terra.com.*

ment in the economic, social, and environmental aspects, which will change life forever. The Madre de Dios region of southeast Peru will serve as an example of what could happen in other parts of the Amazon where the highways will intersect. This area well-known for its reservations such as Manu, Tambopata, Bahuaja-Sonene, and Alto Purus. These areas are unique in biodiversity and genetic resources. This region has been isolated from the Pacific Ocean due to the nonexistence of asphalted highways. In summary, the roads would facilitate immediate access to the immense natural resources of the forest, with the potential risks and opportunities that it implies.

THE TRANSAMAZONIC CONNECTION—WILL IT BE USEFUL FOR THE TRADE OF THE AMAZON BRAZIL WITH THE ASIA-PACIFIC REGION?

The interior of Brazil has a growing trade with the countries of the Asia-Pacific region, particularly with China and Japan. Their main export product is soybean grain. For this, one has to use the big fluvial ports or the Atlantic Ocean. Then, one uses the Panama Canal as a connection bridge with China and Japan. To have an idea of the current production of the aforementioned regions, the total export of soybean grain from Brazil to China was 4.14 million tons, while to Japan, 710,000 tons were exported. The export of the Brazilian products uses multimodal connections, including highways or rivers.

The routes for the export from Amazonic Brazil (GEIPOT, 2000) are:

- Route 1. Manaos/Itacoatiara (Brazil)—Panama—Shanghai (China).
- Route 2. Porto Velho (fluvial port, Brazil)—Itacoatiara (fluvial port, Brazil)—Shanghai (China).

Description of the Future Alternative: Interior Brazil—Pacific Ocean

The routes that connect the interior of Brazil with China and Japan through the ports of the Pacific Ocean will be analyzed. It has always been commented that an interoceanic connection would be favorable to trade within the interior of the continent. This statement coincided with the increase of the export of Brazilian soybean to China and Japan. In the future, an integrated system of intermodal transport will exist through the Andes that connects the Atlantic and the Pacific oceans. This network includes highways, rail, and fluvial routes.

Route 1A (alternative route to the Route 1): Manaos/Itacoatiara (fluvial port, Brazil). Iquitos (Peru)—Yurimaguas—Paita (seaport, Peru). Shanghai (China).

Firstly, one travels from Manaos/Itacoatiara countercurrent until

Iquitos, where transshipment to a smaller craft should be made. Then, one arrives at Yurimaguas, where the load is moved by a 30-ton truck to Paita. From there, a ship would take the load to Shanghai.

Route 2A (alternative route to the Route 2): Porto Velho (Brazil)—Matarani (seaport, Peru). Shanghai (China).

From Porto Velho, the load is transported by road to the Pacific coast in Matarani, then by ship to Shanghai.

The Andes Impact

The existence of the Andes has a direct impact on the transport cost by road and railway. Nowadays, scarce traffic exists between Brazil and the Pacific Ocean. The main cause is the lack of asphalted roads between Brazil with Peru and Bolivia. Special operating conditions in the Andes are also required, such as additional fuel costs, the necessity to adjust the motors to height, and the risk of navigating the tunnels and steps in winter. However, infrastructure improvements in execution of this project will facilitate more trade among the countries on both sides of the Andes.

In Peru, the effect of the height has been studied in the transport by road. The suitable numbers are the conversion factors that one has to multiply to the price of the transport cost, according to the height where it circulates (MTC Peru, 2002).

- Altitude from 0 to 1000 m or gradient 0-3%   1.00
- Altitude from 1000 to 2500 m or gradient 3-5%   1.20
- Altitude more than 2500 m or gradient 5-7%   1.40

The routes of Brazilian soybean export to Peru would have to take into consideration the factors in the cases of routes 1a and 2a.

Determination of Transport Cost by Road and Port Costs in the Pacific Side

The transport cost by road depends on each individual situation. Among the internal conditions are the expense in fuel, remunerations, and tires (MTC Peru, 2002). For the external side, they are the volume to transport, the product type, the value of the load, and the negotiation. This data has been compared in Brazil, Peru, and Bolivia. The effect of the height has already been analyzed. In summary, the average transport cost by road, at sea level, is US$0.0276/(ton*km) for shorter distances up to 1,000 km. For 1,500 km or further, the value is US$0.023/(ton*km). If one needs to ponder the value of the height, one multiplies it by the conversion factors described previously.

The port cost in the Pacific Ocean varies from US$5 to 7/ton of bulk cargo. One could consider US$5/ton for all the ports: Matarani,

Arica, Iquique and Antofagasta. This is very similar to the port costs in the Atlantic, around US$6/ton. On the other hand, the ports of the Pacific Ocean have natural conditions to receive ships that transport soybean grain. However, they need to improve their infrastructure.

Analysis of the Alternatives

The competitiveness of each of the routes has been described in detail in previous sections. Appendix 1 (p. 347) shows all the results:

• *Route 1 vs. Route 1a.* For the case of the bulk cargo, a difference exists of more than 100% with regard to the route used now.

• *Route 2 vs. Route 2a.* The alternative for the ports of the Pacific Ocean is 50% more expensive than the route utilized today.

Some inferences can be made from the obtained results:

a) The multimodal systems are efficient to shorten the distances and times of a trip, but do not necessarily reduce the transport costs. This is of particular importance for bulk cargo, in which the financial cost is low due to the monetary value for load ton.

b) The alternative of the Pacific Ocean is not profitable because of the great terrestrial distance that has to be traveled. The transport by road competes against the fluvial system.

c) Estimations have been carried out based on the current trade structure of the Brazilian interior regions, so the soybean grain was selected as an example. A change is not seen in the type of commercial structure for the coming years (GEIPOT, 2000).

The main analysis is to determine if a return load exists from the ports of the Pacific Ocean toward the interior of Brazil. Although the determination of new trade flows is very delicate, one will investigate each one of the following routes:

• Route 1a: Peru—Brazil. It is not considered a higher return load, beyond the commercial exchange between these two countries.

• Route 2a: Peru—Brazil. It is possible to transport of 300,000 tons annually from the Peruvian coast to Porto Velho. This would partially assure the return load. On the other hand, it does not evaluate the possibility of exporting Peruvian phosphates from the new agricultural lands that would exist as a result of the Amazon deforestation.

The Time of Journey

It is very difficult to calculate the difference in time because each situation has to be analyzed individually. However, ships that leave Peru or Chile arrive in Shanghai or Kobe within 10 days of those that leave Brazil (Hoffmann, 2000). The importance of time is high only if the value of load is high.

The Value of Load

For all cases, it is assumed that the monetary value of the load, per ton, is small because it is dry bulk cargo. The transport of containers with products of more value would demand a revision of the data, but not of the methodology used.

In any event, one would have to weigh the financial cost of saving time on the trip against the total logistical costs. However, the situation would get complicated due to the necessity of containers and transshipments in Panama or Los Angeles.

WHAT COULD ONE EXPECT FROM THE CONNECTION BETWEEN BRAZIL AND PERU THROUGH THE AMAZON FOREST?

It is believed that the physical infrastructure of the Amazon forest will facilitate the use of the forest's natural resources. At present, the forest activity represents the most important extractive activity in the areas of Peru and Brazil. However, the Amazon forest in general, and certain regions in particular, have great biodiversity and genetic resources. The infrastructure projects will pass very near these critical habitats. In particular, the case of the Madre de Dios region of southeast Peru will be studied.

Current Situation of the Madre de Dios Region

The Madre de Dios region, situated completely in the Amazon, covers an area of 8.7 million hectares, with waters that come from the heights of the southern Andes of Peru. It borders Brazil to the north and Bolivia to the east. It is one of the most isolated areas in Peru and South America. Its connection with the Pacific Ocean is by a road that is impassable several months a year. The connection with Brazil is similar.

In the economic aspect, it represents less than 0.37% of Peru GDP (Growth Domestic Product), around US$230 million. Their main activities are concentrated on wood and chestnut extraction. In recent years, there has been an increase of tourism, due to a worldwide attraction to its protected natural areas. Inside the heterogeneity of economic activities developed in the region, three economic aspects can be distinguished: (1) The extractive front, comprised of the activities of wood and chestnut extraction; (2) the agricultural front that includes the migratory agriculture and the extensive cattle raising, located around the highways and the main waterways; and (3) the conservation front and the legacy of an indigenous territorial economy that harbors diverse indigenous towns, ecotourism companies, oil lots, bioinversion initiatives, and group of protected natural areas.

The region has a population of 100,000 inhabitants, of whom 40,000 live in its capital, Puerto Maldonado. The rest of the people work in the rural area, mostly in the business of wood extraction. Many of them were not born in the region, but have migrated from the southern Andes of Peru.

Madre de Dios is known in the world for its biodiversity and genetic resources, many of which are very unique species. Specialists consider it a "hot spot." This has given way to the creation of natural areas protected from regular human activity: Manu, Tambopata, Bahuaja-Sonene, and Alto Purus. The government and many NGOs, like Conservation International and World Wildlife Fund, have been working there for several years. The research of biological material has not been concluded because every year new species are classified. It has registration records of birds, butterflies, and dragonflies, as endemic species. Therefore, it has half of the biodiversity and endemism of Peru. Until now, they have registered 214 species of mammals, 755 of birds, 123 of reptiles, 124 of amphibians, 117 of spineless aquatic, 259 of fish, and 1,572 of butterflies.

On the other hand, the region has indigenous reservations that do not have any relevant contact with Western society. The Peruvian state has assured them, by law, territories that they have occupied for thousands of years.

Potential Consequences of the Asphalted Highway in the Madre de Dios Region

The asphalting of the highway is an event that will change the life of the Madre de Dios region forever. It will physically integrate the area with the rest of Peru and the Brazilian occident. The consequences of this can be divided into three areas that are interrelated to each other.

Economic Outcomes

Madre de Dios will continue having as a main activity the use of wood. The Peruvian state has defined an area of 2.5 million hectares for reforesting. At present, only 8 m^3 per hectare is used, mainly for mahogany and cedar extraction. The highway will reduce the transportation cost, and it will facilitate the use of other species. It could reach the extraction rate of 30 m^3 per hectare of more than 20 species of trees. The annual extraction would be 4 million m^3 of wood.

In addition, a new use of lands will be given to many of the areas adjacent to the highway. It will increase the agricultural activity (occupying up to 1 million hectares) in products that can be sold in the rest of Peru.

Social Outcomes

The favorable economic conditions due to new activities will attract migration from the Andean south to work in the wood activity. Why will this take place? Because the Andean regions have a higher level of poverty (around the 75% of population), while Madre de Dios has 35%.

Other delicate consequences are centered on the changes in the indigenous way of life, as well as the probable conflicts in occupying land in order to take advantage of resources.

Environmental Outcomes

These are the less foreseen consequences when infrastructure projects in the Amazon forest are planned. However, there are some precedents in the Brazilian area. Because of that, if one gives a free occupation of the territory, the lands would demean 50 kms to each side of the highway. This is of particular relevance because of the proximity of the road to the natural areas of Manu and Tambopata.

In the worst possible case, a strong social pressure would exist to modify the territorial ordinance done by the Peruvian government. These lands would be used for migratory agriculture of low quality, which would worsen the quality of floors in the area. In addition, the increase of illegal loggers cannot be discounted.

Present and Future of Influence Areas of Transamazonic Connections Between Peru and Brazil

The scenario presented in Madre de Dios is an example of what could happen to the rest of the Amazon forest as a consequence of transamazonic connections. Increased development has negative and positive aspects, which should be foreseen before the construction of the highways.

In South America, a regional initiative exists for physical integration. It is called IIRSA, supported by all regional governments. Unfortunately, they have not put enough emphasis on reducing the negative impacts to the Amazon environment. They have too optimistic a vision. The initiative of integrating the Amazon countries will have a beneficial outcome if opportunities and problems are analyzed as a whole.

Because the transamazonic connections will not be used for trade between Brazil and Asia, there will be less economic pressure to use the forest indiscriminately.

Highway construction will bring accessibility to remote areas as well as increased development. Thus, there would be greater economic occupation of lands. We cannot forget that there is a context of socioeconomic vulnerability in South American countries, and due to that, there are some risks that must be prevented.

Strategic Environmental Evaluation

A strategic environmental evaluation will be necessary. It would provide: (i) a comprehensive environmental and social diagnosis of the project's several areas of influence; (ii) an ample process of public consultation and interaction with the national government and with the various local social sectors involved; (iii) the analysis of the project's indirect, synergetic, accumulative, and long-term impact, resulting from the interaction with other projects; (iv) the construction and evaluation of long-term scenarios.

However, the most important thing is assuring that the suggestions of the environmental evaluation are taken into consideration.

SUMMARY AND CONCLUSIONS

In the coming years, South America will have completed the infrastructure that connects the Atlantic and Pacific oceans through the Amazon forest. The territories of this region have today reduced population, but this will change in the future.

The first objective of the paper was to determine if the transamazonic roads would be useful for the trade between Brazil and China. It has been concluded that the Pacific Route will not replace the Panama Canal for soybean export. The most important parameter used for this is the transport cost. The analyzed routes would present higher unitary costs for the alternative use of the Pacific Ocean. In the primary analysis of the operative transport cost, the problem of the load asymmetry in the terrestrial transport has not been considered. On the other hand, a saving of time exists if Amazonic Brazil uses the ports in the Pacific Ocean. This would be of particular importance only for products of high monetary value, due to the capital cost involved.

The second aim of the paper was to study some consequences of these roads. The main outcome of the complete existence of infrastructure will be increased development, including a higher traffic of goods and people, as well as new uses of the land, and migration toward the forest, among others. Negative impacts are environmental pollution, the conversion and degradation of the use of land, and the change in the native way of life.

The Peruvian and Brazilian governments have to assure the sustainable development of the Amazon forest. This task would be "easier" because Brazil will not use it as a connection to Asia. For that, they have to respect and follow the signed agreements and environmental evaluations related to the Amazon. Otherwise, they will increase the negative consequences for the regional and global environment.

REFERENCES

Arrospide, Ramón. *The Peruvian Interoceanic*, Lima (1990).

GEIPOT, *Exit Alternatives for the Soybean Export*, GEIPOT, Brasilia, Brazil (2000).

Hoffmann, Jan. "The Potential of Pivot Ports on the South American Pacific Coast," *Journal of ECLAC*, 71 (August 2000), 121-143.

INRENA. *National Inventory of Biodiversity*, Lima (1997).

MTC Peru (Ministry of Transports of Peru), "Methodology of Determination of Costs for the Freight Transport," *The Peruvian Newspaper*, February 3, 2002.

Research Institute of Peruvian Amazon (IIAP). *Propuesta Zoneamiento Ecológico-Económico de Madre de Dios*, Lima (2001).

Ridia, Michael. *The Future Connection Between Interior Brazil and the Asia-Pacific Region Through Ports in Western South America. Will it Replace the Panama Canal?*, Lima (2004, unpublished).

Schneider et al. *Sustainable Amazon* (World Bank: Brasilia, 2000).

World Bank. *Roads and the Environment Handbook*, Washington, D.C.

INTERNET REFERENCES

www.conservation.org
www.iadb.org (Inter-American Development Bank, Sustainable Development Department
www.iiap.org.pe
www.iirsa.org
www.inrena.gob.pe
www.siamazonia.org.pe
www.enapu.com.pe (National Port Enterprise of Peru)
www.worldbank.org

APPENDIX 1

TRANSPORT COSTS IN THE ROUTE AMAZONIC BRAZIL–SHANGHAI AT PRESENT AND ALTERNATIVE ROUTES IN THE FUTURE

CURRENT TRANSPORT OF SOYBEAN

Preliminary Considerations
1. Average costs of transport in Brazil for the soybean grains are used.

0.023 US$/ton-km	highway of more than 1,500 km
0.014 US$/ton-km	for route Porto Velho-Itacoatiara
0.00166 US$/ton-km	approx. long distances and ships PANAMAX

2.*: Itacoatiara is a fluvial port that is near to Manaos.

Route 1: Manaos/Itacoatiara* (Brazil)—Panama—Shanghai (China)

Maritime Way		Total Cost
	US$/ton	US$/ton
21,087	35	35

Route 2: Porto Velho (fluvial port)—Itacoatiara (fluvial port, Brazil)—Shanghai

River		Maritime Way		Port Cost	Total Cost
km	US$/ton	km	US$/ton	US$/ton	US$/ton
1,056	14.8	21,087	35	6	56

FUTURE ALTERNATIVE ROUTES

Preliminary considerations
1. Average costs of transport are used for soybean.

0.023 US$/ton-km	highway of more than 1,500 km
0.01626 US$/ton-km	railroad of more than 1,000 km

2. In some routes, a conversion factor must be used (explained in present study).

Route 1A: Manaos/Itacoatiara*—Iquitos (fluvial port, Peru)—Yurimaguas (fluvial port)—Paita (maritime port, Peru)—Shanghai

Road		River		Maritime Way		Port Cost	Total Cost
km	US$/ton	km	US$/ton	km	US$/ton	US$/ton	US$/ton
850	26	2,550	21	15,550	21	9	77

Notes: 1. Transport costs by river includes routes: Manaos/Itacoatiara—Iquitos (1,900 km) and Iquitos—Yurimaguas (650 km).

2. Port cost includes all transshipments.

Route 2A: Porto Velho (Brazil)—Matarani (maritime port, Peru)—Shanghai

Road		Maritime Way		Port Cost	Total Cost
km	US$/ton	km	US$/ton	US$/ton	US$/ton
2,150	55	16,500	23	5	83

Sources: GEIPOT (2000), MTC Peru (2002), World Bank (2001). Field Work (2003) and personal estimations of the author.

APPENDIX 2

BIODIVERSITY OF SOME GROUPS IN THE PERUVIAN FOREST

Taxonomic Group	No. of Species in Peruvian Amazon
Superior Plants	7,372
Ferns	700
Non-Flying Mammals	263
Bats	100
Birds	806
Reptiles	180
Amphibians	262
Continental Fish	697
Spiders	2,000
Lepidopterons (day)	2,500

Source: Regional Diagnostic of Biodiversity in Peru. INRENA (1997).